ATLAS OF HISPANIC-AMERICAN HISTORY

Revised Edition

George Ochoa
and Carter Smith

Facts On File
An imprint of Infobase Publishing

To Melinda and Martha
—G. O.

Atlas of Hispanic-American History, Revised Edition

Copyright © 2009 by Media Projects Inc.

Media Projects, Inc. Staff:
Editor: Carter Smith
Principal Writers: George Ochoa and Carter Smith
Production Editor: Laura Smyth
Indexer: Diane Brenner

Facts On File, Inc.
An imprint of Infobase Publishing
132 West 31st Street
New York NY 10001

Library of Congress Cataloging-in-Publication Data
Ochoa, George.
  Atlas of Hispanic-American history / George Ochoa and Carter Smith.—
Rev. ed.
     p. cm.
  Includes bibliographical references and index.
  ISBN 978-0-8160-7092-3 (hc : alk. paper)—ISBN 978-0-8160-7736-6
(pb: alk. paper) 1. Hispanic Americans—History. 2. Hispanic
Americans—History—Maps. I. Smith, Carter, 1962- II. Title.
  E184.S75O287 2008
  973'.0468—dc22

                                    2008020664

Text design by Laura Smyth
Cover design by Takeshi Takahashi
Maps and graphics by Dale Williams

Printed in China

CREATIVE USA FOF 10 9 8 7 6 5 4 3 2 1
           (pbk) 10 9 8 7 6 5 4 3 2 1

This book is printed on acid-free paper.

CONTENTS

ACKNOWLEDGMENTS

The author and editor wish to thank the many people who have contributed greatly to this project. It was first conceived by Facts On File's Eleanora von Dehsen. Eleanora and her noble successors, Nicole Bowen and Owen Lancer, have exhibited perseverance, patience and expertise. It was a pleasure working with them.

The maps, too, were a collaborative effort. For the first edition, most were prepared by David Lindroth, a very skilled independent illustrative cartographer. For the revised edition, Dale Williams of Facts On File did a magnificent job reformatting David's original maps and creating a considerable number of entirely new maps as well. Laura Smyth also deserves enormous thanks for her excellent work as production editor for the revised edition.

On the personal side, the author thanks his wife, Melinda Corey, and daughter, Martha Corey-Ochoa for their help and patience during the writing of the first edition of this book. Likewise, the editor thanks his wife, Monique Avakian, and daughter, Erin Smith, for their support and patience, as well.

NOTE ON PHOTOS

Some of the illustrations and photographs used in this book are old, historical images. The quality of the prints is not always up to modern standards, as in many cases the originals are from old negatives or the originals are damaged. The content of the illustrations, however, made their inclusion important despite problems in reproduction.

INTRODUCTION

A Hispanic is a person who descends from one of the world's Spanish-speaking peoples. Behind that simple definition lies the complex history that created the world's Spanish-speaking peoples: a history of migration, empire-building, cultural and ethnic blending, conflict, and change. The complexity of that history may be glimpsed in the difficulty of defining exactly where Hispanic America is and who is a Hispanic American.

The term "Hispanic America" is most often used to refer to the 18 Western Hemisphere countries that were once colonies of Spain and in which Spanish is still the predominant language: Mexico, Guatemala, El Salvador, Honduras, Nicaragua, Costa Rica, Panama, Cuba, the Dominican Republic, Colombia, Venezuela, Ecuador, Peru, Bolivia, Paraguay, Argentina, Uruguay, and Chile. These countries, also called Spanish America or Spanish-speaking America, are part of the broader region of Latin America, which comprises all those American nations and territories where the predominant language is derived from Latin. Spanish is one of those languages, as is Portuguese, which is spoken in Brazil, and French, which is spoken in Haiti, Martinique, and French Guiana.

Sometimes "Hispanic America" is used more broadly to mean any part of the Americas where Hispanics live in large numbers, including parts of the United States. Sometimes it refers exclusively to the community of Hispanics in the United States. Similarly, depending on the context, a Hispanic American may be a resident of one of the Western Hemisphere's Spanish-speaking countries or a Hispanic who lives in the United States.

This book generally uses the term "Hispanic Americans" in the restricted sense of Hispanics living in the United States. There is good reason for all Americans to learn more about this ethnic group, since it currently includes 35.3 million people, or 12.5 percent of the U.S. population. During the 1990s, Hispanics surpassed non-Hispanic African Americans to become the country's largest minority group, and they are expected to account for one-quarter of the population by 2055. Yet it is not possible to tell the story of these Hispanic Americans without telling about Hispanic America in the largest possible sense: the community spanning the Western Hemisphere that owes at least part of its heritage to Spain.

Besides the Spanish legacy, there are two other major parts of the Hispanic American heritage: the Native American and African components. Most, though not all, Hispanic Americans have a mix of Spanish and Native American genes; some also have African genes. Therefore, Hispanic-American culture blends Spanish, Native American, and African traditions. Puerto Rican historian Arturo Morales Carrión has gone so far as to say, "A simple definition of the Hispanic could be: a person with a willingness to mix and therefore a person with a disposition to create new types of human relationships and new types of cultural forms...."

The result of all this biological and cultural blending is not a homogeneous mass, but a diverse collection of societies and nations. Indeed, devotion to local traditions is as much a feature of Hispanic culture as is a willingness to mix. This is not surprising, since both features are characteristic of Spain itself, which from antiquity has been marked by the blending of peoples and by separation into distinct regions. Hispanics coming to the United States for the first time are unlikely to identify themselves first as "Hispanic"; more likely, they will consider themselves Cuban, Mexican, or Colombian.

Just as there is no single Hispanic culture, there is no single Hispanic race. Hispanics may be white, black, Native American, or any mix thereof. That is why the U.S. Census Bureau notes in its documents that "persons of Hispanic origin may be of any race." Although many non-Hispanic Americans persist in regarding Hispanics as members of a race, the very nature of being Hispanic, with its tangled mix of ethnic stocks and influences, undermines the notion of race as a clear and distinct category.

Despite their diverse origins, Hispanic Americans are aware of their common heritage and identity. That identity is fraught with controversy, even concerning the name "Hispanic." Some people in this community prefer to call themselves "Latinos," rejecting the English coinage "Hispanic" for its emphasis on Spain (Hispania is Latin for Spain). "Latino," by contrast, is an authentic Spanish word that does not directly mention Spain, though it does credit ancient Rome's Latin language, from which the Spanish language derives. Most people regard both "Latino" and "Hispanic" as acceptable terms, and this book uses them interchangeably.

Because the blending of cultures is one of the central characteristics of Hispanic America, readers will find that the pages of *Atlas of Hispanic-American History* recount the stories of how and when that blending took place, as well as the tensions spurred along the way. And because by its very nature the blending of Hispanic cultures involves the crossing of borders—both geographical and cultural—an atlas is an ideal form through which to tell the tale. Through the use of maps, charts, and other illustrations, the story of Hispanic America proceeds in these pages from detailing the Spanish, African, and Native American roots of today's Hispanic-American cultures. Topics include the Spanish conquest and colonization of Mexico, South and Central America, and much of the Caribbean; the Spanish exploration and settlement of the Gulf Coast and Southwest of the present-day United States; the conflicts between Mexico and the United States over that territory—as illustrated by the fight for the independence of Texas and the U.S.-Mexican War; the emergence of Cuban and Puerto Rican communities in the United States following U.S. victory in the Spanish-American War; and the arrival of new Hispanic immigrants from other regions of Latin America, such as Colombia, Peru, and Central America. The book will discuss the ways in which Hispanic immigrants have adapted to life in the United States—the discrimination they have faced, the obstacles they have overcome, and the contributions they have made. The impact of Hispanic culture on American history as well as on American society in the early 21st century has been and continues to be dramatic. In fact, Hispanic culture and American culture are more inextricably intertwined than ever. This book celebrates that vibrant story.

THE ROOTS OF A PEOPLE
The Many Cultures of Hispanic America

Spain occupies 85 percent of the Iberian Peninsula, the boxy region that forms the southwest corner of Europe. Portugal, on the western edge, occupies the remainder. Larger than California but not as large as Texas, Spain has a total area of 194,884 square miles, including the Balearic Islands in the Mediterranean, the Canary Islands in the Atlantic, and two enclaves in Morocco, Ceuta, and Melilla. In the north, the Pyrenees Mountains form a natural barrier between Spain and France. Also in the north lies the Bay of Biscay; to the west, the Atlantic Ocean and Portugal; and to the east and the southeast, the Mediterranean Sea. At Spain's southern tip is the Strait of Gibraltar, which at its narrowest is less than eight miles wide, all that separates the Iberian Peninsula from North Africa.

From antiquity, the people of Spain exhibited both the penchant for blending and the devotion to local traditions that would characterize Hispanic America. The region's geography encouraged both traits. Via its Mediterranean coastline, Spain received seafaring traffic from

Contemporary Spain

Africa, southern Europe, and Asia; via mountain passes through the Pyrenees, Spain received migrants from northern Europe. All of these peoples contributed many elements to Spain's dynamic ethnic mix: Iberians, Celts, Phoenicians, Greeks, Romans, Jews, Alans, Vandals, Suevi, Visigoths, and Moors (all of which are discussed further below). But once in Spain, each group of settlers tended to become isolated by geography, thanks to the series of mountain ranges and rivers that cut across the Meseta, Spain's broad central plateau, chopping the country up into discrete regions. Mountains also border the Meseta, further slicing up the peninsula, with the Cantabrian mountains in the north and the Sierra Morena mountains in the south. The result has been a wide-ranging collection of distinct local cultures, at times fiercely independent of each other. Today these cultures are preserved within autonomous regional governments, all of which are united under Spain's constitutional monarchy.

SPANISH HISTORY TO 1492

Spain's identity as a diverse melting pot society has been a primary feature of its history since at least 3000 B.C., when a people known as the Iberians arrived on the peninsula. In time, they were joined by Phoenicians (ca. 1200 B.C.), Celts (ca. 1000 B.C.), Greeks (ca. 700 B.C.), Carthaginians (ca. 250 B.C.), Romans (ca. 200 B.C.), Visigoths (ca. A.D. 400), and Muslims (ca. A.D. 711). As will be seen, each of these groups has left an imprint on Spain, its history, and its culture.

FROM PREHISTORY TO CARTHAGE

The Iberian Peninsula has been populated since Paleolithic times, as is testified by magnificent cave paintings at Altamira that date back some 14,000 years. In about 3000 B.C., a people called the Iberians crossed the Strait of Gibraltar from North Africa and settled in the peninsula, ultimately occupying its southern two-thirds as far as the Ebro River valley in the northeast. The names "Ebro" and "Iberian" come from this people's word for "river," iber. They were joined, at about 1000 B.C., by the Celts, who came over the Pyrenees from France and mingled with the Iberian stock, particularly in the west, north, and center of the peninsula. The new mix was called Celtiberian. To this day, people in the northern Spanish regions of Galicia and Asturias are more likely to have Celtic blond hair and blue eyes than the typically dark-haired people in the southernmost region of Andalusia.

From across the Mediterranean came the Phoenicians, beginning in the 12th century B.C. Traveling from their base in Sidon and Tyre in what is now Lebanon,

THE END OF THE WORLD

To the ancient Greeks and Romans, Spain marked the western end of the known world. According to Greek and Roman mythology, Hercules, the fabulously strong son of Zeus, visited Spain, under the rays of the setting sun, to accomplish two of his 12 labors—capturing the oxen of Geryon and stealing the golden apples of the Hesperides. At what is now the Strait of Gibraltar, it is said Hercules raised two columns, the Pillars of Hercules, which correspond to modern Gibraltar and Ceuta. He also left an S-shaped legend around the pillars reading Non plus ultra, Latin for "Do not go beyond there."

In *The Buried Mirror: Reflections on Spain and the New World*, Mexican writer Carlos Fuentes argues that Spain's place at the edge of the Greco-Roman world helped to shape its national character: "Spain became something like the cul-de-sac of the Mediterranean. You went westward to Spain and there you stopped. . . . Spanish culture was fashioned to the highest degree by this finality, this eccentricity, of the country's geographic position. If you went to Spain, you stayed there, because there was nothing after it. Or you went back east, where you came from."

It is fitting that this end of the world was the embarkation point for Columbus's journey of discovery, which transformed Spain from the end of the world into the sovereign of much of the New World.

A Roman theater at Medellín, Spain (©Philip Baird/www.anthroarcheart.org)

these expert mariners and merchants established trading posts in the southern peninsula. The Greeks began to establish their own trading posts in the 7th century B.C.

In the 3rd century B.C., much of the Iberian Peninsula was conquered by Carthage, a powerful Phoenician city in what is now Tunisia in North Africa. They bequeathed Spain its name, calling it "Ispania," or "land of rabbits," for the preponderance of rabbits they found there. (Rabbit stew remains a favorite dish of Spanish country dwellers.) The Romans later adapted the name as "Hispania," which became the basis for the Spanish national name "España" and the English name "Spain."

Carthaginian rule was short-lived. During the Second Punic War with Rome (218–201 B.C.), Carthage was forced to surrender the peninsula to Rome, which went on to hold sway there from 205 B.C. until A.D. 409. The Iberian Peninsula was eventually segmented into three Roman provinces: Lusitania, roughly corresponding to modern Portugal; Baetica, in what is now southern Andalusia; and Hispania Tarraconensis, the rest of the peninsula.

ROMAN SPAIN

Rome's influence on Spanish history was profound. While permitting local traditions to flourish, the empire unified Spain's disparate regions, most visibly in a system of highways, more subtly with the introduction of Roman law and central administration. Imperial expansion developed the peninsula into a thriving source of grain and mineral wealth, including silver and gold; the separation between a few wealthy landowners and a vast peasantry that arose in Roman times became a hallmark of many Hispanic societies. In the country's interior, where only villages had stood, Rome founded such cities as Corduba (modern Córdoba) and Hispalis

ISLAMIC EXPANSION INTO SPAIN

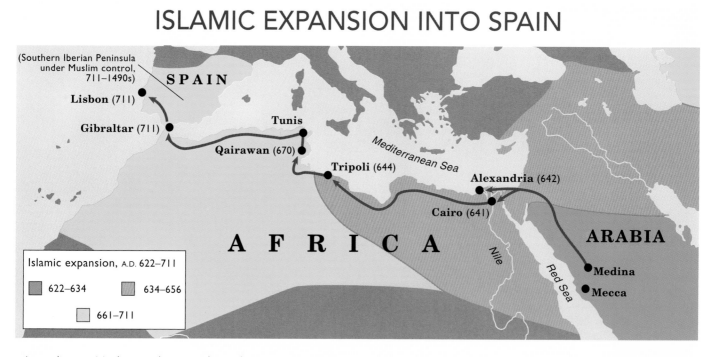

According to Muslim teaching, in about the year A.D. 610, the archangel Gabriel visited Muhammad, a Bedouin trader, and revealed to him the word of God, whom Bedouins called Allah. In time, Muhammad received further teachings concerning Allah's greatness and the need to recognize Him as the only god. Muhammad thus became Allah's messenger, preaching the message he had received to the people of Mecca, the trading city where he lived. His followers were called Muslims, which means "those who surrender to Allah."

Muhammad's message that all believers—whether rich or poor—were equal in the eyes of Allah angered the wealthy citizens of Mecca, who ordered that all Muslims be restricted to a certain section of the city. In a.d. 622, Muhammad and some of his followers left Mecca for the village of Yathrib (later known as Medina, "the city of the Prophet"). There, Muhammad found a more receptive audience to his message. In 628, he and his Muslim followers captured a caravan headed for Mecca. Then, in 627, an army from Mecca was forced to make peace with Muhammad's forces after failing to conquer Medina. In 630, Muhammad returned to Mecca, declared the Black Stone of Kaaba to be an Islamic shrine, and ordered that all idols to gods other than Allah be smashed.

Although Muhammad died two years later, his successors took up the cause of spreading the Muslim faith. By 634, Muslims had captured most of the Arabian peninsula, and by 652, they held the once-powerful Persian Empire in the east and a swath of North Africa to the west, stretching from Egypt to Tripoli. After continuing west across North Africa, the Muslim conquerors crossed the Strait of Gibraltar into Spain in 711. Spain remained in Muslim hands for the next 700 years.

(Seville). Rome built public works that still remain, such as the Segovia aqueduct (1st century A.D.), and made Spain a center for poetry and thought. Most notably, Rome left Spain the Latin language, the ancestor of modern Spanish and Portuguese, along with French, Italian, and other Romance languages.

By facilitating travel in the Mediterranean basin, Roman rule inadvertently helped Christianity to reach Spain, some time in the 1st century A.D. Until Rome proclaimed official tolerance for Christianity in the 4th century, Christians in Spain were often persecuted, with tales of glorious martyrdom becoming part of the country's lore. Fervent Roman Catholicism, with a willingness to blend in local pagan traditions, became an enduring characteristic of Hispanic culture. Judaism also grew in Spain under Roman rule, as Jews who had been expelled from their Near Eastern homeland of Judaea added yet another element to Spain's ethnic and cultural mix.

VISIGOTHIC SPAIN

After six centuries of rule, the declining Roman Empire lost its hold on Spain. In a.d. 409, Germanic peoples—the Alans, Vandals, and Suevi—swept through the Pyrenees and occupied much of the peninsula, effectively ending Roman rule. At Rome's request, another Germanic people, the Visigoths, entered Spain in 412 and soon became the dominant power, even after the Roman empire ceased to exist (476). With their base in

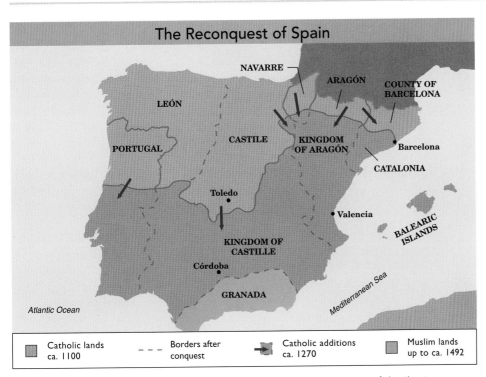

The Reconquest of Spain

NAVARRE

ARAGÓN

COUNTY OF BARCELONA

LEÓN

CASTILE

KINGDOM OF ARAGÓN

Barcelona

PORTUGAL

CATALONIA

Toledo

Valencia

BALEARIC ISLANDS

KINGDOM OF CASTILLE

Córdoba

Mediterranean Sea

GRANADA

Atlantic Ocean

Catholic lands ca. 1100

Borders after conquest

Catholic additions ca. 1270

Muslim lands up to ca. 1492

Beginning in about the year 1000, Christians in the northern regions of the Iberian peninsula began a struggle to reconquer the lands conquered by Muslim invaders in 711. As the map above illustrates, by 1492, only Granada in Spain's south remained in Muslim hands. In that year, however, the combined forces of Isabella of Castile and Ferdinand of Aragón retook that territory, uniting all of the peninsula under Christian rule.

Toulouse in present-day France, the Visigoths ruled Spain for three centuries, until 711. Their rule was, in some ways, a continuation of Roman rule, with Roman law and culture and Latin speech remaining in force, although with Visigothic adaptations.

MOORISH SPAIN

In 711, the rule of the Visigoths came to an abrupt end with the arrival of a new religion: Islam. Founded in Arabia by the prophet Muhammad in the 7th century and spread by military conquest across the north of Africa, Islam came to the Berbers, a North African people also known as the Moors. The Moors, in turn, brought Islam to Spain, crossing the Strait of Gibraltar in 711. By 718, they had conquered most of the Iberian Peninsula. The Moors tried to advance into France but were stopped near the city of Poitiers in 732 by the Frankish ruler Charles Martel.

Almost as soon as the Muslim conquest of Spain was completed, the Christian reconquest of Spain began. The Reconquest, or Reconquista, did not take

place all at once but spanned more than five centuries (ca. 1000–1492). It began when Pelayo, a Christian Visigothic chieftain, defeated the Moors at Covadonga in 722, securing his rule of the independent kingdom of Asturias in mountainous northern Spain. By the 11th century, Christian control of Spain had spread to other parts of the north, notably the kingdoms of León (which included Asturias), Navarre, Castile, and Aragón. The rulers of Christian Spain advanced steadily into Muslim lands, but they spent as much time warring with each other and with their nobles as with the Muslims. The reign of King Alfonso VII (1126–1157) was typical: although he united the thrones of León and Castile, he failed in his bid to rule Aragón as well, and after his death, even León and Castile fell into civil war.

Meanwhile, the Moors under the Umayyad dynasty of emirs (756–929) and caliphs (929–1036) developed an advanced civilization in southern Spain. The capital of Moorish Spain, Córdoba, became the greatest western European city of its day, marked by universities, public lighting, limited toleration for Christianity and Judaism, and free

WHY PORTUGAL IS NOT SPANISH

The earliest European competitors in the Americas were Portugal and Spain. Yet to the Romans, Visigoths, and Moors, Portugal was just another part of their Iberian lands, with a status no different from that of a Spanish province. It was only in 1139 that Alfonso Henriques, the count of Portugal, declared his realm's independence and took the title King Alfonso I.

Alfonso and his successors expanded their kingdom into Moorish territory, until, in 1249, the Moors were expelled from Algarve, completing the Portuguese reconquest. Under King John I, who reigned from 1385 to 1433, Portugal successfully defended itself against attack by Castile, formed an alliance with England, and fostered a new age of overseas exploration and conquest. Portugal's overseas adventures were aided by its position on Europe's Atlantic coast and by its development of the caravel, a light ship equipped for ocean voyages. By 1500, Portugal had captured Ceuta in Morocco; colonized the Atlantic islands of Madeira, the Azores, and Cape Verde; begun to colonize the West African coast; staked a claim to what would be their colony of Brazil; and discovered a sea route from Europe to India around the southern tip of Africa. Still, Portugal did not become the dominant power in the Americas, losing to Spain and others. Portugal itself came close to being subsumed into Spain. In 1580, Spanish king Philip II annexed Portugal, which remained part of Spain until 1640, when a revolt restored Portugal's independence. Ever since, Portugal has been independent, and its one time colony of Brazil, where the national language is still Portuguese, has not been part of Hispanic America.

schooling for the poor. Philosophy, astronomy, mathematics, and medicine were all studied; literature, art, and architecture flourished. The Moors irrigated arid lands and encouraged trade. Among the elements they introduced to Spanish culture were oranges and rice, lutes and paper, Islamic musical and architectural styles, and landmarks like the fortified palace Alhambra, which still stands in Granada.

COMPLETION OF THE RECONQUEST

In 1036, the Umayyad dynasty ended, with the caliphate splitting into rival kingdoms. The Christian kings in the north took advantage of the Moors' growing disunity to expand into the south. In 1094, the great national hero El Cid (Rodrigo Díaz de Bivar) captured Valencia in southeastern Spain from the Moors. At the battle of Navas de Tolosa in 1212, the Christians under King Alfonso VIII of Castile defeated the reigning Moorish rulers, the Almohads, and Islamic control of southern Spain mostly disintegrated. Moorish rule continued in the kingdom of Granada in the south but was increasingly threatened by Christian unification. In the 1480s, Ferdinand V of Aragón and Isabella I of Castile, who had unified most of Christian Spain following their marriage in 1469, waged a sustained war against Granada. In 1492, Granada fell. After more than 700 years, Moorish rule of Spain was over.

Ferdinand and Isabella centralized authority, taking power away from the nobles and putting it in the hands of the monarchy. Viewing themselves as guardians of the Roman Catholic faith against heresies and false religions, they established the Spanish Inquisition in 1478 to search out heretics, and in 1492 they required all Jews to convert or leave; Muslims faced the same demand in 1502. About 150,000 Jews left Spain, eventually settling in such places as the Netherlands, the Middle East, and the Americas. Most Muslims converted to Christianity. But both Muslim and Jewish converts, known as conversos, were suspected of secretly retaining their former beliefs, and as such remained targets of the Inquisition. Infamous for its ready use of torture and capital punishment, the Inquisition was not abolished until 1834.

Determined to make Spain a great power, Ferdinand and Isabella wanted to build trade with East Asia, especially China, India, and Indonesia, known collectively as the Indies. To that end, they financed the exploratory voyage of Italian mariner Christopher Columbus, who embarked westward in 1492 and first brought the Spanish into contact with the Americas. (More will be said about Columbus later in this chapter and in chapter 2.)

Spanish society on the eve of the birth of Hispanic America was a unified, autocratic, stratified, and expansionist society, fresh from a great military victory against a rival religious and political power, and zealously dedicated to the preserving and expanding the reach of the Roman Catholic faith. Yet it was also a society that was built on millennia of ethnic intermingling, with a unique stew of cultural influences, a wide array of regional differences, and a long history of interregional conflict.

THE NATIVE AMERICAN HERITAGE

Native Americans are those people whose ancestors lived in the Americas and developed indigenous societies before the arrival of Columbus. They are also called American Indians, in commemoration of Columbus's mistaken notion that the American territories he reached were part of the Indies, or East Asia.

ORIGINS

How the ancestors of modern Native Americans—Paleo-Indians—arrived is shrouded in mystery. The traditional view is that they came principally from the northeast Asian region of Siberia, across what is now the Bering Strait between Siberia and Alaska. During the last ice age, from about 20,000 to 14,000 years ago, glaciers locked up large quantities of water, lowering sea levels enough to create a land bridge, known as Beringia. The first Americans, according to this view, walked across Beringia from Siberia to Alaska, spreading from there across the Americas. Though this view is

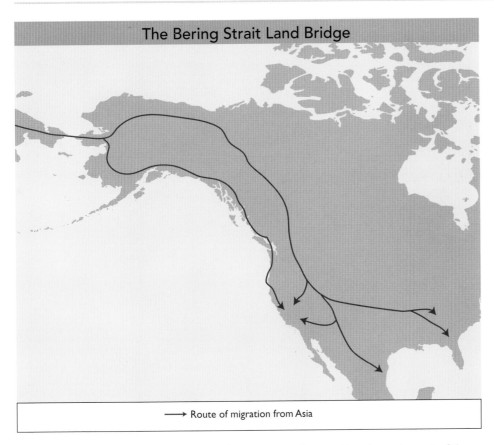

The Bering Strait Land Bridge

⟶ Route of migration from Asia

According to one of the most common theories regarding prehistoric settlement of the Americas, the first Americans crossed the Bering Strait land bridge between Siberia and Alaska some time between 14,000 and 20,000 years ago. In time, these early peoples settled across North America, Central America, and eventually South America. The map shown here illustrates possible migration routes in North America.

still widely held, many scholars now argue that there were other avenues of migration as well, including oceangoing travel in the Pacific Rim region, sea travel across the Bering Strait after Beringia was submerged, and perhaps even transatlantic voyages from Europe.

The date of the earliest human arrival in the Americas is no clearer than the route taken. The earliest widely accepted archaeological evidence, at Monte Verde, Chile, dates from 12,500 years ago. Another early culture is the Clovis culture, associated with Clovis, New Mexico, and dating from 11,500 years ago. But earlier sites keep being uncovered: for example, some archaeologists believe that a site at Cactus Hill, Virginia, dates from 15,000 years ago. Analysis of contemporary people's DNA and linguistic studies of differences between Native American languages indicate that the common ancestors of New World and Old World populations may have lived even earlier, perhaps 20,000 to 40,000 years ago.

CULTURAL DEVELOPMENT

Whatever the point of origin or time of arrival of Native Americans, they were living throughout North, Central, and South America by 11,000 years ago. At first, they lived by hunting, gathering, and fishing. About 9,000 years ago, in the valley of Tehuacán in south-central Mexico, plant domestication began, about a thousand years after it had been independently developed in the Old World. In subsequent millennia, agriculture spread to many regions of the Americas, becoming a major source of food and developing much of the world's current diet: crops first cultivated by Native Americans include potatoes, tomatoes, corn (also called maize), red peppers, peanuts, cacao (from which chocolate is made), and pineapples, not to mention less healthy substances such as tobacco and coca (the plant that is used today to make cocaine). However, unlike their Old World counterparts, Native American farmers did not have large domesticated animals. Dogs

ART AND ARTIFACTS OF MESOAMERICA

Colossal Olmec head

Zapotec bas-relief sculpture

Toltec column

Aztec calendar

The art and artifacts of pre-Columbian Mesoamerica have given historians and archeologists some limited insight into the many cultural traditions of the peoples who populated the region during the centuries before the arrival of Europeans. Among the earliest examples is the carved basalt-stone head seen above, which came from the Olmec people, who flourished on Mexico's gulf coast by 1200 B.C. As large as nine feet high and as heavy as 200 tons, the heads were carved from stone blocks brought from distances as great as 50 miles without the benefit of wagons. The bas-relief sculpture is an artifact of the Zapotec of the Oaxaca Valley,

whose civilization lasted from 600 B.C. until about the 15th century. The sculptures, depicting men, are thought to represent corpses of enemies. From the Toltec, who dominated much of central Mexico between A.D. 950 and about 1200 came the 15-foot-tall column seen above. So great was the Toltec civilization that centuries later, the Aztec (who arrived in central Mexico in about 1300) still spoke of them in mythic tales. The Aztec, who claimed to be descended from the Toltec, would themselves attain the status of legend. Among their achievements is their calendar stone, shown above, which symbolized cycles and eras that played parts in their legends.

and turkeys could be found on their farms, as could llamas and guinea pigs in South America, but no sheep, cows, or horses (none of which yet lived in the Americas). Some cultures developed metallurgy on a limited scale, but the wheel as labor-saving device was never invented.

Whereas hunting and gathering supports only a small number of people relative to land area, systems of agriculture support large numbers. The systems also encourage people to stay in one place, rather than moving regularly as hunters do, thus permitting the development of towns and cities. Surplus crops provide leisure for at least some people, facilitating the development of arts, sciences, and often stratification by class, with the leisured people at the top and the hard-working peasants at the bottom. Following this model the Americas, long before Columbus, became the site of several flourishing urban civilizations, including the Maya, Aztec, and Inca civilizations, all of which contributed to the Hispanic-American heritage.

MESOAMERICA

Mesoamerican civilizations is the collective name for the pre-Columbian civilizations that arose in the region stretching from central Mexico through upper Central America. It was here, at about 7000 b.c., that plant domestication in the Americas began. By 1200 b.c., in the midst of Mexico's eastern jungles, the Olmec people were building pyramid temples, palaces, and great stone monuments. In about 600 b.c., the Zapotec, another Mesoamerican people, developed a system of hieroglyphics, the first known writing system in the Americas.

By 400 b.c., Olmec power was waning, and another people was emerging: the Maya, based in the Yucatán Peninsula but eventually extending their power as far south as Guatemala and Honduras. During their Classic period, from about A.D. 300 to 900, they too raised pyramids, as well as making great advances in writing, mathematics, astronomy, calendar keeping, agriculture, and architecture. But after 900 many of the lowland Mayan cities were mysteriously abandoned. Despite this collapse in the southern reaches of the empire which ended the Classic period, Mayan civilization survived in the Yucatán until the Spanish arrived in the 16th century. This latter period is known as the Post-Classic period.

The Maya shared present-day Mexico with another Mesoamerican people, the inhabitants of Teotihuacán in central Mexico northeast of what is now Mexico City. A small settlement in 400 B.C., Teotihuacán developed into a major city by the 1st century a.d. and flourished until about 700, dominating the valley of Mexico. After Teotihuacán went into decline, the Toltec arrived in the region, migrating south from northern Mexico. During the 10th century, the Toltec built an empire in central Mexico, gaining control of neighboring peoples, including the Maya, through warfare. The Toltec

empire collapsed in the 12th century, and in the 14th century another remarkable people, the Aztec or Mexica, began to gain dominance in central Mexico. Their capital, Tenochtitlán, located at present-day Mexico City, was founded by 1325. They formed military alliances with other peoples, establishing an empire that stretched from central Mexico into northern Guatemala. This empire was still powerful when the first Spanish explorers arrived in the early 15th century.

When the Spanish conquered Mexico and Central America, the Aztec were the most prominent people in the region. Their capital, Tenochtitlán, was a dazzling city of 250,000 people, built on an island with causeways linking it to the mainland. They expanded upon the achievements of previous Mesoamerican peoples by constructing enormous pyramids to honor the gods; by practicing an elaborate system of astronomy and

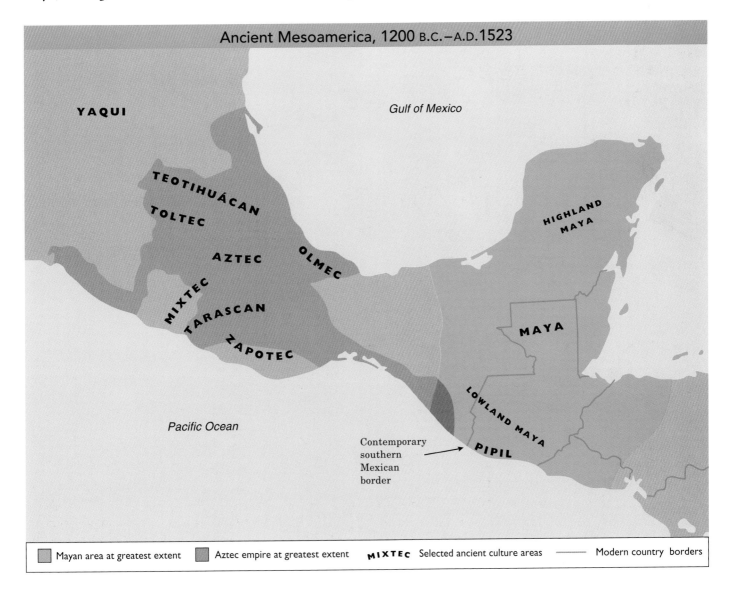

Ancient Mesoamerica, 1200 B.C.–A.D. 1523

YAQUI

Gulf of Mexico

TEOTIHUÁCAN

TOLTEC

AZTEC

OLMEC

HIGHLAND MAYA

MIXTEC

TARASCAN

ZAPOTEC

MAYA

Pacific Ocean

LOWLAND MAYA

Contemporary southern Mexican border

PIPIL

Mayan area at greatest extent   Aztec empire at greatest extent   **MIXTEC** Selected ancient culture areas   —— Modern country borders

calendar keeping; by educating their young not only in food preparation and fishing, but also in sculpting, painting, and writing detailed histories, in the form of pictographs, or picture writing.

Aztec society was highly stratified, with masses of slaves and commoners serving a small elite group of priests, warriors, and other nobles. Trade thrived in city markets, supported by the labor of farming villages. The Aztec worshiped many gods, including Huitzilopochtli, the sun and war god; Coyolxauhqui, the moon goddess; Tlaloc, the rain god; and Quetzalcoatl, the feathered serpent god associated with death and resurrection. Human sacrifice was central to Aztec religion, with slaves and prisoners of war regularly killed on the altar block as offerings.

The Aztec were not the only people whom the Spanish encountered in Mexico and Central America. The Aztec empire consisted of a diverse and sometimes tense collection of 300 city-states, and there were many rival states outside the empire,

such as the Tarascan empire, as well as an assortment of Mayan states. Other peoples of the region included the Mixtec, known for their metalwork and stonework; the Zapotec; the Yaqui; and the Pipil.

The Inca

Another advanced civilization encountered by the Spanish was that of the Inca in the central Andes Mountains of South America. As with the Aztec in Mesoamerica, the Inca benefited from the arts and sciences of their predecessors in the region, including the Chavín, Tiahuanico, Mouche, Nazca, Aymara, and Chimú peoples. About A.D. 1200, the Inca, who spoke Quechua, settled in the valley of Cuzco in what is now Peru. In the 15th century, they established an empire around Cuzco and swiftly expanded it until it stretched more than 2,500 miles from north to south and 500 miles from east to west. Encompassing parts of

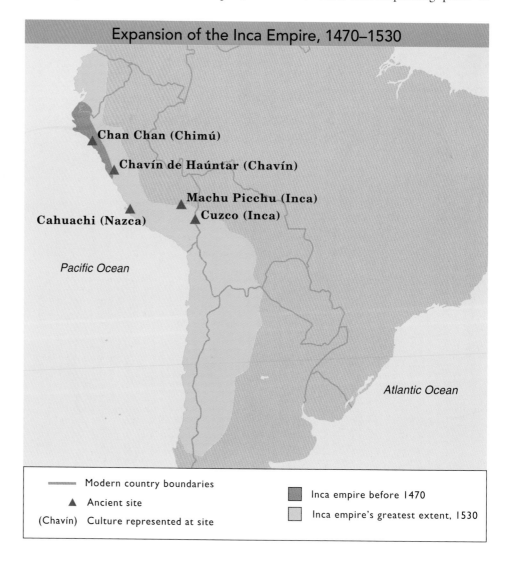

Expansion of the Inca Empire, 1470–1530

Chan Chan (Chimú)

Chavín de Haúntar (Chavín)

Machu Picchu (Inca)

Cahuachi (Nazca) Cuzco (Inca)

Pacific Ocean

Atlantic Ocean

——— Modern country boundaries

▲ Ancient site

(Chavín) Culture represented at site

Inca empire before 1470

Inca empire's greatest extent, 1530

Machu Picchu (Corbis)

present-day Ecuador, Peru, Bolivia, Chile, and Argentina, it resembled a long snake curling through the Andes Mountains.

Like the Aztec empire, the Inca empire was highly stratified and centralized, with a large farming population subordinated to a small ruling class. The empire was theocratic, with the Inca emperors regarded as representatives of the sun god. Animal sacrifices figured in religious ceremonies; so did human sacrifices, though not to the extent practiced by the Aztec. The Inca built a network of stone roads to unify the empire, raised great temples and palaces, dug irrigation canals, built rope suspension bridges, and fostered development in art and music. They used the abacus and kept numerical records using knotted strings.

OTHER SOUTH AMERICAN PEOPLES

In the northern Andes, the Chibcha of what is now Colombia were politically powerful, with numerous towns, villages, palaces, and temples. The Chibcha exhibited great artistry in making gold ornaments and cultivated extensive agriculture and trade. In the northern tropical forests of what is now Venezuela, by contrast, the various Native peoples lacked political or cultural unity.

In southern South America, in what are now Paraguay, Uruguay, Argentina, and Chile, the Native peoples were similarly diverse and decentralized. Many lived in villages and subsisted on hunting, gathering, and fishing. Two of these

Anasazi cliff dwellings at Canyon de Chelly, in Arizona (Library of Congress)

groups were the Araucanian people of Chile and Argentina and the Guaraní of Brazil, Paraguay, Uruguay, and Argentina. Around the Strait of Magellan in Chile, the Ona and Yahgan hunted seals and lived in sealskin-covered wigwams.

BEFORE THE UNITED STATES

Spain at its zenith claimed vast tracts of what is now the United States, and in those regions they encountered still more Native American peoples. They can be roughly categorized by culture area—a geographic region in which a particular climate and ecology encourages certain kinds of cultural adaptations. The Southwest culture area included parts of what is now the U.S. Southwest—Arizona, New Mexico, and southern Colorado—and what is now northern Mexico. Plant cultivation in this mostly arid region dates from 3000 B.C. When the Spanish came, the peoples they encountered included the Akimel O'odham (Pima) of Arizona, a

farming people who lived near riverbanks in villages of domed huts, irrigated their fields, and were governed by an elected chief and a council. They were the descendants of the Hohokam, who migrated into Arizona from Mexico in about 300 B.C. The Spanish also encountered the Pueblo, descendants of a people called the Anasazi, who flourished about A.D. 700. Like their ancestors, the Pueblo grew maize, beans, and squash, excelled in pottery making and weaving, and lived in multistoried, terraced apartment buildings of adobe called pueblos. Peoples in this group include the Zuni and the Hopi.

Also living in the Southwest at the time were nomadic hunting and gathering people, such as the Navajo (Dineh) and Apache, who had migrated there from the north in the 1400s. Able warriors, they were accustomed to raiding Pueblo towns for food. They hunted bison, or buffalo, and lived in buffalo-hide tipis and brush huts.

Not all Native peoples that would come into contact with the Spanish were

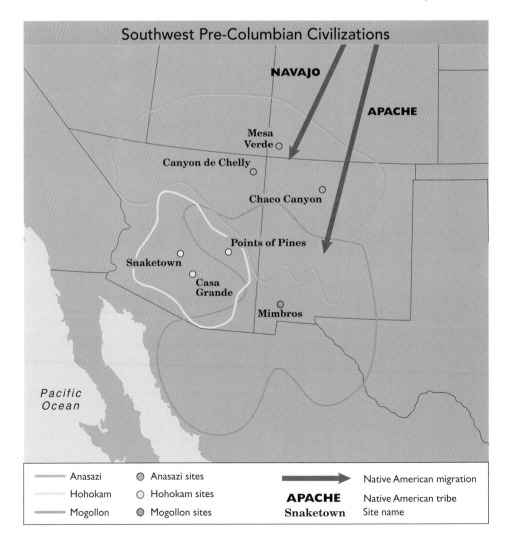

PRE-COLUMBIAN CULTURES IN THE CARIBBEAN

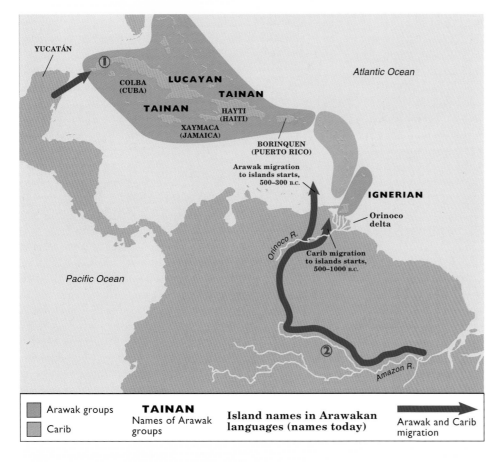

Arawak groups	**TAINAN**	Island names in Arawakan	
Carib	Names of Arawak groups	languages (names today)	Arawak and Carib migration

Island Carib and Arawak (A.D. 1492)

A common misconception during the Spanish colonization of the Caribbean was that the Arawak were peace-loving while the Carib were warlike cannibals. (Cannibal is actually a corruption of the word Carib.) This misconception dates back to Columbus: as a way to make money from his exploration he proposed enslaving the Indians and selling them in Europe. The Spanish crown restricted capture and enslavement to tribes who had attacked Europeans or were cannibals. As a result, many tribes in the Caribbean and South America were labeled as cannibals by the colonists to justify their enslavement. There is little evidence that the Carib actually practiced cannibalism.

① Earliest Settlers (ca. 5000 B.C.)

Archaeologists think that one or more waves of Stone Age settlers may have crossed from the Yucatán beginning as early as 5000 b.c. As late as Columbus's arrival, there were reports of a primitive, cave-dwelling people (today called the Guanahatabey) living in western Cuba, but archaeologists cannot confirm that they actually survived into the time of the conquest.

② Origins (ca. 3000 B.C.)

The Arawak and the Carib descended from groups living in the central Amazon region of South America perhaps 5,000 years ago. Over the centuries, these peoples moved north into the Orinoco valley, and from there to the islands of the Caribbean.

of the Southwest culture area. In California, Native Americans at the time of the Spanish conquest subsisted on hunting, gathering, and fishing. In the Southeast, a semitropical region extending from central Texas to Florida, a number of peoples lived in long-established villages and farmed such crops as maize, beans, and squash. Among these peoples were the Natchez of the lower Mississippi River valley, a rigidly stratified society of sun worshippers who built temple mounds. Other agricultural peoples of the Southeast who were based in permanent villages were the so-called Five Civilized Tribes: the Cherokee, Choctaw, Chickasaw, Creek, and Seminole.

INDIGENOUS PEOPLES OF THE CARIBBEAN

The Caribbean islands or West Indies—the first New World location reached by explorers from Spain—were populated by two competing peoples: the Arawak or Taíno, and the Carib. In this tropical culture area, people lived by farming, fishing, and hunting. Arawak on the large Caribbean islands had elaborate societies headed by hereditary chiefs who ruled over other classes. The Arawak were skilled at pottery making, weaving, and working with wood and metal—including gold, which they used for ornaments. Also inhabiting the Caribbean islands were the Carib, who gave the region its name. The Carib were known for their skill in warfare and able canoeing.

THE DIVERSITY OF INDIGENOUS AMERICA

Although the numerous and distinct peoples that the early Spanish explorers encountered in the New World did share some common cultural attributes, that is not to suggest that the hundreds of distinct peoples that populated the Americas shared a single homogenous identity. On the contrary, these peoples—who lived in climates ranging from the high Andes of South America and the desert Southwest of North America to the tropical islands of the Caribbean—varied greatly in their fundamental cultural traits, with vast differences in their diets, languages, living arrangements, and religious beliefs; their

economic, political, military, and social structures; and their clothing styles, arts, crafts, and musical styles. Some lived in vast empires and others in small nomadic groups. Some were hunters and gatherers and others were farmers. Nonetheless, upon contact with the Spanish, many of these varied Native American cultures contributed distinctive elements to the wide-ranging mixture that would become what would become Hispanic America.

THE AFRICAN HERITAGE

In a sense, all Americans, like all other human beings, are of African descent. It was in Africa that hominids, or humanlike primates, first emerged at least 5 million years ago. Many scientists now believe that modern humans first evolved in Africa about 100,000 to 200,000 years ago, spreading from there to other continents, where they became the ancestors of all the world's peoples. But the links between Africans and Hispanic Americans are more recent than that. The people of Spain are themselves a blend of North African and other ethnic groups. Black Africans, those from sub-Saharan Africa, were transported across the Atlantic as slaves to Spain's American colonies, where they contributed to the cultural and genetic heritage of Hispanic America.

AFRICAN EMPIRES

Africa contains more than 3,000 distinct ethnic groups, speaking more than 1,000 languages. It is impossible here to do justice to such a long and complex history. Instead, this section briefly recounts the history of sub-Saharan Africa prior to the start of the transatlantic slave trade, since that is the region from which most of the New World's African people came.

South of the Sahara Desert, in the semiarid savannah region of what are now southeastern Mauritania, eastern Senegal, and southwest Mali, the kingdom of Ghana was the dominant power from the 5th to 12th centuries A.D. It was powerful for its control of trans-Saharan trade, in which gold and slaves from the south were exchanged for salt and cloth from the north. Ghana disintegrated early in the 13th century, under pressure from

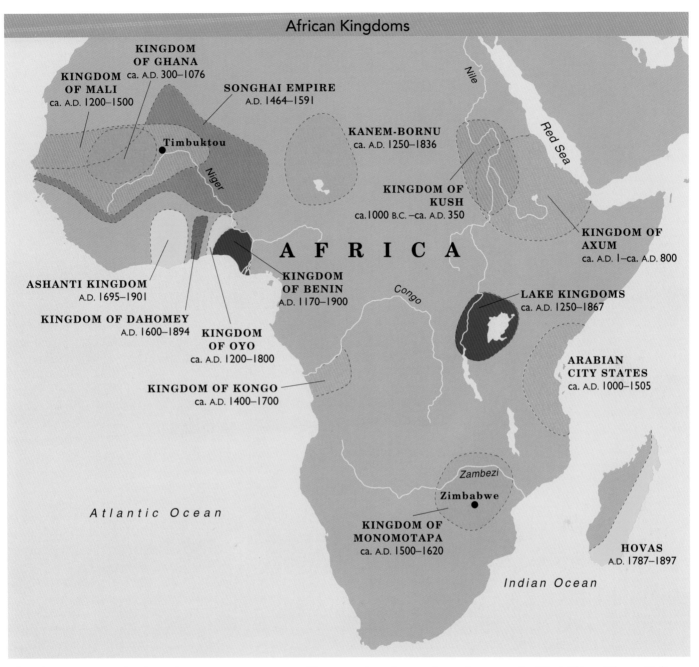

African Kingdoms

KINGDOM OF GHANA
ca. A.D. 300–1076

KINGDOM OF MALI
ca. A.D. 1200–1500

SONGHAI EMPIRE
A.D. 1464–1591

Timbuktou

Niger

KANEM-BORNU
ca. A.D. 1250–1836

Nile

Red Sea

KINGDOM OF KUSH
ca. 1000 B.C.–ca. A.D. 350

KINGDOM OF AXUM
ca. A.D. 1–ca. A.D. 800

A F R I C A

ASHANTI KINGDOM
A.D. 1695–1901

KINGDOM OF DAHOMEY
A.D. 1600–1894

KINGDOM OF OYO
ca. A.D. 1200–1800

KINGDOM OF BENIN
A.D. 1170–1900

Congo

LAKE KINGDOMS
ca. A.D. 1250–1867

ARABIAN CITY STATES
ca. A.D. 1000–1505

KINGDOM OF KONGO
ca. A.D. 1400–1700

Atlantic Ocean

Zambezi

Zimbabwe

KINGDOM OF MONOMOTAPA
ca. A.D. 1500–1620

HOVAS
A.D. 1787–1897

Indian Ocean

The African continent has been home to numerous magnificent empires. Among the earliest were the West African Ghana, Mali, and Songhai. Other early kingdoms, such as Ashanti, Oyo, and Kongo, also thrived. The locations and dates for many of Africa's most important kingdoms are shown here.

competing states. The empire of Mali, in what is now the Republic of Mali, then became the dominant power. It had emerged in the 11th century, governed by Mandinka people, and reached its zenith in the early 14th century, when it stretched more than 1,000 miles from the Atlantic Ocean to beyond the Niger River. Internal discord drove the empire into decline later that century. Songhai, a kingdom that gained independence from Mali in 1335, then rose to power in West Africa, reaching its peak in the 15th and 16th centuries.

Important as these empires were in the history of West Africa, many of the people who would come in bondage to Hispanic America hailed not from these semiarid realms but from farther south— the heavily rain-forested coasts of the Atlantic Ocean and the Gulf of Guinea. This region includes the coastal areas of what are now modern Senegal, Gambia, Guinea-Bissau, Guinea, Sierra Leone, Liberia, Côte d'Ivoire, Ghana, Togo, Benin, Nigeria, and Cameroon. Slaves also came from west central Africa, the region that is now Equatorial Guinea,

Gabon, Angola, the Republic of Congo, and the Democratic Republic of Congo (formerly Zaire). (Africa's two nations known as Congo trace their roots back to the Kingdom of Kongo, which was founded in the 15th century and collapsed in the wake of European colonialism in the 18th century.)

The West African coast had its share of powerful states. In eastern Senegal, the Tukulor people established the Tekrur state, which dominated its area from the 11th to 14th centuries. The kingdom of Benin, in what is now Nigeria, was a powerful force in trade with Europe from the 15th to 18th centuries, and it also produced magnificent bronze sculptures. Benin was later eclipsed by the Oyo Empire, led by the Yoruba people, who emerged in Nigeria in the 17th century and survived into the 19th century. The kingdom of Dahomey in what is now Benin and the Ashanti (Asante) confederation in what is now Ghana also lasted from the 17th to 19th centuries.

Despite the existence of states like these, ruled by kings or princes, many people in West Africa lived in stateless communities: the Ibo, for example, who lived in the forests of what is now Nigeria east of the Niger River; and the Tiv, who lived along the Benue River, which flows through what are now Cameroon and Nigeria. The status of people in these societies was based on kinship affiliations, with village elders administering justice and each family worshipping its personal gods and harvesting its own crops, particularly yams, palm oil, and kola nuts. The wood sculptures and music of some of these stateless peoples were as remarkable as works produced in the centralized kingdoms.

THE SLAVE TRADE

Even before the transatlantic slave trade began, African societies captured, sold, and used slaves. But the pace of the slave trade greatly increased after 1444–1445, when Portuguese explorers reached Cape Verde, an archipelago off the West African coast, and the mouth of the Senegal River in what is now Senegal. The Portuguese soon began trading with the Africans, seeking primarily gold but also pepper, ivory, and slaves. Portuguese trade soon extended down the West African coast; in the 1480s, it reached what are now Angola and the Republic of Congo.

At first, the trade in slaves was light, with captives shipped mainly to Europe to work as domestic servants. These slaves, heavily Europeanized, were the first Africans to come to the New World, entering as servants of the Spanish conquistadores. They shared their masters' religion, language, and culture, and became known as ladinos, a word derived from a Latin term for "cunning" or "learned." By contrast, slaves shipped to the Americas directly from Africa, unfamiliar with European language or culture, became known as bozales, a word that also referred to the muzzles used on dogs or horses.

The slave trade began to grow in the late 15th century, when Portugal and Spain were establishing sugar plantations on such Atlantic islands as Madeira, the Canaries, and São Tomé. The plantations needed agricultural workers, so slaves were imported directly from Africa. Their unpaid labor helped generate considerable profits for their owners. Desiring similar wealth from the Americas, Spain, began to import vast numbers of slaves in the mid-16th century for its American empire. Africans were brought to Peru and Mexico to toil at everything from mining and textile manufacture to skilled crafts such as metalworking. But they were especially in demand in the West Indies, where Spanish brutality and disease had killed off much of the Native American population, eliminating them as potential workers for the sugar plantations that were beginning to sprout there.

The slave trade boomed as the years went on. From Columbus's discovery of the New World in 1492 until 1600, Spanish America imported about 75,000 African slaves. In the 17th century, the number imported was 292,000; from 1701 to 1810, the total was 578,600. Nor was Spain alone in this commerce. By 1810, the various American empires—including those of Spain, Portugal, Britain, France, the Netherlands, and Denmark—had imported a total of more than 7 million African slaves. Portugal dominated the transatlantic slave trade for more than a century, but Spain, Britain, and other European powers eventually joined in the business. The European slavers were aided by African

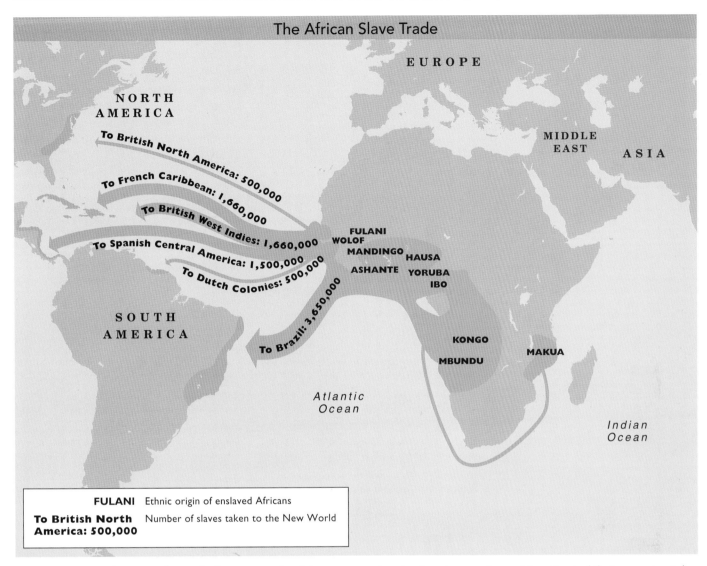

The African Slave Trade

Between 1505 and 1870, millions of Africans were forcibly transported to the Americas as slaves. It is estimated that approximately one in six enslaved Africans died en route to their destinations. All told, almost 9.5 million Africans made the journey, with roughly 1.5 million destined for Spain's American colonies.

states, such as Benin, Dahomey, and Oyo, that collected slaves from the interior and traded them for European goods at the coast.

At first, most slaves came from Senegambia—modern Senegal and Gambia—where the major ethnic groups included the Wolof, Fulani, Tukulor, Serer, and Mandingo. Gradually, the area for enslaving Africans expanded south and east along the coast to the Bight of Biafra, which extends from modern Nigeria to modern Gabon; enslaved peoples from this region included the Yoruba, Ibo, and Fang. In the 17th century, Angola's Orimbunda, Mbanda, and Kongo peoples became a major source of slaves.

Once enslaved, Africans were grouped with other African captives who spoke different languages and came from far-off societies—an intentional strategy on the part of traders to prevent communication that might foster mass revolt. This strategy had long-term consequences as well, making it difficult for slaves to preserve for their descendants the memory of their original homes. Even so, enslaved Africans found ways of saving some traces of their religious, culinary, and musical heritage.

Great Britain outlawed the slave trade within its empire in 1807, but that did not end slavery in Hispanic America. There slavery did not begin to be abolished until the 1820s, when Chile and Mexico, which had newly won independence from Spain, outlawed the institution of slavery. In other parts of Hispanic America, slavery persisted until late into the 19th century, with Cuba the last holdout: slavery was not fully abolished on that Spanish island colony until 1886.

THREE WORLDS COLLIDE

Christopher Columbus's discovery brought together two of the three founding peoples of Hispanic America: Native Americans and Spaniards. In the decades that followed, Spain built a vast New World empire, forcing Africans to work in its colonies as slaves. So entered the third of the three founding Hispanic-American peoples.

AMERICAN EMPIRES

Several trends combined to drive European discovery and conquest of the Americas. First was the unification of small European states between the 16th and 18th centuries into centralized, highly competitive nation-states, including Spain, Portugal, France, and England (referred to as Great Britain after the unification of England and Scotland in 1707). Development of new techniques in shipbuilding and navigation also helped foster exploration, as did the desire of Christians to bring the Gospel to peoples who had never before heard it. But perhaps the most powerful motive for exploration was greed: the hunger of merchants to acquire new wealth and the longing of monarchs to increase the power of their kingdoms at the expense of other states.

Goods from Africa and Asia, such as gold, silk, and spices, were in great demand in Europe, but most of the profits from trade in these commodities went to the Islamic and Italian middlemen who controlled the trade routes. These established trade routes led mostly overland and across the Mediterranean. The easiest way to circumvent the middlemen was to establish new trade routes along the African coast or around the southern tip of Africa. In the course of seeking one such trade route—westward from Europe to Asia—Columbus stumbled on the Americas. That discovery opened up the possibility of building vast new empires, realms that would produce yet more riches for the profit of the European states that controlled them.

By the mid-18th century, the European powers had established many thriving colonies in the Americas. Spanish America encompassed much of what is now the western and southwestern United States, all of Mexico, and much of Central and South America. The most extensive non-Spanish part of South America was Brazil, claimed by Portugal. North America was the site of violent jockeying for power between France and Britain, Spain's rivals in the continent. By 1763, France had been forced out, with Britain's domains extending west from the Atlantic Ocean to the Mississippi, and south from Canada to the Gulf of Mexico.

In the West Indies, Spain possessed Cuba, Puerto Rico, and part of Hispaniola. Other islands in the West Indies were under English, French, and Dutch control.

Despite its vast possessions, Spain by the 18th century was a declining world power, its treasury sapped by too many wars in Europe and abroad defending its colonial interests. At home, religious persecution of Jews and Muslims had driven merchants of both faiths from the country, forcing Spaniards to import more and more of their goods from northern Europe instead of buying them at home. The late 18th and 19th centuries saw a wave of wars of independence in the New World that neither Spain nor other European powers were able to resist. By the 1820s, when most of Spain's colonies won their independence, 300 years of Spanish rule had already begun the blending of peoples that would characterize Hispanic America.

THE MAKING OF HISPANIC AMERICA

According to some estimates, North and South America just prior to European colonization were inhabited by more than 90 million Native Americans: about 10 million north of present-day Mexico; 41 million in Mexico and Central America; 39 million in South America; and nearly half a million in the Caribbean islands. No one knows the exact figures, because by the time Europeans began counting, the Native American populations had been decimated. Europeans introduced diseases, such as smallpox and influenza, that killed off large numbers of Native

European Claims in North America, 1700

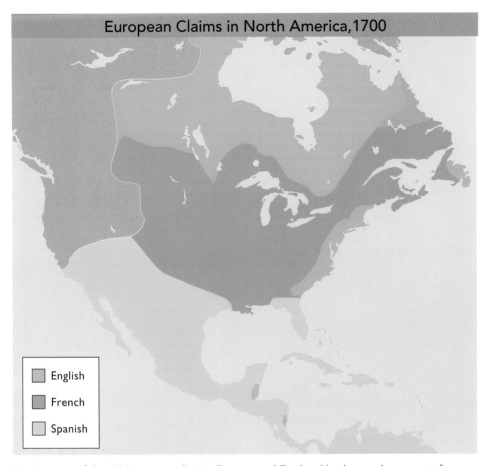

- ■ English
- ■ French
- ■ Spanish

By the start of the 18th century, Spain, France, and England had carved up most of North America into colonies. England competed for control of the Atlantic seaboard with France, while France and Spain battled over control of the Gulf Coast. Although the Spanish held most of Cuba, Puerto Rico, and Santo Domingo (present-day Haiti and the Dominican Republic), by 1700 English, French, and Dutch forces had begun challenge them for control of the Caribbean as a whole.

Americans who lacked immunity to them. War, forced labor, and the brutality of their European conquerors killed off more. In the Spanish colonies, Native Americans were forced to work for Spanish masters under extreme conditions, while their indigenous cultures were suppressed and destroyed.

The Africans who were forcibly brought to the New World suffered their own torments, beginning with a miserable and often fatal passage across the Atlantic, chained in the holds of slave ships, where they fell victim to disease, malnutrition, and overcrowding. Once in Spanish America, their condition varied, depending on the amount of labor they were given. Plantation and mill workers suffered the worst, while domestic servants and artisans fared somewhat better. Physical punishments, including whipping, branding, and death by hanging, were bestowed for a variety of transgressions.

While some have argued that despite the hardships placed upon them, Native Americans and enslaved Africans in Spanish colonies fared better, in some ways, than their counterparts in English colonies, the evidence for this view is mixed at best. While Catholic missionaries such as Bartolomé de Las Casas were moved by the plight of Native Americans and successfully pushed for laws that somewhat improved their treatment, tens of millions of Native Americans died of overwork and European disease. While the English avoided contact with Native Americans, regarding them as barely human, the Spanish only regarded them as human if they converted to Christianity. Those who did not convert were often tortured to death. In regard to Spanish treatment of Africans, Spaniards again distinguished between those who had been Christianized in Europe before arriving in the Americas and those who arrived directly from Africa. For these

THE VIRGIN OF GUADALUPE

On December 1531, ten years after the Spanish conquest of Mexico, a dark-skinned Virgin Mary appeared to an Indian boy named Juan Diego on Tepyac Hill, outside Mexico City. To prove her divinity, she had him pick roses, which, significantly, were in bloom in December. When he delivered these to the Spanish bishop, the Virgin's picture appeared on the mantle in which he had been carrying them. As the news of this miracle spread through Mexico, Indian conversion to Catholicism accelerated. Today, the Virgin Mary is the patron saint of Mexico, known as Our Lady of Guadalupe or the Virgin of Guadalupe. Approximately 80 to 90 percent of Mexicans and Mexican Americans are Roman Catholic to this day, including roughly 30 percent of the Mexican population that are classified as Native American or predominantly Native American.

The story of Our Lady of Guadalupe accelerated Mexican Indians' bond with Catholicism for various reasons: she had appeared before one of the oppressed and vanquished; she had the physical appearance of a dark-skinned woman; she communicated in Nahuatl, the language of the Indians; when she appeared, her face blocked the sun—the focal point of the native religions—establishing the precedence of the new faith brought by the Spaniards over the old Aztec religion. All of these factors emphasized to the Indians that they were worthy of respect.

Andalusia and other parts of southwestern Spain. (Even today, the Spanish spoken in the Americas resembles the Spanish that was spoken in Andalusia in 16th and 17th century colonial times.) These early Spanish settlers brought with them their customs, culture, religion, and language—visible throughout the history of Hispanic America in everything from the baroque architecture of colonial churches to the widespread playing of that homegrown Spanish instrument, the guitar; from the persistence of authoritarian political institutions in many Latin American countries in the face of popular strivings for democracy to the devotion to local identity that has often thwarted attempts at wider union.

RACE AND SOCIAL STATUS IN HISPANIC AMERICA

With few European women present, Spanish colonists freely—and often forcibly—took Native American and African women as wives and concubines. African slaves and freedmen often married Native Americans. The Spanish discriminated among the resulting children, with those of entirely Spanish descent at the top of the social ladder, and many racial gradations of class below. Yet the result was the creation of a multicultural people. By 1800, there were only 3.2 million people of solely Spanish descent in the colonies, less than 20 percent of the total population.

It is not surprising then that Hispanic America bears as many traces of Native America and Africa as it does of Spain. The traces are everywhere: in the Mexican shrine of the Virgin of Guadalupe, which, according to legend, stands where an Aztec mother goddess was worshiped; in corn tortillas that have been eaten in Mexico since the time of the Aztec; in the hammock, created by the Arawak of the West Indies; in the Santería religion of Cuba, which blends Yoruba gods and Catholic saints; and in merengue music of the Dominican Republic, born of both African and Spanish influences.

Africans, life was torment—including branding, whipping, and other forms of torture. Nonetheless, Africans on the Spanish plantations of the Caribbean, like their counterparts on British and French islands, managed to preserve many more aspects of their traditional cultures than Africans in the British colonies of North America, and later the United States. Because the slave populations in the Spanish Caribbean often far outnumbered the European populations, many more African traditions managed to survive and, in time, mix with both Spanish and Native American traditions.

Those who had migrated freely from the Old World to the Americas, the Spanish themselves, had come to explore, conquer, convert Indians, make fortunes, and escape poverty. Most came from

SPAIN IN THE AMERICAS

For more than 300 years, from the late 15th to the early 19th century, much of the Americas belonged to Spain. Spanish ships were the first to reach the New World, and Spanish conquistadores, or conquerors, quickly overran Native American resistance and established great empires. Spanish colonial America came to stretch from what is now Chile northward, deep into what is now the United States. The long period of Spanish rule in the New World, with its glories, atrocities, and complex interweaving of cultures, set the stage for the future history of independent Latin America.

DISCOVERY AND GENOCIDE

Ironically, Spain's American empire was not founded by a Spaniard. Known to the Spanish as Cristóbal Colón, Christopher Columbus (1451–1506) was born Cristoforo Colombo, in Genoa, then a republic in what is now Italy. Influenced by Genoa's tradition of maritime trade, he became a mariner himself and developed an unusual theory about how to sail to Asia. The result was not only the "discovery" of the Americas but the establishment of Spain's first American colonies—and the first of many acts of genocide against Native Americans.

The Voyages of Columbus

In an age when explorers were trying to discover new sea routes to the riches of the Far East, Columbus proposed to get there by sailing west. Most educated people agreed that the Earth was spherical, but many believed that the ocean separating East Asia and western Europe was too vast to cross. Based on geographical analysis and many wishful assumptions, Columbus argued that the distance from the Canary Islands to Japan was only 2,400 nautical miles; in fact, it is more than 10,000. If he had been right, then Japan

would have been only as far from Europe as Haiti. In any case, Columbus proposed to attempt the journey, sailing west from the Canary Islands, propelled by the easterly trade wind. The king of Portugal refused to fund his proposal, but after much discussion, Ferdinand and Isabella of Spain agreed to do it. Among other things, their bargain stipulated that Columbus would be titled Admiral of the Ocean Sea, would be viceroy and governor of any lands he discovered, would receive a hereditary peerage, and would get 10 percent of any gold or other precious merchandise obtained from his lands.

On August 3, 1492, Columbus set sail from Palos, Spain, with a modest expedition consisting of 90 men, most of them Spanish, and three ships: the Santa Maria, probably less than 100 feet long;

"I promise, that with a little assistance afforded me by our most invincible sovereigns, I will procure them as much gold as they need..."

—Christopher Columbus, in a letter dated March, 1493, reporting to one of his patrons what he had found in the Caribbean

Christopher Columbus (Library of Congress)

DID COLUMBUS DISCOVER AMERICA?

Although Christopher Columbus is credited with the European discovery of America, he was not the first European to reach the New World. About A.D. 1000, an Icelandic explorer named Leif Ericson (975–1020) reached a land he called Vinland, in what is probably Newfoundland. He may have been preceded there somewhat earlier by another Norseman, Biarni Heriulfson. In any case, the Norse established at least one settlement in the New World, identified in the early 1960s in the ruins at L'Anse-aux-Meadows in northern Newfoundland. But the settlement did not survive long, and aside from being recorded in Icelandic sagas, the discovery was forgotten.

To Columbus belongs the more enduring claim to the title of discoverer: once he set foot there, Europe never forgot what he had found, and the two halves of the world were never again separated. Of course, from the Native American point of view, the Americas were discovered when their prehistoric ancestors first colonized them.

To avoid asserting the European point of view over the Native American one, some historians prefer the neutral term contact over discovery. But even in terms of contact, Columbus has a claim to distinction. The first contact between Europeans and Native Americans that led to lasting interaction was the work of Columbus. Whatever that is good or ill that may be said about him, he deserves the credit (or blame) for that.

and the caravels Pinta and Niña, each probably less than 70 feet long. Columbus himself commanded the Santa Maria, while two Spanish brothers commanded the other ships: Martín Alonzo Pinzón on the Pinta and Vicente Yáñez Pinzón on the Niña. After stopping for provisions at the Canary Islands, on September 6 they sailed due west for regions unknown.

By late September, the expedition's progress was dramatically slowed by doldrums and weak winds, causing crew members to threaten mutiny. A month after setting sail, the expedition had covered 2,700 miles, surpassing Columbus's estimate of 2,400 miles for the entire journey. Rather than disclose his miscalculation to his rebellious crew, he began keeping two logbooks: one with fake caculations, and a second accurate but secret account. At 2:00 a.m. on October 12, Rodrigo de Triana, the Spanish lookout on the Pinta, spotted land. After sunrise the explorers anchored their ships and stepped ashore on an island in the Bahamas that the Native peoples called Guanahaní. Columbus, a deeply religious Catholic, knelt and thanked God; then, claiming the island for Spain, he christened it San Salvador, or "Holy Savior."

The people who lived on San Salvador, the Arawak or Taino, soon came out to meet the newcomers. The Arawak bore gifts of parrots, cotton, and wooden spears, which they readily exchanged for the trinkets the Spanish offered, such as glass beads and hawks' bells. A handsome people who went naked or nearly naked, they impressed Columbus with their hospitality and guilelessness. "Of anything they have," wrote Columbus, "if you ask them for it, they never say no; rather they invite the person to share it, and show as much love as if they were giving their hearts." Columbus wrote at first that he had high hopes of converting them to Christianity, using not force but love. Despite these good intentions, they were soon to be exterminated, with Columbus's help.

Columbus called them Indians, since he believed he had already reached the Indies, or East Asia. He was convinced that the advanced civilizations of Japan and China lay nearby, and with them the treasures he was seeking, especially gold. Some of the Arawak wore gold ornaments in their noses, a sign to Columbus that vast gold reserves were close at hand. Following hints from the Arawak, he sailed from island to island, landing on Cuba and Hispaniola (from española, "Spanish lady"), the latter now divided into the Dominican Republic and Haiti. But the great gold fields did not materialize, nor

A Currier and Ives lithograph depicting the landing of Columbus at San Salvador, in the West Indies (Library of Congress)

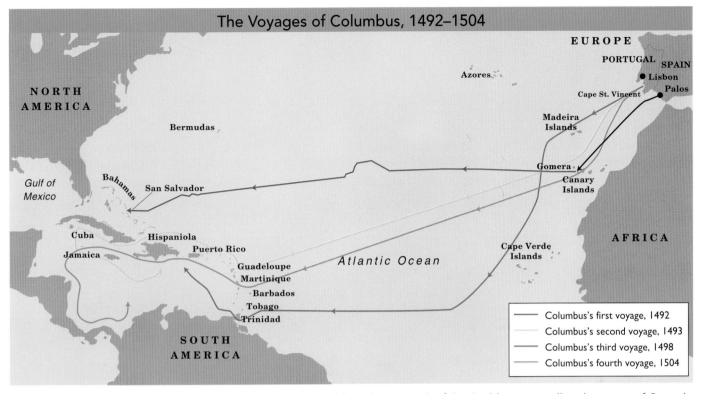

The Voyages of Columbus, 1492–1504

EUROPE

PORTUGAL SPAIN

● Lisbon

Cape St. Vincent Palos ●

NORTH
AMERICA

Bermudas

Azores

Madeira
Islands

Gomera
Canary
Islands

Gulf of
Mexico

Bahamas

San Salvador

Cuba

Hispaniola

Jamaica

Puerto Rico

Guadeloupe
Martinique

Barbados

Tobago

Trinidad

Atlantic Ocean

Cape Verde
Islands

AFRICA

SOUTH
AMERICA

	Columbus's first voyage, 1492
	Columbus's second voyage, 1493
	Columbus's third voyage, 1498
	Columbus's fourth voyage, 1504

Christopher Columbus made four expeditions to the New World, exploring much of the Caribbean, as well as the coasts of Central and South America.

did any signs of advanced civilization. Worse, on Christmas Day 1492, the flagship Santa Maria broke up on a coral reef off Hispaniola. But Columbus, ever the optimist, took it as a sign that God wanted him to found a settlement on that lush and well-watered island. Using timbers from the ship's wreckage, his crew constructed a fort called Navidad, or "Christmas." Columbus left fewer than 40 men there with orders to keep looking for gold and to treat the Native peoples well. On January 4, 1493, he set sail with the Niña and Pinta for Spain, which he reached on March 15.

Ferdinand and Isabella were pleased to receive him, and they confirmed the titles he had been promised. Then they sent him out on a second voyage, this one much larger, intended not just to explore but to establish a colony. The expedition consisted of 17 vessels and about 1,200 men, including priests to do the converting and soldiers to do the conquering. Lasting nearly three years, from September 25, 1493, to June 11, 1496, it was the first European expedition to visit many West Indian islands, including Puerto Rico, Jamaica, Dominica, Guadeloupe, and Antigua. In addition, Columbus returned to Navidad on

Hispaniola, where he found the fort destroyed and all the settlers killed. Columbus learned that the garrison had demanded gold, food, and labor from the Taino. As eminent historian Samuel Eliot Morison described it, "the Spanish garrison, roaming about Hispaniola in search of more gold and girls, ran afoul of a stout cacique [chief] named Caonabó, who killed them and destroyed Natividad." Or as a contemporary Spanish diarist euphemistically wrote, "Bad feelings arose. To eliminiate this outrage . . . [the Taino] attacked the Christians in great force."

Columbus established the new colonies of Isabella and Santo Domingo, both in what is now the Dominican Republic. Santo Domingo is today that nation's capital and the oldest surviving European city in the Americas. The new colonies were plagued by dissension and the same unbridled mistreatment of the natives that had likely led to the destruction of Navidad. A pitched battle broke out between the Spanish and the Arawak. The Spanish, with their intimidating firearms and war dogs, won the battle decisively, bringing all of Hispaniola under control. But when Columbus returned to Spain, he had little to show for his efforts. The fabled gold reserves

THE DAY OF THE RACE

Columbus has many faces. He is alternately celebrated as the heroic discoverer of America, praised as an intrepid master mariner, criticized as an inept geographer and navigator who got lucky, and vilified as the founder of the European tradition of genocide against Native Americans. While Hispanic Americans share the general ambivalence about Columbus, they also have a special regard for him, one that leads many Hispanic Americans to celebrate October 12, the day of discovery that Anglo-Americans call Columbus Day, as El Día de la Raza, "The Day of the Race." For it was Columbus who first brought together the peoples of the Old World and the New under the banner of Spain, founding, in a sense, a new people: the Hispanic Americans.

The Papal Line of Demarcation, 1493, and the Treaty of Tordesillas, 1494

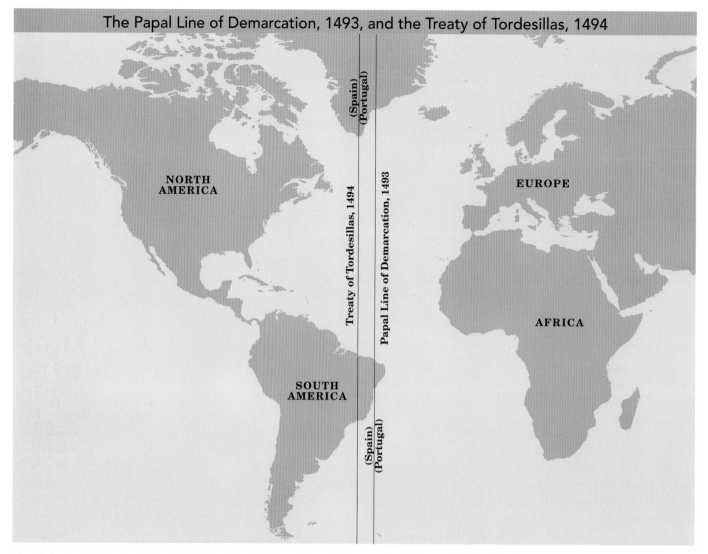

NORTH
AMERICA

(Spain)
(Portugal)

Treaty of Tordesillas, 1494

Papal Line of Demarcation, 1493

EUROPE

AFRICA

SOUTH
AMERICA

(Spain)
(Portugal)

Shortly before Columbus's New World landing, Spain petitioned the pope for full control of any lands encountered. In 1493, Pope Alexander VI granted to Spain all lands west of a line running 100 leagues west of the Cape Verde Islands. Under this demarcation, Spain received most of the Americas, while Portugal received lands that would become Brazil. When King John II of Portugal objected, the two countries negotiated a treaty—signed at Tordesillas, Spain, in 1494—to move the line 270 leagues farther to the west.

Spanish galleons such as the one shown here dominated the seas during the 16th century. This ship, the Victoria, was captained by Juan Sebastio de Elcano, a member of Ferdinand Magellan's crew. When Magellan himself was killed in the Philippine Islands after crossing the Pacific in 1521, Elcano completed the journey around the globe, arriving back in Spain the following year. (private collection)

had not yet been found, nor the rich civilizations of China and Japan. Even so, the Spanish sovereigns sent him out on two more voyages.

On the third voyage, which took place between May 1498 and October 1500, Columbus went to Trinidad and came ashore on the mainland for the first time, visiting what is now Venezuela. By then, however, a number of colonists had complained to the Spanish crown about Columbus's tyrannical style, leading Ferdinand and Isabella to ask for his resignation as governor. When he refused, he was arrested and returned to Spain in shackles. While the sovereigns recognized his service to the crown, and thus released him and approved plans for a fourth voyage, they did not restore him to the governorship of Hispaniola.

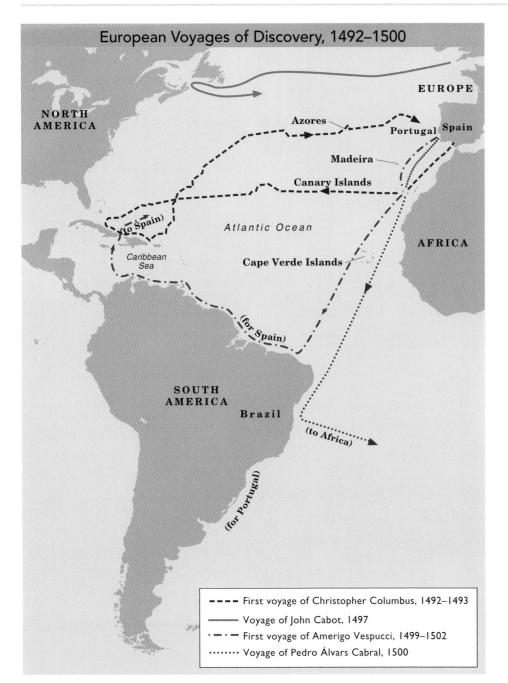

European Voyages of Discovery, 1492–1500

NORTH
AMERICA

EUROPE

Azores

Portugal Spain

Madeira

Canary Islands

Atlantic Ocean

(to Spain)

*Caribbean
Sea*

AFRICA

Cape Verde Islands

(for Spain)

SOUTH
AMERICA

Brazil

(to Africa)

(for Portugal)

- - - - First voyage of Christopher Columbus, 1492–1493
——— Voyage of John Cabot, 1497
- · - · First voyage of Amerigo Vespucci, 1499–1502
········· Voyage of Pedro Álvars Cabral, 1500

Following Christopher Columbus's first voyage to the Americas, other explorers followed almost immediately in his wake, particularly from Spain and Portugal. Voyages from both of those nations typically began with a stop in the islands off Africa's west coast to take on supplies. By 1497, England had joined Portugal and Spain in chartering an American expedition when the country sent Italian mariner John Cabot (Giovanni Caboto) on an exploratory mission across the North Atlantic, where he traced the coasts of present-day Labrador, Newfoundland, and New England.

On the fourth voyage, which began in May 1502 and ended in November 1504, Columbus concentrated on trying to find a westward passage to the mainland of Asia, which he still felt sure must lie near Hispaniola and the other islands that he had explored. Cruising along the coast of Central America in search of a passage to the Pacific Ocean, he landed in what are now the nations of Honduras,

Nicaragua, Costa Rica, Panama, and Colombia, and even briefly established a settlement in Panama. He died in Spain in 1506, having become a wealthy man from his expeditions but nonetheless thinking himself slighted by the crown and cheated out of part of his financial rights. He did acknowledge that what he had found did not correspond to any previously known lands: it was, he said, an

AMERIGO VESPUCCI

(Library of Congress)

Early in the 16th century, Spain and other European powers gradually ceased to think of the lands across the Atlantic as an arm of Asia and realized they were a "new world." Italian navigator Amerigo Vespucci (1454–1512), who explored parts of South America on Spanish expeditions, called it just that in his 1504 pamphlet Mundus Novus, or "New World." Vespucci was a shameless self-promoter who is widely believed to have lied in claiming to have reached the American mainland before Columbus. Yet his use of the term "New World" stuck, and his claim of discovery persuaded German cartographer Martin Waldseemüller to label the New World "America" on a map in 1507. That name stuck too, pushing out other proposed terms like "Columbiana."

As for Columbus's dream of reaching Asia by sailing west from Europe, that dream was first realized by another expedition. In 1519–1522, Portuguese navigator Ferdinand Magellan (ca. 1480–1521) led a Spanish expedition that successfully sailed west from Spain, through the South American strait now called the Strait of Magellan, past Indonesia and the southern tip of Africa, and finally back to Spain. The expedition was the first to circumnavigate the globe, as Columbus had hoped but failed to do. Technically, Magellan himself also failed, for he was killed in a fight with native peoples in the Philippines in 1521, leaving the completion of the voyage to others.

Columbus in Hispaniola (Library of Congress)

"In [Hispaniola], there are mountains of great size and beauty, vast plains, groves, and very fruitful fields, admirably adapted for tillage, pasture and habitation..."

—Christopher Columbus, March, 1493

otro mundo, or "other world." Even so he died still convinced that the New World he had landed in was very close to or perhaps even connected to Asia, and that with a little more sailing, he might have reached his original goal.

RIVAL EXPEDITIONS

Even while Columbus was still exploring, Spain acted quickly to solidify its claims in the New World. As Catholic sovereigns, Ferdinand and Isabella believed the pope had the responsibility to authorize monarchs to evangelize the pagan peoples in newly discovered territories and, for this purpose, to grant temporal sovereignty to monarchs over those territories. They appealed to Pope Alexander VI, who was Spanish himself, to grant them this sovereignty in the New World,

and this he did in a series of bulls in 1493 that established what has become known as the Papal Line of Demarcation. The precise terms of the arrangement dissatisfied Portugal, which managed to get them modified in the Treaty of Tordesillas of 1494. Under the revised arrangement, Portugal was given title to all lands east of a line of demarcation 370 leagues west of the Cape Verde Islands, while Spain won title to all lands west of the line.

The agreement was meant to protect Spain's interest in the New World and Portugal's interest in Africa, but it had an unintended consequence. When eastern Brazil, which lay east of the line of demarcation, was reached by Portuguese explorer Pedro Álvares Cabral (ca. 1468–1520) in April 1500, it gave Portugal a claim to vast territory that would become Brazil. This claim was upheld despite the fact that he had been beaten to Brazil in January 1500 by the Spanish explorer Vicente Yáñez Pinzón (ca. 1460–ca. 1523). Hence Brazil became a Portuguese, colony, with Salvador founded in 1549, São Paulo in 1554, and Rio de Janeiro in 1567. It remains to this day a Portuguese-speaking nation.

During the years 1492 to 1500, one other European nation, England, sent an expedition to the New World. Heading that expedition was Italian-born English navigator Giovanni Caboto, or John Cabot (ca. 1450–1499), who explored the coasts of Labrador, Newfoundland, and New England in two voyages in 1497 and 1498. Like Columbus, he was searching for a short route to Asia and was convinced that Japan and China lay right around the bend. France sent expeditions for the same purpose in the early 16th century. Italian explorer Giovanni da Verrazano (ca. 1480–1527) explored North America's Atlantic coast for France in the 1520s, and French explorer Jacques Cartier (1491–1557) explored Canada in the 1530s and 1540s.

Despite this budding foreign competition, exploration of the New World in the late 15th and early 16th centuries was almost entirely a Spanish affair. Spain moved so rapidly to capitalize on Columbus's discoveries that vast regions of the American interior were already shipping wealth to Spain while European rivals were still skirting the coasts. Spain's first holdings were in the place Columbus had first colonized: Hispaniola.

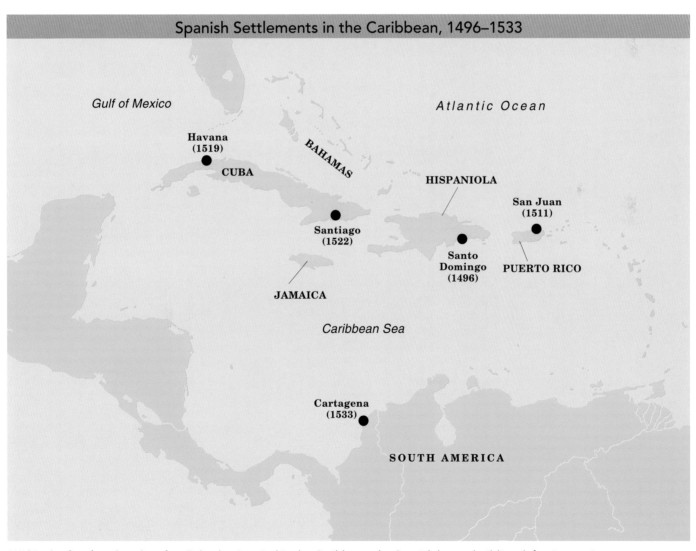

Spanish Settlements in the Caribbean, 1496–1533

Within the first few decades after Columbus's arrival in the Caribbean, the Spanish began building defensive garrisons to protects Spain's colonists and also to safeguard Spain's treasure ships. While the era of English and French pirates in the Caribbean did not begin in earnest until the late 16th century, as early as 1525 word had spread throughout Europe of the riches Spain was shipping out of its new American lands. In 1505, a fort was constructed at Santo Domingo, followed by others in San Juan (1511), Havana (1519), Santiago (1522), and Cartagena (1533).

Havana in the 17th century (Library of Congress)

> *"[The] Spaniards still do nothing save tear the natives to shreds, murder them and inflict untold misery, suffering and distress, tormenting, harrying and persecuting them mercilessly."*
>
> —Bartolomé de Las Casas, Spanish missionary

HISPANIOLA

The early history of Spain's first American colony, Hispaniola, was marked principally by the genocide of the indigenous population. This phenomenon was repeated elsewhere in the Caribbean, including Cuba and Puerto Rico. Estimates for the number of Native Americans living in the Caribbean before Columbus are uncertain; there may have been hundreds of thousands, perhaps millions. However many Native Americans there were, they were virtually exterminated. Of the few who survived, most intermarried with Europeans and Africans, losing their pre-Columbian way of life, although a small community of Carib still live on a reservation on Dominica.

Why did this genocide occur? It was not that Columbus or his sovereigns were entirely lacking in good intentions. Columbus at times urged his men to treat the Native Americans well. In 1495 Queen Isabella forbade Columbus to send American Indians to Europe for sale as slaves, and in 1501 she instructed Hispaniola's governor that the Native peoples should be "well treated as our subjects and our vassals." Some missionaries of conscience went to Hispaniola, most

notably Bartolomé de Las Casas (1474–1566), who in 1502 went to Hispaniola, serving as advisor to the colonial governor. In 1512 Las Casas became the first person in the Americas to be ordained a priest, and he later became an outspoken advocate for Native Americans. Yet none of these good intentions were enough to stop the wholesale slaughter.

Seeking an explanation for Spanish extermination of Native Americans, some historians have pointed to the Spanish experience of the Reconquest. The centuries-long effort to wrest land away from the Moors on the Iberian Peninsula, seizing and subjugating their domains, had made the Spanish warriors battle-hardened and contemptuous of non-Spanish people. They were thus prepared to conquer and rule ruthlessly and absolutely. Spanish nobility considered treasure won in warfare to be honorable, while manual labor was beneath the dignity of a gentleman. As the later conquistador Hernán Cortés is said to have put it, "I came to get gold, not to till the soil like a peasant." Columbus tried at first to control the excesses of the men who accompanied him on his voyages, wanting to treat the Native Americans as fellow Christians, but as a foreigner he had little sway over them. He also had a conflict of interest that sometimes put him on the side of brutality: he wanted to use Native Americans to produce the gold he felt he needed to justify his expeditions to the crown. In any case, Columbus had little say in the matter after 1500, when the crown removed him and his brothers from the governance of the New World.

Atrocities against the Native Americans of Hispaniola, many of them well documented by Las Casas, were legion. Soldiers murdered and tortured, took slaves, stole provisions, and raped women at will. For sport, Arawak babies were dashed against rocks or fed to dogs. To test the sharpness of their swords, soldiers would cut open the nearest Native American. At one point all adult Arawak were ordered to deliver a certain amount of gold every three months, at which time they would receive a token to wear around their necks as proof of delivery. Anyone found without his token would have his hands cut off.

When the Arawak resisted with their inferior weapons, the massacres grew worse. The Spanish decided unofficially that for every European killed, 100 Indians would be executed. The Native Americans tried to hide in the hills or flee to neighboring islands, but the Spanish presence soon pervaded the Caribbean, and there was nowhere to hide. As the Native Americans abandoned their crops, many died of starvation. Countless others died of diseases brought in by the Spanish to which the Native Americans had no natural immunity.

Other islands suffered similar fates. The Spanish launched successful campaigns to conquer Puerto Rico in 1508, Jamaica in 1509, and Cuba in 1511—the three large islands that, with Hispaniola, compose the Greater Antilles. The Native American populations of all these islands were soon wiped out. In 1542, describing the Spanish Caribbean in his blistering A Short Account of the Destruction of the Indies, Las Casas wrote: "All those islands . . . are now abandoned and desolate."

THE ENCOMIENDA SYSTEM

Hispaniola saw the development of a system known as the encomienda—

Bartolomé de Las Casas (Library of Congress)

Enslaved Indians work at the command of a Spanish overseer. (Library of Congress)

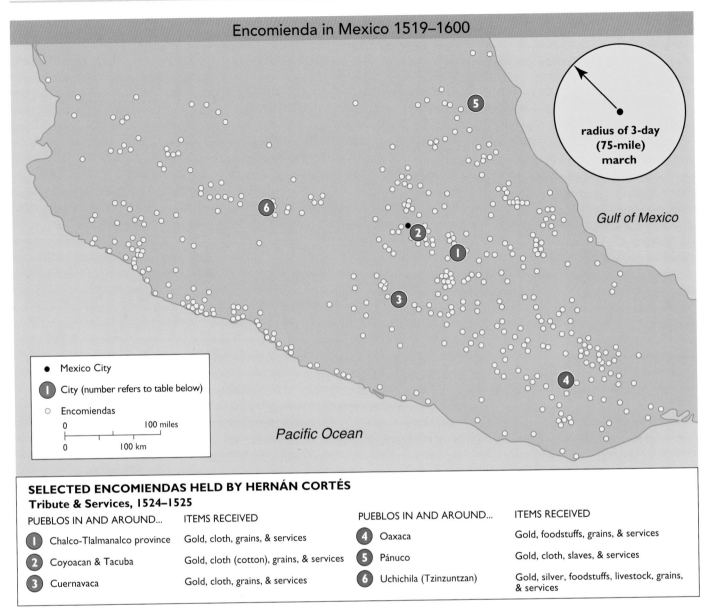

Encomienda in Mexico 1519–1600

radius of 3-day (75-mile) march

Gulf of Mexico

Pacific Ocean

- Mexico City
- City (number refers to table below)
- Encomiendas

0 ——— 100 miles
0 ——— 100 km

SELECTED ENCOMIENDAS HELD BY HERNÁN CORTÉS
Tribute & Services, 1524–1525

PUEBLOS IN AND AROUND...	ITEMS RECEIVED	PUEBLOS IN AND AROUND...	ITEMS RECEIVED
1 Chalco-Tlalmanalco province	Gold, cloth, grains, & services	4 Oaxaca	Gold, foodstuffs, grains, & services
2 Coyoacan & Tacuba	Gold, cloth (cotton), grains, & services	5 Pánuco	Gold, cloth, slaves, & services
3 Cuernavaca	Gold, cloth, grains, & services	6 Uchichila (Tzinzuntzan)	Gold, silver, foodstuffs, livestock, grains, & services

commission or grant—which would spread throughout Spanish America. It originated in the 1490s with informal repartimientos, or allocations, in which a group of Native American laborers would be assigned to a certain Spanish settler. As the system developed, the settler was designated as the encomendero, or recipient, of the labor of a given Native American cacique, or chief, and his people living in a certain location. The encomendero received from his laborers tribute payments, often in the form of in-kind goods like crops and clothing, as well as personal services around his house or farm. Technically, the encomendero was supposed to provide for the Indians' conversion and instruction in the Catholic faith, though in practice most settlers were mainly interested in profiting from their subjects' labors. Encomenderos on Hispaniola used their Native Americans to grow food for them and pan for placer gold in streams.

As the colonial economy of Hispaniola developed, encomenderos were typically the wealthiest and most influential of the colonists, those who profited most from commercial agriculture and mining. Las Casas and other reformers tried to abolish or ameliorate the encomienda system, which amounted to virtual serfdom for Native Americans. Outright slavery also existed, but the encomienda was more important to the colonial economy. The New Laws of 1542, enacted under pressure from Las Casas, prohibited enslavement of Native Americans and provided for the abolition of the encomienda system, but resistance from encomenderos persuaded the king merely to modify it so as to increase royal control. Since many encomenderos died without heirs, and since their encomiendas then reverted to the crown, the royal treasury gradually became the greatest beneficiary of the encomienda system. By the 18th century, other types of labor arrangements became more influential in colonial society.

AFRICANS IN HISPANIOLA

As the Native American population of the West Indies died or was killed off, Spanish colonists looked to Africa for a source of forced labor. And as the region's gold supply faded, they looked to export products as a source of income—chiefly sugar, but also ginger, tobacco, hides, and tallow. The first African slaves were shipped to Hispaniola in 1502, and the first sugar mill in the Caribbean was erected on Hispaniola in 1516. By 1527 the colony had 25 sugar mills in operation, and by 1565 as many as 30,000 African slaves may have been sent to Hispaniola.

Despite this vigorous beginning, the sugar industry in the Caribbean did not come into its own until the mid-17th century, when the English and French reoriented their West Indian colonies decisively toward sugar production on large plantations. After that, importation of African slaves increased dramatically. But the precedent had already been set on Hispaniola, where Africans began to mingle with Europeans and Native Americans to shape the culture of Hispanic America.

THE CONQUEST OF MEXICO

When Columbus came to the New World, he had dreamed of finding advanced urban civilizations like those of China and Japan. These did exist, but they were not discovered until after his death. The first European to conquer one of them was Hernán Cortés (1485–1547), who overthrew the Aztec Empire of Mexico. How he accomplished this, when the people of the empire outnumbered Cortés's original party on an order of 100,000 to one, is one of the most amazing stories in the history of Hispanic America.

BEFORE CORTÉS

Hernán Cortés was not the first person to venture onto the North American mainland. On his fourth voyage (1502–1504), Columbus explored the coast of Central America. In 1510 Vasco Núñez de Balboa (1475–1519) established a settlement in Darién in what is now the nation of Panama, and in 1513 he became the first European to see the Pacific Ocean from the west coast of the Americas. Despite Balboa's success, a general conquest of the region did not immediately follow. Balboa fell afoul of rivals and was beheaded for treason. As for Darién, the colony suffered from illness, famine, and the usual depredations of colonists against Native Americans.

In 1511 Diego Velázquez conquered Cuba, and from that base he launched expeditions to the Yucatán Peninsula on the mainland of present-day Mexico. The first of these expeditions, led by Francisco Fernández de Córdoba, ended in military disaster—and Córdoba's own death—at the hands of the Maya. Nonetheless, it served to encourage further efforts: Mayan cities were replete with temples, plazas, and gold and copper jewelry, indicating a civilization wealthier and more advanced than any yet encountered by the Spanish in the New World. A second expedition was ordered out, headed by Velázquez's nephew Juan de Grijalva. This time, the Spaniards brought with them a cannon. Thus armed, Grijalva

Vasco Núñez de Balboa (Library of Congress)

Diego Velázquez (Library of Congress)

Hernán Cortés (Library of Congress)

easily defeated the people of Champotón in battle, and then traded successfully for gold. In doing so, he learned of an even mightier civilization than the Maya: that of the Aztec in the Mexican interior. Grijalva's success and this new information about even greater riches led to orders for a third expedition—this time headed by Hernán Cortés.

Cortés Arrives in Mexico

Hernán Cortés, an ambitious young man of noble lineage but little money, had come to the New World in 1504, when still in his teens. He aided Velázquez in the conquest of Cuba, became alcalde, or mayor, of Santiago de Cuba, and successfully angled to be named captain of the third expedition to the mainland. In February 1519 Cortés set sail from Cuba with an expedition designed for conquest: 11 ships; about 500 European soldiers; 12 arquebuses, or muskets; 14 cannon; and an assortment of horses and war dogs. Native American and African servants also accompanied the expedition.

Upon landing in Yucatán, Cortés insisted that his men treat the Native Americans they encountered well, with the aim of winning support for the conquest he envisioned. Good treatment did not extend to their gods, whose idols he smashed and replaced with crosses. He was always ready to read Native peoples the Requerimiento, or Requirement, a document that informed them of Christian doctrine and also required them to swear immediate allegiance to both the pope and the king of Spain. Cortés, like many Spanish soldiers trained through fighting Moors, combined zeal for spreading the message of Christianity with a passion for military conquest.

While exploring the coast, Cortés captured the town of Tabasco in what is now Mexico and had the good fortune to find two interpreters. One was Jerónimo de Aguilar, a Spanish priest who had been shipwrecked and held captive for years by the Native Americans, and who had learned to speak Mayan. Another was Malinche, a slave woman who spoke both Mayan and Nahuatl, the language of the Aztec or Mexica. Cortés could give messages in Spanish to Aguilar, who could relay them to Malinche in Mayan, who could pass them to the Aztec. Malinche was baptized Marina and became a mis-

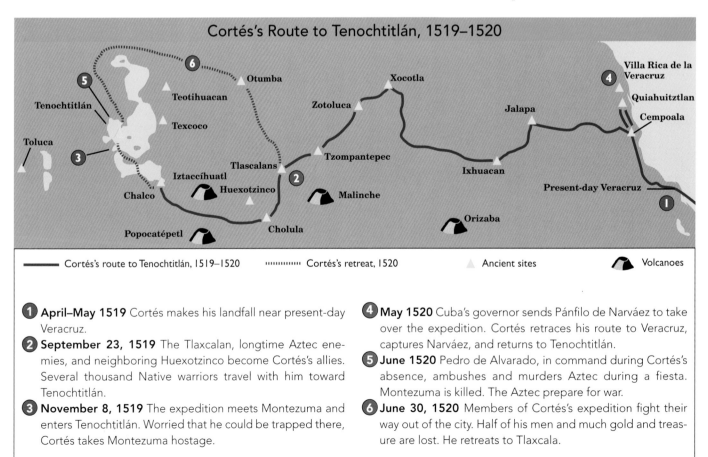

Cortés's Route to Tenochtitlán, 1519–1520

Villa Rica de la Veracruz
Quiahuitztlan
Cempoala
Jalapa
Xocotla
Otumba
Teotihuacan
Zotoluca
Texcoco
Tenochtitlán
Ixhuacan
Toluca
Tzompantepec
Present-day Veracruz
Tlascalans
Iztaccíhuatl
Huexotzinco
Malinche
Chalco
Orizaba
Popocatépetl
Cholula

——— Cortés's route to Tenochtitlán, 1519–1520   ·········· Cortés's retreat, 1520   ▲ Ancient sites   🌋 Volcanoes

① **April–May 1519** Cortés makes his landfall near present-day Veracruz.

② **September 23, 1519** The Tlaxcalan, longtime Aztec enemies, and neighboring Huexotzinco become Cortés's allies. Several thousand Native warriors travel with him toward Tenochtitlán.

③ **November 8, 1519** The expedition meets Montezuma and enters Tenochtitlán. Worried that he could be trapped there, Cortés takes Montezuma hostage.

④ **May 1520** Cuba's governor sends Pánfilo de Narváez to take over the expedition. Cortés retraces his route to Veracruz, captures Narváez, and returns to Tenochtitlán.

⑤ **June 1520** Pedro de Alvarado, in command during Cortés's absence, ambushes and murders Aztec during a fiesta. Montezuma is killed. The Aztec prepare for war.

⑥ **June 30, 1520** Members of Cortés's expedition fight their way out of the city. Half of his men and much gold and treasure are lost. He retreats to Tlaxcala.

In 1585, Spanish priest Father Diego Durán published an illustrated manuscript on Mexico's history. In it, he included his depiction of a confrontation between Spaniards and the Aztec. (Library of Congress)

tress to the married Cortés, bearing him a son. She was loyal and devoted to him, serving him not only as an intepreter but as a guide and advisor.

Before attacking the Aztec Empire, Cortés founded the coastal settlement of La Villa Rica de la Vera Cruz, "The Rich City of the True Cross" (present-day Veracruz, Mexico). There he established a government that he declared independent of his superior, Velázquez, with whom he had quarreled bitterly before leaving Cuba. Instead of pledging loyalty to Velázquez, Cortés claimed to be subject only to the Spanish crown. He also made his authority absolutely clear to his men, first by crushing a mutiny and, then in a dramatic gesture, by destroying all of his expedition's ships—thus preventing the timid or rebellious among his crew from sailing home. With no way back to Cuba, his men had nowhere to go but forward under his command.

CORTÉS AND MONTEZUMA

A daring general and a cunning politician, Cortés used every advantage in his single-minded drive to conquer the Aztec Empire. He needed every advantage he could get, for his position was almost laughable: an army of 500 against an empire of tens of millions, with an extensive, battle-hardened warrior class and a practice of sacrificing and eating defeated enemies.

But Cortés did have advantages. The Aztec had never enountered muskets and cannon and were appropriately terrified by their fire, noise, and destructive power. With their steel armor and strange white skin, the conquistadores looked like gods or demons rather than men. Riding horses, which looked like giant deer to the Native Americans, and holding ferocious dogs on leashes, it seemed as if they commanded even wild animals. They had no fear of Native American gods and smashed their idols without receiving divine punishment, which seemed to suggest that they themselves were divine or at least worshipped a higher god. They won their early battles easily and were magnanimous at first to their defeated enemies, giving them a reputation for both invincibility and graciousness.

Another Spanish advantage was the vacillation of the Aztec emperor Montezuma II (ca. 1466–1520), who

Montezuma (Library of Congress)

"And when we saw all those towns and villages in the water, and other great towns on dry land, and that straight and level causeway leading to Mexico, we were astounded. These great towns…and buildings rising from the water. All made of stone, seemed like an enchanted vision.… Indeed some of our soldiers asked whether it was not all a dream… It was all so wonderful that I do not know how to describe this first glimpse of things never heard of, seen, or dreamed of before."

—Bernal Díaz del Castillo, one of Cortés' soldiers, writing about seeing the Aztec capital of Tenochtitlán for the first time in his eyewitness account *The Conquest of New Spain.*

distrusted Cortés from the beginning but failed to destroy him when he had the chance. While Cortés was still at Veracruz, Montezuma sent emissaries laden with gold and silver, requesting that the Spanish not venture inland to his capital city of Tenochtitlán, now Mexico City. The gifts only whetted the conquistador's appetite and made him more determined than ever to take control of this rich land.

Some attribute Montezuma's vacillation to his belief in the legend of Quetzalcoatl. According to this account, Montezuma believed that his reign would see the return of the great Quetzalcoatl, a god of peace and fertility who had been driven away by a hostile god. Quetzalcoatl would come as a white-skinned, bearded man traveling across the water from the land where the sun rises. Montezuma supposedly feared that Cortés was that man and that upon arrival he would take over the empire. However, some historians argue that this story is not well-founded and that Montezuma's uncertainty in dealing with Cortés was sufficiently explained by his fear of the unknown and his overestimation of Cortés's resources.

Perhaps the most important weakness of the Aztec Empire was its disunity. Its subjects feared the Aztec but also hated them for enslaving and sacrificing some of their people and exacting heavy

taxes from the rest. For their part, the Aztec feared rebellion and were constantly spying in search of rebels. On several occasions, Cortés masterfully played the rebels and the Aztec against each other, indicating to one that he had come to liberate them and to the other that he had come to safeguard their rule.

On August 8, 1519, Cortés and about 300 soldiers began the 250-mile march inland from the coast to Tenochtitlán. "To conquer the land or die" was his slogan. They encountered heavy resistance from the Tlascalan, an independent people who eventually surrendered and formed an alliance with Cortés against the Aztec, their ancient enemies. Montezuma, fearful of Cortés but unwilling to launch an army against him, permitted him to enter the Aztec capital on November 8, 1519. Built on an island in a lake, the city of 250,000 people was larger than any in Spain and dominated by great flat-topped temples. But Cortés was not intimidated by its obvious power and wealth or by how ludicrously he was outnumbered. Given a palace to live in, which he fortified as a headquarters, and freedom to move around the city at will, he resisted his soldiers' wish to take what gold they could and run away. He was determined to conquer or die.

Accordingly, when visiting Montezuma one day, he took the Aztec emperor

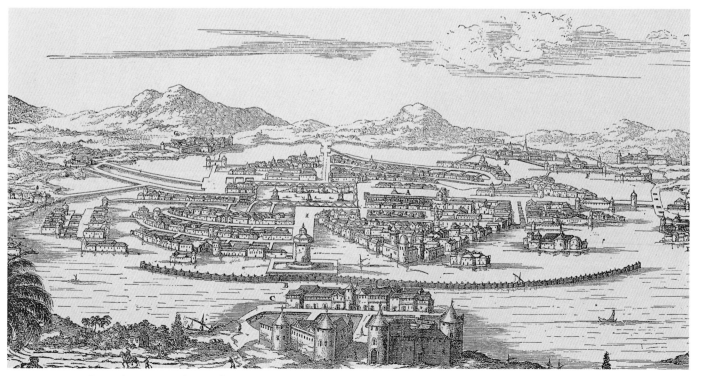

Mexico City in the 16th century (Library of Congress)

prisoner and forced him to take up residence in the Spanish headquarters. He required Montezuma to swear allegiance to the Spanish king, Charles I, who had come to the throne in 1516 and reigned to 1556 (he also reigned simultaneously as Holy Roman emperor Charles V, 1519–1558). Cortés also ordered Montezuma to provide a great tribute in gold and jewels. But before he could fully establish his control of the Aztec Empire, Cortés had to pause to crush a different enemy: Velázquez.

The governor of Cuba had sent an expedition under Pánfilo de Narváez (ca. 1480–1528) to arrest his rebellious captain, and Cortés now learned that they had arrived on the coast. Cortés left 200 men at Tenochtitlán under the command of Pedro de Alvarado and swiftly marched to meet his enemies. He defeated Narváez and convinced most of that leader's men to join him, giving him an army of more than 1,000.

By the time that Cortés returned to Tenochtitlán, Alvarado had made a mess of things, launching an unprovoked massacre that prompted a revolt against the Spanish. The Aztec allowed Cortés to rejoin Alvarado in their headquarters only so they could surround and attack all the Spanish at once. A battle ensued, forcing the Spanish to retreat inside their fortress. Cortés persuaded Montezuma to address his people from a rooftop and urge them to cease their rebellion. In contempt for what they viewed as a show of weakness, his people stoned and shot arrows at the emperor. The Aztec leader died of his wounds three days later.

THE FALL OF THE AZTEC EMPIRE

With Montezuma gone, Cortés had no shield against the fury of the Aztec. On June 30, 1520, a rainy night commemorated in Mexican history as the Noche Triste, or "Sad Night," Cortés ordered a retreat from the city while the Aztec slept. But the Aztec awoke, raining arrows on the fugitives. Cortés's men carried portable bridges to fill gaps in the causeways leading out of the city and across the lake. But the bridges collapsed and many soldiers drowned in the lake, dragged down by all the gold they were trying to

"Be advised that I, being free, do not have to pay tribute to anyone, nor do I believe there is a king greater than I."

—Atahualpa

Francisco Pizarro (Library of Congress)

Atahualpa (Library of Congress)

carry out. More than 400 Spanish died, along with thousands of their Native American allies, and many horses and weapons were lost. Still more were lost on July 7 when the new emperor, Cuitláhuac, Montezuma's brother, caught up with them at Otumba. Yet Cortés defeated a much larger force there and managed to reach safe terrritory in Tlaxcala.

Despite the disaster of Noche Triste, which he viewed only as a setback, the unstoppable Cortés remained determined to conquer the Aztec. He reorganized his army and brought in reinforcements from Veracruz. He built up an army of 200,000 Native American allies, drawn from those who hated the Aztec. Sailing ships called brigantines were built for an assault on the lake-bound capital.

The march on Tenochtitlán began. Cortés first seized outlying cities and then laid siege to the capital for three months. A smallpox epidemic, introduced by the Spanish, raged within the city. On August 13, 1521, the emperor Cuauhtémoc—successor to Cuitláhuac, who had died of smallpox—was captured, and Tenochtitlán fell.

Cortés razed the city, and on its ruins he built Mexico City, capital of the new colony of New Spain. Colonists flowed in from Spain to make it the greatest city in the Spanish American empire, with churches, palaces, a printing press built in 1535 (the New World's first), and a university in 1551.

The Native Americans of the Aztec Empire were made to swear allegiance to their new Spanish overlords, just as they had once done to their Aztec overlords. Native Americans who had worked for the Aztec now worked for the Spanish, who introduced the same encomienda system that had reduced the Caribbean peoples to virtual slavery. Under Nuño de Guzmán, who replaced Cortés as ruler in 1528, abuses against Native Americans were common, from rape of women to branding of slaves.

Some priests, such as Juan de Zumarraga, Mexico's first bishop, did what they could to alleviate Native American suffering, founding schools and convincing King Charles I to replace Guzmán. But the priests' main priority was to root out Aztec religion and replace it with Christianity. Despite their efforts, some old traditions blended with the new, and subtle forms of resistance sprang up.

In statues of Roman Catholic saints, Native American sculptors sometimes hid figurines of the old gods and goddesses.

As for Cortés, his personal triumph did not last long. The Spanish crown feared he was becoming too powerful, so they ordered him out of office and back to Spain in 1528. He never regained the governorship and bickered constantly with the court over his rights. More expeditions followed for Cortés—to Honduras and the Pacific coast of Mexico—but his star had faded, and he died in retirement near Seville.

A SPANISH EMPIRE

With the conquest of Mexico, there seemed to be endless possibilities for empire in the New World. In the years that followed, Spanish conquistadores acted exactly as if there were no limits. In Peru, Francisco Pizarro conquered yet another empire, that of the Inca. The Caribbean became a Spanish sea, Central America a Spanish land-bridge, and colonies sprouted from California to Chile. By the early 18th century, Spanish America was a thriving entity: centrally controlled but full of potential for disunion; ripe with extremes of rich and poor; and blending Spanish, Native American, and African peoples and traditions.

PIZARRO AND THE INCA

Like Cortés, Francisco Pizarro (ca. 1476–1541) was a daring and unscrupulous man of little money but gentle birth (illegitimate, in Pizarro's case) who came to the New World to seek his fortune. After arriving in 1510, he served under Balboa in Central America and, in 1519, settled in Panama, which he used as a base for exploration to the south. Eager to follow Cortés's example of conquering an empire, he was thrilled to learn in his travels of the existence of the Inca Empire, a vast and wealthy state based in Cuzco, Peru, that governed millions of people throughout the Andes. With royal backing from Charles I and fewer than 200 men, Pizarro sailed from Panama in 1531 and landed in Peru in 1532.

Like Cortés, Pizarro was aided by an epidemic of Spanish-introduced smallpox. This one had killed the Inca emperor Huayna Capac in 1525, opening the door to a power struggle between two of his sons, Huáscar, the favorite of the court elite, and Atahualpa, whose armies controlled the newly conquered regions

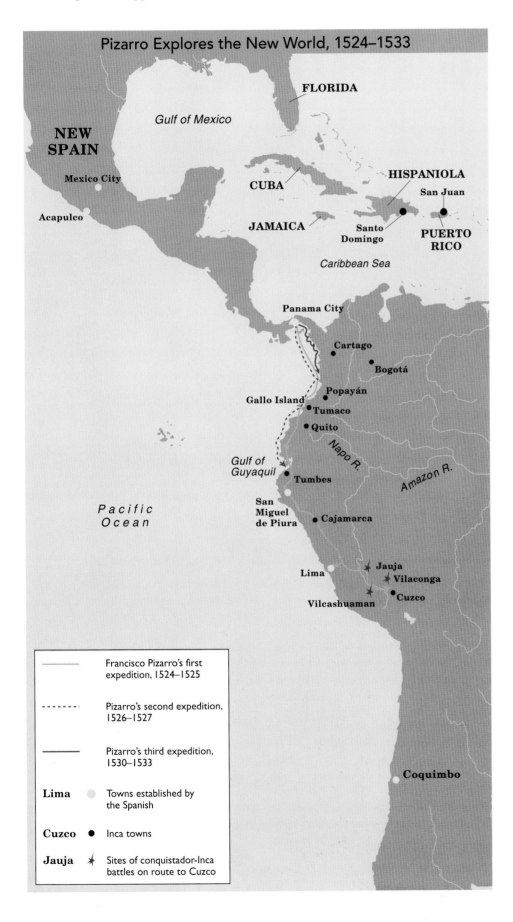

Pizarro Explores the New World, 1524–1533

FLORIDA

Gulf of Mexico

NEW SPAIN

Mexico City

Acapulco

CUBA

JAMAICA

HISPANIOLA

San Juan

Santo Domingo

PUERTO RICO

Caribbean Sea

Panama City

Cartago

Bogotá

Popayán

Gallo Island

Tumaco

Quito

Napo R.

Amazon R.

Gulf of Guyaquil

Tumbes

San Miguel de Piura

Cajamarca

Pacific Ocean

Lima

Jauja

Vilaconga

Cuzco

Vilcashuaman

Coquimbo

————	Francisco Pizarro's first expedition, 1524–1525
- - - - -	Pizarro's second expedition, 1526–1527
————	Pizarro's third expedition, 1530–1533
Lima ●	Towns established by the Spanish
Cuzco ●	Inca towns
Jauja ✳	Sites of conquistador-Inca battles on route to Cuzco

New Spain in 1600

Santa Fe

NEW
SPAIN

FLORIDA

Gulf of Mexico

Mexico City

CUBA

HISPANIOLA

San Juan

Acapulco

JAMAICA

Santo
Domingo

PUERTO
RICO

Atlantic
Ocean

Caribbean Sea

Cartagena

NEW
SPAIN

Pacific
Ocean

Panamá

Bogotá

PERU

BRAZIL

Lima

Santiago

Atlantic
Ocean

Buenos Aires

Spanish claims

Portuguese claims

Viceroyalty borders

of Ecuador and Colombia. At the moment Pizarro arrived, Atahualpa had just defeated and captured his half-brother Huáscar in a civil war and was marching triumphantly toward Cuzco to take power. To overthrow him, Pizarro used every tactic of Cortés's: playing Native American factions against one another; making false promises; terrifying the locals with firearms, steel swords, and horses; and capturing the ruler.

The conquest began in 1532, when Pizarro lured Atahualpa into a trap and took him prisoner. Pizarro accepted Atahualpa's offer of a roomful of gold as a ransom, but rather than letting Atahualpa go, Pizarro had him garroted. Huáscar was already dead, on Atahualpa's order, so Pizarro installed a new puppet emperor, Manco Inca. In 1535, viewing Cuzco as

too far inland to serve as a viable capital, Pizarro founded Ciudad de los Reyes, "City of the Kings," near the coast as the region's new capital. It soon became known as Lima, a corruption of the Quechua Indian name Rímac, meaning "Talker."

Manco proved to be less compliant than Pizarro had hoped. Supported by Native Americans, Manco led a revolt against the Spanish in 1536. He lost and retreated to Vilcabamba, where an independent Inca kingdom survived until 1572, when the last pretender to the Inca throne, Manco's son Tupac Amaru, was defeated.

By then Pizarro was long dead. Despite his achievement in conquering for Spain an even richer empire than that of the Aztec, he enjoyed not even Cortés's simple reward of dying in bed. In 1537 a civil war broke out between him and his longtime partner in conquest, Diego de Almagro. Pizarro's forces defeated and executed Almagro in 1538, but a faction still loyal to Almagro assassinated Pizarro in 1541. Spain tried to relieve the chaos in 1542 by making Peru a viceroyalty, one that comprised all of Spanish South America and Panama except for Venezuela. But the first man appointed as viceroy was killed by rebels led by Pizarro's brother Gonzalo in 1546. By the end of the 1540s, the king's new representative, Pedro de la Gasca, had defeated Gonzalo Pizarro and executed him, putting the colony of Peru under firm royal control.

OTHER CONQUESTS

News of the riches to be had in the New World drew an influx of colonists, who hastened to launch their own entradas, or entries into new lands. Like the expeditions of Cortés and Pizarro, these expeditions were generally mounted with royal license but with private funding. They were partnerships of a few hundred men, in which the members would invest capital to purchase equipment and supplies, band together in whatever trailblazing and fighting there was, and split the proceeds of gold, loot, or encomiendas, with the organizers and biggest investors receiving the largest shares. Though present-day people would call them soldiers, and though they were headed by a man called a captain, the members were not part of a regular army and often had little military experience. They came from all walks of life, from notaries to carpenters to seamen to lower nobility. The captain was usually a nobleman, or hidalgo, who had already achieved some distinction in the area that served as the expedition's base. They were often driven by Native American rumors of wealthy empires like the Seven Cities of Cíbola in the American Southwest or the land of the ruler El Dorado in South America. These and other legendary places failed to materialize as imagined, but the drive to find them spurred exploration and conquest.

The most important bases for expeditions were Mexico, the Caribbean, Panama, and Peru. Expanding southward from Mexico, Cortés's lieutenant Pedro de Alvarado brought what are now

DISEASE AND THE COLUMBIAN EXCHANGE

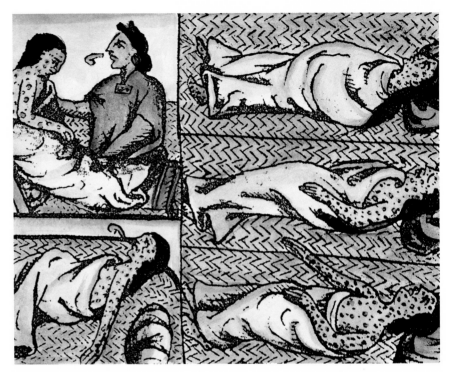

Native Americans, such as the smallpox victim shown above, were highly susceptible to European viruses like smallpox because they had no natural immunity. (Granger Collection)

Upon first encountering the plant known to the Aztec as the xitomatl, Europeans feared it was poisonous. The Aztec drink xocolatl made them nauseous. But in time, these two crops—known in English respectively as the tomato and chocolate or cacao—became staples of the European diet. So did such other distinctively American foods as the potato, maize, red pepper, peanut, cashew nut, squash, cranberry, and avocado. In turn, Europeans introduced to the Americas a variety of Old World plants and animals—wheat, grapes, olives, apples, peaches, oranges, pigs, sheep, goats, cows, chickens, donkeys, and horses. Bananas, coffee, and sugar, the production of which is now closely identified with Latin America, were all introduced from the Old World. The swapping of biological species between Old and New Worlds is known as the Columbian exchange or Atlantic exchange.

There were good and bad consequences of this exchange for both hemispheres. The available food supply increased in both regions, but introduction of alien species sometimes wreaked havoc on local ecologies—as when the hooves of Spanish cattle destroyed Native American grassland that was food for game. New World dandelion seeds were inadvertently shipped to Europe, Old World rats shipped to America. The exchange also included microbes of which neither Old nor New World societies of the time had an understanding. For example, syphilis, believed by many historians to have been a New World illness, may have came back with Columbus to ravage Europe. In the Americas, Old World microbes such as smallpox and influenza killed whole populations of Native Americans. For example, in Mexico, the estimated Native American population of 25.2 million people in 1519 plummeted following Spanish contact—to 16.5 million by 1539, 6.3 million by 1549, and just 1 million by the 1620s. Perhaps the worst gifts from the New World to the Old were two Native American crops that yielded popular but harmful products: tobacco and coca, the source of cocaine. Outside of dangerous microbes, perhaps the most harmful Old World product introduced to the New World was alcohol, which in time would have an even more widespread impact than cocaine.

CARLOS DE SIGÜENZA Y GÓNGORA

Carlos de Sigüenza y Góngora was one of New Spain's greatest intellectuals. Born in Mexico City in 1645, he studied astronomy and mathematics with his father, who had been a tutor for the royal family of Spain. De Sigüenza published his first poem in 1662, and in 1671, an almanac. In 1672, he became chair of mathematics and exact sciences at the University of Mexico and was ordained a priest the following year. He then became chaplain of the Hospital del Amor de Dios (now Academia de San Carlos) from 1682 until his death in 1700.

Throughout his career, de Sigüenza bridged the divides between science, the arts, and religion. In addition to his poetry, he also was one of New Spain's foremost non-fiction writers, publishing *El Mercurio Volante,* the first newspaper in New Spain, in 1693, and also producing works of history, philosophy, cartography and cosmography. In fact, his reknown stretched will beyond the Spanish colonies, as the French King Louis XIV attempted to convince him to move to Paris.

It was de Sigüenza's lifelong interest in the native peoples of the Americas that won him what may have been his greatest acclaim. At the Hospital del Amor de Dios, he met historian Juan de Alva Ixtlilxochitl, a descendent of the kings of Texcoco, a city-state in the central Mexican plateau. De Alva, whose family line also included several of the last Aztec rulers, granted de Sigüenza access to his family's richly detailed papers, and in 1668, de Sigüenza began what would become his lifelong study of Aztec and Toltec writings.

Among the documents found in de Alva's family papers was purported to be a "map" or codex that documented the legendary 1531 apparition of the Virgin Mary as Our Lady of Guadeloupe (see sidebar on p. 20). A devotee of the Virgin Mary, de Sigüenza had written poetry in her honor as early as 1662; because of his association with the codex, he now became even more closely associated with the legend.

De Sigüenza also continued his work in a wide variety of fields during the latter part of his career. In 1680, he was commissioned to design a triumphal arch for the arrival of a new Viceroy of New Spain, Cerda y Aragón. He also wrote histories of Ancient Mexico, arguing that the Olmecs had migrated to the New World via the lost city of Atlantis, and that the Apostle Thomas had evangelized natives of the New World shortly before the death of Christ.

In 1691, de Sigüenza prepared the first map of all of New Spain, and also drew hydrologic maps of the Valley of Mexico. The following year, King Carlos II of Spain appointed him as royal cartographer of New Spain. As royal geographer, de Sigüenza mapped Pensacola Bay and the mouth of the Mississippi during a 1692 expedition in search of defensible frontiers against the French.

That same year, a serious drought and the loss of a significant portion of the year's wheat crop due to disease led to a severe food shortage throughout New Spain. Although de Sigüenza was able to identify the cause of the wheat disease as a small insect called chiahuiztli, the food shortages led to an uprising on June 8, 1692. On that day, a mob attacked the viceroy's palace with stones and set the archives on fire. Putting his life at risk, de Sigüenza saved most of the documents and some paintings, this preserving preserved a host of colonial Mexican documents that would otherwise have been lost. Two years later, he retired from the University. He died in 1699, leaving his body to science and his papers to the Jesuit College of San Pedro and San Pablo.

Guatemala, Honduras, and El Salvador under Spanish control in the 1520s and 1530s, ruthlessly suppressing determined Native American resistance. Subduing the Quiche and Cakchiquel of Guatemala, Alvarado burned captured chiefs to death and branded and sold prisoners as slaves. The Maya of the Yucatán, with their decentralized societies and guerrilla tactics, were harder to subdue: the last independent group was not conquered until 1697. Elsewhere in Central America, Panama City was founded in 1519, and the first Spanish colonies were founded in Nicaragua in the 1520s and in Costa Rica in the 1560s.

Expanding northward from Mexico, the conquistadores established new provinces such as Nueva Galicia, where a rich silver deposit was discovered in 1546, leading to rapid founding of mines. The northern frontier pushed into what is now the American Southwest in 1540–1542, with the expedition of Francisco de Coronado (1510–1554). The American Southeast was explored in 1539–1542 by Hernando de Soto (ca. 1500–1542), who had served under Pizarro in Peru and who sailed from Cuba.

In South America, Spanish control spread south from Panama and north from conquered Inca strongholds in Peru and Ecuador. The Chibcha or Muisca civilization, centered around what is now Bogotá, Colombia, fell in the 1530s to conquistador Gonzalo Jiménez de Quesada. Soon all of Colombia and Venezuela were under Spanish rule. Conquistadores pushed south from Peru as well, with Bolivia conquered in 1538 and Santiago, Chile, founded in 1541. But the Araucanian people of Chile proved difficult to subdue; they launched a major rebellion in the 1550s, and warfare with them continued into the 19th century, even after independence from Spain.

To the east of Chile, the estuary Río de la Plata, or "River of the Silver," which lies on the southeast coast of South America between modern Uruguay and Argentina, had been discovered by Spanish navigators as early as 1516. Colonization there began with an expedition under Pedro de Mendoza that was launched directly from Spain in 1535 and resulted in the founding of Buenos Aires in 1536. The settlement was later temporarily abandoned, but a new settlement at Asunción in what is now Paraguay (founded 1538) provided a permanent base for expansion. Settlers from Peru began the permanent colonization of Argentina in 1553, with Buenos Aires resettled in 1580. Uruguay was conquered relatively late, with the first permanent Spanish settlement not established until 1624.

GOVERNMENT

The conquistadores enjoyed the glory and the first rush of wealth from the New World. But the Spanish crown, which licensed their adventures and took a share of their spoils, had no intention of allowing these ambitious, individualistic men to chop up the empire into personal fiefdoms. Having mastered the art of centralized, autocratic control among the fractious warlords of the Iberian Peninsula, Spain exercised that control in Spanish America. The conquistadores were pushed aside as Cortés and Pizarro had been, their domains put under the authority of royal officials. A royal council called the Council of the Indies was established in 1524 to supervise the government of the empire.

New Spain, with its capital at Mexico City, and Peru, with its capital at Lima, were declared viceroyalties. The Viceroyalty of New Spain encompassed all Spanish territory on the North American mainland as far south as what is now Costa Rica. The Viceroyalty of Peru at first encompassed all of Spanish South America except for the Venezuelan coast (governed from Santo Domingo). In the 18th century, however, New Granada (roughly corresponding to present-day Ecuador, Colombia, and Panama) and Río de La Plata (modern Bolivia, Chile, Argentina, Paraguay, and Uruguay) broke off from Peru to became separate viceroyalties.

The viceroyalties were segmented into kingdoms or audiencias, so called for the audiencia, or tribunal, that headed each unit in association with a governing executive. Within a kingdom, at the provincial level, corregidores, or provincial governors, were in charge of administration and justice. Some kingdoms, called presidencies, were governed by a president while others, called captaincies-general, were governed by a captain-general. In principle, these officals were subordinate to viceroys, but in practice they had considerable independence, especially the captains-general, whose job was to protect colonies deemed particularly vulnerable to foreign attack, such as Guatemala, Cuba, Venezuela, and Chile. The de facto autonomy of the kingdoms made it difficult to unite them once Spain left the New World. Many present-day Latin American countries correspond roughly to the colonial kingdoms.

By the 1580s, at the peak of Spain's world power, the Spanish empire in the Americas was mostly under firm royal control. It had passed from the initial period of exploration and conquest to one of consolidation and stability. Many places in Spanish America were claimed but not subdued, with Spanish settlements still sparse and Native Americans still putting up strong resistance. Nonetheless, Spanish control gradually increased over these areas, until the time came when Spain was forced out of the Americas, not by Native Americans, but by the descendants of its own colonists.

ECONOMY

The economy of New Spain was dominated by a small elite of wealthy landowners, miners, factory owners, and merchants. At first the landowners were mainly encomenderos, but as encomiendas came under increasing royal control, other labor arrangements became more important. In many places, a system developed for exacting compulsory or draft labor from Native Americans, with Native American communities providing a quota of laborers for a prescribed time, and the laborers receiving minimal wages in return. In New Spain the system was called repartimiento (not to be confused with the forerunner of the encomienda system), in Peru

The Rise of Latin America's Mestizo Population

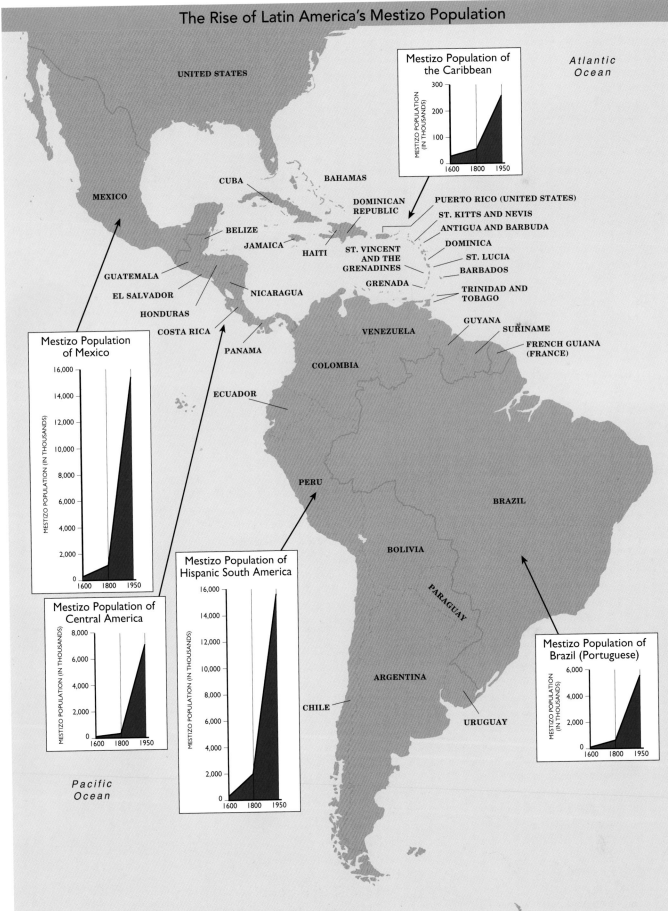

mita. In the 17th century, this system gradually declined in importance compared with free wage labor, in which hacendados, owners of haciendas, or large estates, contracted directly with laborers. Wages were so low that the peasants, who were not free to leave until their debts were paid off, were often forced into perpetual debt to their employers, a condition of servitude known as debt peonage.

Another way the Spanish exploited Native American communities was to require them by law to buy goods at fixed high prices, even if the goods were not wanted, a system that (confusingly) was also called repartimiento or reparto de bienes. The most abject form of servitude was found in the enslavement of Africans, who were bought and sold as chattel, chiefly to work on the plantations of the Caribbean, or to work in mines or as artisans and domestic servants throughout the colonies. But Native American labor was cheaper, and the Spanish colonists preferred to use that where available.

The most valuable exports from the colonies were gold and silver. In the mid-16th century, Honduras and Guatemala enjoyed a boom from gold strikes, Mexico and Bolivia from silver strikes. In 1591–1595, the port of Lima, the exit point for Bolivian metals, alone shipped 23.9 million pesos of silver. Second in importance were agricultural goods: tobacco, sugar, hides, cacao, and cascarilla, used as a flavoring and fragrance. Imports included slaves, iron, textiles, wine, brandy, olive oil, spices, and miscellaneous luxury goods, such as furniture and books.

Following mercantilist theory, which regarded possession of precious metals and control of trade as the basis for a nation's wealth, the Spanish crown excluded foreign competitors from colonial trade, closely supervising commerce through the Casa de Contratación, "House of Trade." Overseas trade consisted mainly of approved annual sailings of fleets, or convoys, to and from a few ports in Europe and the New World. From the 1570s Spanish America also traded with Spain's Asian colony of the Philippines. In the 18th century, trade was increasingly carried out by single, licensed ships, or register ships, less vulnerable than fleets were to naval attack during the century's many wars. Despite these attempts to control trade, smuggling of contraband to and from foreign merchants was rampant.

RACE AND CLASS

Despite the influx of Spanish people during the colonial period, Hispanic America by the end of that era was predominantly Native American and mestizo, a mix of white and Native American. In the Caribbean, the Native American population was virtually exterminated, and Native Americans in other areas of the New World also suffered precipitous population declines as a result of Spanish cruelty and European diseases. But in most places, the populations of Native Americans had stabilized by the late 17th century and begun to recover in the 18th century.

One set of estimates puts it this way: by the end of the colonial period, out of an estimated Spanish-American population of 17 million, Native Americans were the single largest ethnic group, about 7 million or 41 percent. About 5.8 million more people, or 34 percent, were of mixed ancestry, predominantly mestizo—blends of white and Native American. There were also some mulattoes, blends of white and black, particularly in slave plantation areas. In addition, there were about 1 million people (6 percent) of entirely African descent, about half of them slaves, working as laborers on plantations and as artisans and domestics in cities, and another half freedpersons. Finally, there were the españoles, or Spanish, people of entirely Spanish descent: about 3.2 million, or 19 percent. English philosopher Francis Bacon remarked, "I have marvelled sometimes at Spain, how they clasp and contain so large dominions with so few natural Spaniards."

Despite the many variations of mixed ethnicity in the Spanish colonies, the Spanish were far from color-blind. On the contrary, they made fine class distinctions among the types of racial blends. At the top of the social ladder were españoles, themselves divided between peninsulares, or colonists born in Spain (by 1800, only 5 percent of españoles), and criollos, or Creoles—those born in the Americas but of full Spanish descent (the remaining 95 percent). Below them were mestizos and mulattoes, and below them were those with entirely Native

*Ah stupid men, unreasonable
In blaming women's nature,
Oblivious that your own acts
     incite
The very faults you censure.*

—Selection from Sister Juana
Inés de la Cruz's
"Hombres necios…"

American or African heritage. As many as 46 other racial gradations were recognized. For example, one whose parents were an African and a Native American was a pardo or zambo; a child of an African and a mestizo was a mestizo prieto. Casta was a general term for any nonwhite person who was not fully Native American.

Race was not the only element involved in determining a person's status. Despite the normally low status of Native Americans, individual Native American leaders—chiefs, or caciques—might have considerable wealth and status. A person of mixed white and Native American descent might be called an Indian if he or she lived in Indian communities, a mestizo if he or she lived in Spanish colonial towns, or Spanish if he or she became rich and influential enough.

EVERYDAY LIFE

Spanish society was urban centered, and Spanish-American societies even more so. Wherever the Spanish went in the New World, they established cities and towns, usually on the same plan. There was a large square in the middle, with the city's principal church on one side, the municipal council building on another, the residence of the royal governor or governor's representative on another, and various shops and wealthy residences on the remaining spots fronting the square. Beyond the square extended a boxlike grid of straight streets, and beyond that a collection of temporary huts, mainly for Native Americans serving the Spanish. With this simple plan, Spanish-American cities could stay small or grow indefinitely large, without losing their central focus on church and crown.

Mexico City and Lima, as the first viceregal capitals, were Spanish America's most prestigious cities, but others grew fast. Potosí in what is now Bolivia rode a silver boom to become the largest city in the Hispanic world by 1650, with a population of 160,000. The often extravagant and ornate architecture in Spanish-American colonial cities embodied a baroque aesthetic. Flamboyant domes, spiraling twisted columns, and heavy sculptural decoration characterized churches and other public buildings.

RELIGION AND THE MISSIONARIES

Religion was a basic part of Spanish colonial life, and priests often accompanied the conquistadores, to minister to their spiritual needs and to begin the process of Christianizing the Native Americans in newly conquered areas. The first archdioceses were established in Mexico City, Lima, and Santo Domingo in 1545, making the colonial church hierarchy separate from that of Spain. The colonial

SISTER JUANA INÉS DE LA CRUZ

Sister Juana Inés de la Cruz
(Library of Congress)

The daughter of a Spanish military officer and a creole mother, Juana Inés de la Cruz (1651–1695) learned to read at age three and to write by the time she was five. Juana begged her parents to let her dress as a boy and attend university, but they refused. At age nine Juana left the Spanish colonial town San Miguel Nepantla, Mexico, to live in Mexico City, where she studied Latin. News of the young girl's intelligence reached the viceroy, who invited her to join his court. At age 17, Juana stunned 40 professors with her knowledge in an oral examination arranged by the viceroy. Although Juana attracted many suitors with her intelligence and beauty, she was determined to lead a scholarly life. Rather than marry, in 1669 Juana entered the convent of San Jerónimo where she devoted the next 23 years to writing poetry and philosophic studies and conducting scientific studies. There she also accumulated a library of more than 4,000 volumes. Over the years, her religious superiors attempted to diminish her scholarly activities. They condemned her controversial belief that women held the right to develop their minds as well as their souls. In defense of women's rights, Sister Juana wrote the poem "Hombres necios que acusséss" ("Foolish Men Who Accuse [Women]") in 1691. Two years later, however, she bowed to pressure from the church, sending officials a letter using her own blood as ink, in which she vowed to relinquish all contact with the world. She then stopped writing, gave away her extensive library and scientific materials, and devoted the remainder of her life to her religious duties. Sister Juana died while nursing her fellow nuns during an epidemic. Several editions of her work were published in Spain in the 18th century, including her well-known autobiography *Repuesta a Sor Filotea de la Cruz* ("Reply to Sister Philotea of the Cross;" published in English as *A Woman of Genius*).

church owned a great deal of property—with lands in which the missionaries worked intensively to Christianize the Native American population becoming known as mission fields—and had considerable political influence and social status, staffed as it was mostly by people of entirely Spanish descent.

Although priests often supported the interests of America's Spanish rulers, they were at times the only authority standing in the way of those rulers' rapacity, urging decent treatment of Native Americans and establishing hospitals and schools that served them. Bartolomé de Las Casas, already mentioned, was an example. Many of those who tended to the spiritual and temporal needs of Native Americans were members of Catholic religious orders, with the Franciscans predominating in Mexico and the Dominicans in Peru; Augustinians and Jesuits were also present. To instruct the Native Americans in the faith, these missionaries learned Native American languages, studied their cultures, and created new forms of organization, including the doctrina, a religious school or center, and the reduccion or congregación, a Native American community formed to facilitate preaching, such as the Jesuit-led Guaraní reducciones of Paraguay.

The culture of Spanish colonies was modeled on that of Spain, but some artists and writers began to innovate in ways that suggested the birth of a new Hispanic-American culture. The Mexican nun Sister Juana Inés de la Cruz (1651–1695) was Spanish America's first major poet, besides being a scholar and early advocate of equal education for women. Native American artists learned to carve and paint saints in European ways, but they added stylistic touches characteristic of pre-Columbian culture. Music blended Spanish instruments with Native American rhythms—a blend still audible in, for example, the huayno, a traditional Peruvian social dance. African culture was often added to the mix, especially in the Caribbean.

FLORIDA AND THE SPANISH CARIBBEAN

Besides colonizing much of what is now called Latin America, the Spanish were the first European colonizers of what is now the United States. Forty-two years before the English would found Jamestown, Virginia, in 1607, England's first permanent settlement in the Americas, the Spanish founded one in St. Augustine, Florida.

Juan Ponce de León (Library of Congress)

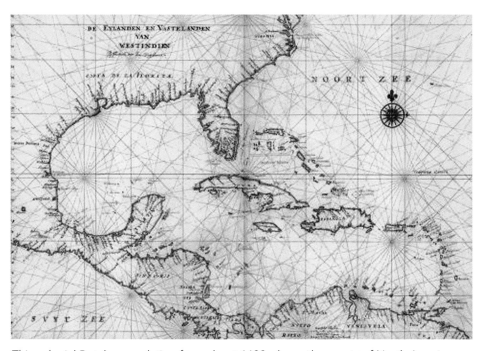

This colonial Dutch map, dating from about 1639, shows the coasts of North America and South America from Virginia through the Yucatan Peninsula in Mexico to Guyana in South America highlighting Cuba, the island of Hispaniola and the West Indies. (Library of Congress)

This 19th century image shows Hernando de Soto entering an Indian Village during the journey in which he became the first European to see the Mississippi River. (Library of Congress)

"Juan Ponz de Leon, giving heed to the tale of the Indians of Cuba and Santo Domingo, went to Florida in search of the River Jordan...then that he might become young from bathing in such a stream."

—Hernando de Escalante Fontaneda in his memoirs

SPANISH FLORIDA

Florida's European discoverer was Juan Ponce de León (1460–1521), who traveled with Columbus on his second voyage (1493–1496) and who conquered Puerto Rico beginning in 1508. According to a dubious legend, he came to Florida searching for a mythical "Fountain of Youth." What is certain is that he landed on the northeast coast near present-day St. Augustine on April 2, 1513, and claimed the land for Spain, calling it Florida because he discovered it in the season of Easter, known in Spanish as Pascua Florida, "Floral Passover." He returned in 1521 and attempted to found a settlement on the peninsula's west coast, facing the Gulf of Mexico, but a Native American attack drove him off, leaving him with an arrow wound that killed him once he reached Cuba.

Spanish exploration of Florida and adjacent areas continued in the coming decades. In 1526, Lucas Vásquez de Ayllón (ca. 1475–1526) founded a colony in what is now North or South Carolina but died of fever that year; the colony foundered soon after. Two years later, in 1528, an expedition headed by Pánfilo de Narváez, former antagonist of Cortés in Mexico, landed on the Gulf Coast at Tampa Bay and marched inland almost to the present-day border with Georgia. But through Narváez's mismanagement, the explorers lost contact with their ships and were forced to build barges to try to sail across the Gulf of Mexico to New Spain. The barges were wrecked near present-day Galveston, Texas, and all but four men were lost. They managed to stay alive and return to tell their astonishing tale. Led by Álvar Núñez Cabeza de Vaca (ca. 1490–ca. 1557), they walked for years across Texas and what is now the American Southwest, becoming the first Europeans to see American bison and making their living as healers among the Native Americans before arriving back in Mexico in 1536.

After this dismal start, Spain had little reason to continue exploring Florida. The terrain was difficult, there was no gold or silver, and the Native Americans

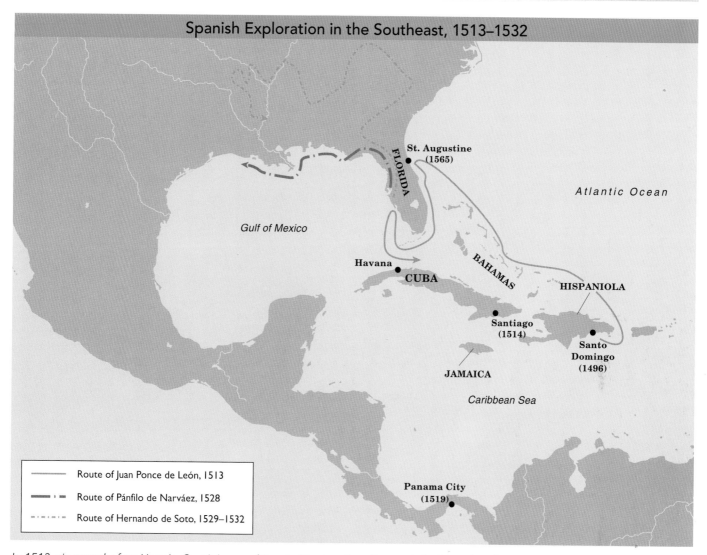

Spanish Exploration in the Southeast, 1513–1532

Atlantic Ocean

St. Augustine
(1565)

FLORIDA

Gulf of Mexico

Havana

CUBA

BAHAMAS

HISPANIOLA

Santiago
(1514)

Santo
Domingo
(1496)

JAMAICA

Caribbean Sea

Panama City
(1519)

Legend:
——— Route of Juan Ponce de León, 1513
— · — · Route of Pánfilo de Narváez, 1528
— · · — · · Route of Hernando de Soto, 1529–1532

In 1513, six years before Hernán Cortés's expedition to Mexico, Juan Ponce de León explored and then claimed Florida for the Spanish crown. In 1528, Pánfilo de Narváez led an expedition along the Gulf of Mexico coast, and in 1539, Hernando de Soto led a mission that crossed the Mississippi River and reached as far west as Texas. Both Cortés and Narváez died in the course of their travels; Ponce de León died shortly after returning to Cuba, from arrow wounds inflicted by the Native Americans he had encountered there.

were skilled fighters. Even so, Hernando de Soto (ca. 1500–1542) came to Florida in 1539, searching for gold. His expedition (1539–1543) slogged across parts of what are now Florida, South Carolina, North Carolina, Alabama, Mississippi, Tennessee, Arkansas, Oklahoma, and Texas. Although he discovered the Mississippi River in 1541 (where he was buried after dying of fever), his expedition's reports did not make Florida or the American Southeast sound any more attractive to Spanish ears. The Spanish claim to the territory languished for two more decades.

What brought Spain back to Florida was not desire for wealth but a strategic interest in keeping foreign rivals from grabbing the peninsula, particularly since

Florida threatened the sea lanes through which Spanish ships carried New World treasure home to Spain. In 1564, a group of Huguenots, or French Protestants, organized by Protestant leader Admiral Gaspard de Coligny and led by the Norman navigator Jean Ribault, had landed near the St. Johns River in February 1562, before moving north to Port Royal Sound. There, on present-day Parris Island, Ribault left twenty-eight men to build a settlement known as Charlesfort. Ribault then returned to Europe to gather supplies for the new colony. However, he was arrested in England, and unable to return.

Under attack by Indians and without Ribault's leadership or adequate supplies, the Huguenot colonists abandoned

Hernando de Soto (Library of Congress)

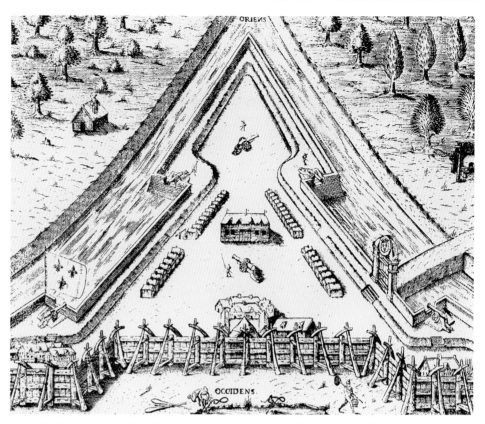

Fort Caroline, built by French Protestants near present-day Jacksonville, Florida (Library of Congress)

Charlesfort, and all but one of the ill-fated colonists set sail to return to Europe. (During their voyage in an open boat, failed colonists were reduced to cannibalism before the survivors reached English waters.) Meanwhile, René Goulaine de Laudonnière, who had been Ribault's second-in-command on the original 1562 expedition, led a group of about 200 new settlers back to Florida, where they founded Fort Caroline (or Fort de la Caroline) at St. John's Bluff on June 22, 1564. The fort was named for the reigning French king, Charles IX. Unfortunately, like those at Charlesfort, the Fort Caroline colonists also suffered from hunger, Indian attacks, and mutiny. Within a year, Fort Caroline also gained the attention of Spain, who saw the colony as a direct threat to its control of the region.

In June of 1565, Ribault, by now released from English prison, returned to Florida. In late August, he arrived at Fort Caroline with a large fleet and hundreds of soldiers and settlers and took command of the settlement. At the same time, the Spanish Governor of Florida, Don Pedro Menéndez de Avilés, had simultaneously been sent from Cádiz, Spain with a thousand men, promises of reinforcements, orders to destroy the French settlement, and authorization from King Philip II to establish Spanish settlements.

Menéndez arrived at the mouth of the St. John's River shortly after Ribault, and retreated 35 miles south. On August 28, the feast day of Augustine of Hippo, Menéndez sighted the land on which to build a new settlement. On September 8, he founded St. Augustine, and then declared all of Florida a possession of Philip II.

Two days later, Ribault's fleet set out in pursuit of the Spaniards with several of ships and most of his troops, but he was surprised at sea by a violent storm lasting several days.

In a daring surprise attack, Menéndez then marched his forces overland, launching a dawn attack on the now-lightly defended 200 to 250 Huguenots at Fort Caroline. The only survivors were about 50 women and children who were taken prisoner and a few defenders who managed to escape; the rest were executed.

Meanwhile, Ribault's fleet was virtually destroyed in the storm, and many of the crew lost at sea. Ribault himself, along with the rest of his crew, were marooned.

Upon discovering the Frenchmen, Menéndez then executed Ribault and several hundred Frenchmen as religious heretics at a place now known as Matanzas ("massacres") Inlet. In 1568, the French counterattacked and burned the fort that the Spanish had built on the site of Fort Caroline, but after the massacre of Ribault and his men, they made no more attempts to colonize the Atlantic seaboard of North America.

The city of St. Augustine, Florida remains the oldest European-founded settlement in North America. In 1566, Martín de Argüelles became the first child of European ancestry to be born in what is now the continental United States. Its Castillo de San Marcos, begun in 1672, is the oldest masonry fort in the continental United States. While the English privateer Sir Francis Drake attacked and burned the city 1586, and English pirates plundered it and killed most of its inhab-

itants in 1668, it remained a Spanish settlement until it was temporarily ceded to Great Britain in 1763. Following the American Revolution the city would again become Spanish territory until it was at last ceded, along with the rest of Florida, to the United States.

Spain's sense of what constituted La Florida was vague at first: roughly the Florida peninsula and anything north and west of it, even as far north as Newfoundland. Spain's more extravagant claims to distant northern lands were challenged in the early 17th century as European rivals at last established their own enduring colonies, including France's Quebec in 1608, England's Plymouth in 1620, and Holland's New Amsterdam (later captured by the English and renamed New York) in 1624. But closer to the southern heartland of Spanish America, Spain did what it could to press its claims.

Spanish homes in St. Augustine, such as this one, were sparsely decorated. Chairs were usually reserved for the men. (Media Projects Inc./Photo by Pat Lods)

A street scene in St. Augustine in the early 17th century (Library of Congress)

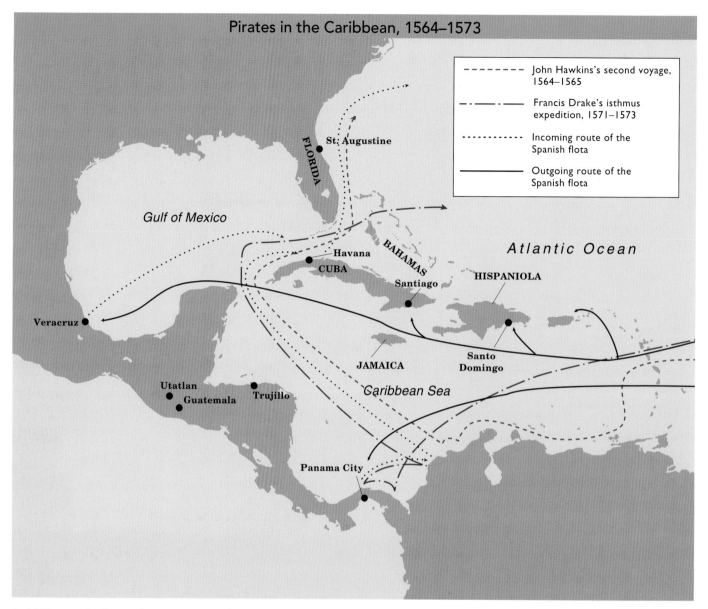

Pirates in the Caribbean, 1564–1573

Legend:
- – – – – – John Hawkins's second voyage, 1564–1565
- – · – · – Francis Drake's isthmus expedition, 1571–1573
- · · · · · · Incoming route of the Spanish flota
- ——— Outgoing route of the Spanish flota

FLORIDA · St. Augustine

Gulf of Mexico

Havana · CUBA · BAHAMAS · Santiago · HISPANIOLA

Atlantic Ocean

Veracruz

JAMAICA · Santo Domingo

Caribbean Sea

Utatlan · Guatemala · Trujillo

Panama City

In 1525, news had spread across Europe of the silver and gold shipped to Spain from the Americas. Angered by Spain's monopoly over the Indies, other nations began plotting to seize Spanish treasure. In the 1500s, the French, English, and Dutch commisioned privateers such as Francis Drake to plunder the Spanish, taking some treasure for themselves and sharing some with their governments. To protect their riches, the Spanish ordered treasure ships sail for Spain just once a year in a heavily guarded fleet known as a flota. When flota became more difficult to attack, privateers and, later, pirates took to attacking smaller merchant ships and coastal towns. The map above shows several of the most famous pirate routes, as well as the inbound and outbound route of the flota.

In the 17th century, Spanish Franciscan priests converted most of the Timucua and Apalachee peoples of northern Florida to Christianity, establishing a chain of missions as far north as Georgia. In 1698 Spain founded Pensacola in the Florida panhandle. But Spain's foothold in the region was weak. English colonists pushed south from Jamestown (founded in Virginia in 1607), settling the Carolinas and Georgia by the early 18th century. English raiders attacked Spanish Florida settlements and destroyed missions. In 1682, French explorers traveling south from their initial foothold in Quebec reached the mouth of the Mississippi River. All the land drained by the river and its tributaries—a vast section of North America—was claimed for France as Louisiana. By the early 18th century, the French in Louisiana were harassing Pensacola and had settlements throughout a territory then known as West Florida, corresponding to the Gulf Coast strip of present-day Alabama, Mississippi, and Louisiana east of the Mississippi River. Squeezed militarily by the British to the north and

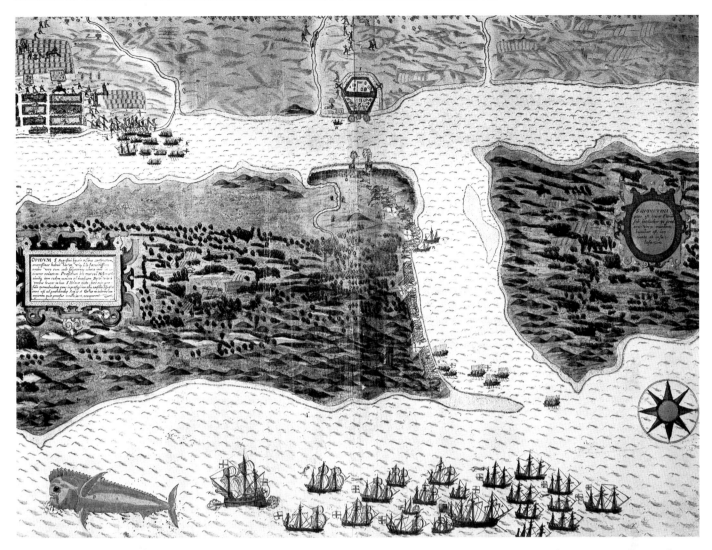

This illustration of Sir Francis Drake's ships attacking St. Augustine appeared in a book published in London in 1589. (Library of Congress)

the French to the west, Spanish Florida was in an unfavorable position by the mid-18th century.

PIRATES OF THE CARIBBEAN

The power struggle taking place in Florida and adjoining regions was mirrored by the struggle in the Caribbean Sea. As early as the 1570s, when Spain and Portugal were alone in having founded New World colonies and Spanish power was at its zenith, Spanish traffic was harassed by English privateers such as Sir Francis Drake (1540–1596) and Sir John Hawkins (1532–1595). As privateers, they acted as agents of their country in harassing the commerce of England's enemy, attacking and plundering Spanish ships and colonial ports. Puerto Rico built strong fortifications in defense, such as the fortress El

Morro, erected to guard San Juan, and in 1595 repelled Drake and Hawkins's attempt to capture the colony.

In the 17th century, privateering gave way to unqualified piracy, robbery on the high seas unsanctioned by rival powers. In the Caribbean, English, Dutch, and French pirates, also known as buccaneers or freebooters, went down in lore and literature for attacking coastal colonies and slow-moving Spanish galleons laden with New World gold and silver. Their name came from the French *boucanier*, a person from Hispaniola or the nearby island of Tortuga who smoked meat on a *boucan*, or barbecue frame. Tortuga and Jamaica were among their bases in what was called the Spanish Main, an area roughly equivalent to the Caribbean region. Another base was the Central American region that is now Belize, a longtime British colony called British Honduras. The line between

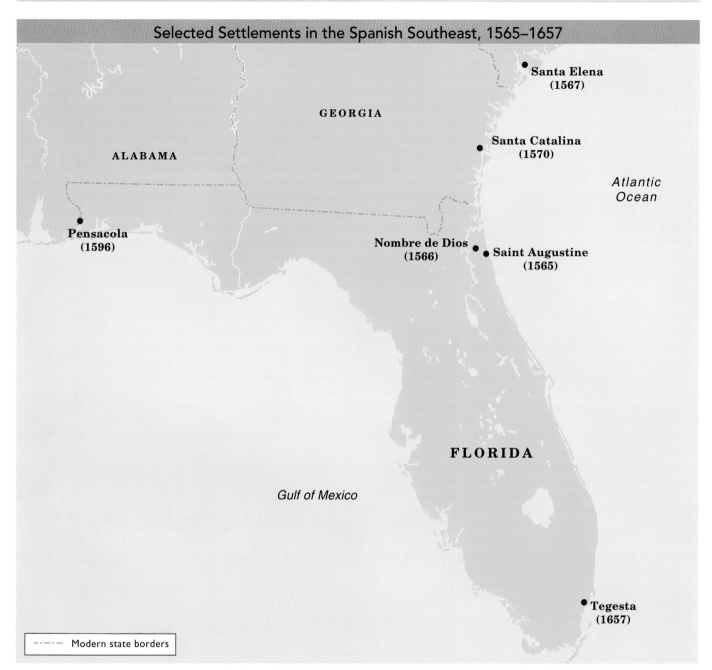

Selected Settlements in the Spanish Southeast, 1565–1657

Santa Elena (1567)

GEORGIA

Santa Catalina (1570)

ALABAMA

Atlantic Ocean

Pensacola (1596)

Nombre de Dios (1566) Saint Augustine (1565)

FLORIDA

Gulf of Mexico

Tegesta (1657)

----- Modern state borders

While the Spanish would in time expand Florida settlement southward during the 17th century, swamplands in southern Florida slowed the pace of development. With the exception of a settlement at Tegesta, most of the earliest settlements were in the north. In fact, although no precise borders existed, the Spaniards viewed what they called La Florida as extending northward into the Carolinas.

buccaneering and privateering was often vague, with the British and French only too happy to see their enemy Spain harassed, even without official approval. Some buccaneers were explicitly hired by their governments to fight as privateers in the War of the Spanish Succession (1701–1714), in which Austria, England, Denmark, the Dutch Republic, Portugal, and several other European nations joined forces against France and Spain. But pirates also menaced the colonies of other nations. The infamous English pirate Blackbeard (Edward Teach, ca.

1680–1718) was killed by the British for his attacks on Virginia, a British colony.

Even aside from the attacks of pirate ships, Spanish control of the Caribbean was greatly weakened by the mid-18th century, for other nations had planted colonies throughout the West Indies. The Netherlands took possession of the Leeward Islands in the 1630s, England of the Bahamas in the 1640s. Jamaica, settled by Spain in 1509, was ceded to England in 1670. The western part of the island of Hispaniola that was to become Haiti was ceded to France in 1697. Just beyond the eastern edge of the Caribbean, foreign powers carved out colonies on the northern coast of South America, colonies that developed into the modern nations of Guyana (a former British colony) and Suriname (a former Dutch colony) and the French overseas department of French Guiana. All this trespassing on what was once considered an exclusively Spanish colonial domain boded poorly for continued Spanish dominance in the New World.

THE SPANISH BORDERLANDS

Soon after the Spanish settled in Florida, they also settled in another part of what is now the United States: the Southwest. To them it was the far north of New Spain. By the end of the Spanish colonial era, far northern territories claimed by Spain included all or part of what are now California, Arizona, New Mexico, Texas, Nevada, Utah, Colorado, Wyoming, Kansas, and Oklahoma. Despite these grandiose claims, these territories were thinly populated by the Spanish, and in many areas Native Americans continued their ancient ways unmolested by Spain. Other European powers contested Spanish claims and encroached on their colonies, particularly in Texas. The area was a frontier, a region at the edge of an expanding state—or, as many historians now prefer to call it, a borderlands area, a region where boundaries are contested or ill defined and different cultures are cohabiting. Within these borderlands were some thriving Spanish colonial communities, particularly Santa Fe, New Mexico; San Antonio, Texas; and San Diego, California.

New Mexico

The first Spanish explorer to enter what is now the state of New Mexico was Álvar Núñez Cabeza de Vaca, the shipwrecked survivor of Narváez's ill-fated Florida expedition (1528–1536) who walked across Texas and New Mexico before returning to New Spain. After him, in search of the legendary riches of the Seven Cities of Cíbola, came Francisco Coronado, whose overland expedition from Mexico (1540–1542) reached present-day Arizona, New Mexico, Texas, Oklahoma, and Kansas. The Coronado expedition encountered such wonders as the Grand Canyon of the Colorado River but no wealthy empires. The fabled Cíbola turned out to be only the pueblos, or adobe villages, of the Zuni people.

For several decades, Spain lost all interest in the territory. But as New Spain grew, and its northern frontier expanded as far as Santa Bárbara, Mexico, soldiers and missionaries again became curious about what lay beyond the Rio Grande. Spain's strategic interest increased when England's first successful circumnavigation of the globe was completed (1577–1580) by none other than the privateer Sir Francis Drake, who explored the California coast as far north as present-day San Francisco and claimed the region for England. Whatever the lands north of Mexico contained, Spain did not want England to possess them.

Beginning in the 1580s, several small expeditions reconnoitered the region they called Nueva México, "New Mexico." Beginning in 1598, Juan de Oñate (ca. 1550–ca. 1630) set forth from Mexico with a royal contract to settle the region and renew the search for precious metals. He founded San Juan de los Caballeros, near present-day Santa Fe, in 1598. For abuses against the Native Americans, he was dismissed as governor in 1607. His successor, Pedro de Peralta, founded the new provincial capital of Santa Fe in 1610.

Nearly 2,000 miles from Mexico City, this far northern outpost of New Spain had little to attract settlers, and it grew slowly as a farming and ranching community, with missions to indoctrinate the Pueblo in the Catholic faith. As usual, the Native Americans got the worst of it, pressed into servitude by various mechanisms and whipped or murdered on the slightest pretext. In 1680, Spanish abuse prompted a Native American rebellion known as the Pueblo Revolt, led by a Tewa shaman of the San Juan Pueblo named Popé and supported by the Hopi, the Zuni, and the people of Acoma. Wanting to restore their old religion and drive out the Spanish, the Pueblo destroyed the missions, killed 400 Spanish, and forced out the rest. For more than a decade, the Pueblo occupied Santa Fe. But the Spanish returned in

AN AMAZING JOURNEY

In 1527 Pánfilo de Narváez set off from Cuba to explore Florida. Believing Florida to be a separate landmass from Mesoamerica, Narváez and his men explored the Gulf Coast by sea until meeting with disaster. First, they lost many men to Indian attacks and disease, then they ran out of food and were forced to eat their horses. Next, after stitching boats together with horsehide to sail back to Cuba, they were caught in a hurricane off present-day Galveston, Texas. After being captured by Indians, survivor Álvar Núñez Cabeza de Vaca escaped into the desert where he wandered for five years before he was imprisoned again. With three other survivors of the Narváez crew—including an enslaved African named Estéban—the four escaped into the desert together. Each time they met Native Americans, Estéban did the talking, shaking a rattle given to him by Plains Indians, offering to heal the sick, and gaining a larger and larger entourage with each stop. At last the men met an Indian wearing a Spanish-made buckle. They had reached the province of Nueva Galicia in northwest Mexico, eight years after leaving Cuba.

The four men were led into the provincial capital of Compostela by 600 local Indians. There the local governor had the Indians arrested and quizzed Cabeza de Vaca about riches to be found in the north. Cabeza de Vaca told reports of seven fabulously rich cities not far from where they had been (these became known as the Seven Cities of Cíbola). This report reached Antonio de Mendoza, the viceroy in Mexico City, who decided to commission his own expedition. Mendoza picked Estéban for the journey and chose Father Marcos de Niza, a priest, to lead the group, since a slave could not be given that role. Returning to Compostela from Mexico City, the Niza party was greeted by the new governor of Nueva Galicia, Francisco de Coronado. From there the party continued north, with Estéban dressed in ankle bells, feathers, and body paint, assuming the role of a traveling shaman. By the time they reached the Mayo River in present-day Senora, Father de Niza was exhausted. He ordered Estéban to go on without him and to send back crosses if he found anything important, with the size of the cross a sign of the importance of the discovery. For a time, crosses arrived, each larger than the last, along with stories of Estéban being showered in jewels and gold. Then the crosses stopped; Estéban had disappeared. According to the Zuni people who live in the region, Estéban was killed by their ancestors in about 1539. Whatever Estéban's fate, when de Niza returned to Compostela, he told Coronado that the slave had been killed at the gates of one of the legendary Seven Cities of Cíbola. Coronado rushed to Mexico City to receive permission to launch a full-scale search—one that would end in failure and frustration when the only cities he found were a few adobe pueblos.

Álvar Núñez Cabeza de Vaca, who is seen in the foreground, wandered for seven years in the American Southwest with his fellow survivors of the ill-fated Narváez expedition until they encountered a group of Spanish soldiers. One member of the group, the African slave Estéban Dorantes, seen here to the left of Cabeza de Vaca, later returned to the region to continue searching for the legendary Seven Cities of Cíbola. (National Park Service)

Coronado searches for the famed Seven Cities of Cíbola. (Library of Congress)

1692, led by Diego de Vargas Zapata Luján y Ponce de León, recapturing Santa Fe that year and reconquering the whole region by 1696.

After their return in the 1690s, the Spanish were marginally more respectful of the Pueblo, permitting them to hold their ancient religious ceremonies. The antagonists also became allies against the Apache—nomadic, buffalo-hunting people who raided them both. While his people had occupied Santa Fe, Popé had made the mistake of trading horses aquired from the Spanish to the Apache, who, like Native Americans throughout the Great Plains, began using the horse not only in hunting but also in raids on Spanish and Pueblo Indians.

Despite the dangers and hardships of New Mexico, colonization increased there during the 18th century. In 1692 the Italian Jesuit missionary Eusebio Kino (1645–1711), working with New Spain, came to what is now Arizona and was then part of the province of New Mexico. There he began founding missions among the Yaqui, Yuma, and Akimil O'odham (Pima). In 1752 the Spanish built a presidio, or fort, at Tubac, the first permanent European settlement in Arizona. By then the Spanish had learned the value both of sending missionaries into frontier areas as vanguards of colo-

nization and of establishing a paid, standing garrison in a presidio to guard the missionaries. The presidio guarding the mission church became a central feature of many far northern colonies, from California to New Mexico to Texas.

By 1800 the Hispanic population of New Mexico was about 20,000. Many of these inhabitants were not Spanish but poor, Spanish-speaking mestizos from New Spain, induced to move north by offers of land—a technique used in colonizing Texas and California as well. Trade grew throughout New Mexico in the 18th century, with Native Americans exchanging skins and buffalo meat for Spanish manufactured goods at annual trade fairs such as those at Taos and Pecos. These fairs were an extension of a complex system of internal trade in New Spain that included El Camino Real, "The Royal Road," the name for the overland trade routes in New Mexico, Florida, California, and Texas connecting the northern frontier with Mexico City. Other important land routes connected Mexico City to the east coast port of Veracruz, center for transatlantic trade with Europe; and to the west coast port of Acapulco, center for transpacific trade with the Philippines.

Illicit trade with the French also took place, as the French, pressing their

Coronado's Exploration in the Southwest, 1540–1542

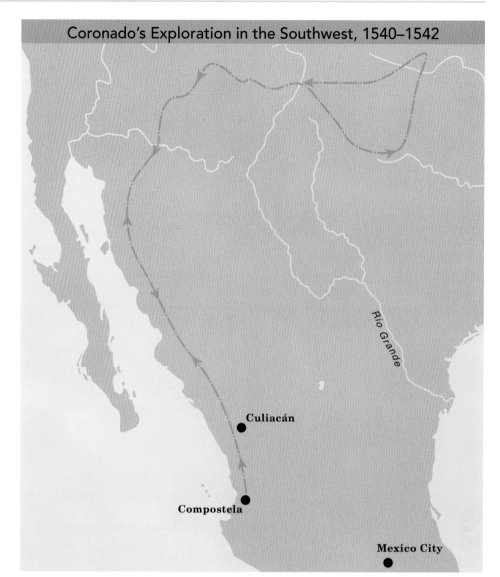

Rio Grande

● **Culiacán**

Compostela ●

Mexico City ●

In search of the legendary riches of the Seven Cities of Cibola, Francisco Coronado and his men journeyed from Mexico (1540–1542) across present-day Arizona, New Mexico, Texas, Oklahoma, and Kansas. The expedition encountered such wonders as the Grand Canyon of the Colorado River but no gold.

territorial claims to Louisiana, established a presence in what are now the states of Kansas, Oklahoma, and Texas. The international jockeying between Spain and France did not end until 1763, when France transferred to Spain its claim to the Louisiana Territory from the Mississippi River to the Rocky Mountains. Even then the conflict was not completely over: this territory was ceded back to France in 1800 and then ceded by Napoleon to the young United States as the Louisiana Purchase in 1803, prompting American explorers to venture west across the plains.

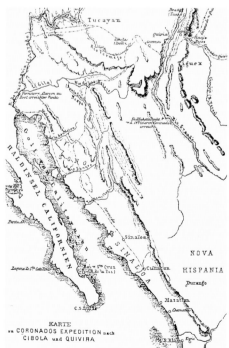

An historic map depicting a portion of Coronado's journey (Library of Congress)

TEXTILES OF SPANISH NEW MEXICO

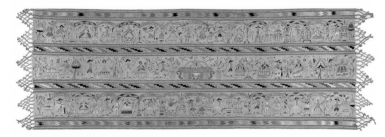

Wool from sheep brought to the Americas by the Spanish, combined with Native American weaving techniques, led to a flourishing textile industry in Mexico's northern territories. Above is a woolen serape, or "wearing blanket," dating from the 19th century. Serapes were especially prized by horsemen. (courtesy of Mark Winter)

The very fine handiwork in this 19th-century New Mexican rebozo, or shawl, suggests that it was reserved for special occasions. The rows of dancing figures (see detail) are thought to represent celebrants at a wedding. (courtesy of Mark Winter)

The fine art of Hispanic weaving is one of the oldest traditional crafts still practiced in present-day New Mexico, dating back as early as the 16th-century exploratory mission of Francisco de Coronado, who counted about 5,000 sheep in his entourage. (Weaving by Native Americans in the region predates this but they did not weave wool until Spanish sheep arrived.) Although Juan de Oñate established the first permanent European settlment in 1598 at San Juan de los Caballeros, it was not until after the territorial capital was founded at Santa Fe in 1610 that traditional Spanish arts and crafts became established in New Mexico. Before long, Santa Fe craftspeople began building enormous treadle looms, looms so large that they were too heavy to transport from Mexico. Most of the weaving was done by men in talleres, or workshops. Prior to the Pueblo Revolt of 1680, most of these workers were enslaved Apache, Ute, and Pueblo.

Not until after the Spanish recaptured New Mexico in 1692 did weaving become common in individual Spanish homes. Because New Mexico's governor Diego de Vargas rewarded his former soldiers with large land grants perfectly suited for sheep farming—and thus for producing wool—the New Mexico textile industry started to thrive, and weavers became the most common kind of craftspersons to be found in New Mexico during the period, working alongside other textile workers such as shearers, carders, spinners, and tailors. Textiles from New Mexico were sent south along El Camino Real (or "The King's Road," the name given to all major Spanish highways in North America that led to Mexico City) to El Paso del Norte and then on to Chihuahua, Sonora, Coahuila, and Durango in Mexico. The styles included the jerga, a checker-pattered woolen rug; the serape (at left, top), a garment worn as a protective outer coat; and the frazada, or blanket, which often included manitas (little hands) or palmas (palms) motifs. Each November a caravan of ox-drawn carts was loaded with textiles and sent south on a dangerous journey, under the watchful protection of as many as 500 soldiers. Usually, several thousand sheep were driven by caravan to Mexican markets. In exchange for wool and textiles, New Mexican merchants received many of the provisions that were otherwise unavailable in the colony, including other kinds of cloth, metal tools and utensils, sugar, chocolate, horses, and mules.

Partly because many of the early textile weavers were genizaro—Indians who had assimilated into Hispanic society, usually as household servants—the New Mexican textile industry has also played an important role in the interplay between Hispanic and Native American cultures. It was Spaniards who introduced the Pueblo and Navajo to sheep and wool. In fact, the Navajo became such masters at the art of weaving that their blankets soon garnered higher prices on the market than those made by Spaniards. Hispanic weavers responded by adding Navajo motifs in the corners of their blankets.

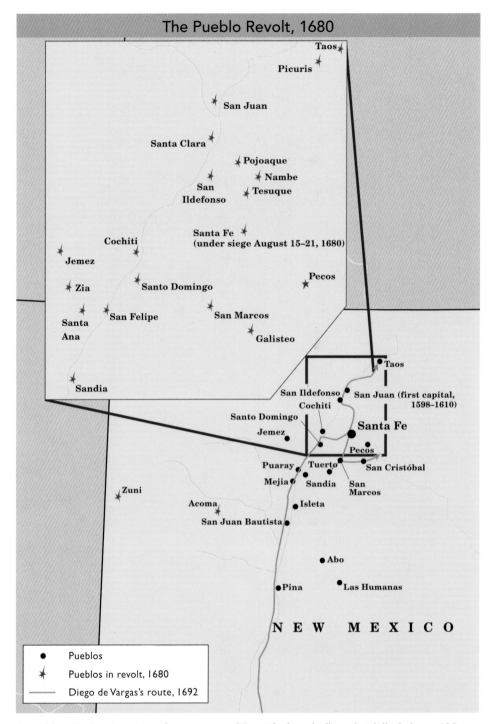

The Pueblo Revolt, 1680

Taos

Picuris

San Juan

Santa Clara

Pojoaque

Nambe

San
Ildefonso

Tesuque

Santa Fe
(under siege August 15–21, 1680)

Cochiti

Jemez

Pecos

Zia

Santo Domingo

Santa
Ana

San Felipe

San Marcos

Galisteo

Sandia

Taos

San Ildefonso

San Juan (first capital,
1598–1610)

Cochiti

Santo Domingo

Jemez

Santa Fe

Pecos

Puaray

Tuerto

San Cristóbal

Mejia

Sandia

San
Marcos

Zuni

Acoma

Isleta

San Juan Bautista

Abo

Pina

Las Humanas

N E W   M E X I C O

● Pueblos

✳ Pueblos in revolt, 1680

——— Diego de Vargas's route, 1692

In 1680, a Native American shaman named Popé led a rebellion that killed about 400 Spaniards and led to the temporary abandonment of Santa Fe. In 1692, Spanish forces under the command of Diego de Vargas retook the city. Seen above are the pueblos in which the rebellion was centered, as well as Vargas's route to Santa Fe.

TEXAS

The Spanish explorers Cabeza de Vaca, Coronado, and Oñate all visited what is now Texas, but Spain showed no major interest in the region until the 1680s, when the French began laying claim to it as part of Louisiana. The Spanish sent expeditions to drive out the French and to found missions and presidios in eastern Texas, but Native American resistance forced the Spanish to abandon these in 1694. Then, in 1714, the French founded a settlement on the Rio Grande in southwestern Texas near what is now Eagle Pass. This was getting perilously close to New Spain. The Spanish reclaimed Texas with a vengeance, in time founding more

Selected Spanish Settlements in Texas, 1699–1725

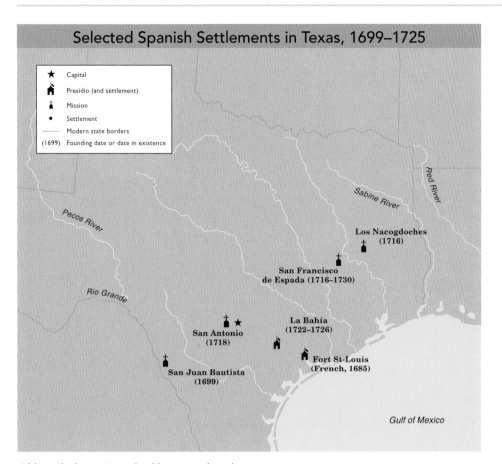

★ Capital
🏠 Presidio (and settlement)
⛪ Mission
• Settlement
—— Modern state borders
(1699) Founding date or date in existence

Red River
Sabine River
Pecos River
Los Nacogdoches (1716)
San Francisco de Espada (1716–1730)
Rio Grande
San Antonio (1718)
La Bahía (1722–1726)
San Juan Bautista (1699)
Fort St-Louis (French, 1685)
Gulf of Mexico

Although the territory had been explored several times in the 16th century, by 1700 few Spaniards had actually settled in Texas. However, competition with France in the early 18th century led to a wave of Spanish fort and mission construction. Seen above are locations of some of the earliest forts and missions in Texas.

than 30 missions in Texas by the end of the 18th century. The most important of these was San Antonio in south-central Texas, founded in 1718, the same year France founded New Orleans near the Gulf Coast just east of Texas.

San Antonio grew into the most important Spanish town in Texas, thanks in part to 56 colonists who migrated here from the distant Spanish-owned Canary Islands in search of new lives. It was incorporated as a city in 1809. The best-known remnant of colonial San Antonio is The Alamo, a Franciscan mission chapel built around 1722 that would become the site in the 1830s of the most famous battle in the war for Texan independence from Mexico.

Spanish Texas was still thinly populated in the early 19th century, with no more than 4,000 Hispanic settlers. The bound-

THE ACEQUIA SYSTEM

The acequia at Mission Francisco de Espada in east Texas (National Park Service)

On the dry plains of the Texas frontier, rain was rare, making acequias, or irrigation ditches, so important to Franciscan missionaries and other settlers that cropland in Spanish Texas was measured in suertes, an amount equal to the land that could be watered in one day.

Ironically, Muslims first introduced the use of acequias to the dry regions of southern Spain during the centuries-long Moorish occupation. Franciscan monks found acequias ideal on the arid nothern frontier of New Spain.

To distribute the water, missionaries and Indians constructed seven gravity-flow ditches, five dams, and an aqueduct—all told, a 15-mile system that irrigated about 3,500 acres of land.

Today the best-preserved acequia in the Southwest stands near Mission Espada in East Texas. Indians on the mission had built a dam at Espada that was completed by 1740, diverting river water into an acequia madre (mother ditch). Using floodgates, an aguador (water master) controlled the volume of water sent to each field for irrigation and for such auxiliary uses as bathing, washing, and power for mill wheels. More than 250 years later, the Espada dam still operates, and water still passes through the Espada Aqueduct—one of the oldest arched Spanish aqueducts in the United States.

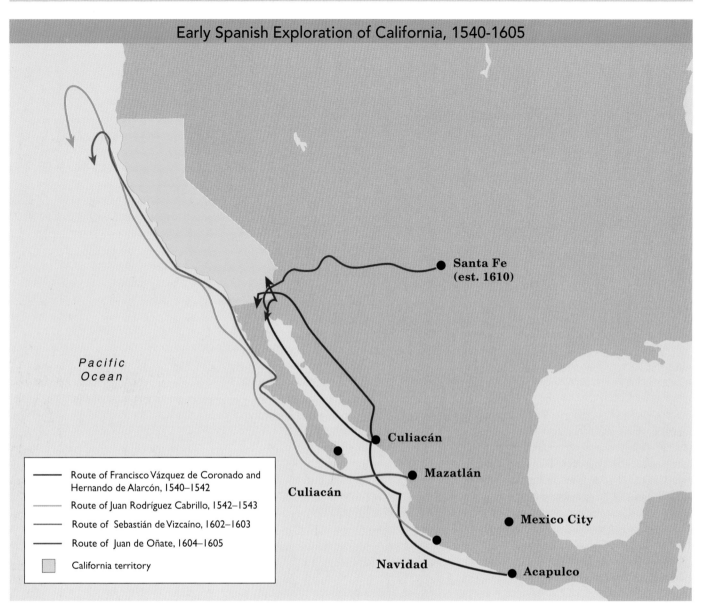

Early Spanish Exploration of California, 1540-1605

Santa Fe (est. 1610)

Culiacán

Mazatlán

Culiacán

Mexico City

Navidad

Acapulco

Pacific Ocean

— Route of Francisco Vázquez de Coronado and Hernando de Alarcón, 1540–1542

— Route of Juan Rodríguez Cabrillo, 1542–1543

— Route of Sebastián de Vizcaíno, 1602–1603

— Route of Juan de Oñate, 1604–1605

California territory

During the mid-16th and early 17th centuries several exploratory Spanish expeditions either surveyed the California coast by sea or traversed part of it by land. While Francisco de Coronado may have crossed into California in search of the legendary Seven Cities of Cíbola, Juan Rodríguez Cabrillo sailed as far north as present-day Washington State.

ary dispute in Texas between the French and the Spanish continued unabated through the colonial era and would play out in a different, more violent form—the Texas independence movement and the U.S.-Mexican War—by the United States and Mexico in the 19th century.

ALTA CALIFORNIA

Baja (Low) California, the peninsula that today is part of Mexico, was discovered by Cortés in the 1530s. The European discovery of Alta (High) California, the region we call simply California, soon followed. In 1540–1543, Portuguese explorer Juan Rodríguez Cabrillo (d. 1543), a

comrade of Cortés in the conquest of Mexico, traveled north along the Pacific coast beyond Baja California and encountered San Diego Bay and other sites. He sailed farther north than present-day San Francisco, then turned back and sailed to San Miguel Island near present-day Los Angeles, where he died of illness, leaving others to finish the expedition.

No apparent gold or silver beckoned in California, so the Spanish left it alone. Drake explored and claimed northern California for England in 1579, but the English also left it alone. Finally, in the mid-18th century, Russian ships began to trade for fur along the Pacific coast north of California, spurring the Spanish to defend their claim to California.

Spanish Exploration of the Western Frontier, 1774–1776

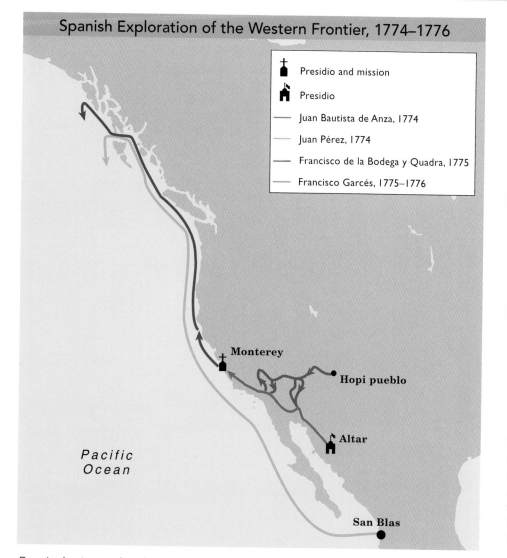

Legend:
- ✝ Presidio and mission
- ⛪ Presidio
- Juan Bautista de Anza, 1774
- Juan Pérez, 1774
- Francisco de la Bodega y Quadra, 1775
- Francisco Garcés, 1775–1776

Monterey · Hopi pueblo · Altar · San Blas

Pacific Ocean

Despite having explored much of the Pacific coast in the 16th century, Spain made no effort to settle it until the 18th century. As had been the case in Texas during the same period, the impetus for settlement was defensive. Spain found competition for the land from both Great Britain and Russia, and by settling the land, the Spaniards felt they could better defend it. The map shown here illustrates the late 18th century expeditions that paved the way for settlement.

La Purísima Concepción, a California mission (National Park Service)

HISPANIC ICONS: RETABLOS

A 19th-century retablo, or religious painting on wood (private collection)

Retablos were Hispanic icons usually painted with organic pigments on wooden panels of varying sizes. Always featuring a religious subject, these paintings were used in both homes and churches throughout the Spanish villages of New Mexico.

Not all religious art was painted on wood. This image of the founder of the Franciscan Order was painted on animal hide and used by missionaries to instruct local Indians in Christianity.

19th-century hide painting of St. Francis of Assisi (International Museum of Folk Art, Santa Fe)

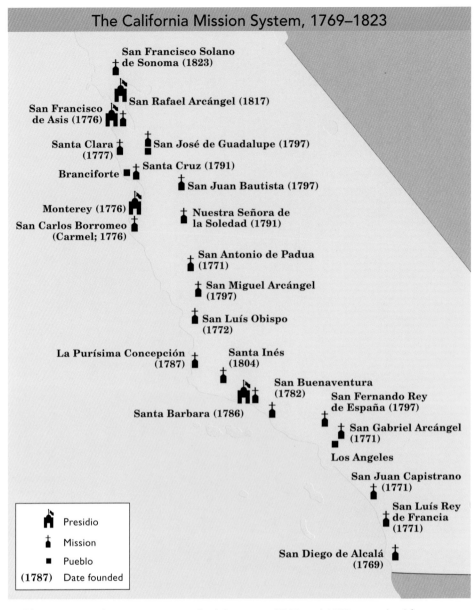

The California Mission System, 1769–1823

San Francisco Solano
† de Sonoma (1823)

San Rafael Arcángel (1817)

San Francisco
de Asis (1776)

Santa Clara † ▮ San José de Guadalupe (1797)
(1777)

Branciforte ■ † Santa Cruz (1791)

San Juan Bautista (1797)

Monterey (1776)

San Carlos Borromeo † Nuestra Señora de
(Carmel; 1776) la Soledad (1791)

† San Antonio de Padua
(1771)

† San Miguel Arcángel
(1797)

† San Luís Obispo
(1772)

La Purísima Concepción † Santa Inés
(1787) (1804)

San Buenaventura
(1782)

San Fernando Rey
de España (1797)

Santa Barbara (1786)

† San Gabriel Arcángel
(1771)

Los Angeles

San Juan Capistrano
† (1771)

San Luís Rey
† de Francia
(1771)

San Diego de Alcalá †
(1769)

Presidio

† Mission

■ Pueblo

(1787) Date founded

California's Spanish mission system, built between 1769 and 1823, stretched from present-day San Diego in the south to Sonoma County in the north.

As in New Mexico and Texas, missions were the advance guard of colonization. The Franciscan priest Junípero Serra (1713–1784) founded a mission and presidio at San Diego. By the 1820s the Franciscans had built a chain of more than 20 missions near the California coast, from San Diego to north of San Francisco Bay. The local Native Americans were taught the Catholic faith while being forcibly resettled near the missions and compelled to work as manual laborers under the direction of the missionaries. Poor Hispanic settlers from New Spain were induced to settle in the pueblos, or towns, that grew up around missions. Cattle ranching became a primary occupation, with hides and tallow among colonial California's chief exports. California cities that originated as missions founded by Father Serra include Carmel (1770), San Francisco (1776), Santa Clara (1777), and Los Angeles (1781). The Spanish presence is still felt in California, not only in Spanish place-names but in the many examples of Spanish colonial architecture that survive, including San Francisco's presidio.

Despite the burst of colonizing energy represented by the California mission system, Spain's heyday as a colonial empire by that time had long since past. By the 1830s, nothing would remain of Spain's American empire but Cuba and Puerto Rico, and those fragments would be gone by the end of the century.

INDEPENDENCE IN THE NEW WORLD

In the late 18th century, the United States became the first American colony to throw off European rule. It succeeded with the help of Spain, including the Spanish colonial governor Bernardo de Gálvez. Ironically, American independence soon came back to haunt Spain, as the new nation absorbed pieces of what had been Spanish America (Louisiana and Florida) and set a revolutionary example to the remaining pieces. Weakened by centuries of war, overspending, and political turmoil, and faced with the difficulty of continuing to enforce authority over distant and rebellious peoples, Spain lost one of the largest empires ever built. By the mid-1820s nothing remained of Spain's American domains except Cuba and Puerto Rico, and even these would be gone by century's end. Most of Spain's other American colonies began new lives as independent nations, and in so doing, they created new traditions for the Hispanic Americans who trace their lineage to them.

SPAIN AND THE AMERICAN REVOLUTION

Given that Spain still held a vast American empire at the time of the American Revolution, it may seem odd that Spain would aid colonial rebels who espoused independence from their mother country. To understand why and how Spain aided American rebels against Britain, one must first realize how different the declining Spain of the late 18th century was from the aggressive young Spain of Columbus's day.

THE RISE AND FALL OF SPAIN

For Spain, the 16th century was more than just the era when its American empire was established. It was also the time when Spain rose to the greatest status it would ever have among European nations and enjoyed a cultural flowering so pronounced as to be called Spain's "Golden Age." Gold and silver from the New World fueled this expansion of Spanish power and wealth, but even more essential was the unique political position enjoyed by Spanish monarchs during that period. At the end of the 15th century, Ferdinand and Isabella had unified Spain and centralized control in royal hands. Throughout the 16th century, their heirs brought Spain to a peak of preeminence it would never know again.

Through canny diplomacy and military prowess, Ferdinand expanded Spain's power in Europe at the expense of its rivals, especially France. He formed an alliance with the Hapsburg dynasty, rulers of the Holy Roman Empire, marrying his daughter Joanna to a Hapsburg heir, making Joanna's son Charles (1500–1558) the heir to the Spanish throne on his mother's side and to the throne of the Holy Roman Empire on his father's side. As a result, when the time for his succession came, Charles reigned simultaneously as both King Charles I of Spain (1516–1556) and Holy Roman Emperor Charles V (1519–1558). Charles governed a vast empire that included Spain, Spanish America, the Philippines (after 1542), the Holy Roman Empire's base in what is now Germany and Austria, the Netherlands, Burgundy (now part of France), and parts of Italy. Though Charles could not even speak Spanish, he became quite popular with his Spanish subjects, as the economy thrived, manufacturing increased, population grew, and the empire swelled.

Charles engaged Spain in a seemingly endless series of wars with France and the Ottoman Empire, increasing Spanish dominance in Italy and the Mediterranean at the cost of much blood and treasure. In 1556, Philip turned over the Spanish crown to his son Philip II (1527–1598; reigned 1556–1598) and the Holy Roman Empire to his brother Ferdinand (1503–1564; reigned 1556–1564). The younger Philip inherited Spain, Spanish America, the Netherlands, and the Italian territories, and he added

New Spain in 1790

	Viceregal Audencia of Mexico
	Captaincy-General of Guatemala
	Captaincy-General of Cuba
★	Viceroyalty capital (Mexico City)

Intendencias and Provinces

① Intendency of Mexico	⑩ Intendency of Oaxaca	⑲ Intendency of Guatemala
② Intendency of Guanajuato	⑪ Intendency of Mérida	⑳ Intendency of San Salvador
③ Intendency of Valladolid	⑫ Province of Nuevo Santander	㉑ Intendency of Comayagua
④ Intendency of Guadalajara	⑬ Province of Nuevo León	㉒ Intendency of León
⑤ Intendency of Zacatecas	⑭ Province of Coahuila	㉓ Province of Costa Rica
⑥ Intendency of San Luis Potosí	⑮ Intendency of Durango	㉔ Intendency of Havana
⑦ Intendency of Vera Cruz	⑯ Intendency of Sonora	㉕ Intendency of Puerto Príncipe
⑧ Government of Tlaxcala	⑰ Government of Old California	㉖ Intendency of Santiago de Cuba
⑨ Intendency of Puebla	⑱ Intendency of Chiapas	

Spain's vast territories in North and Central America and the Caribbean were collectively known as the Viceroyalty of New Spain. At the heart of New Spain was the Viceregal Audencia of Mexico. An audencia, or tribunal, combined the functions of a court and an executive office. Other regions of New Spain, including the Louisiana Territory and Florida, were part of a military district known as the Captaincy-General of Cuba. The present-day nations of Central America formed another military district, known as the Captaincy-General of Guatemala. Within both the Viceregal Audencia of Mexico and the two military districts were a series of smaller jurisdictions. Known as gobiernos, these smaller districts were reorganized in the 1780s and were usually called intendencias or provinces.

Portugal and its overseas possessions in 1580. Philip II continued the wars against France and the Ottoman Empire and began new wars, including campaigns against Protestant rebels in the Netherlands and an ill-fated assault on England with a great fleet known as the Spanish Armada (1588), most of which was destroyed.

Literature flourished during Spain's Golden Age, which began during Philip II's reign and continued into the middle of the 17th century. Writers of the period included novelist Miguel de Cervantes

Saavedra, author of the novel Don Quixote de la Mancha; playwrights Lope de Vega Carpio and Calderón de la Barca; mystics St. Teresa of Avila and St. John of the Cross; and poet Luis de Góngora. But Spanish wars continued into the next century too, even while the supply of precious metals from the New World dwindled and Spanish intolerance drove away such valuable subjects as the Moriscos, Christianized Muslims who were expelled in 1609. Epidemics in the 1590s further reduced the population. To pay for its wars, the crown raised taxes and took out loans it could not repay, leading to economic instability. Domestic revolts began to plague Spain, even while its foreign wars dragged on, notably the continuing conflict in the Netherlands and the Thirty Years' War (1618–1648), a general European conflict. Spain's European empire began to fragment. Portugal broke free in 1640, and the Netherlands was recognized as independent in 1648.

By the time of the War of the Spanish Succession (1701–1714), Spain had drastically declined in stature. That war began when the Bourbon king Louis XIV, ruler of Spain's onetime nemesis, France, tried to put an heir of his on the Spanish throne, raising the possibility that France would absorb Spain and become too powerful a threat to its European rivals, including England, the Netherlands, and Austria. England, which had once feared the mighty Spanish Armada, was no longer concerned about Spanish power but French power. The resulting conflagration embroiled most of Europe. It ended with a Bourbon dynasty established in Spain, on the condition that Spain and France not be united, and with most of Spain's remaining European possessions passing to other countries. England gained the strategically important Spanish territories of Gibraltar, at the southernmost tip of the Iberian Peninsula, and Minorca, an island in the Mediterranean Sea. It also won coveted trading rights in Spanish America, including the asiento, a monopoly for selling African slaves.

During the 18th century, the Bourbon rulers of Spain, particularly Charles III (1716–1788; reigned 1759–1788), concentrated on internal reform and careful attempts to recoup some of the nation's lost overseas prestige.

Government was made more effective, the military was strengthened, the American empire was reorganized, the economy began to rebound, and the population climbed. Overseas, Spain cultivated its alliance with France, seeking to gain some edge against the rising might of Great Britain (as England and Scotland were called after their union in 1707). In the Seven Years' War (1756–1763), Spain joined France as an ally against Britain, only to discover it had sided with the loser. In the peace that ended that war, Britain forced France to sign over Canada and other North American possessions, while Spain was forced to surrender Florida. As some compensation, France ceded Louisiana west of the Mississippi River to Spain.

Under these circumstances, Spain was delighted to learn in the 1770s that Britain had a new trouble: the rebellion of 13 North American colonies on the Atlantic seaboard.

STRANGE BEDFELLOWS: SPAIN AIDS THE REBEL CAUSE

The Thirteen Colonies had been founded along the Atlantic coast, beginning with Virginia in 1607 and ending with Georgia in 1733. In 1775 they erupted in rebellion against Britain over what the colonists considered unjust attempts to tax them without representation and take away their substantial measure of self-government. In 1776, with the American Revolution (1775–1783) already raging, representatives of the Thirteen Colonies signed a Declaration of Independence in which they proclaimed themselves a "free and independent" nation called the United States of America.

France and Spain saw an opportunity in Britain's difficulty. The two countries were ruled by absolutist monarchs with colonial possessions of their own, but their long-term interest in preventing anti-monarchical colonists from setting a worldwide example mattered less to them than their short-term interest in curbing British power. France longed to avenge its defeat in the Seven Years' War and improve its world trade position relative to Britain. The French also feared that their West Indian colonies were vulnerable to British attack as long as Britain possessed the Thirteen Colonies. Spain

CATTLE FOR THE ARMY

Texas is rarely mentioned in most accounts of the American Revolution. But this territory, then a northern frontier region of New Spain, indirectly supported the United States by supplying beef to the soldiers of Bernardo de Gálvez. Gálvez, the governor of the Spanish-controlled Louisana Territory, was sympathetic to the American cause of independence from Great Britain, largely because Spain and Great Britian—together with France—were competing for control of the Mississippi River valley. In 1777 Gálvez began secretly supplying gunpowder, lead, and clothing to the American army and protecting their ships from British attack by pretending to seize them until British ships had gone. Within two years, however, word reached Gálvez that the British intended to attack Louisiana, and in the spring of 1779, Spain declared war on Great Britian. To wage war, Gálvez's troops would need not only weapons but food.

Cattle and other livestock had been raised on Texas ranches since the 1730s, and Texan ranchers had driven their cattle to Louisiana even while it was still in French hands and such trade was prohibited. In 1779, with Gálvez in need of food for his troops, cattle imports from Texas were finally made legal. The cattle drives from Texas to Louisiana began with an order for 1,500 to 2,000 head of cattle. More herds followed, usually accompanied by an escort of soldiers. The risks were great: not only did the Comanche frequently attack, but rival cattle owners often ended up suing each other. Yet the benefits were also great. A cow that sold for four pesos in Texas might sell for 11 in Louisiana; the valuable contraband, like clothing or tobacco, that one might smuggle back home to Texas despite Spain's restrictions on intercolonial trade was an added incentive. In 1788 the Texas-Louisiana livestock trade was once again banned, a victim of peace and Spanish mercantilist policy.

wanted to protect the security of its valuable colonies in Mexico and the West Indies by increasing its holdings in North America. To that end, the Spanish wanted to win back East Florida, corresponding roughly to present-day Florida, and West Florida, the Gulf Coast strip from the Apalachicola River to the Mississippi. Spain also wanted to expand across the Mississippi River into the eastern Mississippi Valley; expel Britain from Central America; and get back the European possessions of Gibraltar and Minorca, lost to Britain during the War of Spanish Succession.

Even while still officially neutral, France and Spain offered assistance to the rebels, providing munitions, lending money, and allowing American merchantmen and privateers to use their ports. In 1778 France formally entered the war as an American ally, and in 1779 Spain joined the war as an ally of France, though not directly of the United States, from which it continued to maintain an official distance.

Much of Spain's military involvement took place far away from the New World and was aimed at tying down Britain's most powerful military asset, its massive and widely feared navy. The number of ships in the British navy outnumbered those of either France or Spain but did not outnumber the two in combination. Spain joined France in launching an attempted naval invasion of Britain (1779), blockading Gibraltar (from 1779 to the war's end) and attacking Minorca (captured in 1782). The Netherlands dispatched its own fleet to menace the English coast, while the French harassed the British in the Caribbean Sea and Indian Ocean. Forced to defend their homeland and far-flung overseas possessions, the British navy was unable to provide needed support to its troops in North America. As a result, when General Charles Cornwallis (1738–1805) was besieged by French ships and American and French troops at Yorktown, Virginia, the British navy was not able to come to his aid. Cornwallis's surrender at Yorktown in 1781, which virtually ended hostilities in North America, was indirectly made possible by the support of the Spanish navy.

In addition to their indirect support in campaigns outside North America, Spanish troops gave comfort to the

Bernardo de Gálvez (Library of Congress)

American rebels closer to home, in clashes with the British along the Gulf Coast and the Mississippi River. The most important figure in these conflicts was Bernardo de Gálvez (1746–1786), governor of Louisiana.

BERNARDO DE GÁLVEZ

Born into a military family, Bernardo de Gálvez first came to the New World in 1765, as a 19-year-old captain assigned to New Spain, where he distinguished himself fighting Apache on the northern frontier. In 1776, now a colonel, he was dispatched to New Orleans and was soon named governor of Louisiana, which France had ceded to Spain 13 years earlier. A speaker of French who soon married a Frenchwoman, Gálvez became popular with the Gallic locals, despite the difference in his nationality. Recognizing Spain's opportunity in the American Revolution, he surreptitiously sent arms and supplies to the rebels. By 1779 Great Britain had learned of Spain's assistance, however, and began threatening Louisiana with attack from forts along the British-controlled western panhandle of Florida. At the urging of Patrick Henry, the governor of Virginia, Gálvez recommended that Spain declare war on Great Britain in order not only to protect Louisiana but to win back West Florida. When Spain

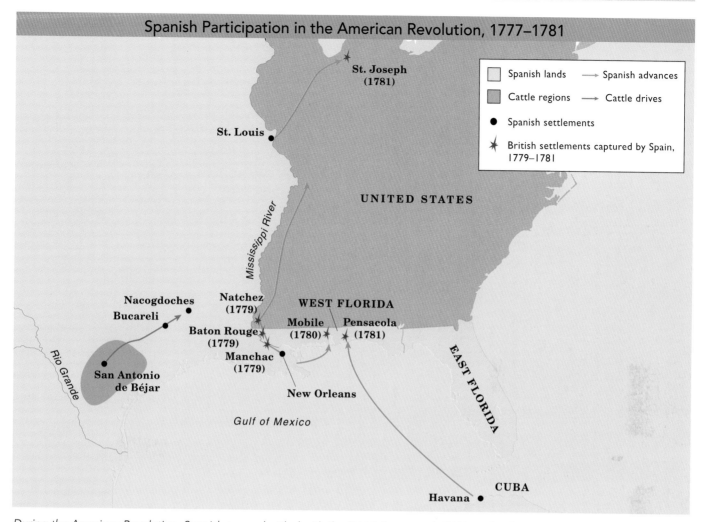

Spanish Participation in the American Revolution, 1777–1781

St. Joseph
(1781)

St. Louis

UNITED STATES

Mississippi River

Nacogdoches
Bucareli

Natchez
(1779)

WEST FLORIDA

Mobile
(1780)

Pensacola
(1781)

Baton Rouge
(1779)

Manchac
(1779)

New Orleans

EAST FLORIDA

San Antonio
de Béjar

Rio Grande

Gulf of Mexico

CUBA
Havana

	Spanish lands	→ Spanish advances
	Cattle regions	→ Cattle drives
●	Spanish settlements	
✳	British settlements captured by Spain, 1779–1781	

During the American Revolution, Spanish troops battled with the British for control of West Florida and the Mississippi River valley. In 1779, Spanish forces under Bernardo de Gálvez captured the British-occupied settlements of Manchac, Baton Rouge, and Natchez on the lower Mississippi, and later Mobile and Pensacola on the Gulf Coast, as well as sweeping far to the north to capture a British trading post named St. Joseph, in what is now Michigan. Critical to maintaining these Spanish offensives was a supply of beef cattle driven east from Texas.

declared war in June 1779, Gálvez quickly organized a small force, including troops from Spain, Mexico, and Cuba. In a lightning series of attacks that fall, he captured five British forts, including Fort Manchac and Baton Rouge (in present-day Louisiana) and Natchez (in present-day Mississippi), driving the British out of the lower Mississippi Valley and thereby eliminating that region's ability to support British forces in the south.

Promoted to general, Gálvez next attacked British outposts on the Gulf Coast, capturing Mobile (in present-day Alabama) in 1780 and Pensacola (in present-day Florida) in 1781. He suffered wounds in the hand and stomach in the hard-fought two-month struggle for Pensacola but survived to be named governor of West Florida and Louisiana and win the title of count of Gálvez. He went

on to become governor of Cuba and viceroy of New Spain before dying in 1786 at age 40. Galveston, Texas, is named in his honor.

WARFARE ON THE MISSISSIPPI

Spain did not limit its North American military attacks to the south. The Spanish aimed to drive the British out of the eastern Mississippi Valley and establish their own claim to the territory, to prevent the Americans from laying claim to it after the war. In November 1780 Captain Balthazar de Villiers crossed the Mississippi River from the Spanish colony of Arkansas Post (in what is now Arkansas) and claimed possession of the east bank in the name of

"To perpetuate in your posterity the memory of the heroic action in which, you, alone, forced your entry into [Pensacola] Bay, [y]ou may put as a Seal in your coat of Arms . . . the Motto: 'I ALONE'"

—King Carlos III of Spain, in a letter to Gálvez

George Rogers Clark (Library of Congress)

Spain. Captain Eugenio Pourré marched from the Spanish outpost of St. Louis (in what is now Missouri) and in February 1781 captured St. Joseph, a British trading post (in what is now Michigan); he then claimed that region for Spain. The British fought back, attacking Arkansas Post in 1783, but failed to capture it.

Spanish designs on the eastern Mississippi Valley were short-lived. During the American Revolution, American soldier George Rogers Clark (1752–1818) captured British forts in Illinois and Indiana and defeated the Shawnee, British allies, in Ohio. In the negotiations that followed the war, Clark's victories allowed the United States to claim the region that constitutes present-day Ohio, Indiana, Illinois, Michigan, Wisconsin, and eastern Minnesota, which was ceded from Britain to the United States in 1783 and became known as the Northwest Territory.

In the peace that ended the war and brought British recognition of American independence, Spain achieved only some of its war aims. It did not win back Gibraltar, obtain recognition of its claims to the eastern Mississippi Valley, or drive the British out of Central America. But it did win East and West Florida and Minorca. In the long run, however, Spain did itself no favors. The new United States would soon bargain itself into possession of Florida and Louisiana, while

the example set by the American Revolution would bring an end to Spain's American empire.

INDEPENDENCE FROM SPAIN

When the American Revolution ended, Spain's empire was larger than ever, with the Floridas now added to its previous holdings. Yet Spain's weakness relative to other powers had not changed, as the coming years were to show. As the 18th century ended and the 19th century began, Spain was forced to cede parts of its American empire to other nations. Finally, in the 1820s it was forced to recognize the independence of nearly all of its American colonies.

LOSSES TO FRANCE AND THE UNITED STATES

The enlightened Spanish monarch Charles III had adroitly steered his country to victory in the American Revolution, but he was succeeded by his incompetent son Charles IV (1748–1819; reigned 1788–1808), who largely ceded power to his chief minister Manuel de Godoy (1767–1851) and proved unable to cope with the challenges raised by the French

Ferdinand VII of Spain (Library of Congress)

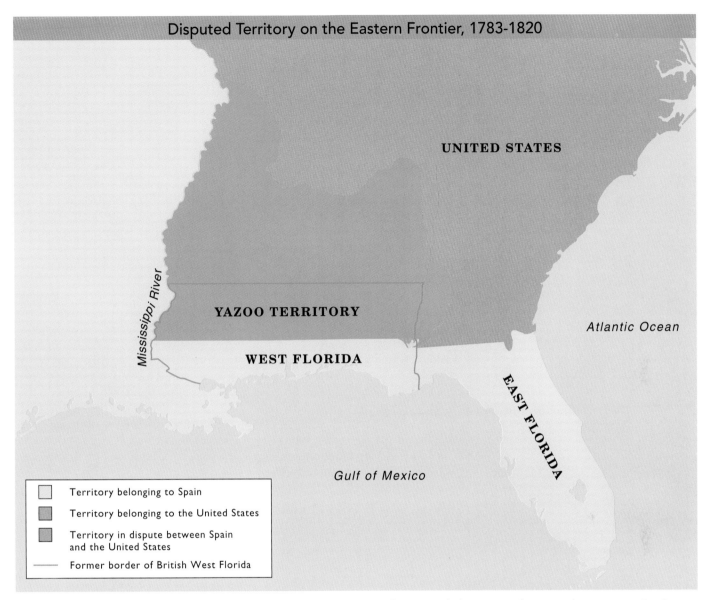

Disputed Territory on the Eastern Frontier, 1783-1820

UNITED STATES

Mississippi River

YAZOO TERRITORY

WEST FLORIDA

Atlantic Ocean

EAST FLORIDA

Gulf of Mexico

☐ Territory belonging to Spain

☐ Territory belonging to the United States

☐ Territory in dispute between Spain and the United States

── Former border of British West Florida

Unclear borders between the United States and Spanish territory in North America led to tension between the two countries. In particular, the Spanish and Americans differed over the border of West Florida, which had been ceded to Spain by Great Britain after the war. In addition, Spain also claimed former British territory as far north as the Ohio and Tennessee rivers. American settlers ignored these claims. By 1820, Spain decided to cede, not only the disputed lands, but the entirety of Florida to the United States.

Revolution (1789–1799). This cataclysmic upheaval, which temporarily abolished the French monarchy and led to decades of war, was partially inspired by the example set by the American Revolution, which Spain had helped bring to fruition. Like other European nations, Spain was terrified to see republicanism take root closer to home and joined in fighting republican France in the Wars of the French Revolution (1792–1795).

So soundly did France defeat Spain that the latter nation was required to surrender the first colony it had founded in the Western Hemisphere, Santo Domingo, in the eastern part of the island of Hispaniola; France already possessed

the western part. The entire island would gain independence from France in 1804, as Haiti, but Santo Domingo, with its distinctively Spanish culture, did not remain part of Haiti for long. It was reconquered by Spain (1809–1821), briefly made independent (1821–1822), then retaken by Haiti (1822–1844). In 1844, as the Dominican Republic, it again won independence, which it has maintained ever since, except for one more period of Spanish rule (1861–1865) and assorted American interventions in the 20th century (see chapters 6 and 7).

In 1796 Spain changed direction and formed an alliance with France against Britain. The result was that Spain became

ON THEIR OWN

The ineffectiveness of Spanish colonial rule was brought home forcibly to the people of Buenos Aires in 1806. That June, a British expeditionary force occupied this city, the viceregal capital of Río de la Plata (which included present-day Argentina and adjoining regions), in pursuance of Britain's war against Napoleon and his then-ally Spain. Far from repelling the attack, the Spanish viceroy fled to the interior, leaving the people of Buenos Aires to fend for themselves. They formed a volunteer army that drove out the British that August and expelled another British force the following year.

The incident taught the colonials several lessons: that Spain was too weak to defend them; that they were strong enough to defend themselves; and that they were ready to organize themselves under the leadership of Creoles rather than peninsulares. Just three years later, in 1810, the people of the region began their revolution against Spain. Said one historian, "The great victory of Buenos Aires had a resounding impact on the world, and above all in the hearts of Americans, who were now made conscious of a force which had been previously unknown."

a puppet of the powerful French leader Napoleon Bonaparte (1769–1821), who became first consul, or dictator, of France in 1799 and emperor of an expanding empire in 1804. His attempts to dominate the European continent led to the Napoleonic Wars (1799–1815), which embroiled numerous nations, westward from Russia to Portugal and southward from Sweden to Naples. In the midst of the wars, in 1800, Napoleon forced Spain to cede Louisiana back to France, thus taking away a large section of its North American empire, and an important buffer between northern New Spain and the aggressive frontiersmen of the young United States. The buffer was lost for good in 1803, when Napoleon decided to sell the Louisiana territory to the United States for $15 million.

The British navy was largely able to cut Spain off from its valuable American colonies, and it won a devastating victory over the allied Spanish and French navies at Trafalgar, on the southwest coast of Spain (1805). The final Napoleonic insult for Spain came in 1808, after a palace revolution that year forced Charles IV to abdicate in favor of his son, Ferdinand VII (1784–1833; reigned 1808, 1814–1833). Seeing the turmoil, Napoleon took the opportunity to occupy Madrid and force both Charles and Ferdinand to abdicate in favor of Napoleon's brother, Joseph Bonaparte.

The Spanish people rose in revolt, as did the Portuguese, whose country had been occupied by Napoleon since 1807. In what was known as the Peninsular War (1808–1814), Britain came to the aid of Spanish and Portuguese rebels, working with Spanish guerrillas to liberate the entire Iberian Peninsula by the time of Napoleon's first abdication in 1814. Though sent into exile that year by his victorious enemies in the Napoleonic Wars (1799–1815), Napoleon escaped, returned, and was not finally defeated until the battle of Waterloo (in present-day Belgium) in 1815.

The Peninsular War, which Napoleon called his "Spanish ulcer," contributed to his defeat by tying down troops and devouring resources. But it also drastically weakened Spain's control of its empire. Not only did it prompt revolutions throughout many parts of Spanish America, but it left one part, Florida, in peril of takeover from a foreign power: the United States.

Florida had been a flash point for contention with the United States since the end of the American Revolution. Borders were disputed and immigrants to Florida from the United States pressed for American annexation. The Treaty of Paris in 1783, which ended the war, failed to establish a clear border between the new United States and West Florida, which had been won by Spain from Great Britain. What is more, because of their

Venezuelan freedom-fighter Simón Bolívar (Library of Congress)

German explorer Alexander von Humboldt (Library of Congress)

military victories against the British in the Mississippi River valley during the war, Spain viewed as its own the land running along the east side of the river up to the Ohio and Tennessee rivers. The American government—and particularly American settlers—ignored these claims, recognizing that the Spanish had little recourse. Finally in 1810 American settlers in West Florida rebelled and established an independent republic, which the United States annexed over Spanish protests. During the War of 1812 (1812–1815), an offshoot of the Napoleonic Wars in which the United States fought Britain over violations of what the United States regarded as its neutral shipping rights, Spain allowed Britain to establish a naval base in Pensacola, and American troops under General Andrew Jackson drove the British out. Later, in the First Seminole War (1817–1819), Jackson invaded Florida again to retaliate for border raids by the Seminole.

By this time, with most of Spanish America in rebellion, the last thing Spain needed was a war with the United States over Florida. So, in the Adams-Onís Treaty of 1819, Spain agreed to cede East Florida to the United States in return for American agreement to assume payment of up to $5 million in claims by American citizens in Florida against Spain. In addition, the United States received recognition of its control of West Florida; Spain gave up its claims to the Oregon Territory; and the border between the Louisiana Territory and New Spain was settled, with American acknowledgement that Texas was not part of Louisiana. In 1821 the United States took formal possession of Florida, cutting away yet another piece of Spanish America. The rest of Spain's once-great empire was then already crumbling away.

INDEPENDENCE FOR SPANISH AMERICA

After three centuries during which Spanish Americans mostly submitted peacefully to colonial rule, Napoleon's 1808 conquest of Spain was the spark that ignited independence movements across Spanish America. As Mexican patriot Carlos María Bustamante put it, "Napoleon Bonaparte...to you Spanish America owes the liberty and independence it now enjoys. Your sword struck the first blow at the chain which bound two worlds."

Yet the roots of Spanish colonial independence movements lay deeper than Napoleon. For years, Spanish Americans had been developing a sense of regional identity, of difference from their European parent country. That sense was often coupled with distaste for the imperial government, which restricted and taxed commerce for the benefit of the mother country; was rife with corruption and ineffectiveness; and habitually assigned the highest offices to peninsulares, people born in Spain, rather than to criollos, or creoles, people of Spanish descent born in the Americas. Even in the late 18th century, a German visitor, explorer Alexander von Humboldt, noticed that Creoles "are frequently heard to declare with pride, 'I am not a Spaniard, I am an American,' words which reveal the symptoms of a long resentment."

Such attitudes were compounded by the influence of Enlightenment philosophy and political liberalism, vividly exemplified by the American and French revolutions fresh in many Spanish-American minds. Venezuelan-born Simón Bolívar (1783–1830), the principal leader of the South American independence movement, was so inspired by French political philosopher Jean-Jacques Rousseau that in his will he bequeathed to the University of Caracas a copy of Rousseau's The Social Contract that had belonged to Napoleon.

Mass social pressures were also fueling revolutionary sentiment. Father Miguel Hidalgo y Costilla (1753–1811), the Mexican priest credited with beginning Mexico's struggle for independence, sought to end the oppression of Native Americans, who followed him in the hope of relieving their poverty. Spanish-American Creoles, who were themselves a social and political elite, generally did not respond well to demands for social justice and equality from the non-European or mixed-race masses. For many Creoles who joined in the struggle for independence, patriotism was tied to making sure that their privileged place would be protected in whatever new nations were established.

The various tendencies toward revolution came to a head in 1808, when

CHANGES FOR BRAZIL

Brazil was not a Spanish colony, but it too gained independence in the early 19th century. When Napoleon occupied Portugal in 1807, the royal family was forced to flee temporarily to the Portuguese colony of Brazil. In 1821, King John VI returned to a liberated Portugal, leaving his son Pedro (1798–1834) in Brazil as prince regent. In 1822, Pedro ignored demands that he return to Portugal, instead declaring Brazil's independence from Portugal—with him as emperor—rather than allowing it to return to colonial status. In 1825, an agreement between Portugal and Brazil was brokered with help from Great Britain, and Brazil was allowed to continue as an independent kingdom.

Despite winning independence for Brazil, Emperor Pedro I lost favor with his subjects, largely because of a series of landowner revolts. In 1831, he was forced to abdicate the throne. Over the next several decades, Brazil was continually involved in costly regional wars that weakened the country while strengthening the military. In 1888 the emperor was overthrown in a military coup and in 1889 Brazil became a republic.

Francisco de Miranda (Library of Congress)

"[In South America,] representative government, native functionaries, a qualified negative on their laws, with a previous security by compact for freedom of commerce, freedom of the press, habeas corpus and trial by jury, would make a good beginning. This last would be the school in which their people might begin to learn the exercise of civic duties as well as rights. For freedom of religion they are not yet prepared. The scales of bigotry have not sufficiently fallen from their eyes to accept it for themselves individually, much less to trust others with it."

—Thomas Jefferson to John Adams, 1821.

Napoleon installed Joseph Bonaparte as king of Spain. Across Spanish America, many colonials reacted with revulsion to the idea of a Frenchman on the Spanish throne and professed their loyalty instead to Ferdinand VII, then Napoleon's captive. Napoleon had hoped to win colonial support for the new monarch, but since that was impossible, he encouraged colonial independence movements as a way of weakening Spanish resistance in the Peninsular War.

In 1810 autonomous governments were formed in what are now Venezuela, Colombia, Argentina, and Chile, nominally under the sovereignty of the captive Ferdinand but in practice separate from the Regency that claimed to govern in his name. The royalist government rejected these claims of autonomy, prompting declarations of complete independence that led swiftly to revolutionary wars. Other countries, pre-occupied with the Napoleonic Wars in Europe, stayed out of the turmoil. Britain, for example, carefully remained neutral between the colonies and Spain, seeking above all to avoid allowing itself or its Spanish ally to become distracted from the war closer to home against Napoleon.

The influence of the Spanish-American wars of independence was profound. Because Spanish-American regions had a tendency to divide into separate countries following independence, the wars meant that today's Hispanic Americans have their roots not in colonies or territories of a single country, Spain, but in a multiplicity of countries, each with its own culture and history.

SOUTH AMERICA AND THE CARIBBEAN

In South America, the forces of independence moved in two general directions: south from what is now Venezuela to Colombia to Ecuador to Peru, and north from what is now Argentina to Chile to Peru. Francisco de Miranda (1750–1816), a longtime advocate of independence known as "The Forerunner," headed the revolution in Venezuela, briefly becoming dictator in 1812 before being overthrown by royalist forces and shipped to prison in Spain, where he died. Simon Bolívar then emerged as the most important revolutionary leader, coming to

be called "The Liberator." In 1819, after years of fighting, the republic of Gran Colombia was established with Bolívar as its president, comprising what are now Venezuela, Colombia, and Panama. An overwhelming victory in 1821 at Carabobo, Venezuela, assured the republic's independence. In 1822 Ecuador joined the republic, thanks to the decisive victory of Bolívar's lieutenant Antonio José de Sucre (1795–1830) at the battle of Pichincha.

Simultaneously, with the southward sweep from Venezuela, José de San Martín (1778–1850) led the northward sweep from the viceroyalty of La Plata, which included what are now Argentina, Bolivia, Paraguay, and Uruguay. Royalist forces were driven out of a substantial part of the region by 1813, and independence was proclaimed in 1816. San Martín pressed the attack into Chile in 1817, defeating the royalists at Chacabuco and occupying the Chilean capital, Santiago. He won a decisive victory at Maipu in 1818.

In 1820 San Martín advanced into Peru, and in 1821 he captured Lima and proclaimed Peru's independence. The following year, with the Spanish continuing to resist, Peru received military aid from Bolívar, who decisively routed the Spanish at Ayacucho in 1824. This was the last major battle in the South American wars of independence, though the last Royalist troops were not forced out of Peru until 1826.

By the time the struggle for South American independence was over, the spark that had started it, Napoleon, was long gone. The Spanish king whose capture had prompted the revolutions, Ferdinand VII, had been restored to the throne in 1814. But he proved to be a harshly conservative ruler, with a talent for driving rebels further into revolt. He revoked the liberal constitution that had been created during his captivity, ruling as an absolute monarch until another revolution in 1820 restored the constitution. The chaos further weakened Spain's hold on its distant colonies. By 1826, while Ferdinand was still reigning, Spain had lost all its colonies except for Cuba and Puerto Rico.

Cuba and Puerto Rico remained colonies during this period for various reasons. For one, they were highly dependent on Spain to buy their sugar

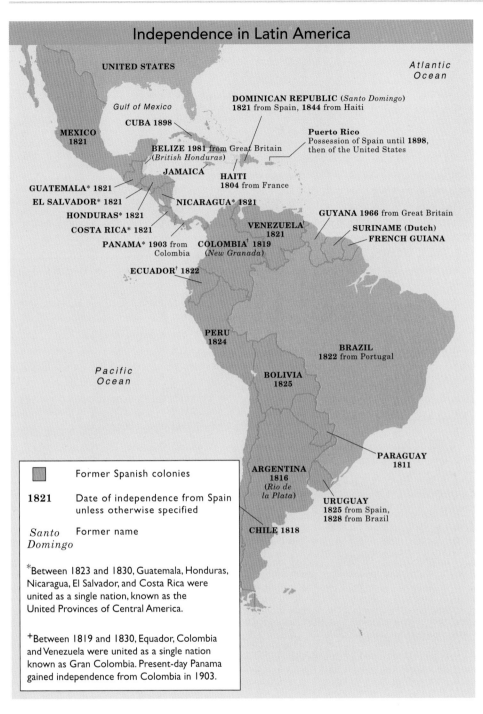

Independence in Latin America

UNITED STATES

Atlantic Ocean

Gulf of Mexico

DOMINICAN REPUBLIC (*Santo Domingo*)
1821 from Spain, **1844** from Haiti

CUBA **1898**

MEXICO
1821

Puerto Rico
Possession of Spain until **1898**,
then of the United States

BELIZE **1981** from Great Britain
(*British Honduras*)

JAMAICA

HAITI
1804 from France

GUATEMALA* **1821**

EL SALVADOR* **1821**

NICARAGUA* **1821**

HONDURAS* **1821**

GUYANA **1966** from Great Britain

COSTA RICA* **1821**

VENEZUELA†
1821

SURINAME (Dutch)

FRENCH GUIANA

PANAMA* **1903** from
Colombia

COLOMBIA† **1819**
(*New Granada*)

ECUADOR† **1822**

PERU
1824

BRAZIL
1822 from Portugal

Pacific Ocean

BOLIVIA
1825

PARAGUAY
1811

ARGENTINA
1816
(*Rio de la Plata*)

URUGUAY
1825 from Spain,
1828 from Brazil

CHILE **1818**

	Former Spanish colonies
1821	Date of independence from Spain unless otherwise specified
Santo Domingo	Former name

*Between 1823 and 1830, Guatemala, Honduras, Nicaragua, El Salvador, and Costa Rica were united as a single nation, known as the United Provinces of Central America.

+Between 1819 and 1830, Equador, Colombia and Venezuela were united as a single nation known as Gran Colombia. Present-day Panama gained independence from Colombia in 1903.

During the first three decades of the 19th century, most of Spain's colonial holdings in the Americas declared and won their independence. Beginning with Paraguay in 1811, a total of 15 different nations emerged from former Spanish colonies. Initially, Guatemala, El Salvador, Costa Rica, and Nicaragua were collectively known as the United Provinces of Central America, and Venezuela, Colombia (including what later became Panama), and Ecuador were together united as Gran Colombia. The map shown here gives the dates of independence for all countries and, where appropriate, the former name of each country.

and other agricultural products. Because of their strategic position in the Caribbean, they were well-defended by Spanish forces against foreign attack, including attack by exporters of revolution. In Cuba, fear of revolt by the black slaves who dominated the population, and who had rebelled successfully in neighboring Haiti, gave many whites an interest in maintaining Spanish rule. These colonies remained the last vestige of the Spanish-American empire until 1898, when the United States wrested them away in the Spanish-American War (see chapter 5).

MEXICO AND CENTRAL AMERICA

In the early morning of September 16, 1810, Father Miguel Hidalgo y Costilla launched the first phase of the Mexican war of independence. A parish priest in the village of Dolores, Hidalgo rang the church bell to gather the townspeople and proclaimed an end to the country's misrule. His call, which became known as the Grito de Dolores, or "Cry of Dolores," was not precisely recorded. It may have included "Death to bad government!" and "Long live the Catholic reli-

Augustín de Iturbide (Library of Congress)

gion!"; it may also have included "Death to the Spaniards!"

Although he was creole and had some creole officers, Hidalgo's was no creole revolution, intended to replace one governing elite with another. It was a mass uprising of the poor and oppressed, Native Americans and mestizos, armed with machetes, knives, stones, and sticks against their oppressors. He led his rebel army from town to town, opening the jails so that prisoners could join them. Their banner was that of the Virgin of Guadalupe, the dark-skinned amalgam of Catholic piety and Aztec roots. Hidalgo's army sacked and looted the houses of the peninsulares, derisively called gachupines (which roughly translates as "blockheads") in Mexico, and sometimes killed even those who surrendered. Vowing to provide for "the liberty of the nation and the rights which the God of nature granted to all men," Hidalgo ordered an end to slavery, an end to the system of exacting tributes from Native Americans, and restitution of lands to Native American communities.

Hidalgo's revolution was frenzied and chaotic, and in the end its chaos destroyed it. Though he had a fair opportunity to capture Mexico City, he turned aside and set up his headquarters in Guadalajara instead. In a climactic battle near the bridge of Calderón in January 1811, his disorganized army was routed by a much smaller but more disciplined and better equipped royal force. Captured and found guilty of heresy and treason, Hidalgo was executed. Mexicans still consider him the father of their nation.

The independence movement did not die but continued under another parish priest, José María Morelos y Pavón (1765–1815), a mestizo lieutenant of Hidalgo's. Relying largely on guerrilla tactics, he gained control of a wide territory on either side of Mexico City, capturing Acapulco in 1813. That year he convoked the Congress of Chilpancingo, which issued Mexico's first formal declaration of independence and published a constitution, one that would have made Mexico a republic and abolished all class distinctions had it been implemented. Instead, starting in 1813, royalist forces rolled back Morelos's conquests. When they finally captured him in 1815, he too was convicted of heresy and executed.

The guerrilla chief Vicente Guerrero continued to carry out raids, but aside from such attacks the independence movement seemed all but dead. Then, in 1820, events overseas tipped the balance. Revolution in Spain restored the liberal constitution that Ferdinand VII had revoked, potentially threatening the privileges of Mexico's ruling elite. Though formerly hostile to the cause of independence, Mexico's conservative leaders now embraced it as, ironically, the best way to preserve the status quo. In 1821, their representative, Colonel Agustín de Iturbide (1783–1824), met with Guerrero and agreed to fight jointly against Spanish authority, under the terms of the Plan of Iguala, which outlined three guarantees: Mexican independence as a constitutional monarchy; establishment of Catholicism as the state religion; and full equality under the law, without respect to race. It also promised no interference with property rights. By appealing to both conservatives and liberals, the plan broke remaining Mexican support for Spanish rule; most military units changed sides, and the last appointed viceroy, Juan O'Donojú, realized that his position was no longer tenable. In the Treaty of Córdoba, signed August 24, 1821, the viceroy recognized Mexico's independence. After 300 years, New Spain had ceased to exist.

Father Miguel Hidalgo (Library of Congress)

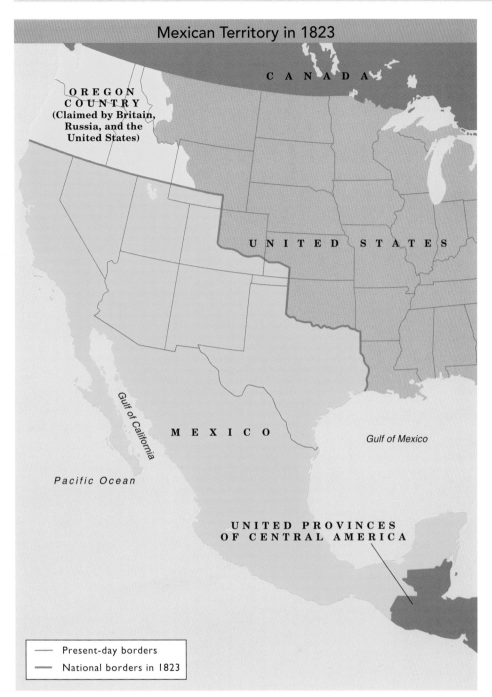

Mexican Territory in 1823

Independence swiftly followed for the region of Central America. The elites of the captaincy-general of Guatemala, which extended from what is now the state of Chiapas, Mexico, through Costa Rica, followed Mexico's path and declared independence from Spain. Under Iturbide, who declared himself Emperor Agustín I in 1822, the region briefly became part of the Mexican Empire. When that empire toppled to republican revolt in 1823, all Central American states except Chiapas split away and, in 1824, became the United Provinces of Central America.

MEXICO'S FAR NORTHERN FRONTIER

With independence, Mexico inherited what had been the Far North of New Spain and would soon become the American Southwest. The people of that region, used to a rugged existence far from the centers of Spanish colonial power, accepted the change in masters peacefully but without much apparent enthusiasm. California's Spanish-born governor Pablo Vicente de Sola, who reluctantly complied with orders to take

The Santa Fe and Spanish Trails, 1822–1829

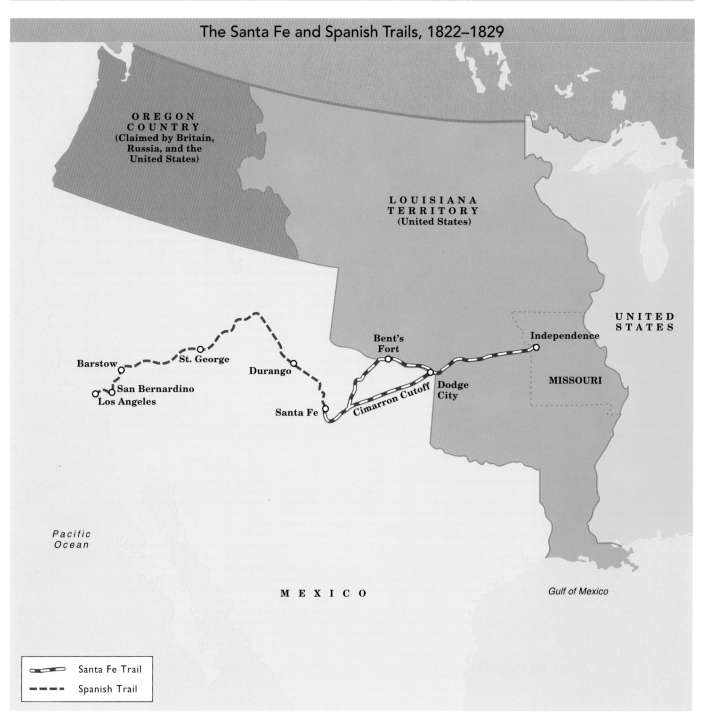

In 1792, Pedro Vial crossed the Missouri, Kansas, and Colorado territories, thus forging the first European trail connecting Santa Fe, New Mexico, with St. Louis. Only in the 19th century, however, would the significance of this journey become realized. In 1821, American merchant William Becknell led a string of pack mules from Franklin, Missouri, in the United States to Santa Fe, New Mexico, thus inaugurating the Santa Fe Trail. For the next 20 years, wagon caravans would leave Independence, Missouri, each spring carrying goods—and Anglo traders—to Santa Fe. In time, a shortcut known as the Cimarron Cutoff was blazed. However, the cutoff crossed 60 miles of waterless plain before reaching the Cimarron River. Travelers on the Cimarron Cutoff were also more vulnerable to attacks by Native Americans than were those taking the longer, more mountainous route. Once in Santa Fe, the trail joined up with what became known as "The Spanish Trail," a route to California that had initially been blazed by Father Silvestre Vélez de Escalante and Father José Juan Domínguez in 1776, before being completed by Antonio Armijo in 1829.

down the Spanish flag, explained his people's silence at the ceremony by saying: "They do not cheer because they are unused to independence."

Under Spain the Far North had been divided into the provinces of Alta California, New Mexico, and Texas, though the boundaries between those provinces and the rest of Mexico were ill defined. Under the Constitution of 1824, which followed the overthrow of Emperor Agustín in 1823, the boundaries changed somewhat. This federalist constitution, which remained in force until 1835—a period sometimes called the federalist era or the First Federal Republic—turned most Mexican provinces into states with considerable autonomy. But the far northern provinces were left as territories under central control or as parts of larger states: the territory of Alta California; part of the state of Sonora y Sinaloa; the territory of Nuevo México; and part of the state of Coahuila y Texas.

Though vast on paper, this far northern region was only thinly Hispanic, with relatively small pockets of frontier pobladores, or settlers, concentrated in what are now California, Arizona, New Mexico, and Texas. There were virtually no Hispanic settlers in what are now Nevada or Utah, then wholly part of the Far North, or in the parts of Colorado, Wyoming, Kansas, and Oklahoma that were also included in the region.

Despite the sparseness of Hispanic settlement in the Far North, the new nation of Mexico regarded the region as a valuable resource. Not only did it have promise as a site for future development, it served as a protective buffer between the Mexican heartland and foreign powers or Native American raiders. In particular, it served to keep central Mexico well insulated from the United States, which had already revealed expansionist designs in obtaining Florida and Louisiana.

On the other hand, the Far North was a constant headache for Mexican government, as the next two decades would show. Precisely because the region was so remote, thinly populated, and weakly defended, it was easily subject to encroachment by Great Britain, the United States, Russia, or any other nation or group of settlers that fancied a piece of it. This latent instability would erupt in the Texas Revolution and the U.S.-Mexican War, which jointly tore most of the Far North away from Mexico and into American possession by 1848.

The Nuevomexicanos

Under Spanish rule, foreigners wandering into the Far North had been regarded as trespassers, likely candidates for the prison cell, or calabozo. Trade with other countries was forbidden or tightly controlled. With Mexican independence, all this changed. Foreign traders were now welcome, once they paid the customs duty and perhaps a local bribe.

Nowhere was the impact of this relatively free trade more visible than in Santa Fe, New Mexico. In 1821, almost as soon as Mexican independence made trade legally possible, American merchant William Becknell led a string of pack mules from Franklin, Missouri (part of the United States since the 1803 Louisiana Purchase), to Santa Fe. There he sold all his goods to the delighted Nuevomexicanos, who gladly paid in silver for the privilege. The trail he took had been known to the Native Americans before Columbus and traversed by Coronado, but it was Becknell who turned it into the traders' gateway known as the Santa Fe Trail.

From 1822 throughout the period of Mexican rule, wagon caravans rolled out of Independence, Missouri, each and every spring, hauling manufactured goods along the Santa Fe Trail. Among these goods were cloth, clothing, tools, kitchen utensils, jewelry, buttons, clocks, combs, needles, candles, pens, and wallpaper. Long a rugged place where items as simple as carpenter's nails were scarce and even the rich lived in plain adobe houses with nearly bare rooms, New Mexico welcomed the abundance of manufactured goods. The American traders, in turn, rejoiced in the big profits to be made and the silver and gold they brought back to their own frontier, where hard currency was scarce. They also brought home hides and wool—products of New Mexico's herding industry—and furs, especially beaver furs, products of the trapping industry then beginning to flourish in the region.

Many of the trappers were themselves Americans, mountain men living a raw existence in the wilderness. Their principal relaxation came in the summers spent trading and carousing at the town fairs, particularly in Taos, located close to the mountain waters where the beavers lived. In their relentless search for fur, the trappers nearly drove beavers to extinction in the region while also blazing trails in many areas claimed but as yet unsettled by Mexico: Nevada,

Californios taunt a cornered bear for sport. (Library of Congress)

Utah, Colorado, and Wyoming. All were reconnoitered by American mountain men, whose home country was soon to absorb the entire region.

American trappers and traders like James Ohio Pattie and Kit Carson also penetrated into Arizona, which had a few Mexican settlements, mostly around Tubac and Tucson. Not only were these settlments frequently attacked by Apache, but they had also suffered from the collapse of the old mission system when the Mexican government began an erratically applied program to secularize mission lands. By 1831 Tucson's total population was only 465 and Tubac's 303—and the population of pobladores in Arizona fell even further during the next 17 years.

Some Mexicans became traders themselves, traveling to Missouri to buy manufactured goods, which they then brought back to New Mexico and the neighboring state of Chihuahua. But the larger flow of people was from the United States to New Mexico, and New Mexico tried to keep them from staying when they arrived. The example of Texas was all too evident: American immigrants could easily grow to outnumber the Mexicans. New Mexico therefore took care to offer few land grants to Americans and to be choosy about those who were admitted. American squatters

sometimes took up residence illegally, but they tried to adopt Hispanic customs so as to be less noticeable.

Trade and foreign contact were not the only things that changed when Mexico became independent. The Plan of Iguala and the Constitution of 1824 both guaranteed racial equality, making it illegal to oppress Native Americans simply because of their race. The frontier provinces, with their need to pull together, had long enjoyed a relatively high degree of racial egalitarianism, with racial intermarriage common and people accepted as "Spanish" (and now as "Mexican") so long as they adopted Hispanic culture—and especially if they made money and rose in class. Now the law supported this tendency.

On the other hand, New Mexican society under Mexican rule was still highly stratified by class. It became even more so as the new abundance of manufactured goods and trading wealth got concentrated in the hands of the rich landowners or patrones, widening the gap between them and the poor. Debt peonage, already in place, increased, particularly through the partido system that dominated sheep-ranching. In this system, similar to share-cropping, the herder cared for a rich man's flock in return for a cash advance and a share, or partido, of the newborn sheep. In good times, the herder could prosper by building up his own flock; in bad times, the herders fell into debt, unable to pay back their advances.

Another class distinction resulted from the system of buying or capturing Native American children, often in military campaigns justified as defensive, and baptizing and raising them as servants. When they grew to adulthood, these genizaro, detribalized Indians, were released, but they generally carried the mark of their low status throughout their lives.

Social tensions in New Mexico peaked in the rebellion of 1837, when many Pueblo people participated in a revolt against an unpopular governor, Albino Pérez. Not a New Mexican, he represented higher taxes and the despised new centralist regime, incurring so much enmity that upon capturing him the rebels cut off his head and played with it as a football. A New Mexican leader, Manuel Armijo, suppressed the revolt and became governor for most of the rest of the Mexican period, without easing the social inequities that had contributed to the revolt.

Despite the frontier existence and social unrest, there were amusements to be had in New Mexico. Most notable was the fandango, a traditional Spanish dance performed at balls that were themselves sometimes called fandangos. The fandango was marked by fast movement and close personal contact between men and women, unlike the more staid dances that prevailed in the United States. The appeal of the dance was enhanced by the outfits favored by New Mexican senoritas, generally more revealing than those of young women in the United States: a low-cut, short-sleeved blouse, a colorful shawl, and a skirt shockingly short by American standards of the time. Said a Missouri trader visiting Santa Fe, "The fandango is a lascivious dance, partaking in part of the waltz, cotillion, and many amorous movements. . . . It is the national dance. In this the governor and most humble citizen move together, and in this consists all their republican boast."

Stephen Austin (Library of Congress)

The Californios

Like Nuevomexicanos, Californios saw changes during the period when Mexico ruled California. Free trade brought the same influx of new goods and new faces as it had brought in New Mexico. Unlike their New Mexican counterparts, Californios were relatively used to foreigners; the ships of American, Russian, British, and French smugglers had all regularly traded contraband in Spanish coastal settlements. But now the ocean traffic greatly increased, with Boston shipping firms coming to dominate the trade, as California hides and tallow were exchanged for all sorts of goods, from clothes to violins. And for the first time, overland trade was opened from the east, with American trappers and traders flowing in along the Spanish Trail from Santa Fe and the Oregon Trail from Missouri. Some Americans traded and went home, but others settled there, many in the Sacramento and San Joaquin valleys, despite Mexican policies that generally sought to discourage them. By 1840 several hundred American settlers lived in California, along with several thousand Californios.

California's economy in this period was based on the rancho, a huge cattle ranch run by a wealthy ranchero. In 1833, the Mexican government secularized the California missions, granting most of the mission lands to private individuals, including landless Hispanic soldiers. The new landowners soon became the dominant force in California, making fortunes from their new ranches. Native Americans who had been forced to work in mission communities fared less well. Released from mission servitude, they entered a new de facto servitude of debt peonage to rancheros, legally unable to quit until their debts to the owners were paid— debts they could never afford to pay. Said a visitor in 1846, "The Indians are the principal laborers; without them the business of the country could hardly be carried on." Even more than the Nuevomexicanos, Californios were renowned for their festive ways, hosting three-day fiestas, or parties, rife with fandangos and other dances such as the jota and the borrego, and annual rodeos, or roundups of cattle, where vaqueros (cowboys) would prove their horsemanship. Yet the idyllic picture of the carefree California don (gentleman) is exaggerated. California was still a frontier, prone to attack by Native Americans and all the vicissitudes of agricultural life. Moreover, with books scarce, education was poor, even for the ruling class. Mariano Guadalupe Vallejo, a prominent citizen, was one of the few literate Californios; many wealthy rancheros could not even write their names.

THE TEJANOS

Unlike New Mexico and California, Texas in the 1820s was bordered by a foreign region steadily growing in population: Louisiana, owned by the United States since 1803. The border between the two regions was not well defined, and even before Mexican independence Americans began flowing into Texas, squatting illegally. Private groups of Americans, sometimes supported by Mexican rebels against Spain, led armed invasions (called filibustering expeditions) that challenged Spanish claims. Two such efforts, both leading to abortive declarations of Texan independence, were suppressed in 1813 and 1819– 1821.

Unable to attract sufficient Hispanic settlers to outweigh the illegal American presence, Spain decided that the best way to defend Texas might be to bring in American immigrants in a controlled fashion, with policies designed to encourage assimilation. Spain therefore accepted the offer of Connecticut businessman Moses Austin to bring American colonists into Texas. The Spanish authorities gave Austin, who had once been a Spanish subject, a generous land grant in exchange for his services as an empresario, or immigration agent. Austin was to bring in 300 settler families, all Catholic or willing to convert to Catholicism, and all swearing allegiance to Spain. He died soon after making the deal, but his son Stephen (1793–1836) inherited the assignment, which was confirmed by Mexico (with the settlers now to become Mexican citizens) after its achievement of independence in 1821.

Stephen Austin brought not only the first 300 American families to Texas but 900 more in fulfillment of later contracts. Other empresarios, such as Green DeWitt and Martín de León, brought in still more Anglo-Americans, or Anglos, so called to distinguish these new settlers, with their British-derived United States culture, from the Tejanos, the Hispanic-American Texans. Many more Anglos flocked in illegally, bringing their African-American slaves with them into a land that had hitherto seen few slaves, and setting up cotton farms and cattle ranches in eastern and central Texas. Driven to migrate by hard times at home, they mushroomed in population, growing to about 35,000 by 1836, or roughly 10 times the number of Tejanos. Most retained their Anglo-American, Protestant ways, proclaiming loyalty to Mexico and Catholicism only on paper, if at all. "Where others send invading armies," said Mexico's secretary of state Lucas Alamán in alarm, "…[the Americans] send their colonists." His words proved prophetic.

MANIFEST DESTINY AND HISPANIC AMERICA

Had Mexico been able to retain all of the territory it possessed upon winning independence, it would be more than twice as large as it is today. California, Arizona, New Mexico, Texas, Nevada, and Utah would all be part of Mexico, as would parts of what are now Wyoming, Colorado, Kansas, and Oklahoma. Instead, soon after Mexico's birth, this immense region passed into the hands of the United States. The takeover occurred in a four-stage process: the Texan Revolution, which made Texas independent (1835–1836); the American annexation of Texas (1845); the U.S.-Mexican War (1846–1848), the conflict between the United States and Mexico that was the first war in which the United States occupied a foreign capital; and the Gadsden Purchase (1853), in which the last piece of the once-mighty Far North was sold to Mexico's erstwhile enemy. Informing the entire process was the vague but popular U.S. notion of Manifest Destiny, which said that Americans were plainly intended by God to spread what they considered to be their superior civilization across the continent, even at the cost of the rights and the lives of Mexicans and Native Americans standing in the way.

These events left the Spanish and Mexicans of the American Southwest in the strange position of being treated like outsiders in their own land by the Anglos who flooded into the region after the war. Their process of conversion from being citizens to aliens, started by the war was completed afterwards through legal and extralegal means. Even today, Mexican Americans sometimes call the region "The Lost Land."

INDEPENDENCE FOR TEXAS

Texans of Anglo-American descent outnumbered Mexican-American Tejanos by as many as 10 to one by the mid-1830s. The Mexican government was well aware

of the danger this large foreign-born population posed to Mexico's sovereignty over the territory. "Texas will be lost for this Republic," Mexican Secretary of State Lucas Alamán warned around 1830, "if adequate measures to save it are not taken." Mexico proved unable to keep Texas, Anglo settlers wanted independence from Mexico, and the Texan Revolution made Texas independent. A contributing cause to the loss of Texas was Mexico's political instability, which reflected the wider political instability of newly independent Hispanic America.

UPHEAVAL IN MEXICO

Mexico began its independent existence bankrupt and devastated by 11 years of revolutionary war. Civil turmoil between warring factions made its early years even harder, a situation mirroring that in many other Hispanic-American nations. Within three years of independence, Mexico had acquired (1822) and deposed (1823) an emperor, Agustín I, and established a liberal, federalist constitution, the Constitution of 1824. During this federalist era, two principal factions formed. On one side were the federalists, who were liberal and egalitarian; they supported religious toleration, relief for the oppressed, and a system of federated sovereign states. On the other side were the centralists, who were conservative and elitist; backed by church and military leaders, they supported state establishment of Roman Catholicism, the interests of wealthy landowners, and a strong centralized, even dictatorial, government.

As early as 1827, President Guadalupe Victoria, a federalist, had to put down an armed revolt by his vice president, Nicolás Bravo, a centralist. Victoria's successor, Vicente Guerrero (1782–1831), also a federalist, was overthrown by his vice president, centralist Anastasio Bustamante (1780–1853), in 1829–1830. Bustamante had Guerrero, a hero of the war of independence, executed by firing squad in 1831. Bustamante

Nicolas Bravo (Library of Congress)

Antonio López de Santa Anna (Library of Congress)

ruled as a dictator, suppressing opposition newspapers and menacing political opponents with military force. Numerous uprisings were launched against him, until forces led by General Antonio López de Santa Anna (1794–1876) compelled him to flee into exile in 1832.

Santa Anna was an amazing figure of Mexico's early history—amazing for the ease with which he switched sides to gain advantage, and even more so for his resilience in coming back time and again as Mexico's leader no matter how thoroughly he had been rejected before. On 11 different occasions from 1833 to 1855, he was Mexico's chief executive. He was a talented military leader who had fought at various times for royalists, independence forces, federalists, and centralists. He dominated Mexican politics in the era in which Mexico lost the Far North.

Santa Anna came to national prominence in Mexico in 1829 by orchestrating the defeat of Spanish invaders at the Battle of Tampico, halting a short-lived Spanish attempt to retake Mexico in the wake of Bustamante's exile. Elected to the presidency of Mexico in 1833 in the wake of this victory, the vain Santa Anna became quickly dissatisfied with the limits of the office when his vice president led a wave of liberal reform through the national and state legislatures. Backed by the centralists, Santa Anna assumed absolute power as dictator in 1834 and revoked the new reforms. Two years later, in 1836, a new conservative Congress formally replaced the federalist Constitution of 1824 with the centralist Constitution of 1836. By this time Texas was in revolt and moving swiftly toward independence. As will be discussed, Santa Anna's turbulent rule would would speed the process.

TURMOIL IN HISPANIC AMERICA

Mexico's experience of bloody political turmoil was all too common in Hispanic America, not only in the years right after independence but throughout the nearly two centuries since. Revolutions, coups, uprisings, civil wars, factional fighting, periods of rule by a dictator or junta (a small group of military officers), persistent wars with neighbors—all have been perennial features of Latin American history. Recent decades have seen stable democratic rule established in most Latin American countries, but the danger of renewed violence remains present in many places.

In the early years of Hispanic America, this violence was accompanied by the disintegration of several large states. Gran Colombia, founded by

Simón Bolívar, splintered by 1831 into the sovereign nations of Venezuela, Ecuador, and New Granada. New Granada, which later became Colombia, splintered further when Panama broke free in 1903. The United Provinces of Río de la Plata broke up when Uruguay became independent in 1828, leaving the remainder to emerge as Argentina. By 1840 the United Provinces of Central America had fragmented into Guatemala, Honduras, El Salvador, Nicaragua, and Costa Rica.

Many reasons have been suggested for Hispanic America's history of fragmentation and violent instability. In many places, barriers of mountains or rain forest made regionalism easy and long-range communication difficult. Regional autonomy was traditional in Spanish culture and had been reinforced by the Spanish colonial divisions, which established the dividing lines for many of the nations. Spain also gave Hispanic America a traditionally autocratic, military, church-reinforced role, with power likely to go to whichever caudillo, or chief (sometimes called a "strongman"), could best his rivals in warfare. This experience was very different from the more democratic traditions the English colonists brought with them to the United States. Chronic economic troubles and widespread poverty also fed civil instability.

Despite this undemocratic heritage, many Hispanic intellectuals had studied the works and deeds of French, English, and American political philosophers and statesmen and were struggling to build liberal, egalitarian republics. United States president James Monroe (1758–1831; president 1817–1825) gave indirect support to their cause when he promulgated the Monroe Doctrine in 1823, warning the European powers not to interfere with the new nations' "free and independent condition." On the other hand, many people in the United States were ambivalent or even hostile about the capacity of Hispanic Americans to govern themselves. John Quincy Adams (1767–1848), then secretary of state and architect of both the purchase of Florida and the Monroe Doctrine, expressed pessimism about the new regimes' future, saying they had inherited Spanish traditions of "arbitrary power" and "civil dissension." Stephen Austin spoke more bluntly, not to say insultingly, writing in a private letter that Mexicans were "bigoted and superstitious in the extreme.... To be candid the majority of the people of the whole nation as far as I have seen want nothing but tails to be more brutes than the apes."

With such attitudes common, it was no surprise that the United States gave less support to the struggle for democracy in Hispanic-American nations than its own civic principles might lead one to expect. U.S. foreign policy in this period was typically based on expediency rather than zeal for democracy. Cuba, for example, remained a Spanish colony, but the United States warned Colombia and Mexico in 1825 not to attempt to liberate it from Spanish rule. Among other reasons, the United States feared that a Cuban war of independence might lead to a Cuban slave insurrection, which might inspire slave insurrections in nearby southern states. Regarding Mexico's Far North, expediency was also the rule, as Mexico soon discovered.

NORTEAMERICANOS IN TEXAS

With Mexico's government in chaos, Anglo-Americans in Texas found it best to ignore the governing officials. By the early 1830s, the Norteamericanos (as they were sometimes known) greatly outnumbered Tejanos and were living by their own rules. In 1826 empresario Haden Edwards went so far as to try unsuccessfully to found an independent republic of "Fredonia" in eastern Texas. The Anglos' restless energy in clearing land and building towns was startling, though Tejanos were appalled by some American customs, such as the habit of saying "God damn!" The phrase, offensive to Tejano Catholics, led to such contemptuous terms for the Anglos as "Godamees" and "Señor God Damn." Americans returned the contempt with a vengeance. Anglo-American William S. Henry wrote of Texas: "It certainly was never intended that this lovely land . . . should remain in the hands of an ignorant and degenerate race. The finger of Fate points . . . to the time when they will cease to be the owners, and when the Anglo-American race will rule with republican simplicity and justice."

Fearing the loss of Texas, Mexico began to enact stricter laws, starting with the outlawing of slavery in 1829. This move had little impact outside of Texas,

John Quincy Adams (Library of Congress)

James Monroe (Library of Congress)

where slavery was rare, but in principle it could have had a large impact on the Anglo-American southerners who had settled in Texas with their slaves. However, under protest from Anglo slaveowners, application of the law to Texas was suspended. Although initially the number of slaves in Texas only increased slowly, in time the land underwent a transformation. The invention of the cotton gin in 1793 had made short staple, upland cotton production economically viable, turning east Texas into ideal cotton country. With the suspension of antislavery laws, the production of cotton began to increase. In just six years, between 1827 and 1833, the number of cotton bales produced in Texas doubled. Following Texan independence and its subsequent admission into the United States, cotton output—and the slave population of Texas—began to skyrocket. In 1860, just prior to the start of the U.S. Civil War, the number of cotton bales produced in Texas reached 60,000.

In 1830 Mexico enacted legislation that was even more direct in its attempts to control the Anglo menace. The new law closed the border to further Anglo-American immigration into Texas, prohibited the slave trade, encouraged Mexicans and Europeans to settle in Texas, and imposed customs duties on imports from the United States. Troops were sent and new forts built to reinforce Mexican authority. Anglo-Americans in Texas responded with outrage, some launching military attacks on customs houses and army posts. Many Texans resorted to smuggling to avoid duties. The influx of Anglo immigrants, though illegal, continued to be at least as heavy as before.

In 1833 a convention of Texans sent Stephen Austin to Mexico City to argue for rescinding the laws and making Texas a Mexican state with its own U.S.-style constitution. In the turmoil of Mexican politics, Austin could not get an answer from the chaos-ridden Mexican government, so after 11 weeks he sent a letter to the city council of San Antonio, back in Texas, advising that Texas form its own state government without the central government's support. "The fate of Texas depends upon itself and not upon this government," he wrote. "The country is lost if its inhabitants do not take matters into their own hands."

Austin's letter had an unintended effect, for the majority of San Antonio city council members were Mexicans. Alarmed by the fiery tone of the letter, they

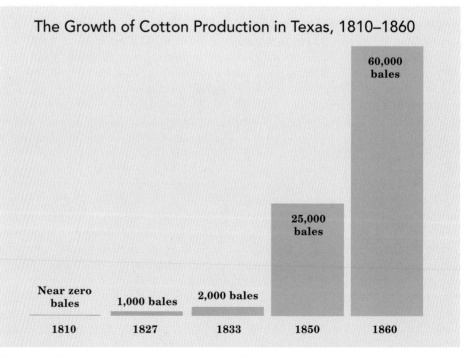

The Growth of Cotton Production in Texas, 1810–1860

				60,000 bales
			25,000 bales	
Near zero bales	1,000 bales	2,000 bales		
1810	1827	1833	1850	1860

Cotton production in Texas increased dramatically with the arrival of Anglo settlers from the United States. After Mexico agreed to exempt Anglos from Mexico's ban of slavery, cotton production began to climb. As available statistics show in the graph above, after Texas gained independence from Mexico (in 1836) and gained admission into the United States (in 1845), production skyrocketed.

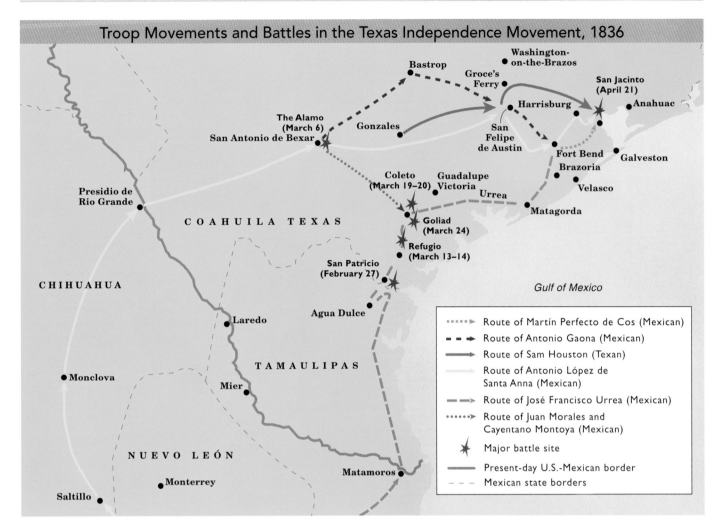

Troop Movements and Battles in the Texas Independence Movement, 1836

Washington-on-the-Brazos
Bastrop
Groce's Ferry
San Jacinto (April 21)
Anahuac
Harrisburg
The Alamo (March 6)
San Antonio de Bexar
Gonzales
San Felipe de Austin
Fort Bend
Galveston
Brazoria
Presidio de Rio Grande
Coleto (March 19–20)
Guadalupe Victoria
Urrea
Velasco
COAHUILA TEXAS
Goliad (March 24)
Matagorda
Refugio (March 13–14)
San Patricio (February 27)
CHIHUAHUA
Gulf of Mexico
Agua Dulce
Laredo
TAMAULIPAS
Monclova
Mier
NUEVO LEÓN
Monterrey
Matamoros
Saltillo

⸱⸱⸱⸱⸱⸱▸ Route of Martín Perfecto de Cos (Mexican)
▬ ▬ ▬▸ Route of Antonio Gaona (Mexican)
⟶ Route of Sam Houston (Texan)
⟶ Route of Antonio López de Santa Anna (Mexican)
▬ ▬ ▬▸ Route of José Francisco Urrea (Mexican)
⸱⸱⸱⸱⸱⸱▸ Route of Juan Morales and Cayentano Montoya (Mexican)
✦ Major battle site
▬▬ Present-day U.S.-Mexican border
– – – Mexican state borders

forwarded it to Mexico City. Santa Anna, now heading Mexico for the first time, judged the letter treasonable and had Austin locked up until 1835. By then Santa Anna had assumed dictatorial power, thrown out the federalist Constitution of 1824, and begun the process of devising a new centralist constitution that would demolish state autonomy.

Rebellion against the new regime began in several Mexican states, including Zacatecas, Yucatán, and Alta California, but nowhere were the consequences more lasting than in Texas. There, Texan delegates, some Tejano but most Anglo, covened at San Felipe de Austin, and, on November 7, 1835, provisionally declared their independence until such time as the Constitution of 1824 was restored, if it ever was.

INDEPENDENCE

A month before what came to be called the Consultation at San Felipe de Austin took place, Texans were already fighting Mexicans in what is generally considered the first battle in the Texan Revolution, or Texan War of Independence. It took place at Gonzales on October 2, 1835, when Texan rebels refused orders to hand over an old cannon they had been given for protection against Native Americans. The rebels raised a banner that read "Come and Take It." Government forces tried, but the Texans routed them and kept the cannon.

The rebels captured the presidio at Goliad a week later, then laid siege to San Antonio, capturing it on December 11 after five days of fierce house-to-house fighting. The victorious rebels permitted their adversary, General Martín Cos, a brother-in-law of Santa Anna, to withdraw with his forces. Now the stakes grew higher. Santa Anna, eager to avenge the defeat, amassed an army of perhaps 5,000 and marched into San Antonio on February 23, 1836. He found the town only thinly defended by a force of about 150 men, all holed up in the fortified mission called the Alamo. It would become the symbol of Texan independence.

The Alamo (Library of Congress)

who had come to aid the rebels in the Texan War of Independence. During the siege, 32 other men joined the defenders, bringing the total force to about 182. Some Tejanos were in the Alamo, including San Antonio colonel Juan Seguín, as was a company of "New Orleans Grays" from Louisiana.

Upon arriving, Santa Anna surrounded the Alamo and raised the red flag, the sign of "no quarter," indicating that the Texans must surrender immediately or die upon being captured. The Texans replied with cannon fire. Santa Anna besieged and bombarded the Alamo for 13 days, then attacked. On March 6, his forces broke through a ferocious defense and captured the Alamo. All 182 Texan soldiers were killed, either in battle or after capture. Only women, children, and slaves in the mission were spared.

Santa Anna had won the battle but lost the war. Word of the Anglo stand at the Alamo reinforced Texan zeal and earned Santa Anna the reputation of butcher, as did his massacre of Texan

Led by William Travis (1809–1836), a South Carolina lawyer who came to Texas in about 1832, the tiny force in the Alamo also included pioneer James Bowie (ca. 1796–1836), who had come to Texas in 1828, and Tennessee frontiersman and politician Davy Crockett (1786–1836),

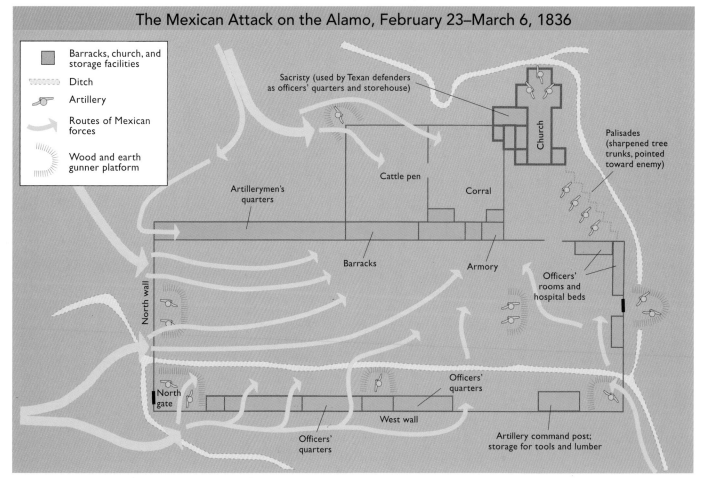

Arrows on the map above illustrate the path of Mexican forces as they scaled the fort's walls during their final assault on the Alamo. Texan defenders, not shown, were stationed throughout all areas of the fort, and most died where they fought.

prisoners outside Goliad on March 27. By that time Texas was committed to seceding from Mexico altogether. On March 2, during the siege of the Alamo, a convention at Washington-on-the-Brazos unequivocally declared independence from Mexico, with David G. Burnet appointed provisional president and Sam Houston (1793–1863) named commander-in-chief.

In the Battle of San Jacinto on April 21, Houston led a force of fewer than 800 men in a surprise attack on Santa Anna's sleeping army of about 1,500. In the 18-minute rout, Houston's soldiers killed Mexicans with vengeful abandon, disregarding many surrender attempts, shouting "Remember the Alamo!" and "Remember Goliad!" Stephen Austin's nephew, Moses Austin Bryan, described it as "the most awful slaughter I ever saw." By Houston's account, 630 Mexicans were killed and 730 taken prisoner, while fewer than 10 Texans died. Houston nearly added one more when an ankle wound he suffered got infected, but he recovered. Among the prisoners he took was Santa Anna, who, in exchange for his freedom, signed treaties recognizing Texan independence and agreeing to withdraw Mexican forces beyond the Rio Grande.

Disgraced by his defeat, Santa Anna was forced out of office and replaced, in 1837, by his predecessor Bustamante, whose government repudiated the treaties and refused to recognize Texan independence. But Mexico was in no position to pursue its claim, what with continuing

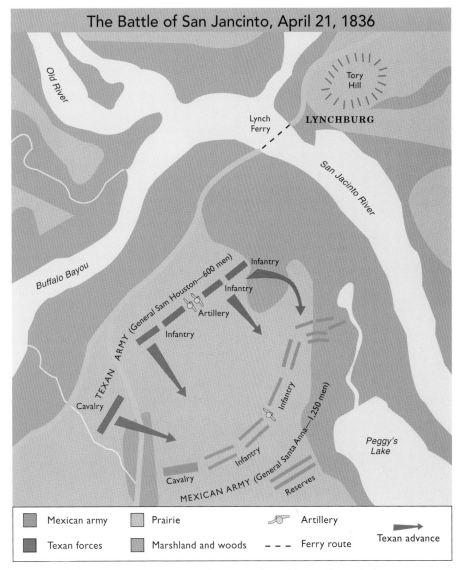

The Battle of San Jancinto, April 21, 1836

▨ Mexican army	▨ Prairie	⚙ Artillery	
▨ Texan forces	▨ Marshland and woods	– – – Ferry route	➤ Texan advance

The broad plain at San Jacinto, near the town of Lynchburg, Texas, helped determine that Sam Houston would need to lead his men in an all-or-nothing struggle against Santa Anna's troops. The open prairie to the south offered no opportunity for retreat, and all other routes were blocked by marshy waters.

General Santa Anna, seen at left-center (wearing white pants and blue jacket) of this 1886 painting by William Huddle, offers his surrender to a wounded Sam Houston following the Battle of San Jacinto. (Texas State Archive)

Sam Houston (Library of Congress)

"Texas, to be respected must be polite. Santa Anna living, can be of incalculable benefit to Texas; Santa Anna dead, would just be another dead Mexican."

—Sam Houston

civil dissension and other troubles, including an invasion by France at Veracruz in 1838. In the first of many comebacks, Santa Anna returned from ignominy to lead the victorious expulsion of the French. He lost part of his left leg in the battle, but his peg leg served as a badge of honor and helped win him another period of dictatorship (1841–1844).

THE U.S.–MEXICAN WAR

While Mexico was occupied with repelling the French, the Republic of Texas, founded in 1836 with Sam Houston as its first elected president, had begun an independent existence. It became known as the Lone Star Republic for its flag with a single star, but the ambition of many Texans, including Houston, was to join the other stars of the United States flag soon through annexation. Some voices in the United States called for annexation, but others resisted. Texas would enter the Union as a slave state, upsetting the already precarious balance of free and slave states in Congress. Further, annexation of Texas would probably lead to war with Mexico, since Mexico still claimed Texas as its own. Eventually the United States did annex Texas, and inevitably, war with Mexico followed in a conflict called the U.S.-Mexican War or, simply, the Mexican War (1846–1848).

The Buildup to War

The years 1836 to 1846 were tense ones in the disputed borderlands that are now the American Southwest. Texas was independent and growing in population, but plagued by debt and embroiled in wars with Native Americans. Mexico did not recognize the Lone Star Republic's independence, invading twice in 1842 but failing to capture any territory. Even if Mexico had recognized Texas, the two nations would have disagreed about boundaries. Texas claimed, on the basis of Santa Anna's forced agreement with Sam Houston, that the Rio Grande from mouth to source was the republic's southern and western border, an assertion that would have allotted Texas parts of what

are now New Mexico and Colorado. Mexico argued that the southern border of Texas since the time of Spanish rule had been and still was the Nueces River, about 150 miles north of the Rio Grande.

Some Texans had even grander notions of their republic's extent, asserting dominion as far as the California coast. In 1841 Texan president Mirabeau Buonaparte Lamar (1798–1859) sent an expedition of 300 merchants and soldiers to Santa Fe, not only to trade but to try to convince the Nuevomexicanos to revolt against Mexico. The expedition of these so-called Santa Fe Pioneers was a disaster. They became lost in the wilderness, suffered attacks from Comanche and Kiowa, and were finally captured by New Mexico's governor Manuel Armijo. The would-be conquerors were marched to Mexico City, from which they were released only after American and British protests.

Tensions rose not only between Mexico and Texas but between Mexico and the United States. In October 1842 American Commodore Thomas Catesby Jones, acting on a rumor that war had broken out, sailed to Monterey, California, and forced the Mexican garrison there to surrender. The embarrassed officer was forced to give Monterey back the next day on learning that he had been mistaken. The incident was a blunder, but it raised Mexico's suspicion of its neighbor's intentions.

Mexico had reason to be suspicious, for California was becoming ever more attractive to the United States. New England shipowners were getting rich on the maritime trade with the California ports of Monterey and San Francisco. New England whalers docked in those ports on their hunting expeditions. In 1844 a treaty opened five Chinese ports to American commerce, increasing the importance of having Pacific harbors available on the American mainland. American merchants had much to trade, because American manufacturing was on the rise, as the country rebounded from a depression that had lasted from 1837 to 1841. Through immigration and natural increase, the population of the United States was burgeoning, nearly doubling from 12.9 million in 1830 to 23.2 million in 1850—and many of those people wanted nothing more than cheap land, no matter how far west it lay. In addition to these factors, the United States had a foreign policy stake in preventing other nations from acquiring California, particularly Britain, which was then contesting the United States for possession of the Oregon Territory, just north of California. For all these reasons, the United States had a strong interest in acquiring Mexico's Far North, especially California. For its part, Mexico—as New Spain had done when settling California and Texas a century before—viewed the northern frontier as a defensive buffer against its expansionist neighbor. Therefore, even though its northern frontier was still relatively sparse in population, Mexico had a strong interest in not letting the United States have it.

As early as the 1820s, the United States had offered to buy Texas, an offer rejected as an insult by Mexico. In 1835 United States president Andrew Jackson (1767–1845; president 1829–1837) offered to buy San Francisco Bay. In 1845 President John Tyler (1790–1862) offered to buy New Mexico and California. Such offers only fueled Mexico's distrust and resentment of the United States.

At the same time, the Anglo-American population in the remainder of Mexico's Far North kept growing. Just as in Texas before the Texan Revolution, Anglo-American immigrants poured into California, attracted by such reports as that of former New Mexican Louis Robidoux, who called northern California "the promised land where the arroyos run with virgin honey and milk. Another Texas." Among those who came was Baden-born John Augustus Sutter (1803–1880), who settled in the Sacramento Valley with a grant of 49,000 acres, to which he attracted many American settlers. After the U.S.-Mexican War (in which Sutter sided with the United States), Sutter became even more famous for the gold found on his lands.

The Mexican authorities tried the same strategies for control that had failed in Texas: clamping down with tougher anti-immigration laws, sending more troops, and trying to encourage immigration from outside the United States. The strategies failed in California too—in part because Californios, who welcomed the local development the immigrants brought and lacked the military strength to expel them, tended not to enforce the restrictions. One young Californio, Pablo

Andrew Jackson (Library of Congress)

de la Guerra, said the foreigners "are about to overrun us, of which I am very glad, for the country needs immigration in order to make progress."

In New Mexico, Governor Manuel Armijo had better luck restricting immigration, but Anglo-Americans could turn up anywhere. Even during the U.S.-Mexican War, one determined group of Anglo-Americans took up residence in a Far Northern region as yet unsettled by Hispanics: the Mormons, who, fleeing persecution in the United States, established their first colony in what is now Utah in 1847.

The threat of war between the United States and Mexico grew in November 1844, when Democrat James K. Polk (1795–1849) was elected president. Polk was an expansionist committed to territorial growth, beginning with annexation of Texas and ideally extending to California. The notion of annexing Texas was becoming increasingly popular, as southern states pressed for addition of a new slave state to aid their cause in Congress, and as British and French influence grew in Texas, making it possible that the United States would permanently lose

John Tyler (Library of Congress)

its chance to acquire the Lone Star Republic.

On February 28, 1845, before Polk had been inaugurated, the U.S. Congress approved a joint resolution inviting Texas into the Union. Mexico protested and broke off diplomatic relations with the United States, but the tide of U.S. expansionist sentiment grew. In the summer of 1845, John L. O'Sullivan, editor of the United States Magazine and Democratic Review, coined the phrase Manifest Destiny, saying it was the United States' "manifest destiny to overspread the continent allotted by Providence for the free development of our yearly multiplying millions." O'Sullivan had not originated this idea; many Americans, including Polk, felt that their country should and would expand from coast to coast, bringing with it the blessings of democracy and free enterprise. Some saw no limits to this destiny—up into Canada, down into Mexico, even into South America or Europe. One American soldier wrote prior to the U.S.-Mexican War that with a "gigantic effort" the United States "could sweep the continent from Panama to the Pole and from ocean to ocean in a year." Others, like Polk, were more restrained; they wanted only North America, from sea to shining sea.

Manifest Destiny was closely linked to the commonplace racism of the day: the view that white Anglo-Americans were superior to the darker-skinned Native Americans and Mexicans currently occupying the coveted lands. Many Americans viewed it as an outrage that a people like the Mexicans, whom they regarded as lazy and degenerate, should stand in their way. Sam Houston wrote that he could "see no reason why we should not go in . . . and take their [the Mexicans'] lands."

Polk made one major effort to acquire the Far North peacefully. In November 1845 he sent diplomat John Slidell (1793–1871) to Mexico to try to gain recognition of the Rio Grande border for Texas and buy New Mexico and California. As a bargaining tool, Slidell was to use claims of damages to American property during Mexico's civil wars, claims that the United States was willing to drop in return for Mexican cooperation. The Mexicans adamantly refused to negotiate with him.

While Slidell was in Mexico, Texas entered the Union, becoming the 28th state on December 29, 1845. At about the same time, another revolt broke out in Mexico, with General Mariano Paredes coming to power on January 2, 1846. As Polk saw it, he had tried peaceful means to acquire Mexico's Far North, and those had failed. His next move was war.

WAR WITH MEXICO

On January 13, 1846, Polk ordered General Zachary Taylor and his 3,550 troops to advance from their position on the Nueces River to the Rio Grande. The president did so knowing that Mexico rejected the American claim to the territory between the rivers and would therefore regard this move as an invasion. On March 28 Taylor arrived at the Rio Grande, across from the Mexican city of Matamoros, and began constructing forts. Shortly thereafter, General Pedro de Ampudia, commander of Mexico's Division of the North, ordered Taylor to withdraw or face hostilities. Taylor refused.

On April 25 a large Mexican cavalry force crossed the Rio Grande. They surrounded a small squadron of American dragoons, killing or wounding 16 and taking the rest prisoner. Taylor sent word to Polk, who informed Congress heatedly, "Mexico has passed the boundary of the United States, has invaded our territory and shed American blood upon the American soil." Some congressmen objected, questioning whether the east bank of the Rio Grande could really be considered American soil, but they were in the minority. Congress declared war on Mexico on May 13, 1846. A subordinate of Taylor's, Colonel Ethan Allen Hitchcock, commented: "It looks as if the government sent a small force on purpose to bring on a war, so as to have a pretext for taking California and as much of this country as it chooses."

The American strategy for winning the war centered on Taylor, who had won two victories on the northern side of the Rio Grande even before the declaration of war: at Palo Alto on May 8 and Resaca de la Palma on May 9. On May 18 Taylor advanced into Matamoros, which the enemy had abandoned, and raised the American flag there. The plan was for Taylor to keep pushing into northern Mexico, while a separate force, the Army of the West, conquered New Mexico and

The U.S. Invasion of Mexico, 1846–1848

Sutter's Fort
San Francisco
(Yerba Buena)
Monterey

Fort Leavenworth

Pueblo
Bent's
Fort

UNITED
STATES

Colorado R.

Arkansas R.

Los Angeles

Santa Fe
Las Vegas

San Diego

Gila R.

Albuquerque

Red R.

Disputed
area

Brazos R.

Sabine R.

Tucson

El Paso

Pecos R.

Texas

Rio Grande

San
Jacinto

Chihuahua

San
Antonio

Laredo

Corpus
Christi

Rio Conchos

Monclova

Mier

MEXICO

Monterrey

Matamoros

Buena Vista

*Gulf of
Mexico*

*Pacific
Ocean*

Cuidad Victoria

Mazatlán

Rio Grande de Santiago

San Luis Potosí

Tampico

Jalapa

Mexico City

Puebla

Veracruz

Acapulco de Juárez

Legend:

✷ Selected battle sites
● Cities
■ Forts
▢ Former Republic of Texas
▢ Disputed area
◄····· Route of Stephen Kearny
◄━━ Route of Zachary Taylor
◄‑ ‑ ‑ Route of Winfield Scott
◄‑·‑· Route of John C. Frémont

At the heart of the U.S.-Mexican War lay the dispute over the size of Texas. After annexing the Lone Star Republic—as independent Texas was called—the United States claimed that the Texas border followed the Rio Grande, not only from the Gulf of Mexico to El Paso in southwest Texas, but also northward from El Paso to include Albuquerque and Santa Fe in New Mexico as well as parts of present-day Colorado and Wyoming. When U.S. troops began building a fort just across the Rio Grande from Matamoros, they suc-ceeded in provoking Mexican troops to fire the first shots. U.S. President James K. Polk used the Mexican action to occupy Mexico and take New Mexico and California. The major battles and routes of advance by leading American commanders are illustrated in the map above.

"Already, the advance guard of the irresistible army of the Anglo-Saxon emigration has begun to pour down upon [California], armed with the plough and the rifle, and marking its trail with schools and colleges, courts and representative halls, mills and meetinghouses. A population will soon be in actual occupation of California, over which it will be idle for Mexico to dream of dominion."

—John O'Sullivan,
   "Manifest Destiny" (1845)

A U.S. Navy warship off the coast of California, 1849 (Library of Congress)

Captain John C. Frémont helps seize California from Mexico. (Library of Congress)

California, and the navy attacked California and blockaded both Mexican coasts. President Polk hoped these strategies alone would convince Mexico to make peace, ending the war swiftly. He had not counted on the stiffness of Mexican resistance, which would keep Mexico in arms for more than two years, not making peace until their capital was taken.

NEW MEXICO AND CALIFORNIA

In June 1846, while Zachary Taylor battled in northern Mexico, the campaign to capture New Mexico and California began. On June 27, Brigadier General Stephen Watts Kearny (1794–1848), commander of the Army of the West, left

Fort Leavenworth in what is now Kansas with about 1,500 troops. After marching more than 1,000 miles along the Santa Fe Trail, Kearney's forces captured Santa Fe, New Mexico, without a fight on August 16. The Neuvomexicanos varied in their responses to the takeover. They had no great love for the Mexican government but were wary of Americans. The attitude of New Mexican official Juan Bautista Vigil seemed a typical one: "No matter what her condition, [Mexico] was our mother. What child will not shed abundant tears at the tomb of his parents?"

By the time New Mexico was captured, California had fallen to the United States as well. Captain John C. Frémont (1813–1890), who had been in the region on an exploratory expedition since the previous year, gave his support to a settlers' revolt at Sonoma, north of San Francisco. At dawn on June 14, the rebels rousted General Mariano Vallejo from his bed, placed him under arrest, and forced him to surrender. Since they were not yet certain that the United States was at war with Mexico, the rebels could not claim the territory in the name of the United States. Instead, they proclaimed California's independence, raising a flag decorated with a grizzly bear. The event was called the Bear Flag Revolt, even though the Bear Flag Republic's flag was taken down and replaced with an American flag once confirmation of the state of war came.

Soon after the Bear Flag Revolt, Commodore John D. Sloat closed in from the sea, capturing Monterey on July 7 and San Francisco three days later. In August, Commodore Robert F. Stockton, who had replaced the ailing Sloat, captured Los Angeles, Southern California's strongest garrison, without opposition. Stockton proclaimed himself governor of the territory, but the Californios only appeared to submit to him. In September Californios, led by Captain José María Flores, rebelled and took back Los Angeles. In the following months, the Californios took possession of most of the towns in the interior. The tide of battle turned when Kearny, who had been advancing west from Santa Fe, arrived in December and fought through enemy lines until he could join Stockton's forces. With Kearny's help, Stockton recaptured Los Angeles on January 10, 1847. At about the same time, the people of New

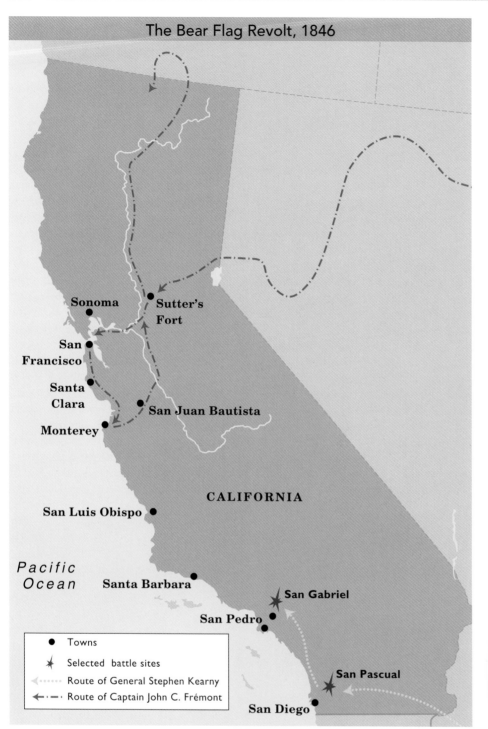

The Bear Flag Revolt, 1846

Sonoma

Sutter's Fort

San Francisco

Santa Clara

Monterey

San Juan Bautista

CALIFORNIA

San Luis Obispo

Pacific Ocean

Santa Barbara

San Gabriel

San Pedro

San Pascual

San Diego

● Towns
★ Selected battle sites
·········◁ Route of General Stephen Kearny
◀—·—· Route of Captain John C. Frémont

The Bear Flag Revolt began on June 14, 1846, when Anglo settlers in Sonoma placed Mexican general Mariano Vallejo under arrest, declaring California an independent republic they called the Bear Flag Republic. The settlers were supported by American explorer John C. Frémont, who had incited tensions the previous March by raising the American flag at Monterey. The real intent of the settlers was not independence for California but annexation by the United States. By early July, the U.S. naval ships under Commodore John Sloat captured Monterey and San Francisco. In August, Commodore Robert Stockton took Los Angeles. U.S. victory was assured when land forces under General Stephen Kearny arrived from Santa Fe to reinforce Stockton's troops.

LEARNING THE LINGO

Like all foreign expeditionary forces, American troops in Mexico during the U.S.-Mexican War faced the problem of communicating with the people whose land they were occupying. Many of them learned more Spanish in Mexico than they had heard in their whole lives. Some of these words they brought home with them. Veterans came home smoking cigarritos, the little paper-wrapped cigars that became known as cigarettes, and giving names like Buena Vista and Palo Alto to towns across the United States.

While in Mexico, some Anglo soldiers struggled with grammars and phrasebooks, but many did the best they could without books. This is how one Illinois volunteer officer described his efforts to communicate with a boardinghouse proprietor and her daughter:

When at fault for a word I take an English one & give it a Spanish ending & pronunciation & make a salaam or two. . . . If that don't go, I throw in a word or two of Latin & French, & occasionally a little German, & conclude with "Senora" or "Senorita." Thus I generally succeed in calling up a smile, & a gentle "Si, Senor" . . . then they let loose a torrent of Castillian on me, & I stand & look knowing, & say "Si Senorita" when I've no more idea of what they are saying than if Moses was talking to me in his native tongue.

Mexico also revolted, but they were crushed at Taos early in 1847.

INVADING MEXICO

While the struggle for California went on, General Taylor moved deeper into Mexico. His victories were aided by the superiority of American weapons over outdated Mexican ones and by the generally poor leadership and training of Mexican soldiers—despite the fact that they often fought tenaciously and courageously, more so than Americans had expected. On September 24, 1846, Taylor captured Monterrey, which guarded an important mountain pass leading into Mexico's interior. On February 22–23, 1847, at Buena Vista, Taylor faced an old fighter against Americans: General Santa Anna of Alamo fame. In exile in Cuba at the start of the war during one of his periods out of power, Santa Anna had convinced President Polk to allow him to pass through the naval blockade so he could regain control of Mexico and negotiate peace. As soon as the general got back home, however, he reneged on the deal and gathered an army of 20,000 to face

Taylor's 5,000 at Buena Vista. Both sides suffered heavy losses, but Taylor held fast, and Santa Anna was forced to withdraw, leaving northern Mexico in U.S. control.

In March 1847 Alexander Doniphan, a lieutenant of Kearny's who had led an expedition from Santa Fe, captured Chihuahua in northern Mexico. But by then the focus of battle had turned to central Mexico. Polk realized that Mexico would not surrender unless its capital was captured, so he determined to seize it. The plan was to land troops at Veracruz, then follow the ancient invasion route to Mexico City that Hernán Cortés had used in overthrowing the Aztec Empire. The man appointed to head the campaign was General Winfield Scott (1786–1866).

On March 9, 1847, near Veracruz, Scott launched the largest amphibious assault yet undertaken by American troops, with 10,000 soldiers wading onto the beach under the cover of naval artillery. After a siege and bombardment, the walled city of Veracruz fell on March 29. Scott marched west to Mexico City as Cortés had, capturing town after town and defeating the Mexicans at Cerro Gordo (April 18), Contreras (August 19), and Churubusco (August 20). Scott was

The Battle of Churubusco, August 20, 1847 (Library of Congress)

General Winfield Scott (Library of Congress)

hampered by high rates of disease and desertion, which had also plagued Taylor's army. However, he was aided by the effective soldiering of his West Point–trained junior officers, who would go on to fight each other in the American Civil War. They included Ulysses S. Grant, Robert E. Lee, George McClellan, P. G. T. Beauregard, and Thomas (later called "Stonewall") Jackson.

Notwithstanding the superior training of the U.S. officers, Mexican forces fought vigorously to defend their country against the American invasion, and some battles were hard-won, such as Churubusco, in which the Americans suffered about 1,000 casualties and the Mexicans 4,000. Particularly fierce were the battles of Molino del Rey (September 8) and Chapultepec (September 13), both fought over fortified positions guarding the entrance to the capital. During the Battle of Chapultepec, in which Americans stormed the castle and military school of the same name, the young Mexican cadets showed great courage, many of them fighting to the death rather than surrendering. Mexicans still commemorate them as Los Niños Héroes, "The Boy Heroes."

With Chapultepec fallen, the road to Mexico City lay wide open. Santa Anna evacuated his troops, and on September 14, 1847, Scott occupied the Mexican capital. Santa Anna tried a last attack on Scott at Puebla, but it failed, and he fled

U.S. Annexation of Mexican Land, 1846–1853

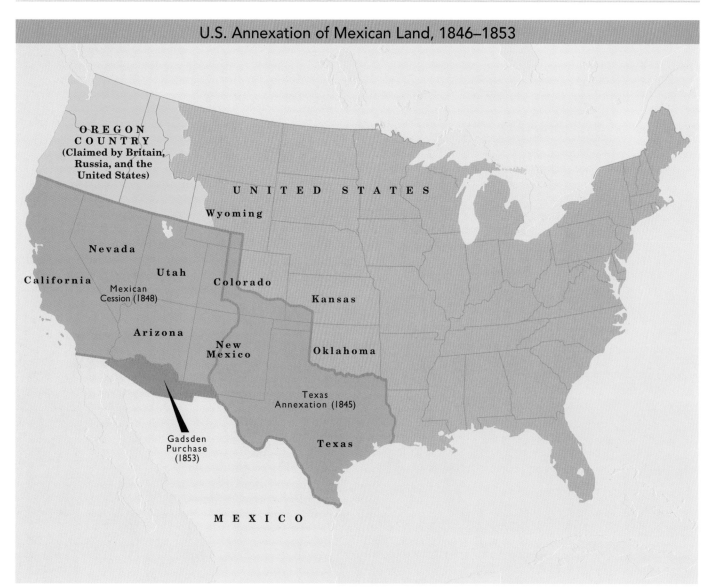

OREGON
COUNTRY
(Claimed by Britain,
Russia, and the
United States)

UNITED STATES

Wyoming

Nevada

Utah

California

Mexican
Cession (1848)

Colorado

Kansas

Arizona

New
Mexico

Oklahoma

Gadsden
Purchase
(1853)

Texas
Annexation (1845)

Texas

MEXICO

into exile once again. The citizens of Mexico City gave some resistance in the form of riots and sniping, but Scott suppressed it within a matter of days. For the first time, the American flag waved over a foreign capital.

THE TREATY OF GUADALUPE HIDALGO

Peace came with the Treaty of Guadalupe Hidalgo, signed in a Mexico City suburb by that name on February 2, 1848. The treaty gave the United States everything it had fought for. Mexico surrendered its claim to Texas and accepted the Rio Grande boundary. In what was called the Mexican Cession, Mexico ceded the remainder of its Far North, including California, New Mexico, and all or part of

what are now Arizona, Nevada, Utah, Wyoming, Colorado, Kansas, and Oklahoma. In return the United States paid Mexico $15 million and took on $3 million in unpaid claims of American citizens against Mexico. Mexican citizens who chose to remain in the acquired territories would be granted "all the rights of citizens of the United States," including full property and civil rights and religious liberty—paper promises that would soon suffer many violations. The two nations ratified the treaty in March, and on June 12 American forces left Mexico City.

About 13,000 Americans had died in the war—1,733 on the battlefield, most of the rest from disease. Thousands more Mexicans died in battle than did Americans, though the precise number is not known. The Whig Intelligencer commented that the $15 million payment to

Mexico showed "we take nothing by conquest. . . . Thank God." But since Mexico had refused to sell its Far North at any price before the war, and was persuaded to do so only under threat of continued occupation, many people then and since have regarded the U.S.-Mexican War as precisely a war of conquest.

The transfer of land from Mexico to the United States was not yet over. In 1853, in what became known as the Gadsden Purchase, American foreign minister James Gadsden convinced Mexico to sell 30,000 square miles in what is now southern Arizona and New Mexico, a region coveted for its mineral wealth and potential as a railroad route. The Gadsden Purchase, for which Mexico received $10 million, established the present-day boundary in that region between Mexico and the United States. The Mexican president who negotiated the transaction was none other than Santa Anna, back again from exile and in need of cash. The purchase once again disgraced Santa Anna and contributed to his being yet again forced out of power, this time for good.

THE ANGLOS MOVE IN

The Treaty of Guadalupe Hidalgo formally made Americans out of the Mexicans who chose to remain in what now was the American Southwest. These thousands of Californios, Nuevomexicanos, and Tejanos were the foundation of today's Mexican-American community. Their experience in the years immediately following the war was largely a sad one, in which their land claims were regularly violated and their civil rights ignored, as Anglo-Americans rushed in to exploit the newly conquered lands. The land grab happened fastest in California, where the lure of gold brought "Forty-Niners" by the tens of thousands, trampling over the old Californio society.

The California Gold Rush

On January 24, 1848, nine days before the Treaty of Guadalupe Hidalgo was signed, Anglo carpenter James Wilson Marshall made a surprising discovery. While building a sawmill for landowner John Sutter on the south fork of the American River northeast of Sacramento, California, Marshall picked up some glittering particles that turned out to be gold. Despite their talent for discovering gold in other parts of the New World, the Spanish had never spotted any substantial deposits in California. This one, in the foothills of the Sierra Nevada, proved to be tremendously rich, especially the mother lode, a great vein of gold ore extending about 120 miles. Gold was also found in other parts of California, including the south and northwest.

Word of the discovery quickly spread, bringing hordes of treasure seekers from around the world, but especially from the United States, traveling overland across the Great Plains, by sea around Cape Horn, or by a combination of ship and muleback across the Isthmus of Panama. Because many prospectors did not get there until 1849 or later, they were known as the Forty-Niners. Because of them, California's population (other than Native Americans), which had totaled only about 8,000 in 1845, rose to more than 90,000 by the end of 1849 and to 220,000 by 1852, the year when gold production peaked at an annual output of about $80 million. San Francisco, a tiny settlement of 812 people in March 1848, contained 25,000 souls by 1850.

Miners at work in California during the 1850s (Library of Congress)

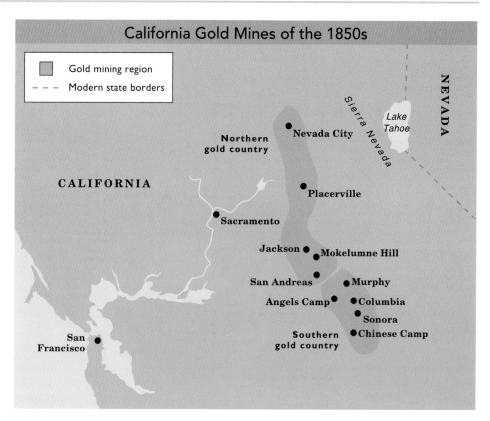

California Gold Mines of the 1850s

Gold mining region
--- Modern state borders

NEVADA

Sierra Nevada

Lake Tahoe

Northern gold country

● Nevada City

CALIFORNIA

● Placerville

● Sacramento

Jackson ● ● Mokelumne Hill

San Andreas ● ● Murphy

Angels Camp ● ● Columbia

● Sonora

Southern gold country ● Chinese Camp

San Francisco ●

The Californios, once the masters of their country, were now a small minority. At first some of them benefited from the California gold rush, especially those who prospected claims of their own or sold supplies to the miners. They were joined by many fellow Hispanics from other parts of the Southwest, Mexico, Peru, and Chile. Mexican Americans knew more about prospecting gold than Anglos did. They taught the newcomers many things, including how to use a batea, a flat-bottomed pan, to isolate gold in streams, and how to crush gold-bearing rocks with a tool called an arrastra. But Anglo miners soon came to see Hispanics as competitors, particularly those from the Mexican state of Sonora, who were more knowledgeable and had more success than they did.

Because mining camps generally arose far from the reach of established law, in areas as yet unclaimed by anyone but Native Americans (whose rights were

Shifting Demographics of the Town of Sonora, California

These graphs illustrate the shifting demographics of the town of Sonora, California. As the gold rush proceeded, Anglo miners forced many miners of other nationalities from the fields.

Other 40
South Americans 80
Chinese 110
Anglos 560
Mexicans 360

Total population in 1850: 1,150

Other 10
South Americans 75
Chinese 40
Mexicans 110
Anglos 1,140

Total population in 1852: 1,375

CHILEAN MINERS

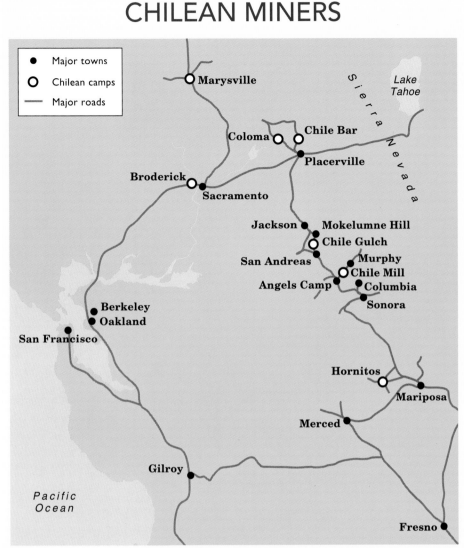

Because of their proximity to quick sea transportation northward, Chileans were among the first fortune seekers to arrive in the California minefields following the discovery of gold there in 1848. Their presence—like that of Mexicans and others from Latin America—angered Anglo miners, who petitioned the California government to pass a foreign miners' tax on all non-U.S.-born miners. Though steep for its time, the tax (which began at $20 per month, but was later lowered) did not dissuade many Chileans from working in the mines. As the gold rush came to a close, some Chileans in 19th-century California returned home, while most shifted to other occupations.

routinely ignored), miners made their own laws, called mining camp codes. The camp codes defined how big a claim could be and specified that all claims had to be continuously worked to stay valid. The codes were often enforced by "vigilance committees" that were little more than lynch mobs. With mining camp sentiment growing against "foreigners," many codes began incorporating clauses that specifically excluded or otherwise discriminated against Mexicans and other Latino miners, as well as against Asians. Many

miners working in Sonora were forced to return to Mexico under the threat of violence. Because all Hispanics looked alike to these Anglos, many Californios were also forced to flee to Mexico, even though they had lived in California all their lives—and even though the Treaty of Guadalupe Hidalgo had made them citizens of the United States.

California entered the Union as a state in 1850, but the state legislature failed to address discrimination against Hispanic and other non-Anglo miners. In

SPANISH COWBOYS

While raising cattle in New Mexico and Texas, the Spanish introduced many of the techniques and customs that English-speaking cowboys would later adopt. Among the elements introduced by Hispanic vaqueros, or cowherds, in what is now the American Southwest were the wide-brimmed hat to shield the face from the sun; the western saddle; chaps (from the Spanish chaparerras), or leather trousers, to protect the legs from high brush; the lasso (from the Spanish *lazo*, or knot); and the practice of using a lasso to round up and rope cattle. So deep is the American cowboy's debt to the Spanish that the quintessential English slang term for the cowboy, "buckaroo," is a corruption of *vaquero*.

fact, the legislature ratified the mining camp codes and added a foreign miners' license tax, which imposed a fee of $20 a month on miners who were not citizens of the United States. In theory, Californios were exempt from this fee; in practice, they were bullied into paying it or leaving, just like all the other "Mexicans." By about 1854, when the gold rush had begun winding down, the new U.S. state of California had been utterly transformed, and the Californios who remained were, more than ever, strangers in a land that had once been home.

LAND OWNERSHIP AND THE LAW

The Treaty of Guadalupe Hidalgo promised that the United States would honor Spanish and Mexican land grants in the former Mexican lands. In reality, that promise was often broken. Through means both legal and violent, most Mexican Americans were effectively stripped of their lands.

Part of the problem was that some Mexican land claims were poorly documented, and often what constituted a legal claim in Mexican law often was not viewed the same way in U.S. courts. Even though one federal report in California in 1850 said that the Mexican grants were mostly "perfect titles" —or complete and indisputably legal under Mexican law— Spanish and Mexican land grants were frequently vast, and even when there were titles, the boundaries were often sketchy. The Pomona Valley of California, for example, was described as "the place being vacant which is known by the name of [Rancho] San José, distant some six leagues, more or less, from the Ex-Mission of San Gabriel, a map of which place we will lay before your Excellency as soon as possible." "More or less" and "as soon as possible" were good enough for officials in Mexico City when determining land rules for a frontier where land was abundant and settlement sparse. The same could not be said for American law courts trying to serve a growing horde of land-hungry citizens. Most of the claims in California did not even have the benefit of antiquity, since a majority were dated within the five years before the American takeover.

Anglo-American settlers did not wait for the courts to resolve the matter. They simply squatted on the disputed land and waited for it to be decreed public, as they assumed it would. In many cases the courts did rule this way, throwing out titles as imperfect or fraudulent, in accordance with the California Land Settlement Act of 1851. This act required all Spanish or Mexican land claims to be submitted to a special land commission within two years; claimants' failure to do so would result in forfeiture. The California Supreme Court, in *Minturn v. Brower* (1864), later ruled that a perfect land grant was not subject to forfeiture under this provision, but the United States Supreme Court reversed that decision and upheld the validity of the 1851 law in *Botiller v. Dominguez* (1889).

Out of 813 Spanish and Mexican claims made to the land commission, 604 were upheld and 209 rejected. But because of the costs of litigation, many Mexican Americans were compelled to sell their land to pay debts. A lengthy appeals process, open to both the claimant and the United States, allowed the cases to drag on for an average of 17 years; consequently, payments to lawyers often bankrupted the claimant. If a claimant was short on cash, he might have to promise the disputed land to the lawyer, who ended up being the beneficiary when the title was upheld. Even if a Mexican American prevailed in court and was able to keep his land, he might find himself in a battle with squatters, who sometimes resorted to rioting to keep what they considered their homes.

In New Mexico, many Mexican Americans lost their land through the slowness of the Office of Surveyor General. Established in 1854 to settle land disputes over Mexican and Spanish grants, it did not make its last decisions until five decades later, by which time most Nuevomexicanos had lost their land in one way or another, often in payments to lawyers. About 80 percent of Spanish and Mexican land grants in New Mexico ultimately passed to Anglo-American lawyers and settlers. Most vulnerable was community land, territory held in common for grazing by a whole community's livestock. This was easily confiscated, because the U.S. legal system did not recognize the Spanish and Mexican concept of community ownership.

In 1781, a group of 44 Spanish, Filipino, Native American and African settlers founded Los Angeles, naming it "El Pueblo de Nuestra Señora la Reina de los Ángeles del Río de Porciúncula" ("The Town of Our Lady the Queen of the Angels on the River Porciúncula"). By 1820 the population had reached about 650 residents, spread out over a number of vast estates. When Mexican rule ended in 1847, and the Mexican government ceded Alta California and other territories to the United States, many of the old Spanish and Mexican ranches were lost to Anglo land speculators.

PROPERTY LAW AND MEXICAN AMERICANS:
Selected Court Cases and Legal Precedents, 1829–1889

According to the Treaty of Guadalupe Hidalgo, Mexicans in the conquered Southwest were "[to] be incorporated into the union of the United States and admitted as soon as possible . . . to the enjoyment of all rights of citizens of the United States. In the meantime, they shall be maintained and protected in the enjoyment of their liberty, their property, and civil rights now vested in them according to the Mexican laws." Unfortunately, the United States did not live up to these assurances. After gold was discovered in California in 1848, lawsuits were filed contesting ownership of Mexican lands. Although many Californios had owned land since the Spanish colonial era, numerous boundaries established by original Spanish land grants were vague. As thousands of Anglos poured into the Southwest, Mexicans found themselves no longer welcome. This seizure of their lands was enforced both by violence and by a series of court decisions and laws that served to legalize the denial of Mexican property rights.

Date	Case/Law	Description
1829	Foster v. Neilson	While Article VI, Clause 2 of the U.S. Constitution holds that all treaties should be considered the law of the land, it accords the same status to federal laws. In 1829, the U.S. Supreme Court took up a case involving a claim for property in present-day Louisiana under a land grant made by the king of Spain. According to the 1819 Treaty of Cession, which ceded the territory to the United States, all lands granted before a specified date "shall be ratified and confirmed by persons in possession of the lands, to the same extent that the same grants would be valid if the territories had remained under the dominion of his Catholic majesty." The Court ruled, however, that the treaty was no more than a promise of future legislative action by the U.S. government, and as such could not be considered a "self-executing treaty."
1833	United States v. Percheman	Four years later, the Court reversed itself, ruling that the 1819 treaty was "self-executing" based on a discovery that the Spanish version of the treaty should have been translated as land grants "shall remain ratified," instead of "shall be ratified." Nonetheless, the contradictory rulings left the enforceability of international treaties open to legislative challenge.
1851	The California Land Settlement Act	This congressional law was a major setback for Californios, who hoped that Guadalupe Hidalgo's promises of property protection would be enforced. The law set a two-year time limit for "each and every person claiming lands in California by virtue of any right or title derived from the Spanish or Mexican government" to submit claims to a special land commission. Any failure to do so would result in forfeiture of land to the U.S. government. During California's climate of gold rush fever, the commission's impulse was to open as much territory to prospectors as possible. In the end, out of 813 claims made to the commission, only 604 were confirmed.
1853	The Gadsden Treaty	In 1853, the United States pressured Mexico into selling part of present-day southern Arizona and New Mexico stretching along the Gila River from present-day Yuma to the Mesilla Valley in New Mexico. Anglo land speculators were interested in the land as a possible route for the Transcontinental Railroad. Many Mexicans, a number of whom had recently relocated to the region after being forced from their lands immediately after the Treaty of Guadalupe Hidalgo was signed, felt again betrayed by Mexico; others took the Mexican government's offer of financial assistance for relocating to Mexico. While the Gadsden Treaty promised the same land protections as the Treaty of Guadalupe Hidalgo had, Mexicans who stayed faced increasing oppression.
1854	Act of July 22, 1854	This congressional act created an office of the surveyor general to settle disputes over Mexican and Spanish land grants in New Mexico Territory. However, it would take that office 50 years to settle just a handful of claims. Before that could happen, many Nuevomexicanos were cheated out of their land.
1862	The Homestead Act	In 1862, Congress passed this act, granting 160 acres of land to any U.S. citizen over 21 years old who was a family head. The act was meant to encourage settlement of unoccupied lands on the western frontier, but it resulted in a flood of Anglo settlers seizing not only Native American lands but Mexican-American lands as well.

Date	Case/Law	Description
1864	*Minturn v. Brower*	The California Supreme Court held that a perfect land grant ("perfect" meaning complete and indisputably legal under Mexican law) was not subject to forfeiture, even if a claimant failed to submit the grant before the land commission as required by California Land Settlement Act of 1851. In reaching this decision, the court distiguished between perfect and imperfect grants, declaring that imperfect grants needed to be confirmed by the U.S. government. Nonetheless, *Minturn v. Brower*'s exemption of perfect titles from the Land Act requirement bolstered the 1833 precedent stating that international treaties such as Guadalupe Hidalgo were "self-executing," or enforceable on their own, and not dependent on subsequent legislation.
1889	*Botiller v. Dominguez*	In *Botiller v. Dominguez*, a Mexican land grantee sought to eject Anglos from his lands. The Anglos claimed the property under the terms of the Homestead Act of 1862. Although the plaintiff's grant was perfect and complete according to Mexican law, it had not been reviewed by the land commission. The U.S. Supreme Court reversed the California court's Minturn v. Brower decision, ruling that regardless of a grant's legality according to Mexican law, the U.S. Congress was within its rights to seize Mexican titles according to the terms set out in the California Land Settlement Act of 1851.

In the formerly disputed portion of Texas between the Nueces River and the Rio Grande, most Mexican and Spanish land claims were upheld, but Mexican Americans gradually lost their land in other ways, such as depression in livestock prices that forced them to sell to wealthy Anglos, or partitioning of land among heirs who then sold their shares to Anglos.

Although differing legal standards and changing interpretations of those standards ultimately deprived many Mexicans of their lands, at the heart of the conflict lay not just courtroom battles but battles over who was a foreigner and who was not. Despite their long history on the land, Californios, Nuevomexicanos, and Tejanos often found that their identities and rights as American citizens were defined by U.S. officials not so much by law as by race.

COOPERATION AND TENSION

Despite the disputes over land, there were many instances of cooperation and friendship between Mexican Americans and Anglo-Americans in the Southwest. The Anglo cowboys of the West adopted most of their cattle-herding techniques and equipment from Hispanic vaqueros, so much so that the Anglos in the early days were more likely to call themselves not cowboys but "white vaqueros," as distinct from "Mexican vaqueros." Anglo-

American miners in the gold rush learned much from Mexican-American miners, and Anglos and Hispanics often joined forces in fighting off the attacks of Native Americans, on whose land both were encroaching. Many Mexican Americans were politically active, working side by side with Anglos to achieve common political ends. But the winning of statewide office for Mexican Americans was rare. After the conquest in 1846, New Mexico did not have a Hispanic governor until 1897, when President William McKinley appointed Miguel A. Otero Jr. to the job.

Mexican Americans gradually adapted to the new Anglo culture, but they also kept alive their distinct identity. They continued to celebrate their own holidays, such as September 16, in honor of Father Hidalgo's 1810 Grito de Dolores, and celebrated common holidays in distinct ways, for example, staging pastorelas, or shepherds' plays, during the nine days before Christmas. At funciones, or public dances, they played Mexican music and ate pan dulce, or Mexican pastries. For those living near the Texas border with Mexico, the line between the countries was only a token boundary, often crossed to visit with family or conduct business.

Yet despite the efforts of many Hispanics and Anglos to live in peace together, there were also many instances of prejudice, hostility, and violence. Many Anglos shared the view that the chief Mexican-American characteristics were

THE DEATH OF JUANITA

Nowhere was Anglo contempt for Mexican-American life more visible than in the lynching of a Californio woman named Juanita by a mob of Anglo Forty-Niners in San Francisco on July 5, 1851. On July 4 the Anglos had assembled to hear a patriotic oration by U.S. senator John B. Weller. Afterward they celebrated frontier-style, getting drunk and carousing. Early in the morning, an Anglo miner named Joseph Cannan broke down Juanita's door and tried, as she testified, to assault her. She killed him with a knife. His friends captured her and brought her to a vigilante "trial," where the mob convicted her of murder and sentenced her to hanging. Juanita asserted that, given the same chance, she would defend herself again in exactly the same way. Then she adjusted her own noose and died. An observer, David P. Barstow, reported that the only murder in this incident was the hanging: "No jury in the world, on any principle of self-defense or protection of life and property, would ever have convicted her."

JOAQUÍN MURIETA

Many legends have circulated regarding the exploits of a Mexican bandit named Joaquín Murieta. While details of Murieta's life are sketchy, it is known that in 1853, the California legislature hired a former Texas Ranger named Harry Love to organize a posse and track down five Mexican desperadoes, apparently all of whom were named Joaquín.

When Love and his men found a group of Mexican outlaws hiding out in Tulare County, California, they killed the leader and one of his men. As proof of their achievement, Love's posse cut off the head of the supposed leader, placed it in a whiskey jar and sent it to the legislature with a demand for a reward. Along with it, they sent the hand of the other man, who they claimed was an associate of Joaquín Murieta named Three Fingered Jack.

The famous head and hand were displayed all around California mining camps and towns for many years, even though many questioned whether they had come from the real Murieta.

When John Rollin Ridge, who was part Cherokee, wrote a fictional account of Murieta's life in 1854, he wrote that Murieta had turned to crime as revenge after his brother was shot and his wife raped. Ridge's novel became so popular that in time it became accepted as truth. The mystery surrounding the real Joaquín only added to the legend's allure.

Now I go out onto roads
To kill Americans
You were the cause
Of my brother's death
You took him defenseless
You disgraceful American
From the rich and the greedy
I took their money
To the humble and poor
I tipped my hat
Oh, what unjust laws
I'm going to become a bandit

—From *The Life and Adventures of Joaquín Murieta*
by John Rollin Ridge

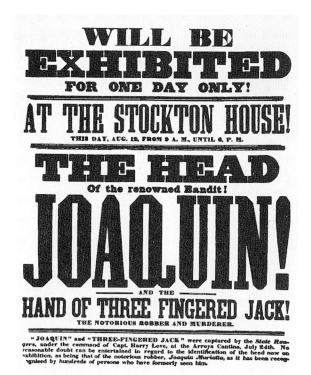

A traveling exhibition featuring a head reputed to be Murieta's toured California in the 1850s. (Dover Publications)

Joaquín Murieta
(Dover Publications)

"ignorance, indolence and cowardice," as one Texan rancher put it. An Anglo visitor to California in the early 1840s called Californios "an imbecile, pusillanimous [cowardly], race of men." Anglos were especially prejudiced toward lower-class, dark-skinned Hispanics. A titled ranchero of the Tejano elite might be accepted socially, but not the poor ranch hand with Native American features.

Prejudice showed itself in many ways. After Texas was annexed in 1845, efforts were made to deny Tejanos their voting rights, through such means as poll taxes and literacy tests. Intimidation of Tejanos was rampant, notably in the Cart War of 1857, when Anglo ruffians tried unsuccessfully to muscle Mexican-American carters, or wagon drivers, out of business, with 75 people killed in the conflict.

With prejudice came a lower value on Mexican-American life. Many Anglos thought it no crime to kill a Mexican, as suggested by a racist joke about the notorious Anglo-American Texan bad man, King Fisher. According to the story, a boy once asked King Fisher how many men he had killed. The outlaw answered, "Seven—just seven." The boy said, disappointed, "Oh, I thought that it must be more than that." King Fisher replied, "I don't count Mexicans."

The prevalence of crime in some places did not help matters. In Texas, border communities were plagued by bandits from Mexico. Even though Mexican Americans suffered from these attacks as well, and even though some of the worst rustlers were Anglo cowboys raiding Tejano ranches, Anglos were inclined to lump all Hispanics together as bandidos, or bandits. Said one Anglo settler in Texas in 1858: "The population of [Cameron] county is about 7,000 no less than 6,000 of which is Mexican of which 5,000 may be recorded as theives [sic]."

The most notorious Anglo group charged with combatting thievery—and one particularly feared by Mexicans and Mexican Americans alike—was the Texas Rangers. The Rangers were an Anglo law enforcement corps organized in 1835 during the Texan independence movement. Originally formed to patrol the disputed frontier against invasion by the Mexican Army as well as against attacks by the Comanche and Apache, the Rangers soon turned their attention to Mexican banditry. In 1842, for example, legendary Ranger William "Bigfoot" Wallace became a folk hero among Texan Anglos and a feared villain among Tejanos when he killed a Mexican horse thief. During the U.S.-Mexican War, Rangers led the U.S. Army into Mexico, operating as both cavalrymen and scouts. When one Ranger was killed in Mexico City sometime after that city's capture, Rangers rampaged through the Mexican capital, slaughtering more than 80 people. During the U.S. Civil War, the Texas Rangers joined the Confederate Army, and although they temporarily disbanded after the war, they re-formed after the end of Reconstruction as an independent law enforcement organization. The brutality of the Rangers was legendary. They once tracked and killed 76 Comanche warriors, stole their horses, and then destroyed all of the food stored by surviving Comanche villagers. It was through episodes such as this one that Mexican Americans came to regard the Rangers as los tejanos diablos, the Texan devils.

Fighting Back

Mexican Americans struggled to maintain their dignity and rights in various legal ways: through the courts, through politics, and through the press. One of the earliest newspapers in Los Angeles was El Clamor Publico, or "The Public Cry" (1855–1859), a Spanish-language weekly founded by an enterprising 17-year-old, Francisco Ramirez. The paper urged better treatment of Hispanic Americans and recommended their emigration to Sonora, Mexico, where its editor eventually went himself. Other Mexican Americans took to violent means, in the form of banditry mixed with social revolution. These were the desperadoes, from the Spanish word desesperadoes, "desperate men." They included Juan Cortina in Texas and Joaquín Murieta, Juan Flores, and Tiburcio Vásquez in California.

These men were known for robbing, rustling cattle, stealing horses, killing, and rampaging. Rich Mexican Americans feared them, as did rich Anglos. But the poor Mexican Americans of the countryside saw them as Robin Hood–like heroes, giving them shelter from the law and celebrating their feats. At least they viewed the desperadoes as heroes in retrospect, as legends grew up around the bandits. With these men, as with so many western heroes and outlaws, it is almost impossible to sort out legend from fact.

Of the "superbandit" Joaquín Murieta, little can be established clearly beyond his death. In 1853, at the behest of the California state legislature, former Texas Ranger Harry S. Love tracked down a man presumed to be Murieta and not only killed him but cut off his head and put it in a whiskey jar as proof of his accomplishment.

The stories of the desperadoes were laced with Mexican-American protest against the new Anglo order. Juan Flores, said to be "uncannily clever with the knife" during the 1850s, when he terrorized the Los Angeles area, was linked to what the locals called the "Juan Flores Revolution." The exploits of Tiburcio

Vásquez, born in Monterey in 1835, were also tied to the anger of Mexican Americans at Anglo abuses. He claimed to have developed a "spirit of hatred and revenge" as a teenager, when he saw Anglos push their way into Californio parties and force Mexican-American women to dance with them. Said Vasquez, "Given $60,000, I would be able to recruit enough arms and men to revolutionize Southern California." In fact, he seems to have devoted his life not to organizing revolt but to stealing livestock and robbing stores and stagecoaches.

Accounts vary of how outlaw Juan Nepomuceno Cortina, known as "Cheno," began his career, but many trace it back to an incident in Brownsville, Texas, in the summer of 1859, when Cortina saw an Anglo marshal pistol-whip a Mexican-American laborer. Outraged, Cortina shot the lawman and gathered a group of raiders who attacked Brownsville in September, killing several Anglos. His rebellion grew as he organized to defend Tejano rights at a time when his people had become, according to Cortina, "strangers in their own country." Cortina called on Mexican Americans "to mak[e] use of the sacred right of self-preservation...because the supremacy of the law has failed to accomplish its object."

In 1860 U.S. troops forced Cortina and his followers to retreat across the Mexican border, but Cortina carried on sporadic raids for the next two decades, ever eluding Anglo pursuit even as he gained political power in Mexico. His legend grew larger than life: the mere rumor of his presence sent Texas towns into panic, and he was blamed for nearly every cattle theft along the border. His career ended in 1875 when, at the request of the United States, Mexican president Porfirio Díaz at last put him in prison.

By the 1870s, posses, soldiers, vigilantes, and old age had hunted down most of the Mexican desperadoes. But they survive in legend as memorials of a time of lawlessness, bigotry, and rage at social injustice.

CHAPTER 5

A TIME OF TRANSITION

The outcome of the U.S.-Mexican War brought the United States its first large population of Hispanic Americans. But there had already been some people of Hispanic descent in the country—immigrants from Spain and Hispanic America—and more would follow in the second half of the 19th century. Near the end of the century, in 1898, another large Hispanic population entered the United States: the people of Puerto Rico, which became an American possession in that year's Spanish-American War. The war also brought Cuba under American hegemony, preparing the way for a century in which the destinies of Cuba and the United States were interwoven.

HISPANIC AMERICANS AND THE CIVIL WAR

In the American Civil War (1861–1865), the northern states (the Union) forced the secessionist southern states (the Confederacy) to return to the Union and accept abolition of slavery. The bitter conflict cost more than 500,000 American lives, more than any other American war. It resulted in part from disagreement about the lands gained during the U.S.-Mexican War. The issue of whether the territories acquired from Mexico should be slave or free sharply divided North and South and contributed to the South's decision to secede.

Soldiers and Spies

The best known Hispanic-American participant in the Civil War is one whom many people are surprised to learn was of Spanish descent: Union naval officer David Glasgow Farragut (1801–1870), the son of Spanish Minorcan immigrant Jorge Farragut, a war hero in his own right. In the U.S. Navy since joining as a midshipman at age nine, David Farragut served in the War of 1812 while still a boy

and participated in the blockade of Mexico during the U.S.-Mexican War. He founded the Mare Island Navy Yard near San Francisco in 1854. Though his home was in Virginia, he backed the Union when Virginia seceded. In 1862 he received command of the West Gulf Blockading Squadron, with orders to capture New Orleans, which he did on April 25. The victory won him promotion to rear admiral and led to more action, most memorably the Battle of Mobile Bay, Alabama, in August 1864.

His objective in that battle was to capture the port of Mobile, but to do so he had to bypass underwater mines, called torpedoes, that blocked the entrance to Mobile Bay. One Union ship had already been sunk by a torpedo, but Farragut led the rest of the fleet through the mined waters, reportedly calling, "Damn the torpedoes—full speed ahead!" The ships got through and Farragut captured Mobile. For his daring victory, he was made the first admiral of the United States in 1866. As commander of the European Squadron after the war, he was later honored with a hero's welcome when he visited his father's birthplace at Ciudadela, Minorca.

Other Hispanic Americans joined Farragut in defending the Union. Two of them, navy seamen, were the first Hispanic-American recipients of the Medal of Honor (also called the Congressional Medal of Honor), the nation's highest military award, first awarded in 1863 to recognize uncommon valor. One of the two was Chilean-born Philip Bazaar, who distinguished himself in the assault on Fort Fisher, North Carolina, in 1865; the other was Spanish-born John Ortega, who saw action aboard the USS Saratoga. In the ensuing years, dozens of other Hispanic Americans would also receive the Medal of Honor.

During the Civil War, some of New York City's Spanish Americans participated in the Garibaldi Guard, also known as the 39th New York Infantry. This polyglot regiment contained volunteers of many ethnicities—Italian, Spanish, German, Hungarian, Swiss, and French—and

IN HIS FATHER'S FOOTSTEPS

David Farragut (Library of Congress)

David Farragut followed in the military tradition of his father, Jorge (or George) Farragut. The elder Farragut had come to North America in the 1770s from Minorca, a once-Spanish colony that then belonged to Britain. During the American Revolution, Jorge Farragut joined the South Carolina Navy as a lieutenant and fought the British at Savannah (1779) and in the second defense of Charleston (1780). Jorge Farragut also participated in the War of 1812.

Jorge Farragut was part of the small community of Hispanic Americans who lived in the Thirteen Colonies prior to the Revolution. That community also included Hispanic Jews who settled in the Dutch colony of New Amsterdam, the future New York, as early as 1654.

fought at Gettysburg (1863) and Petersburg (1864–1865).

Some Hispanic Americans fought on the Confederate side. Hispanic Americans were concentrated in states and territories that had formerly belonged to Spain—states and territories that now, due to their southern location, were predisposed to join the Confederacy. Of these, the states of Florida, Louisiana, and Texas all became Confederate, while the new state of California and New Mexico Territory stayed in the Union. Hispanic Americans in these regions were divided, some joining the Union, some the Confederacy. In Texas, an estimated 2,250 Tejano soldiers fought for the Confederate army, and 950 for the Union Army.

The highest-ranking Mexican American serving in the Confederate army was Col. Santos Benavides, who commanded the regiment that defended Laredo, Texas, during the war and drove Union forces back from Brownsville in 1864. Tejanos also served in the Confederate cavalry. The 10th Texas Cavalry, commanded by Major Leonides M. Martín, a Tejano, was also notable for its large number of Hispanic members.

The Civil War in the Southwest

Though remote from the Union and Confederate capitals, the New Mexico Territory became the focus of intense fighting in the early part of the Civil War. Right on the border of the Confederate state of Texas, New Mexico was seen as a gateway through which the Confederacy could expand westward to Colorado and

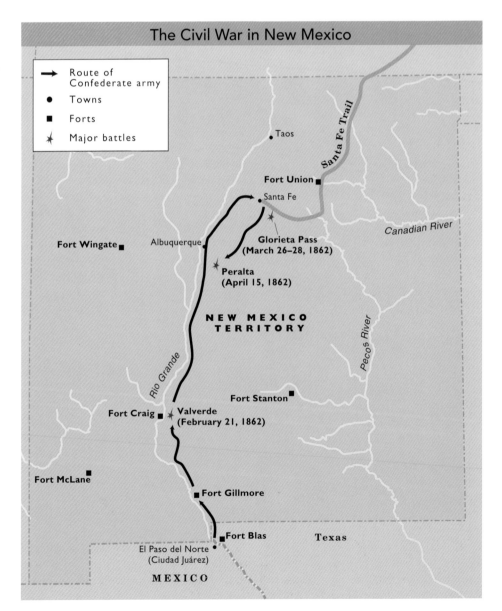

The Civil War in New Mexico

→ Route of Confederate army
● Towns
■ Forts
✦ Major battles

Santa Fe Trail

● Taos

■ Fort Union

● Santa Fe

Canadian River

■ Fort Wingate
Albuquerque

✦ Glorieta Pass
(March 26–28, 1862)

✦ Peralta
(April 15, 1862)

NEW MEXICO TERRITORY

Rio Grande

Pecos River

■ Fort Stanton

Fort Craig ■ ✦ Valverde
(February 21, 1862)

■ Fort McLane

■ Fort Gillmore

■ Fort Blas   **Texas**

El Paso del Norte ●
(Ciudad Juárez)

MEXICO

California. Wealthy rancheros in New Mexico had cause to be sympathize with Confederate plantation owners since they shared similar concerns in operating rural, agricultural businesses. But overpowering that sentiment was suspicion of Texas, which had a history of trying (and failing) to conquer New Mexico, dating back to the 1841 Santa Fe Expedition.

In July 1861 a Texan force crossed the western border and captured what is now southern New Mexico, claiming that region and Arizona as Confederate territory. The Confederates went on to capture Albuquerque and Santa Fe in 1862. Their victory was short-lived, however. At the Battle of Glorieta Pass that spring, in a clash sometimes known as the Gettysburg of the West, Union soldiers destroyed the Confederate supply train and forced the Confederates to withdraw from New Mexico Territory. Nuevomexicanos who fought for the Union in that battle included Lieutenant Colonel Manuel Chaves and other members of the New Mexico Volunteers, a predominantly Hispanic unit. Among the other Hispanic-American soldiers who served with the Union army in the West, patrolling the borders and skirmishing with Confederates, was Major Salvador Vallejo, an officer in a California unit, and Miguel E. Pino and Roman Anthony Baca of the New Mexico Volunteers.

Manuel Chaves (Library of Congress)

The American Civil War had one other major impact on Nuevomexicanos. During the war, what had been a single territory was divided into two separate entities. In 1863 the Union organized the Arizona Territory out of the western portion of what had been New Mexico

A WOMAN IN BATTLE

Among the more unusual Hispanic Americans to have served the Confederacy was Loreta Janeta Velasquez. According to her 1876 memoir *The Woman in Battle*, this intrepid Latina took on male garb as Lieutenant Harry Buford, in which guise she fought valiantly at the First Battle of Bull Run (1861) and the Battle of Shiloh (1862). By her account, she also raised a battalion in Arkansas; served as a spy and blockade runner; met Union president Abraham Lincoln and Confederate president Jefferson Davis; and had a chance to shoot Union general Ulysses S. Grant from a concealed position but decided against it because it would have been "too much like murder." Both contemporaries and later historians have cast doubt on her stories, which have little corroborating evidence. But she remains a colorful character in the annals of Hispanic-American military lore.

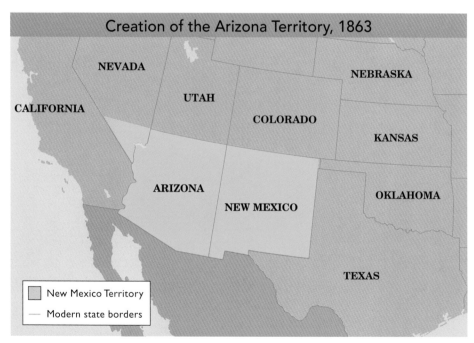

In 1863, New Mexico Territory was divided into separate territories. Most of the western half became Arizona Territory. Another portion later became part of southern Nevada. Both New Mexico and Arizona entered the Union in 1912.

Emperor Maximilian of Mexico
(Library of Congress)

Territory, leaving New Mexico with its present-day borders. The two southwestern territories would join the union as states a half-century later, in 1912.

Cinco de Mayo

With the United States distracted by the Civil War, foreign powers were emboldened to intervene in Hispanic America in defiance of the Monroe Doctrine. Spain regained possession of the Dominican Republic in 1861, holding it until 1865, when a combination of popular rebellion and U.S. intervention forced Spain to give up the territory again. In 1861 the liberal government of Mexican president Benito Juárez (1806–1872) suspended payments on foreign loans, prompting France, Spain, and Great Britain to send troops to Veracruz in pursuance of their claims. Mexico reached a settlement with Great Britain and Spain, both of which withdrew their troops in 1862. But the forces of French emperor Napoleon III (Louis-Napoléon) remained, in what became known as the Mexican-French War of 1861–1867.

With the support of Mexican conservatives, Napoleon planned to establish a puppet monarch in Mexico, one who would be subservient to France. With that end in view, French forces marched from Veracruz toward Mexico City. They were temporarily stopped at the Battle of Puebla on May 5, 1862, the date that became known as Cinco de Mayo (Fifth of May). In that battle, Mexicans under General Ignacio Zaragoza and Brigadier General Porfirio Díaz routed the French, forcing a long delay in their advance while reinforcements came from France.

The following year, a greatly expanded French army captured Puebla and Mexico City. In 1864, Maximilian, archduke of Austria, was installed in Mexico City as emperor of Mexico. Based as it

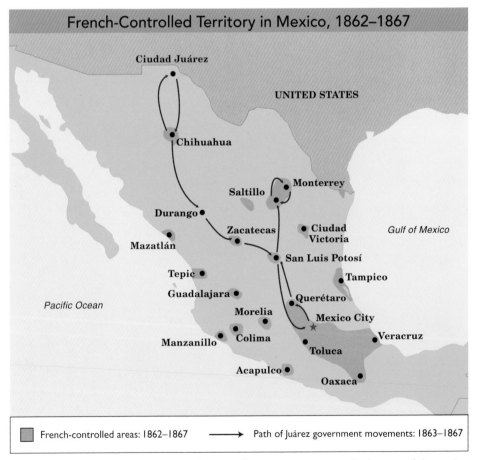

Between the years 1862 and 1867, the French government controlled many of the major cities in Mexico. In 1864, France installed the Austrian prince Ferdinand Maximilian to rule as Emperor Maximilian I. His reign was short-lived, however, as the forces of Mexico's liberal president Benito Juárez finally retook control of the country in 1867 after France withdrew its military support for Maximilian.

A Cinco de Mayo parade in Mogollon, New Mexico, in 1914. (Library of Congress)

was on the continuing presence of French troops, Maximilian's empire was short-lived. As soon as the Civil War was over, the United States, which had never recognized the empire, pressured France to withdraw from Mexico and permitted surplus U.S. munitions to flow to Mexican rebels. France bowed to U.S. pressure and to other considerations (such as the looming threat from its rising European neighbor Prussia) and withdrew its forces in 1866–1867.

As the French withdrew, the forces of president-in-exile Juárez reconquered the country, aided by 3,000 discharged Union veterans. The imperial side was aided by 2,000 Confederate veterans, but their support was not enough. In 1867 Maximilian was court-martialed and shot, and Juárez was reelected president. He died in 1872 during an uprising by the hero of Cinco de Mayo, Díaz, who went on to rule Mexico as a virtual dictator for much of the period 1876–1911.

Cinco de Mayo remains a major holiday for people of Mexican descent, celebrated as a festival in Los Angeles and other cities with large Mexican-American populations.

came from Spain, Cuba, Puerto Rico, and Mexico, among other points of origin. Their numbers at this time were small in comparison with the flood of non-Hispanic immigrants. Immigrants from Spain numbered in the tens of thousands, while immigrants from Germany, Ireland,

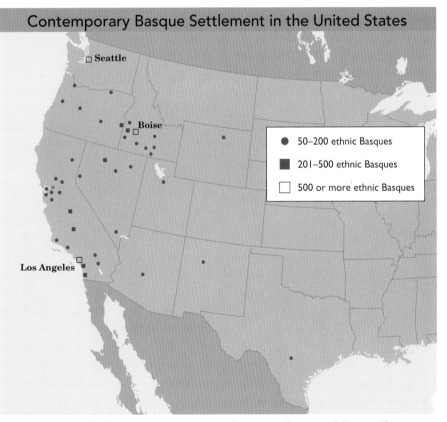

The map above highlights major Basque settlement in the United States. The vast majority of Basque Americans live in the western United States. Miami and New York City, neither of which is shown above, are the only cities in the eastern United States with Basque populations numbering as many as 50 persons.

NEW FACES, OLD CONFLICTS

The 19th century saw a great tide of immigration to the United States, and Hispanics were part of that tide. They

"In choosing sheepherders, the best will be found among the Mexicans, Basques, or Portuguese. These latter two do not, as a rule, take service except with their own people: their aim is ultimately to possess a share in the herds, and to rise to the position of owners."

—Major W. Shepherd, *Prairie Experiences in the Handling of Cattle and Sheep*, 1885

and Italy each numbered in the millions. It was not until the 20th century that the number of Hispanic immigrants climbed into the millions as well. Nevertheless, Hispanic newcomers formed part of the quilt of ethnic groups that marked late 19th-century America.

IMMIGRATION FROM SPAIN

The late 19th century was a time of turmoil in Spain. In 1868 a revolution deposed Isabella II (1830–1904; reigned 1833–1868), who had succeeded her father Ferdinand VII. During the six years that followed, Spain was ruled successively by a regent, an elected monarch, three presidents, and a prime minister. Civil war, political unrest, and economic depression plagued the nation. Not until 1874 was a relatively enduring regime instituted, when the Bourbon monarchy was restored with Isabella's son, Alfonso XII (1857–1885; reigned 1874–1885), as king.

In the face of such instability, some Spanish people did see fit to emigrate, but relatively few came to the United States. Most emigrants settled in the remaining Spanish colonies (Cuba and Puerto Rico) or Hispanic-American countries, where the language and cultural barriers were smaller. Still, immigration to the United States from Spain did increase at the turn of the century, reaching 8,731 during 1891–1900 and 27,935 during 1901–1910.

Among the Spanish newcomers were the Basques. In a sense, these people were not Hispanic, because their native language was not Spanish but Euskera, a language believed to be unrelated to other European languages. As speakers of Euskera, Basques call themselves Euskaldunaks. They are probably the oldest ethnic group in Europe, having preserved their distinct cultural identity from antiquity to the present. They have a long history of valiantly defending the autonomy of their homeland in north central Spain and southwestern France. Despite the autonomous culture of the Basques, their destiny has long been intertwined with that of Spain. Basques first came to the New World with the Spanish conquistadores and they have contributed to Spanish history such famous figures as St. Ignatius of Loyola (1491–1556), founder of the Jesuits, a Roman Catholic order.

Basques enjoyed autonomy in Spain from the time of Ferdinand and Isabella to 1876, when the Spanish Basque provinces were absorbed by the crown. Many Basques then emigrated to the United States, settling mainly in the West, particularly Nevada, Idaho, Oregon, California, and Wyoming. Skilled shepherds, they flourished in the sheepherding industry and enriched the region's culture with such traditions as the Basque festivals still held in Reno and Elko, Nevada. The Idaho Basque Museum and Cultural Center in Boise commemorates Basque contributions. One of the best-known Basque contributions is the game jai alai, imported into Cuba about 1900 and imported from there to the United States in the 1920s.

IMMIGRATION FROM CUBA

In the late 19th century, the last vestiges of Spain's once mighty American empire were Cuba and Puerto Rico. Both of these Caribbean islands were rocked by independence struggles and economic hardship during this period, prompting their residents to leave them for the United States.

In Cuba the most significant conflict before the Spanish-American War in 1898 was the Ten Years' War (1868–1878), which began shortly after the revolution in Spain that deposed Isabella II. For much of the 19th century, Cubans had been demanding increased political power, abolition of slavery, tariff reform, and equal rights for Creoles and peninsulares; Spain had responded by increasing repression, banning political meetings, and raising taxes.

On October 10, 1868, Cuban rebels under Carlos Manuel de Céspedes (1819–1874) declared independence in the town of Yara, in what became known as El Grito de Yara, "The Cry of Yara." During the ensuing Ten Years' War, about 200,000 people died as rebels waged guerrilla warfare and Spanish troops harshly counterattacked. The Treaty of El Zanjón ended the war in 1878, promising abolition of slavery and other reforms. (A much shorter conflict, the Guerra Chiquita, or "Little War," of 1879–1880, followed but was no more successful in gaining independence.)

Slavery was abolished in 1886, but other promises were never fully kept. A

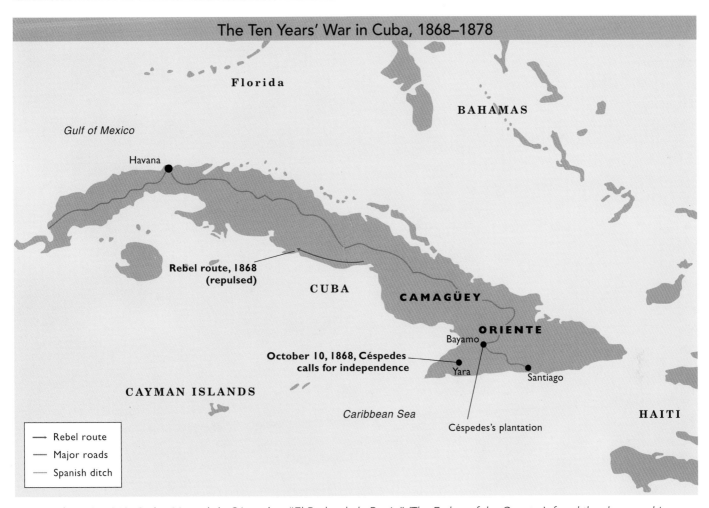

The Ten Years' War in Cuba, 1868–1878

Florida

BAHAMAS

Gulf of Mexico

Havana

Rebel route, 1868 (repulsed)

CUBA

CAMAGÜEY

ORIENTE

Bayamo

October 10, 1868, Céspedes calls for independence

Yara

Santiago

CAYMAN ISLANDS

Caribbean Sea

Céspedes's plantation

HAITI

— Rebel route
— Major roads
— Spanish ditch

On October 10, 1868, Carlos Manuel de Céspedes, "El Padre de la Patria" (The Father of the Country), freed the slaves on his plantation at Bayamo—an act of sedition against Spain that led to an armed revolt. In the resulting Ten Years' War, Céspedes proclaimed Cuba's independence and was named president by the rebels. The Spanish managed to confine the revolt to the eastern provinces of Camagüey and Oriente by building a fortified trench the width of the island. Dissension among the rebels led to Céspedes's dismissal in 1873, and the war ended in truce in 1878. Although the war did not win independence for Cuba, it did lead to the abolition of slavery in Cuba in 1886.

severe economic depression in the mid-1880s compounded Cuban woes. Jobs were scarce, and abolition of slavery meant that 200,000 former slaves were now competing for existing jobs. Under these conditions, thousands of Cubans immigrated to the United States. Some came as revolutionary exiles, regrouping and planning for the next war of independence—one they hoped would be successful; some came mainly in search of work. Cuban émigrés traveled as far as New York City, but most settled in Florida, where the climate was similar to home and the proximity to Cuba afforded an ideal launching ground for revolution. Cuban immigrants settled in many parts of Florida: Key West, Jacksonville, St. Augustine, the Martí City quarter of Ocala, and Tampa. But they made their greatest mark at this time in the district of Tampa known as Ybor City.

Ybor City was a company town named for Vicente Martínez Ybor, who founded it and built the first cigar factory in the Tampa area in 1886. Within a decade, more than a hundred cigar factories had been constructed in the vicinity. Cigar making was a traditional Cuban art, one that dated back to the island's pre-Columbian Taino and Ciboney inhabitants. Under Spanish rule, Cuba's cigar makers had established a worldwide reputation for excellence. In Ybor City, incorporated into Tampa in 1887, they established a new center of cigar-making prestige.

Known as the Havana of America, Ybor City in the late 19th century became a place of Cuban social clubs and cafés, Spanish-language newspapers, and grocery stores called bodegas that catered to Caribbean tastes. Its factories maintained

"I arrived in Ybor City in the middle of a torrential rain storm. The streets were paved with mud—not gold. All I remember was the mud, the heat, and the mosquitos. And that night, my first night in Tampa, I vowed I would return to Cuba within the year."

—José de la Cruz, Cuban immigrant to Ybor City, Florida, where he worked as a lector in a cigar factory

Vincente Ybor's cigar factory (National Park Service)

CUBA LIBRE

Viva Cuba Libre!, or "Long Live Free Cuba," was the slogan of late 19th-century revolutionaries fighting for an independent Cuba. The phrase "Cuba libre" is best known today to Americans as the name of a cocktail consisting of one part rum, two parts Coca-Cola, and lime juice or a slice of lime (often just called a rum and Coke). That formula says something about the process by which Cuba became a nation. Rum, the Cuban national beverage, represents the efforts of Cuban patriots to achieve independence; Coca-Cola, the archetypal American soft drink, represents American involvement in that struggle and also the domination of Cuba by the United States once independence was achieved.

Cuban traditions, like a flexible work schedule and an unlimited personal supply of cigars. One distinctive custom was la lectura, in which a lector, or reader, sat on a scaffold above the workers and read aloud in Spanish from newspapers and books while they rolled cigars. Workers customarily chose the readers and the materials they read. Attempts to curtail these amenities were regularly thwarted by strikes.

While busy earning a living in the United States, Cubans did not forget the cause of Cuban independence. The most prominent voice in that movement became José Martí (1853–1895), who lived in the United States from 1881 to 1895, after his revolutionary activities in Cuba forced him into exile. Most of his time was spent in New York City, though he also visited Cuban émigré communities in Florida.

A renowned poet as well as patriot, Martí supported himself in the United States through journalism and employment as a consul for Uruguay and Argentina. Meanwhile, he founded and led the Cuban Revolutionary Party, publishing hundreds of essays in his party's journal, Patria, and in periodicals from the New York Times to La Nacíon of Buenos Aires. He spoke at innumerable gatherings, raised funds for the cause, and argued that Cuba should be free not only from Spain but from racism, political

oppression, and economic exploitation. Martí's revolutionary work reached its climax in 1895, when he returned to Cuba for the Cuban War of Independence.

IMMIGRATION FROM PUERTO RICO

In the late 19th century, the people of Puerto Rico, like the people of Cuba, began to push hard for independence from Spain. On the night of September 23, 1868, Puerto Rican patriots armed with machetes, knives, and guns marched into the western city of Lares, captured it, and declared Puerto Rico independent. Their victory was short-lived, however. Spanish troops soon crushed the revolt, which came to be known as El Grito de Lares, "The Cry of Lares." The episode is not forgotten. Puerto Ricans still celebrate it on September 24 as a holiday.

During these years, some Puerto Rican patriots were forced into exile in the United States, where they continued to work for their island's independence. New York City was a center for these émigrés, among them physician Ramón Emeterio Betances, a strong advocate dfor abolition of slavery, freedom of speech, and freedom of religion. Another was the journalist Francisco Gonzalo "Pachin" Marín, publisher of the revolutionary newspaper El Postillón, who moved to New York in

1896. In 1898 Eugenio María de Hostos founded the League of Patriots in New York City. Other Puerto Rican patriots in New York City included Luis Muñoz Rivera, who helped persuade Spain to grant a measure of autonomy to Puerto Rico in 1897, and Santiago Iglesias Pantín, the father of Puerto Rico's labor movement. Despite the presence of these exiles, however, the Puerto Rican community in New York and elsewhere on the mainland United States would not achieve significant size until after the Spanish-American War made Puerto Rico an American possession.

CONFLICT IN NEW MEXICO AND THE SOUTHWEST

While Florida and New York played host to new groups of Hispanics, New Mexico continued to be the site of conflict between Anglo-Americans and the Mexican Americans whose ancestors had been there for centuries. In the decades after the Civil War, New Mexico became a dangerous and lawless place. Cattle ranchers, mostly Anglos arriving from Texas, competed for range space with mostly Hispanic sheepherders. Both kinds of ranchers competed with newly arrived homesteaders who came to New Mexico to plant farms. Nuevomexicanos cried injustice when communal village lands were claimed and divided up by what they viewed as Anglo land-grabbers. Meanwhile, Anglos and Hispanics alike fought wars with Native Americans, and desperadoes from better-policed western regions fled to the territory for fresh raiding.

Cycles of violence and retribution were rampant, as one group attacked another, prompting retaliatory counterat-

Mexican American Catholic church, in Deming, NM (Library of Congress)

tacks. In the 1870s the violence took the form of the Lincoln County War, a prolonged struggle between rival cattle interests and their armed henchmen. Most Mexican Americans sided with rancher John Chisum against his opponent Laurance Gustave Murphy, in a war that began with the murder of one of Chisum's associates, John H. Tunstall. The violence was marked by racial hatred on both sides. In one incident in Lincoln County, an Anglo gang led by cattle rustler John Selman shot down two Hispanic men and two Hispanic boys. Lincoln County's Mexican Americans were reportedly roused into planning revenge on "the first Americanos, in particular Tejanos, that came their way."

The Lincoln County War did not end until a new governor, General Lew Wallace, working with Mexican-American militia leader Juan Patrón, restored peace around the end of the decade. Patrón was later shot dead in a saloon by a cowboy some believed to have been hired by the Murphy gang.

Some Mexican Americans emerged from this period as folk heroes. In one incident in the 1880s, Nuevomexicano deputy sheriff Elfego Baca shot a Texan and was confronted by a lynch mob of Texans determined to exact "justice." Reportedly, Baca single-handedly held off the mob for three days, killing four and wounding several. He went on to become an influential New Mexican political leader.

Impressive as the gunfighting was, the real drama in post–Civil War New Mexico took place behind the scenes. There, an informal alliance took shape, linking a small group of Anglo bankers, businessmen, lawyers, and politicians to about 20 families of rich Hispanic Americans, or ricos. Known as the Santa Fe Ring, they conspired to buy up New Mexican land, using every political and legal means at their disposal. The ring controlled the governorship and most territory offices and was supported by the territory's most influential newspaper, the New Mexican. Through the Santa Fe Ring's machinations, many poor Nuevomexicanos were deprived of their lands. By 1894, one of the leaders of the Santa Fe Ring, lawyer Thomas B. Catron, held title to about 2 million acres. He later became one of New Mexico's first U.S. senators.

To counter the loss of land, Nuevo-mexicanos resorted to legal and illegal techniques of their own. Formed in the 1880s, Las Gorras Blancas, "The White Caps," were a group of armed horsemen in white masks and black coats who sabotaged the property of Anglo and rico landowners. Specifically, they cut apart the barbed-wire fencing and railroad ties that they considered to be intruding on common land. In the 1890s, they gradually disappeared as popular opinion turned against lawlessness and the governor threatened military action.

Legal means were also used to speak out for los pobres, or poor Nuevo-mexicanos. Voices that supported them in the 1890s included the Spanish-language newspaper *La Voz del Pueblo* (The Voice of the People), the early national trade union the Knights of Labor, and the political organization The United People's Party (El Partido). But the redistribution of land and power from Hispanic to Anglo continued largely unchecked.

A similar transition occurred in other formerly Mexican territories, including California, Texas, and Arizona. Mexican Americans everywhere faced prejudice and loss of economic and political power, and they fought back as best they could. In Santa Ana, California, in 1892, a lynch mob broke into jail and hanged Hispanic ranch worker Francisco Torres for having killed his Anglo foreman, despite the fact that Torres claimed to have acted in self-defense. In Arizona, Mexican-American mine workers were assigned the dirtiest work (called "Mexican work") and were paid half of what Anglo workers were paid. In Texas, Hispanic anger at Anglo injustice resulted in the El Paso Salt War of 1877. Salt beds that had been regarded as community property were claimed as private property by enterprising Anglos, who began to charge local pobres for the use of what they had previously enjoyed for free. Mexican Americans erupted in rioting, which was brutally suppressed when the governor brought in hired gunmen from New Mexico.

Despite the lawlessness and injustice Mexican Americans faced in the post–Civil War Southwest, the region increasingly became a magnet for

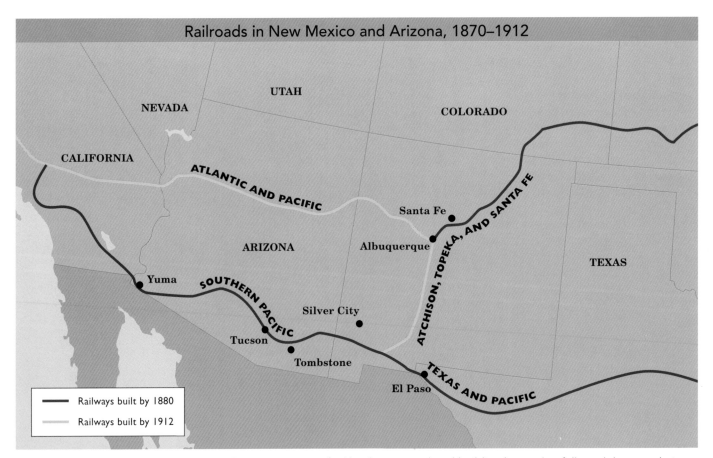

Struggles over land ownership in the Southwest were intensified by the great railroad building boom that followed the completion of the transcontinental railroad in the 1860s. The major railroads of that era are shown above.

During the 1880s, vigilante groups like that shown here roamed the Great Plains, Southwest, and elsewhere, cutting barbed wire and pulling up railroad ties. In New Mexico, a Hispanic group known as Las Gorras Blancas (The White Caps) were particularly active. (Nebraska Historical Society)

Mexicans south of the border. The railroad reached New Mexico in 1879 and Arizona in 1880, bringing new development and job opportunities. Railroad lines began connecting the region to Mexico in the 1880s, providing an easy immigration route out of Mexico. Under the dictator Porfirio Díaz, poverty and oppression were widespread in Mexico, encouraging Mexican workers to leave for the American Southwest, where there was high demand for laborers at ranches, railroads, mines, and farms. Mexican laborers were all the more valued after the Chinese Exclusion Act of 1882, enacted as a result of anti-Asian prejudice, halted the influx of what had been a larger number of Chinese workers. Thus Mexican immigration to the Southwest began to grow in the late 19th century—though not as much as it would in the century to come.

Partly because of Anglo-American prejudice against the Spanish-speaking population in the Southwest, New Mexico and Arizona were compelled to wait a long time before being accepted into the Union as states. In 1912, New Mexico and Arizona became, respectively, the 47th and 48th states.

WAR WITH SPAIN

As the 19th century drew to a close, Cuba's struggle for independence reached a boiling point. Cuba's struggle became bound up with expansionist sentiment in the United States, where some influential voices wanted Spain out of the hemisphere so the United States could take over its colonial role. While colonial expansion was the impetus, U.S. actions were justified by invoking the precedent of the Monroe Doctrine—the policy that European colonialism would not be tolerated in the Americas, and that the United States would ensure the independence of North, South, and Central America by force if necessary. It is ironic then that during the last years of the 19th century, the United States would go to war with Spain over this policy, not only in the Caribbean, but thousands of miles away in the Philippine Islands as well.

This propaganda cartoon urges the United States to come to the aid of Cuba against Spain. "Columbia," a female symbol of the United States, sleeps while a figure representing Spain dominates a Cuban. Looking on disapprovingly are statues of the Revolutionary-era generals Von Steuben from Prussia and Lafayette of France, who both came to the aide of the rebelling American colonies, represented here by a bust of George Washington

THE UNITED STATES LOOKS TO CUBA

Long before Spain and the United States went to war over Cuba, some Americans had looked with longing on the fertile, strategically located island just 90 miles from Key West, Florida. As early as 1809, Thomas Jefferson stated, "We must have Cuba." John Quincy Adams, who had engineered the annexation of Florida, viewed American annexation of "the pearl of the Antilles" as all but inevitable, writing as secretary of state in 1823:

> There are laws political as of physical gravitation, and if an apple, severed by a tempest from its native tree, cannot choose but to fall to the ground, Cuba, forcibly disjoined from its own natural connection to Spain, and incapable of self-support, can gravitate only towards the North American Union, which, by the same law of nature, cannot cast her off from her bosom.

In keeping with Adams's view, the United States repeatedly offered to buy Cuba from Spain. In 1848, in the heyday of Manifest Destiny, President James K. Polk offered $100 million for it. Spain adamantly turned down all such offers, viewing them as insults to national pride.

Even without American ownership of Cuba, the United States had tremendous leverage over Cuban affairs, since it was the chief market for Cuba's primary export, sugar; Cuba sold nearly 70 percent of its annual sugar crop to the United States. American influence became even stronger as American corporations bought up Cuba piecemeal. By 1895 Americans had invested about $50 million in sugar plantations, mines, railroads, and other businesses in Cuba. These businessmen were eager to see their investments in the revolution-wracked island protected by American military force.

Other factors joined in fueling American support for military action in Cuba in the late 1890s. Humanitarians were appalled by reports of Spanish atrocities in Cuba, particularly the suffering in the concentration camps that had been set up by order of Spanish governor-general Valeriano Weyler. Expansionists such as Theodore Roosevelt (1858–1919), then assistant secretary of the navy, wanted to see the United States project more strength and influence on the world stage—and in an age of imperialism by European powers, such strength could best be shown by acquisition of an overseas empire. An economic depression that began in 1893 was starting to subside as the economy expanded, and many Americans believed that new foreign markets would keep the expansion going. And finally, the newspapers, which found they could boost circulation by spotlighting Spanish atrocities and urging American intervention, encouraged pro-war sentiment. In an era notorious for its sensationalistic "yellow press," publishing magnates William Randolph Hearst, owner of the New York Journal, and Joseph Pulitzer, owner of the New York World, vied with each other to see who could best whip up public sentiment for war.

Some Cubans hoped for U.S. aid in the war against Spain, and even supported annexation by the United States. But others insisted on an independent Cuba, warning that American aid could endanger that independence. Nor did they wish to see Cuba become a small-scale imitation of the United States. Writing in exile in the United States, Martí criticized American culture for its "excessive individualism and reverence for wealth" even while praising its free institutions. Above all, Martí advised against allowing the United States to join the struggle for Cuban independence. "Once the United States is in Cuba," he warned, "who will get her out?"

José Martí and the Cuban War of Independence

In 1895 Cuban émigré José Martí decided the time was right to resume the war for independence. Among other considerations, he wanted to set Cuba free before the United States moved to annex it. That January, under his guidance, three yachts loaded with munitions secretly prepared to set sail from Florida to Cuba, there to join a planned uprising. Unfortunately for Martí, the plan was leaked and the ships were seized by American authorities. Undaunted, Martí left for the Dominican Republic to prepare for another invasion.

On February 24, 1895, the Cuban War of Independence (1895–1898) began with El Grito de Baire, a revolutionary proclamation in the town of Baire that prompted an uprising in eastern Cuba. In April, Martí, along with two other patriot leaders, Máximo Gómez y Báez and Antonio Maceo, reached Cuba. Although a brilliant writer and political leader, Martí was inexperienced as a soldier, and he survived for little more than a month in Cuba. On May 19, 1895, he was killed during a skirmish with Spanish troops at Dos Rios. He has been honored ever since as the father of Cuba and a martyr for his people.

With Gómez as commander in chief and Maceo as second in command, the rebels established a provisional government in eastern Cuba. Outnumbered and outgunned by the Spanish army, but supported by the majority of peasants in the countryside, they avoided open battle and instead waged guerrilla war. Raiding outposts, ambushing small units, and destroying railroads and bridges, they gradually advanced to the west and neared Havana, the capital. Yellow fever and other tropical diseases indirectly aided them by plaguing the new recruits from Spain more than they did the native-born guerrillas.

In 1896, in an attempt to reverse its losses, Spain sent a new military governor, Valeriano Weyler (1838–1930), a veteran of the Ten Years' War. From Havana, Weyler launched a major offensive against the eastern provinces. In so doing he quickly became the most hated man in Cuban history.

THE MEDIA WAR

Reporter Richard Harding Davis learned the hard way how far his publisher William Randolph Hearst would go to sell newspapers. While in Cuba reporting on the war of independence in 1896, Davis wrote a story about how the Spanish subjected a Cuban woman to being searched on board an American ship in Havana harbor. The story ran in Hearst's New York Journal with an illustration by Frederic Remington that showed lascivious Spanish officers surrounding a naked girl, and a headline that asked: "DOES OUR FLAG PROTECT WOMEN? INDIGNITIES PRACTISED BY SPANISH OFFICIALS ON BOARD AMERICAN VESSELS."

Americans responded with appropriate outrage, buying nearly a million copies of the paper (a record) and calling for the defense of national and womanly honor. Only later did the rival New York World reveal that a matron, not male officers, had searched the woman. Davis, whose accurate reporting had been twisted by the Journal, swore never to work for Hearst again.

WELL, I HARDLY KNOW WHICH TO TAKE FIRST!

A cartoon shows American president William McKinley serving up new territories to a hungry Uncle Sam. (Library of Congress)

With the poor people of the earth

I want to cast my lot

The brook of the mountains

Gives me more pleasure than the sea

Guantanamera, guajira Guantanamera

—José Martí, "Versos Sencillos (Simple Verses)," a poem later adapted as lyrics to the song "Guantanamera"

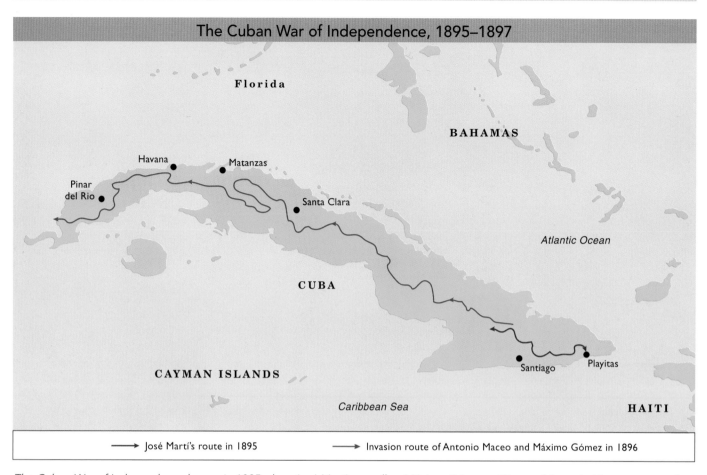

The Cuban War of Independence, 1895–1897

→ José Martí's route in 1895   → Invasion route of Antonio Maceo and Máximo Gómez in 1896

The Cuban War of Independence began in 1895 when José Martí, as well as Máximo Gómez y Báez and Antonio Maceo, returned to Cuba to wage a guerrilla war against the Spanish colonial government. Although the inexperienced Martí was killed shortly after arriving in Cuba, Gómez and Maceo were veterans of the Ten Years' War of 1868–1878. Making their way across Cuba, they launched surprise attacks on Spanish infantry, and in an effort to destroy any economic benefit that Spain might reap from its Cuban colony, they burned railways, factories, and plantations. The route they followed across Cuba is shown above, as is the route of Martí.

Believing that the guerrillas could not survive without the aid of peasants in the countryside, Weyler rounded up civilians and placed them in concentration camps. Those who resisted were shot. The farms they left behind were burned. Disease, starvation, and inhuman conditions killed more than 100,000 of the reconcentrados, or "reconcentrated people," in the camps, rousing humanitarian sentiment worldwide, particularly in the United States. Amplified by the yellow press, the clamor for the United States to enter the war grew louder.

By the end of 1896, Weyler drove the rebels back to the eastern end of Cuba, but the United States made clear to Spain that his brutality was raising the risk of American intervention. To try to avert this outcome, in 1897 Spain recalled Weyler, closed the concentration camps, and offered home rule to Cuba. Still, American war fever against Spain grew. President William McKinley resisted the

cries for intervention, hoping that Spanish reforms would suffice to keep the United States at peace. But war fever erupted into war when the battleship USS Maine was destroyed in 1898.

REMEMBER THE *MAINE*

On January 25, 1898, the battleship USS *Maine* steamed into Havana harbor on what was officially billed as a "friendly call," a courtesy visit made with the consent of the Spanish government. Unofficially, the United States wanted its armed forces close at hand in case American property and persons in Cuba were endangered by the tumult on the island.

On the night of February 15, 1898, while the ship was still in the harbor, an explosion sank the Maine, and 260 crew members died. The yellow press had no doubt about the cause: "THE MAINE

The USS Maine *explodes in Havana harbor.* (Library of Congress)

EXPLOSION WAS CAUSED BY A BOMB—SUSPICION OF A TORPEDO," declared the New York World headline on February 18. The New York Journal cried, "REMEMBER THE MAINE! TO HELL WITH SPAIN." With Spain denying responsibility for the explosion, some Americans urged their countrypeople not to jump to conclusions. The New York Sun argued that there should be "no lynch law for Spain." A U.S. court of inquiry determined in March that a mine had sunk the ship and held Spain responsible for the breach of maritime security, but it did not go so far as to accuse Spain of a deliberate act of war. Still, most Americans were convinced that Spain had deliberately destroyed the ship. Theodore Roosevelt wrote: "The Maine was sunk by an act of dirty treachery on the part of the Spaniards I believe."

In all likelihood, Spain did not deliberately sink the Maine. Spain had no interest in going to war with the more powerful United States and tried hard to preserve peace through diplomacy after the explosion. Some have argued that Cuban rebels sank the ship to draw the United States into the war, but in fact the rebels were close to winning the war, and many patriots agreed with Martí that their independence would be at greater risk with the United States in the war than out of it. Some have argued that the United States sank the ship to create a pretext for war, though there is no evidence for that assertion. The most likely explanation is that the explosion was caused when ammunition stored in the battleship was ignited by spontaneous combustion. Most Americans ignored this possibility in the stampede for war.

In March, the U.S. Congress appropriated $50 million for war preparations. On April 19 Congress declared its recognition of Cuban independence and demanded that Spain withdraw from Cuba or face military action. At the urging of Senator Henry Teller, a provision known as the Teller Amendment was included, asserting that the United States had no intention of ruling Cuba once peace was achieved, and that it would "leave the government and control of the island to its people." Spain did not withdraw, and on April 25 Congress declared war.

The war was swift and one-sided in favor of the Americans. The United States quickly decided to make Spain wage a two-front defensive battle by launching an offensive not only against Spain's territories in the Caribbean, but also against the Philippines. On May 1 the U.S. Asiatic Squadron, led by Commodore George Dewey, destroyed

Future U.S. president Theodore Roosevelt leads his "Rough Riders" up San Juan Hill. (Library of Congress)

the Spanish fleet in Manila Bay in the Philippines without loss of a single American life. In June a U.S. force of regular troops and volunteers under General William Shafter landed on the Cuban coast east of Santiago de Cuba and took control of key fortifications. Among the volunteers was Theodore Roosevelt, who quit his position as assistant secretary of the navy to form the First Volunteer Cavalry Regiment, or "Rough Riders." The regiment included several Hispanic Americans, among them Captain Maximiliano Luna, a Nuevomexicano whose family had been in New Mexico since the 17th century. Roosevelt led his Rough Riders in a daring assault on Kettle Hill, flanking a Spanish fortification on San Juan Hill. The victory advanced not only the war effort but also Roosevelt's political career, which would soon bring him to the White House (president 1901–1909).

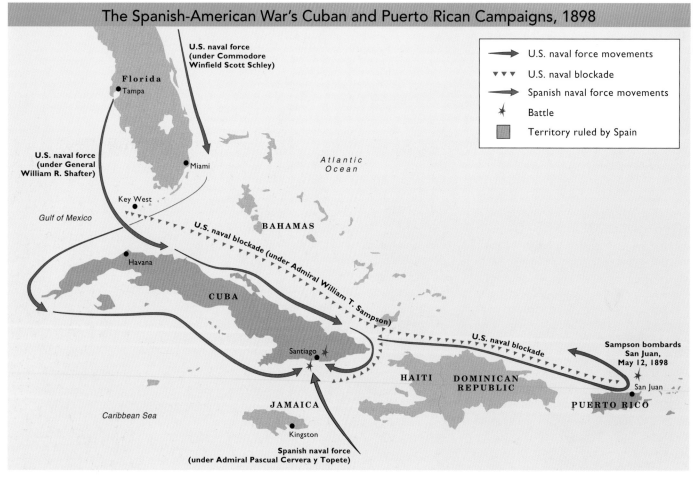

The Spanish-American War's Cuban and Puerto Rican Campaigns, 1898

U.S. naval force (under Commodore Winfield Scott Schley)

U.S. naval force (under General William R. Shafter)

Florida
Tampa

Miami

Atlantic Ocean

Gulf of Mexico

Key West

BAHAMAS

U.S. naval blockade

Havana

U.S. naval blockade (under Admiral William T. Sampson)

CUBA

Santiago

HAITI

DOMINICAN REPUBLIC

U.S. naval blockade

Sampson bombards San Juan, May 12, 1898

San Juan

PUERTO RICO

JAMAICA

Caribbean Sea

Kingston

Spanish naval force (under Admiral Pascual Cervera y Topete)

Legend:
→ U.S. naval force movements
▾▾▾ U.S. naval blockade
→ Spanish naval force movements
✳ Battle
▨ Territory ruled by Spain

Following the sinking of the USS Maine in 1898, the U.S. Congress declared war on Spain, supporting Cuba's fight for independence. On June 14, 1898, 17,000 U.S. naval troops set sail for Cuba from Tampa, Florida. On the advice of the local Cuban rebel leader General Calixto García, U.S. troops landed at Daiquirí and Siboney. Together with Cuban forces, U.S. troops took Spanish strongholds at Las Guásimas, El Caney, San Juan Hill, and Kettle Hill, leading to the Spanish defeat at Santiago. Soon after, U.S. troops invaded Puerto Rico, defeating the Spanish there.

The land assault in Cuba forced the Spanish Caribbean fleet to leave the shelter of Santiago. U.S. naval forces destroyed the fleet on July 3 as it tried to escape westward, and Santiago surrendered to Shafter on July 17, effectively ending the war in Cuba. An American force led by General Nelson Miles occupied Puerto Rico shortly afterward. Manila fell in August. The fighting had ended in just four months. U.S. battle casualties had been relatively light, with 385 battle deaths. Many more Americans—2,061—died of other causes, especially yellow fever.

The Treaty of Paris, signed on December 10, 1898, ended the Spanish-American War. By the terms of that treaty, Spain renounced all of its claims to Cuba, leaving the island for the moment under U.S. control, even though the United States had earlier denied any intention of permanent control through the Teller Amendment. Puerto Rico and Guam were ceded outright to the United States, and the Philippine Islands were sold to the United States for sum of $20 million. Spain emerged from the war with the last vestiges of its storied empire gone. The United States, on the other hand, emerged as a colonial power, with two Hispanic-American islands in the Caribbean now under its sway.

THE "BIG STICK": THE UNITED STATES IN LATIN AMERICA

In the aftermath of the Spanish-American War, the United States, itself once a colony that had waged a war of independence to free itself of foreign domination, found itself for the first time with overseas colonies of its own. Although Cuba would be at least politically independent during the early years of the 20th century—if not economically independent as well—the United States would claim the Philippines and the islands of Guam and Puerto Rico as dependent territories. For more than four decades, these territories were governed by U.S. appointees, who were charged with carrying out policies devised in Washington, D.C. Even Cuba was not truly independent: for almost 60 years, its economy was dominated by U.S. business interests, and the country even needed to grant the United States the right to intervene in its affairs "in order to maintain Cuba's independence." During the early 20th century, the close ties between the United States and both Cuba and Puerto Rico created a greater sense of the historical links between the United States and Hispanic America. At the same time, these ties also sowed the seeds of resentment that laid the ground for a century of conflict.

LUIS MUÑOZ RIVERA AND THE FIGHT FOR PUERTO RICAN INDEPENDENCE

Although the Spanish-American War liberated Puerto Rico from Spain, it had the immediate effect of derailing Puerto Rican progress toward greater self-government. In December 1897 Puerto Rico had already received a Charter of Autonomy from Spain. General elections were held in March 1898, and on July 18 the island legislature met for the first time. Luis Muñoz Rivera (1859–1916), the patriot who had spearheaded the movement for autonomy, was made head of the powerful

A rural schoolhouse in Puerto Rico at the turn of the 20th century (Library of Congress)

A CHRONOLOGY OF THE LIFE OF LUIS MUÑOZ RIVERA

1859 Luis Muñoz Rivera is born in Barranquitas, Puerto Rico.

1887 Muñoz Rivera cofounds the Autonomist Party of Puerto Rico. The party's main goal is independence from Spain.

1890 Muñoz Rivera founds La Democracía (The Democracy), a newspaper dedicated to Autonomist ideas.

1893 In order to learn more about political systems, Muñoz Rivera travels to Spain to study its government. When he returns home, he assists in drafting the Plan de Ponce, an outline for Puerto Rico's administrative autonomy and political freedom.

1895 Muñoz Rivera becomes part of a four-member commission, which meets with the leader of the Liberalist Party of Spain, Práxedes Mateo Sagasta. Together, the Liberalist parties of Spain and Puerto Rico agree that if the Spanish Liberalists come to power, Puerto Rico will have an autonomous government.

1897 Sagasta approves the Autonomist Charter and appoints Muñoz Rivera secretary of state and chief of the cabinet in Puerto Rico's Spanish colonial government.

1898 The United States invades Puerto Rico and ignores the Autonomist Charter.

1899 Muñoz Rivera founds the newspaper El Territoria (The Territory), providing a place for Puerto Ricans to express the ill-effects of the U.S. trade blockade. That same year, Muñoz Rivera unsuccessfully tries to negotiate a free-trade agreement between Puerto Rico and the United States; he moves to New York.

1901 In New York, Muñoz Rivera founds the Puerto Rico Herald, a bilingual newspaper focusing on Puerto Rico's relations with the United States.

1904 Muñoz Rivera returns to Puerto Rico and founds the Unionist Party upon his arrival.

1906 Muñoz Rivera is elected to the Puerto Rican House of Delegates as a Unionist and is reelected twice, serving until 1910.

1910 Muñoz Rivera is elected resident commissioner to the U.S. House of Representatives. He learns English in order to fight for a revision of the Foraker Act. In response, U.S. president Woodrow Wilson says the Unionist Party must end its fight for independence before the United States will amend the act.

1916 The U.S. House of Representatives passes the Jones Act and sends it to the Senate for approval. Muñoz Rivera returns to Puerto Rico. He dies soon thereafter.

1917 The U.S. Congress passes the Jones Act, which grants Puerto Ricans U.S. citizenship and sets up a two-chamber legislative assembly with a 19-member Senate and a 39-member House of Delegates, both of which are elected by the people.

"If the U.S. flag in Puerto Rico covers an American territory, we Puerto Ricans, by natural rights, are perfect U.S. citizens. U.S. citizenship should not be imposed on a Puerto Rican if he does not want it, but if there is a law making all Puerto Ricans ipsofacto U.S. citizens, then the ideals of the people of Puerto Rico would be achieved."

—Jose de Diego, April 9, 1910, U.S. House of Representatives

executive council, serving below a Spanish governor whose authority had been greatly reduced. Muñoz's tenure proved short-lived. On July 25, 1898, U.S. forces landed in Puerto Rico. By August the island was under U.S. control, and the Treaty of Paris in December formally made the island an American possession. Muñoz tried to continue serving as head of the cabinet under an American military governor but found his position so weakened that he resigned early in 1899.

Muñoz and most other Puerto Rican leaders did not at first seek immediate independence. They hoped for an end to U.S. military government, U.S. citizenship for Puerto Ricans, status for Puerto Rico as an organized territory, and eventual statehood. Instead, the Foraker Act

of 1900 established a civil government but did not make Puerto Ricans U.S. citizens or offer substantial self-government. The U.S. Congress, in which Puerto Ricans had no voice or vote, kept control of Puerto Rican affairs.

Meanwhile, unemployment and poverty were on the rise in Puerto Rico. American sugar companies were buying large plots of land from Puerto Rican landowners, converting much of the island's farm land to sugar production. Farmers who had grown their own food now labored at growing sugar, with their livelihoods dependent on the chronically unstable price of that commodity. Poverty was aggravated by a population explosion, the result of U.S.-introduced health and sanitation measures that reduced mortality without providing a means out of destitution.

Under these circumstances, Muñoz began to speak out for independence, writing in his New York-based paper, the Puerto Rico Herald: "If the United States continues to humiliate and shame us, we can forget about statehood and support independence, with or without U.S. pro-tection." In 1910 Muñoz was elected resident commissioner, the island's chief representative and the highest office a Puerto Rican could reach at the time. From this position Muñoz lobbied Congress tirelessly for greater liberty for Puerto Rico. He was aided by the outbreak of World War I (1914–1918). Even before U.S. entry into the war in April 1917,

THE FIRST SIGHT OF NEW YORK

One result of Puerto Rico's attachment to the United States was an increase of migration from the island to the mainland. The greatest waves of migration would come after World War II, but migration increased earlier as well: New York City's Puerto Rican population rose from 1,513 in 1910 to 69,967 in 1940.

Many of those who came were professionals and tradespeople, seeking a way out of the island's poverty. One was Bernardo Vega (1885–1965), a tabaquero, or cigar worker, who found work in New York City's cigar factories, which also employed Cuban and Spanish immigrants. Vega came to New York City in 1916 on the Coamo, a ship that brought thousands of Puerto Ricans to the mainland. In his memoirs, he recalled his first sight of the city from aboard ship:

We saw the lights of New York even before the morning mist rose. As the boat entered the harbor the sky was clear and clean. The excitement grew the closer we got to the docks. We recognized the Statue of Liberty in the distance. . . . In front of us rose the imposing sight of skyscrapers—the same skyline we had admired so often on postcards. Many of the passengers had only heard talk of New York, and stood with their mouths open, spellbound. . . .

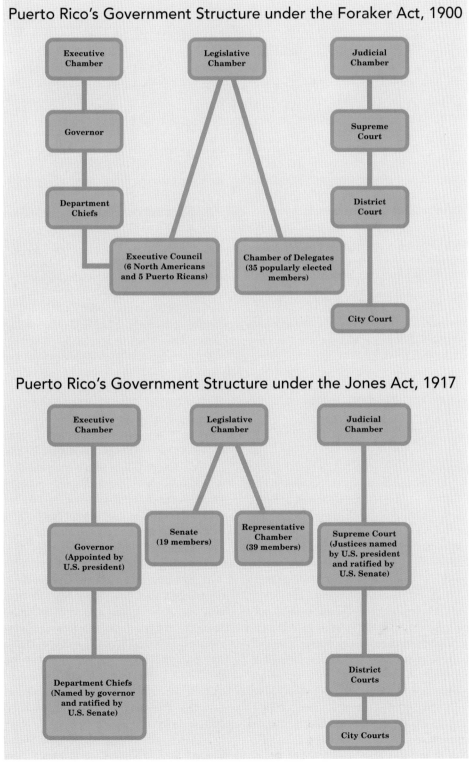

Puerto Rico's Government Structure under the Foraker Act, 1900

Puerto Rico's Government Structure under the Jones Act, 1917

American leaders were fearful of German efforts to turn Latin American governments against the United States. New proposed legislation, the Jones Bill, promised to bolster Puerto Rican loyalty by giving Puerto Ricans greater self-rule.

Muñoz died in November 1916, too soon to see his efforts bear fruit. In March 1917, the Jones Act became law. It made Puerto Ricans citizens, gave them a Bill of Rights consistent with the U.S. Constitution, and gave Puerto Rico its own elected legislature, though subject to veto by an appointed governor. It did not confer statehood or independence, but it gave a greater degree of self-government. Puerto Ricans were exempt from federal income tax and could not vote in national elections. Significantly, it also made Puerto Ricans subject to the draft. After the United States entered World War I a month later, many Puerto Ricans found themselves serving in the armed forces of a country that had only recently made them citizens.

Economically, Puerto Ricans remained disadvantaged. Puerto Rican senator José Celso Barbosa (1857–1921) wrote, "We now enjoy under the American flag the same political rights as any other Americans. But economically we have advanced very little. One cannot say one controls a country if one does not control its wealth."

CUBA: IMPERFECT INDEPENDENCE

Before fighting Spain for Cuba's independence, the United States had declared in the Teller Amendment its intention to "leave the government and control of the island [of Cuba] to its people." But the end of the Spanish-American War left Cuba under military occupation by the United States, which was reluctant to leave. The island was in shambles, its sugar plantations and mills devastated by war. The rebels' ragtag provisional government had little influence outside eastern Cuba and seemed unlikely to be able to maintain peace and order. American businesspeople who had invested in the island wanted their interests protected, as did wealthy Cuban conservatives. Furthermore, the United States wanted to preserve Cuba as a strategic base for control of the Caribbean.

For all these reasons, the United States soon backpedaled from its promise to leave Cuba to the Cubans. American authorities left rebel leaders like Gómez out of positions of real power and summarily rejected a Cuban plan for immediate independence. The military government provided many helpful services, including emergency relief for the poor, reconstruction of public works, and improvement of health and sanitation. But U.S. officials thwarted Cuban aspirations for self-rule. Military governor Leonard Wood wrote to President McKinley: "The people . . . know they are not ready for self-government and those who are honest make no attempt to disguise the fact. . . . This is not the work of a day or of a year, but of a longer period."

American control of Cuba was institutionalized with the Platt Amendment, named for U.S. senator Orville Platt, who introduced it in Congress in 1901. The amendment provided for long-term leases for U.S. naval bases in Cuba, required the Cuban republic to maintain low public debt, forbade Cuba to enter into treaty relations unacceptable to the United States, and effectively gave the United States the right to intervene militarily to preserve order and protect American lives and property. The United States threatened to continue occupying the island until Cuba incorporated the Platt Amendment into its constitution. Faced with that ultimatum, Cuba reluctantly accepted the amendment, and U.S. forces withdrew in 1902. The republic they left was independent in name only; its sovereignty was compromised by the domination of its economy by U.S. corporate interests. In accordance with the Platt Amendment, the U.S. naval base at Guantánamo Bay, Cuba, was established in 1903 and remains there to this day.

Corporate domination of Cuba increased during the occupation, with American investments in Cuba rising from $50 million in 1895 to $100 million in 1902. Among the new investors was banana magnate Minor Keith, who founded United Fruit Company in 1899 and bought 200,000 acres in Cuba for $400,000. United Fruit Company would play an important role in Caribbean and Central American politics throughout the 20th century.

In the decades that followed, the United States several times applied its

U.S. DOMINATION OF THE CUBAN ECONOMY

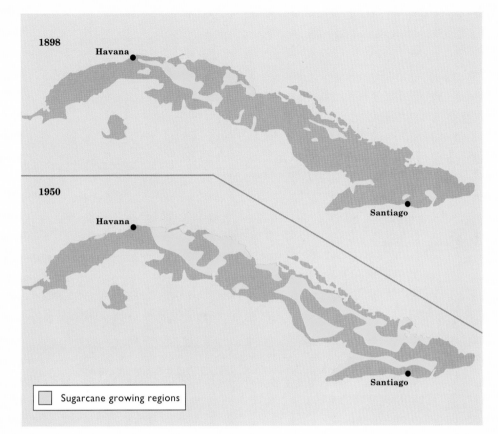

In the aftermath of the Spanish-American War, not only did the United States gain the rights to maintain a naval base at Guantánamo Bay and to intervene in Cuban political affairs as it saw fit, but American business interests also established far-reaching economic control over the island's economy by rapidly expanding the Cuban sugar industry. American corporations bought up many of Cuba's sugar mills, planted enormous plots of sugarcane (destroying jungles in the process), and paid off corrupt government officials in return for special treatment. American efforts increased sugar production in Cuba so rapidly that many laborers from other Latin American and Caribbean countries had to be recruited to work in the island's sugar fields and refineries. Throughout the first two decades of the 20th century, world sugar prices rose along with production. Upon the end of World War I, however, an oversupply of sugar on the world market caused prices to plummet. Although sugar production—and prices—rallied somewhat during the 1920s, they collapsed once more at the start of the Great Depression in 1929. The map above illustrates the amount of land allotted to sugar production in 1898 and 1950. The chart below illustrates the dramatic rise in production between 1860 and 1937.

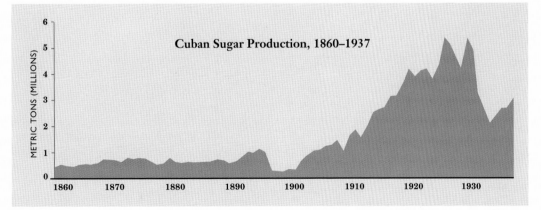

U.S. business interests transformed Cuba's economy from a locally based subsistance economy into one that relied on exporting its resources to the United States. As a result, following the passage of the Platt Amendment in 1901, sugar production in Cuba skyrocketed.

KEY POINTS OF THE PLATT AMENDMENT, 1901

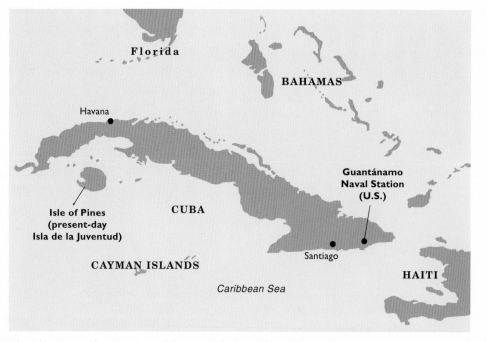

The Platt Amendment granted the United States the right to establish a permanent naval base at Guantánamo Bay, on the southeast coast of Cuba. Its principal articles are as follows:

I. Cuba must not enter into any treaties with any other country that will compromise its independence or permit any other countries to control any part of the island.

II. The Cuban government must not allow its public debt to increase beyond that which its ordinary revenues can pay.

III. Cuba must consent to allow the United States to intervene in order to maintain Cuba's independence, the guarantees of its constitution, and the obligations of the Paris peace treaty.

IV. Cuba must ratify and validate all actions taken by the United States during its occupation of the island.

V. Cuba must take action to sanitize its cities in order to avoid the spread of any infectious diseases on the island, in nearby ports, or to any people involved in trade and commerce with the island.

VI. Cuba must permit the status of the Isle of Pines to be determined at a future date.

VII. Cuba must sell or lease to the U.S. land to be used for coaling or for a naval station in the interest of maintaining Cuban independence and for the defense of her people.

VIII. Cuba must establish a permanent treaty with the United States that will agree to the provisions set forth above.

Platt Amendment right to intervene in Cuba. U.S. forces landed in Cuba in 1906 in response to an uprising by liberals against the moderate government; the United States ended up occupying the island until 1909, this time training Cubans to form a permanent army, which would later become the power base for the dictator Fulgencio Batista. The United States sent troops again in 1912, this time in response to an insurrection in Oriente Province of African Cubans, who were protesting their exclusion from the island's government. U.S. troops occupied Cuba from 1917 to 1923.

Cubans hated the Platt Amendment, which to them symbolized Cuba's compromised independence. One Cuban professor wrote: "We are bound and gagged . . . by your dollars, by your bankers, by your politicians, by your Platt Amendment. . . . We are exiles in our own land." Although the amendment was abrogated by U.S. president Frankin Roosevelt in 1934, by then the damage to Cuban independence had been done. The United States had established a tradition of domination that would continue until revolutionary leader Fidel Castro came to power in 1959.

PANAMA

American control of Puerto Rico and Cuba in the early 20th century was part of a larger U.S. foreign policy shift toward greater overseas influence. The year 1898 made the United States a two-ocean power, with territories in the Caribbean Sea and the Pacific Ocean. The latter included not only the Philippines and Guam but also Hawaii, annexed separately in the same year as the Spanish-American War.

Nowhere was expanding American influence felt more strongly than in Latin America. Ever since the drafting of the Monroe Doctrine in 1823, the United States had viewed itself as having the right to prevent expansion of European power in the Western hemisphere. President Theodore Roosevelt took this doctrine one step further. As an army volunteer, Roosevelt had helped establish American control of Cuba through his heroics in the Spanish-American War. In 1904 Roosevelt set out what became known as the Roosevelt Corollary to the Monroe Doctrine: that the United States had the right and duty to exercise "international police power" in Latin America, intervening at its discretion to correct "flagrant cases" of "chronic wrongdoing" or political impotence "which results in a general loosening of ties of civilized society." This policy established an official rationale for expansion of U.S. power in Latin America. It became known as the "big stick" policy after an adage that Roosevelt liked to quote: "Speak softly and carry a big stick; you will go far." The U.S. Navy, able to carry guns and troops anywhere in the world, was the "big stick."

Prior to articulating the Roosevelt Corollary, Roosevelt had already acted in its spirit in Panama, which at the turn of the 20th century was still part of the South American nation of Columbia. The United States and other countries had long been interested in digging a canal across Central America to provide a short sea route from the Atlantic to the Pacific. The addition of overseas possessions in both oceans made the building of such a canal even more urgent. In 1901 the Hay-Pauncefote Treaty between the United States and Britain gave the former nation free rein to build and regulate a canal across the Isthmus of Panama, provided that the zone remain neutral and open on equal terms to other nations' shipping. The government of Colombia agreed in subsequent negotiations to grant use of the necessary strip of land, but the Colombian senate refused to ratify the agreement.

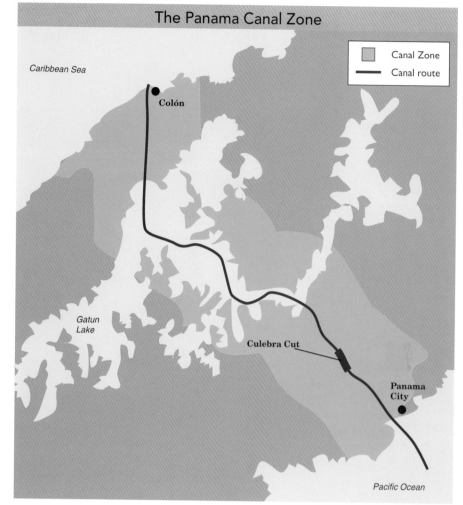

The Panama Canal Zone

Roosevelt's solution in 1903 was to encourage and support militarily a revolution in Panama against Colombia. The revolt was led by the canal's chief engineer.

That year the United States and the newly independent nation of Panama signed the Hay-Bunau-Varilla Treaty, which gave the United States rights in perpetuity over the canal and a Canal Zone on either side. It also gave the United States the right to intervene militarily in Panama to protect order, a right exercised often in the coming years. Panama received a guarantee of its independence and financial compensation: an initial payment of $10 million and an annuity of $250,000 that began in 1913 and was later raised.

A marvel of engineering that stretches 51 miles (82 kilometers), the canal was completed in 1914. Completion required the virtual eradication of malaria and yellow fever in the canal area and the excavation of an estimated 175 million cubic yards (143 million cubic meters) of earth. The political marvel was almost as great: an entire country was created principally

U.S. INTERVENTION IN CENTRAL AMERICA, 1903–1936

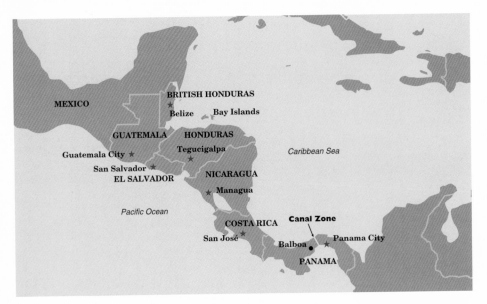

NICARAGUA
1909 Liberal dictator José Santos Zelaya discusses the possible construction of a canal with Germany and Japan; in response, the United States encourages the conservative opposition and then dispatches the U.S. Marines.

1912–1933 U.S. Marines occupy Nicaragua almost continuously; the United States controls Nicaraguan finances.

1916 The Bryan-Chamorro Treaty gives the United States the right to build a canal in Nicaragua.

1925–1926 The marines briefly withdraw, but land again to ensure the second term of conservative President Adolfo Díaz.

1927–1933 Augusto Sandino leads an uprising to resist U.S. occupation; the United States encourages the development of the Nicaraguan National Guard to put down the uprising.

1933 The marines withdraw.

HONDURAS
1905–1925 Several U.S. military troop landings occur.

1928 United Fruit Company buys the Cuyamel Fruit Company and begins to emerge as an important foreign political interest.

EL SALVADORA, HONDURAS, AND GUATEMALA
1906 The U.S. warship Marblehead is sent to settle a war between Guatemala and the combined forces of Honduras and El Salvador.

HONDURAS AND EL SALVADOR
1907 The United States intervenes to prevent war between Honduras and El Salvador.

GUATEMALA
1920–1921 When President Estrada Cabrera is overthrown by liberals, the United States supports a military coup to replace the liberal regime.

COSTA RICA AND PANAMA
1921 U.S. troops intervene in a Panama–Costa Rica border dispute.

PANAMA
1903 The United States supports Panama's movement for independence from Colombia. The Hay-Bunau-Varilla Treaty authorizes the United States to build a canal and to maintain it "in perpetuity."

1904 U.S. troops land to suppress protests against the treaty.

1908–1918 Four more troop inverventions occur.

1914 The Panama Canal opens.

1918 U.S. troops intervene first during presidential elections and again in the Chiriqui province, where they protect United Fruit Company lands for two years.

1934–1936 The Hull-Alfaro Treaty makes Panama a U.S. protectorate.

for the purpose of enhancing U.S. power and has been tied closely to the United States ever since.

Panamanians, like other Latin Americans with experience of the Roosevelt Corollary, resented U.S. domination of their country and long struggled to reduce that domination. A treaty ratified in 1939 removed the right of the United States to intervene in Panama's internal affairs, while giving the United States the right to intervene for the purpose of defending the canal. A 1977 treaty gave Panama possession of the canal beginning in 2000, but did not take away the right of the United States to defend the canal's neutrality. The most recent American military intervention in

Panama took place in 1989, when the United States sent troops to capture dictator Manuel Noriega and force him to stand trial in the United States for drug trafficking.

The racism common among Anglo-Americans of the time against Hispanics laced much of Roosevelt's "big stick" foreign policy. Anglo-Americans regarded themselves as superior, upright, and mature, while considering Hispanics as inferior, corrupt, and childlike. Roosevelt justified his actions in Panama by calling Colombians "an inferior people" and remarking, "You could no more make an agreement with the Colombian rulers than you could nail currant jelly to the wall." He made light of potential Panamanian resistance to U.S. domination in a letter to his brother-in-law in 1905: "Sometime soon I shall have to spank some little brigand of a South American republic."

NICARAGUA

In the early years of the 20th century, the American "big stick" was increasingly used in other parts of Central America. Americans were not newcomers to the region; American businesses had been investing in Central America since the 1840s, opening mines and growing cash crops, especially bananas and coffee. One American, William Walker (1824–1860), went so far as to conquer Nicaragua in a private filibustering expedition, getting himself declared president in 1856 before being ousted in battle in 1857. He was executed by a Honduran firing squad in 1860 while attempting another invasion of Nicaragua.

Even without Walker's adventures, the turbulent politics of Central America was a constant threat to American business interests. Insurrections, revolutions, and wars between neighboring countries were chronic. After 1900, the U.S. Navy regularly patrolled the Caribbean coast of Central America, protecting American lives and property in port towns. On one occasion in Honduras in 1907, a U.S. shore party landed to police a town abandoned by its own military during a war with Nicaragua. The United States lent military and diplomatic support to the overthrow in 1909 of Nicaraguan dictator José Santos Zelaya, who was regarded as

HISPANIOLA'S TURBULENT HISTORY, 1790–1924

1791	Slave insurrection takes places on Saint-Domingue, the French colony on the western portion of the island of Hispaniola, which the rebels call Haiti (after ayti, the native Arawak word for the island).
1793–1798	All of Hispaniola is occupied by Britain.
1801–1808	Santo Domingo, the Spanish colony on the eastern half of Hispaniola, is occupied by Haiti.
1804	Jean-Jacques Dessalines and his generals declare independence in Haiti.
1805	Dessalines crowns himself emperor.
1806	Dessalines is assassinated.
1807–1820	Haiti splits between an authoritarian state in the north led by Henry Christophe and a republic in the south led by Alexandre Pétion.
1808	The people of Santo Domingo revolt against Haiti and set up a republic.
1809	Spain regains control of Santo Domingo.
1820	Following the death of Christophe, Jean-Pierre Boyer, the successor to Pétion, reunites the north and south of Haiti and eliminates the forced labor system.
1821	Spanish rule is overthrown in Santo Domingo by popular uprising.
1822	Haitian forces invade Santo Domingo.
1822–1844	Haiti rules all of Hispaniola. Jean-Pierre Boyer leads a campaign to erase Spanish culture from Santo Domingo.
1843	Boyer is ousted.
1843–1844	Santo Domingo, led by Pedro Santana, overthrows Haitian rule and establishes the Dominican Republic.
1844–1874	Control of the Dominican Republic alternates between armed bands led by Santana and his rival Buenaventura Báez.
1861–1865	At Santana's request, Spain reoccupies the country.
1866–1882	A period of chaos and disorder ensues.
1882–1899	A period of ruthless dictatorship under Ulises Huereaux takes place, ending with Huereaux's assassination in 1899.
1899–1919	Further chaos under several generals bankrupts the Dominican national treasury. The United States arranges to control the finances and customs receivership of the nation, resulting in virtual domination by the United States.
1906–1911	A period of relative stability under President Ramón Cáceras ends with his assassination in 1911.
1911–1919	A sequence of brief presidencies takes place.
1916–1924	The U.S. Marines occupy the Dominican Republic.

a destabilizing force contrary to American interests in the country. In 1912, U.S. Marines landed to protect the government of Adolfo Díaz, who was friendly to the United States, against an insurrection. A small force of marines remained after the rebellion was quelled, inciting nationalist anger.

Anti-American guerrilla warfare prevailed in Nicaragua until the marines left in 1925. In response to a coup, the marines came back in 1926, occupying the country until 1933; for most of that time they were plagued by a renewed guerrilla campaign led by Augusto César Sandino (1895–1934).

THE DOMINICAN REPUBLIC

The Dominican Republic was another focal point for the American "big stick." In 1905, in response to the near collapse of the Caribbean nation's finances, Roosevelt arranged for the United States to administer its customs department. His aim was to ensure that customs money went to repay debts to creditors rather than to line the pockets of corrupt government officials. The arrangement, which lasted until 1941, was part of a policy that became known as "dollar diplomacy" during the administration of William Howard Taft (1857–1930; president 1909–1913). Dollar diplomacy was the use of the leverage provided by American economic might to extend American influence abroad. American bankers and industrialists were encouraged to invest overseas; the United States financed public debt in places as far-flung

as Nicaragua, Haiti, and China. Wherever possible, notably in the Dominican Republic and Nicaragua, Americans were put in charge of collecting customs and administering finances.

Though the aim of dollar diplomacy was to achieve political stability by "dollars instead of bullets," in practice these efforts were often enforced by bullets. In response to civil turmoil, U.S. Marines occupied the Dominican Republic from 1916 to 1924.

For Latin Americans, dollar diplomacy, the "big stick," and the Roosevelt Corollary were all different names for the same thing: American disrespect for their right to govern themselves. The same disrespect had been shown in the annexation of Puerto Rico and the legalized domination of Cuba, despite the undeniably good intentions of many Americans in assisting to drive Spanish colonial forces out of those islands. The situation made for tense relations throughout the 20th century between Latin America and the United States.

CHAPTER 6

THE AGE OF WORLD WARS

The first half of the 20th century was a time of tumultuous change for peoples throughout the world. The most cataclysmic events of the period—World War I, the Great Depression, World War II—were worldwide in scope and affected all Americans, including Hispanic Americans. In addition, certain events of more restricted scope were of particular importance to Hispanic Americans, including the Mexican Revolution, the Spanish Civil War, and the crafting of the Good Neighbor Policy between the United States and Latin America. These events contributed in various ways to the growing tide of Hispanic migration to the United States. Civil turmoil in Latin countries drove waves of refugees, while the policies of the United States regarding Latin America shaped the conditions under which immigration took place.

A REVOLUTION IN MEXICO

The Mexican Revolution (1910–1940) created modern Mexico. At the cost of decades of civil war and political turmoil, with more than 1 million people killed from 1910 to 1920, the Mexican people won some of the long-sought political benefits that had eluded them since independence from Spain: an enduring constitution (the Constitution of 1917), a democratic system of government featuring an orderly transfer of power, separation of church and state, greater freedom from foreign control of their domestic economy, and improvements in the rights and material conditions of workers and Native American peoples. The personalities of the revolution were larger than life, from the cruel Mexican dictator it overthrew, Porfirio Díaz, to revolutionary leaders like Francisco "Pancho" Villa and Emiliano Zapata. The revolution's chaos and violence prompted more than one episode of U.S. intervention and drove hundreds of thousands of Mexican refugees across the border into the United States. It also marked the beginning of a century of rapid growth in the Mexican-American population.

DÍAZ'S DICTATORSHIP

José de la Cruz Porfirio Díaz (1830–1915) first earned fame as a soldier, fighting the United States in the U.S.-Mexican War and the French at the Battle of Puebla on Cinco de Mayo. After failing to win the presidency in the elections of 1867 and 1871, General Díaz led an unsuccessful revolution (1871–1872). He revolted again in 1876, this time successfully overthrowing the government of President Sebastián Lerdo de Tejada, and had himself installed as president in 1877. Complying with a constitutional provision that prohibited immediate reelection, he stepped down in 1880, allowing a surrogate to take power in his stead. In 1884 Díaz was reelected and had the constitution amended so that he could remain in office indefinitely. By 1911 he had been president for 27 consecutive years and had held sway over Mexico for 35 years.

Díaz ruled as a dictator, repressing dissent vigorously. Opposition politicians were assassinated, and journalists critical of his regime were jailed or forced into exile. Díaz's repressive methods yielded a rough orderliness, as his rural police, the rurales, cracked down violently on bandits and rebels. To some Mexicans this Pax Porfiriana, or "Porfirian Peace," was a welcome change from the frequent revolutions of previous years. Further, the peace enabled Díaz to concentrate on modernizing and developing Mexico as no previous leader had done.

Devoted to positivism, a contemporary philosophy that emphasized rational policies and social order, Díaz and his ministers reorganized the nation's finances, balancing the budget and restoring foreign trust in the Mexican government's credit. Díaz encouraged foreign investment on a vast scale, attracting foreign capital with tax and legal breaks and welcoming immigration from Europe.

THE FLORES MAGÓN BROTHERS

Among the most influential figures in the Mexican Revolution were Ricardo (1873–1922) and Enrique Flores Magón (1877–1954). In 1905, a year after moving to the United States as an exile from his home country, Ricardo founded the Mexican Liberal Party, a reform party that would lead unsuccessful revolts against Díaz in 1906 and 1908. Living in exile in St. Louis, Missouri, the Flores Magóns published denunciations against Díaz in their newspaper *Regeneración* (Regeneration). After meeting the anarchist writer Emma Goldman in 1911, Ricardo shifted from his reform-minded liberal philosophy to espouse radical anarchism. In 1911, a year into the Mexican Revolution, the Flores Magón brothers waged a military campaign known as the Magonista Revolt. During the Magonista Revolt, Liberal Party rebels operated from revolutionary communes in Baja California organized by Magón.

With the aid of foreign money and expertise, railroad and telegraph lines were built; mining, textile, and other industries boomed; ports were improved; hydroelectric plants rose; and foreign trade mushroomed. Most of Mexico's industries were foreign owned and staffed at the highest levels by foreigners, particularly Americans who enjoyed privileges not granted to Mexicans. But Díaz repressed any critics bold enough to complain about the country's growing domination by foreigners.

With "order and progress" as his guiding lights, Díaz brought about an era of prosperity that benefited Mexico's middle and upper classes. However, the poor, the vast majority of Mexicans, were left out. Through various legal and illegal means, the country's Native Americans were deprived of their ancient communal lands, the ejidos. Land ownership became more concentrated; by 1910 only 2 percent of the country's population held title to land. Wealthy landowners devoted their acreage to cash crops such as sisal (hemp), coffee, and rubber, harvested by debt peons living in hunger, illiteracy, and squalor. Little land was left available for the growing of subsistence crops by the poor. As a result, food prices rose while wages stayed the same.

After 1900, the mass social discontent of the poor began to merge with other rumblings against the Porfiriato, as the regime was called. In 1905, Ricardo Flores Magón (1873–1922), a Mexican exile living in the United States, founded the Mexican Liberal Party, a reformist, anti-Díaz party. An economic depression in 1907–1908 affected even the middle and upper classes, reducing their support for Díaz's order and progress. Nationalist sentiment began to grow, as Mexicans everywhere felt that the country had been taken over by American and other foreign businessmen. In 1906 a strike by copper miners against an American company at Cananea, a Mexican city near the border, was brutally suppressed by 275 Arizona Rangers imported for that purpose by the company. Many Mexicans considered the incident an insult to national sovereignty.

In 1910 Díaz, as usual, won reelection to the presidency. But the end was near. His imprisoned opponent in the election, Francisco Madero (1873–1913), fled to San Antonio, Texas. There he rejected the election results, declared himself provisional president of Mexico, and called for the Mexican people to rise up against Díaz, beginning on November 20. The uprising that resulted surprised even Madero.

THE MEXICAN REVOLUTION

Beginning on November 20, 1910, locally based guerrilla forces throughout Mexico responded to Madero's call to arms. The movement's members and supporters included people from all social classes who had had enough of Díaz. In response to this opposition, Díaz tried his best to crush them militarily, but despite his efforts, powerful revolutionary forces grew, particularly the peasant armies under Pancho Villa (1878–1923) in the north and Emiliano Zapata (1879–1919) in the south.

In 1911 Madero returned to Mexico as the political head of the revolution. Ciudad Juárez fell to the rebels on May 8, followed by other cities. Accepting the inevitability of his ouster, Díaz resigned on May 25, 1911, and then fled to Paris, where he died in exile four years later. Madero was elected provisional president (1911–1913) in November.

Though Madero himself had called for revolution, he failed to understand the

Emiliano Zapata (MPI Archives)

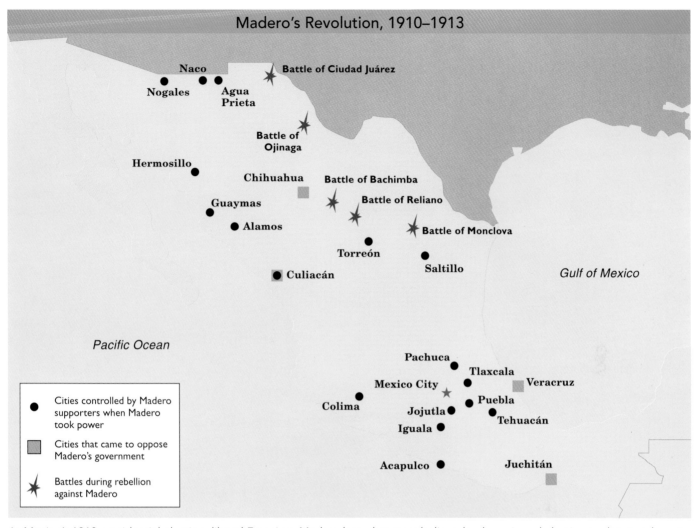

Madero's Revolution, 1910–1913

Naco

Battle of Ciudad Juárez

Nogales   Agua
           Prieta

Battle of
Ojinaga

Hermosillo

Chihuahua   Battle of Bachimba

Battle of Reliano

Guaymas

Alamos

Battle of Monclova

Torreón   Saltillo

Culiacán

Gulf of Mexico

Pacific Ocean

Pachuca

Tlaxcala

Mexico City   Veracruz

Colima   Puebla

Jojutla   Tehuacán

Iguala

Acapulco   Juchitán

- ● Cities controlled by Madero supporters when Madero took power
- ■ Cities that came to oppose Madero's government
- ✴ Battles during rebellion against Madero

In Mexico's 1910 presidential election, liberal Francisco Madero lost what most believed to be a rigged election to dictatorial president Porfirio Díaz. After the election, Madero fled to Texas, joining Ricardo and Enrique Flores Magón, two influential leaders of the anti-Díaz movement. Returning to Mexico, Madero and his forces captured the city of Ciudad Juárez and proclaimed a new government. After rebels quickly won a number of other battles, Díaz was forced to resign, and in 1911 Madero was elected president. Continued conflicts made Madero's presidency a brief one. He was assassinated in 1913.

forces he had unleashed. The scion of a wealthy landowning family, he was dedicated to liberal reforms, such as free elections, but not to the social and economic reforms, such as land redistribution, that peasant leaders like Villa and Zapata demanded. Too slow to implement change and unable to maintain order among the various revolutionary factions, Madero was threatened by new uprisings in 1912 and 1913.

At this point the United States intervened, under the direction of President William Howard Taft. Many American businessmen had property and investments in Mexico. They had no desire to see their property expropriated by Mexican radicals or their normal business dealings interrupted by endless revolution. In February 1913—with encour-

agement from the U.S. ambassador to Mexico, Henry Lane Wilson—Madero's commander in chief, General Victoriano Huerta, overthrew Madero in a coup and became president. Placed under arrest, Madero was killed, reportedly in an attempt to escape.

Huerta ruled dictatorially (1913–1914) until he himself was forced from office in 1914 by the combined forces of Villa, Zapata, and Constitutionalist leader Venustiano Carranza. The overthrow of Huerta was aided by another U.S. intervention, this time driven by President Taft's successor, Woodrow Wilson, who regarded Huerta as a usurper. Wilson permitted arms to flow across the border to the anti-Huerta forces, and in response to a supposed insult to the American flag, U.S. naval forces captured the port of

Mexican rebels (MPI Archives)

The U.S. government sent General John J. Pershing (front, center) in 1916 to capture Pancho Villa following the Mexican revolutionary's raids on Columbus, New Mexico. (Library of Congress)

Veracruz, depriving Huerta of arms supplies. Huerta fled into exile in 1914, and Carranza became president (1914–1920).

Carranza, like Madero, was a political reformer but not a social revolutionary, and he was soon opposed by his more radical allies, Villa and Zapata. Civil war again wracked the nation. In 1915 the tide began to turn when one of Carranza's generals, Álvaro Obregón, defeated Villa at the bloody battle of Celaya. By 1916 both Villa and Zapata were contained, respectively, in the north and south.

President Wilson officially recognized Carranza's victorious government, which may have spurred Villa's decision to turn against the United States. In January 1916 Villa's men stopped a train in Chihuahua and murdered 15 American mining engineers. Two months later his forces raided Columbus, New Mexico, killing a number of citizens and destroying part of the town. The attacks prompted Wilson to send a punitive expedition of about 6,000 troops under General John Pershing to Mexico to capture Villa. Pershing searched for Villa for several months, clashing with Mexican troops

and ignoring protests by Carranza, but Villa successfully eluded them.

With Villa and Zapata still in arms but contained, Carranza oversaw the framing of the Constitution of 1917. This document became the enduring basis of Mexican government. It contained many progressive social provisions that Carranza found objectionable and refused to implement, but that his successors would implement to some degree. The Constitution of 1917 called for separation of church and state, with church property to become government property without compensation. It also provided for nationalization of mineral resources, alarming foreign corporations who claimed ownership. It discouraged the alienation of the Native American ejidos by authorizing land redistribution. Finally, the constitution abolished debt peonage, mandated a minimum wage and unemployment insurance, and granted workers' rights, including the right to strike.

Carranza resolutely ignored many of the Constitution's provisions and continued to wage war against Zapata, who had established an independent government in the south and was implementing his own program of land redistribution. On April 10, 1919, Carranza's forces lured Zapata into an ambush and assassinated him. Carranza was felled himself a year later, the victim of widespread outrage when he attempted to control the presidential election so a puppet would succeed him. In 1920 his minister of war, Álvaro Obregón (president 1920–1924), overthrew him, and Carranza was assassinated while trying to flee the country.

With Obregón's rise to power, the Mexican Revolution's most violent phase at last came to an end. The leading revolutionaries would soon be gone: Zapata was already dead; Villa would be assassinated in 1923. The country was left devastated by a decade of civil war: crops and cities burned, railroads torn up, starvation rampant across the country, the economy in tatters. Obregón oversaw a period of reconstruction in which reforms were gradually begun and power transferred peacefully to his elected successor, Plutarco Elías Calles (president 1924–1928). Lázaro Cárdenas (president 1934–1940), who redistributed 44 million acres of land and nationalized the property of foreign oil companies, was the last leader to commit himself fully to carrying

Women played an important role during the Mexican Revolution, not only caring for rebel soldiers, but often taking up arms themselves. (MPI Archives)

Mexican-American Population Distribution, 1900

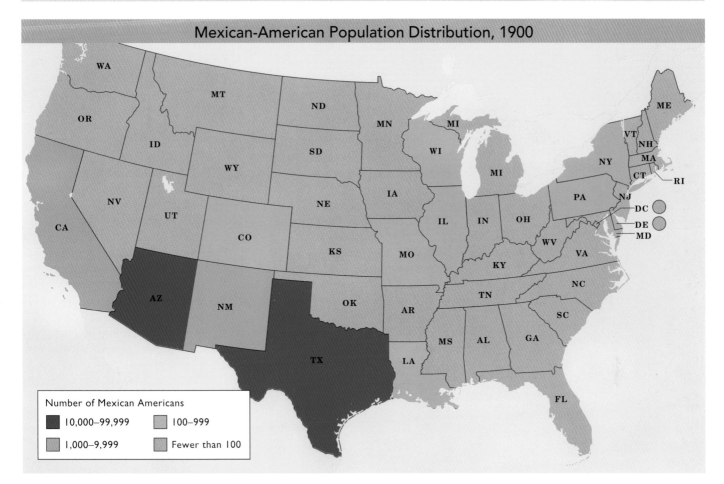

Number of Mexican Americans
- ■ 10,000–99,999
- ■ 1,000–9,999
- ■ 100–999
- ■ Fewer than 100

out the promises of the Mexican Revolution, which is generally regarded as having ended when he left office. Long before Cárdenas took office, however, many Mexicans had already fled the country to seek a better life in the United States.

MEXICAN IMMIGRATION TO THE UNITED STATES

The violence and chaos of the Mexican Revolution drove Mexicans across the border into the United States in unprecedented numbers. In the decade of 1911–1920, 219,004 Mexicans were recorded as immigrating to the United States—more than four times as many as in the previous decade, when just 49,642 did so. In the following decade (1921–1930), the number of Mexican immigrants to the United States more than doubled, to 459,287. According to the census, the Mexican-born population grew more than 13-fold in 30 years, from about 103,000 in 1900 to 1,400,000 in 1930.

Two distinct waves of Mexican immigration from 1900 to 1930 can be distinguished. The first wave, which lasted from 1900 to 1914, included the many Mexicans who were abandoning Díaz's regime in its last years as well as those leaving Mexico in the first years of the Revolution. The second, much larger wave, from 1914 to 1929, came as the revolution intensified at home and as World War I and its aftermath created labor shortages and an economic boom in the United States.

The newcomers included many poor people but also well-to-do businessmen and political refugees of various sorts: politicians, army officers, intellectuals, and journalists. Some of the better-educated and better-capitalized immigrants started businesses, including Spanish-language newspapers and bookstores to serve a small but growing Mexican-American middle class. The poorer, unskilled refugees were fortunate to arrive just as commercial agriculture was booming in the West and Southwest.

Several factors fed the agricultural boom. New dams were opening deserts to irrigation and planting. Cattle ranches and small family farms were losing ground to large, mechanized plantations. Refrigerated train cars had been invented, permitting growers to ship fresh produce over long distances to cities with burgeoning populations. Under these circumstances, the region's agricultural capitalists needed masses of laborers to pick the crops, preferably laborers who would work for little money. They warmly welcomed the Mexican refugees to fill that role, particularly since many Mexicans were seasonal migrant laborers who would stay long enough to pick the crops and get paid, then return to Mexico.

California's Imperial Valley, where the state's first cotton was planted in 1910, became a favorite destination of Mexican immigrants. By 1918 people of Mexican descent were the largest group of agricultural workers in the valley. In Colorado, Mexican Americans picked sugar beets; elsewhere, they picked citrus fruits, grapes, melons, lettuce, spinach, tomatoes, and carrots. They also worked in other industries in the booming region—on railroads, in copper and coal mines, and in factories. As in the late 19th century, Mexican Americans were

aided by laws excluding Asian laborers, including the 1902 Chinese Exclusion Act and the 1907 Gentleman's Agreement with Japan. By 1909 Mexican Americans constituted 98 percent of the work crews employed by the Atchison, Topeka, and Santa Fe Railways west of Albuquerque. By 1928, 75 percent of unskilled construction workers in Texas were Mexican Americans.

Though big business welcomed the labor supply, many Anglo-American and Mexican-American residents of the Southwest reacted with alarm. Some prosperous Mexican-American families that had been in the region since before the U.S.-Mexican War regarded the newcomers with disdain; after all, these refugees were mostly poor and uneducated, without distinguished lineages. To this day, the term hispano, which in its broadest sense means simply "Hispanic or Spanish person," is used in New Mexico in a restricted sense to mean people who claim descent from the region's original Spanish settlers, as distinct from all those

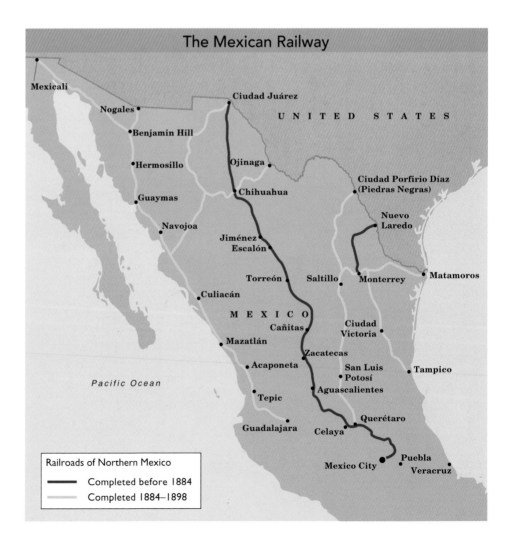

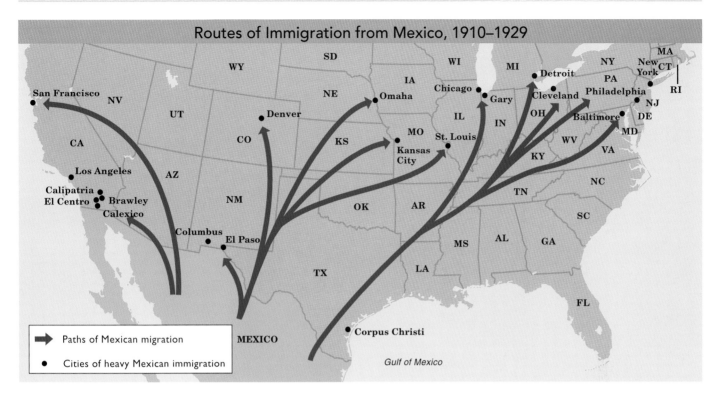

Routes of Immigration from Mexico, 1910–1929

Paths of Mexican migration

Cities of heavy Mexican immigration

MEXICO

Gulf of Mexico

who have come more recently from Mexico.

Anglo-Americans were even more prone to prejudice against the newcomers from Mexico. Mexican laborers were accused of being communist sympathizers, of being supporters of the outlaw Pancho Villa, of practicing sexual debauchery and thievery, of being unassimilable in American society, and of being charges of the state. U.S. representative S. Parker Frieselle of California put it bluntly in a 1926 debate in which he opposed restriction of Mexican immigration: "We, gentlemen, are just as anxious as you are not to build the civilization of California or any other western district upon a Mexican foundation. We take him [the Mexican immigrant] because there is nothing else available to us."

THE FAMILY BUSINESS

Leonides Gonzales was an example of middle-class flight from Mexico during the Mexican Revolution. The mayor of his hometown in Durango, Mexico, in 1911 he crossed the Rio Grande to San Antonio, Texas, with his wife Genevieve, to flee the turbulence of the revolution. In San Antonio, Gonzales became managing editor of the Spanish-language newspaper *La Prensa*. In 1916, with the revolution still raging across the border, his son Henry Barbosa Gonzales was born. Inheriting his father's taste for politics, Henry Gonzales grew up to win election to the U.S. House of Representatives in 1961, becoming the first Mexican American from Texas ever elected to national office. He retired in 1997.

Mexican beet workers and the shacks they live in near Rocky Ford, Colorado, 1915
(Library of Congress)

"As soon as I saw it, I knew it would arouse the country more than any other event."

—Sen. Henry Cabot Lodge (R-Mass.) on the Zimmermann Note

WORLD WAR I AND ITS AFTERMATH

While the Mexican Revolution helped "push" Mexicans to the United States, World War I helped "pull" them. Beginning with U.S. entry into the war in 1917, the great conflagration put 4.7 million Americans in uniform, leaving jobs empty on the home front just as the economy pumped up for war production. Mexican immigrants, still fleeing the upheaval of the Revolution, were eager to take those jobs. The period saw not only immigration from Mexico but internal migration within the United States, as Mexican Americans moved from the Southwest to the industrial Midwest and elsewhere. Many Mexican Americans served in the armed forces as well, defying negative stereotypes to distinguish themselves in combat.

After the war's end, as the U.S. economy continued to thrive, Mexicans kept immigrating to the United States. They took advantage of the relative lack of restrictions on immigration from Mexico compared with new restrictions placed on immigration from Europe and Asia in the 1920s. Yet some limits on Mexican immigration existed. Beginning in 1924, they were enforced by the U.S. Border Patrol, beginning a long-standing

HISPANICS IN HOLLYWOOD: DARK LADIES, BANDITOS, AND BUFFOONS

The history of Hispanic actors in early American film is rife with stereotypes, locked into place by racism and the economic pressures to produce a steady stream of films quickly and cheaply. Prior to 1903, when Edwin S. Porter's 12-minute *The Great Train Robbery* was released, films had virtually no plots whatsoever. Rather, the main draw for the public was the novelty of the moving picture itself—a horse galloping full speed toward the camera, for example. Filmmakers quickly realized that the emotional audience response generated through special effects could be harnessed to the development of more complex plots. In 1915, D.W. Griffith released his three-hour epic *The Birth of A Nation*, the profoundly racist tale of the Ku Klux Klan rising up against venal northern whites and animalistic southern blacks to restore the glory of the humiliated South.

While Griffith held racist personal views, he was not alone in using racial minorities as the film's antagonists. Even prior to *The Birth of A Nation*, filmmakers appealed to the middle class majority with "moral lessons" in which the good triumphed over evil. Westerns were especially popular for these messages, and perfectly in keeping with belief in white America's manifest destiny to conquer the West. Invariably, when mixed-blooded Indian and Mexican outsiders threatened the safety of the pure, innocent heroine, the Anglo male hero would save the day, embodying just enough superior moral and physical strength and bravery to beat back the more primitive enemies.

Economics played a role in enforcing these stereotypes. By the 1920s and 1930s, Hollywood's studio system demanded a steady stream of product in the marketplace. Quantity took precedence over quality, and a set formula of plot and character conventions came to the fore. With these constraints in place, Hispanic actors faced a choice. They could maintain their Hispanic identity and accept stereotyped roles, or they could mask their heritage. For example, after appearing in such fare as *The Three Mesquiteers*, the part-Spanish American actress Rita Cansino adopted the stage name Rita Hayworth in 1937, and went on to become the redheaded pin-up girl of Hollywood legend.

For many Hispanic actors, the choice was even more limited—accept stereotyped roles or do not work at all. These stereotyped roles included the bandito, the buffoon, the dark lady, and in time the caballero. Born in San Luis Potosí, Mexico, Lupe Velez starred in a series of films as the "Mexican Spitfire"—a hot-blooded, hot-tempered, and passionate woman with a thick Spanish accent, who always lost out in love to her Anglo competition. The bandito appeared at the height of the Mexican Revolution. While Pancho Villa evaded real life capture by the U.S. Army, silent cowboy movie star Tom Mix never failed to best the Mexican bandit. Whether the character was a dark lady, bandito or buffoon, he or she could expect to be killed, mocked, punished, or occasionally reformed by the Anglos.

One exception to this trend was the "gay caballero." This character was most famously personified by the swash-buckling Zorro and the Cisco Kid. A charming lothario, the caballero was an outsider who rode into town, saved the day, and broke a few women's hearts before leaving town again.

That Zorro and Cisco ultimately always left town and never did more than flirt with his female admirers is important. If they were allowed to settle down and marry the Anglo heroine, this might have offended the sensibilities of white audiences. (Of course, if these figures ever did settle down and marry, the movie franchises would end.)

The gay caballero, like other Hispanic film stereotypes, would last for decades. As late as 1952, in the film *California Conquest,* the noble Don Arturo Bodega (played by a Hungarian-borne actor Cornel Wilde rather than a Latino), helps the forces of John C. Frémont take California from its Mexican settlers. After doing so, he proposes to his Anglo co-star, who says, "You would give up a lot to be an American, wouldn't you?" Even at that late date, the Latino lead was expected to deny his identity in order to be accepted.

relationship of mistrust between the both legal and illegal Mexican immigrants and the government agency that was charged with enforcing immigration policy.

Once in the United States, Mexican Americans faced considerable prejudice and ill treatment. Most of the immigrants were poor farmers or laborers who could not read or write. Anglo business owners saw them as cheap sources of labor whom they could pay far less than white workers. For example, an Anglo wagon driver in the 1920s might be paid $4.50 a day, while a Mexican would get just $2.50. Anglo workers resented Mexican workers since they feared they would take their jobs, and therefore Mexicans were banned from joining Anglo unions.

The Mexican-American community coped in various ways: by developing self-help organizations, such as mutualistas and their own labor unions; by maintaining close family ties; and by keeping alive a sense of Mexican cultural dignity.

HISPANIC AMERICANS AND WORLD WAR I

World War I (1914–1918) had been raging for three years when the United States joined the struggle of the Allied Powers, which included Britain, France, Russia, and Serbia, against the Central Powers, which comprised Germany, Austria-Hungary, the Ottoman Empire, and Bulgaria. On April 6, 1917, the United States declared war on Germany, in response to German submarine attacks and to the "Zimmermann note," an intercepted telegram from German foreign minister Arthur Zimmermann that proposed a German-Mexican alliance against the United States, with Mexico to win back its lost territories in Texas, New Mexico, and Arizona. Though unprepared for war, with an active U.S. Army of only about 200,000 men, the United States quickly mobilized, instituting a draft and building up an army of nearly 4 million, 2 million of whom served overseas in the American Expeditionary Force (AEF). The AEF first landed in France on June 14, 1917, at first in small numbers, later in great ones, until the war ended with an Allied victory on November 11, 1918.

Whether they were U.S. citizens or merely intended to become citizens, Hispanic males aged 21–31 in the United

GOODBYE, LAREDO

Tejanos drafted to fight in World War I sang a Spanish song called "Registro de 1918" ("Registration 1918"), so called for the draft registration cards they had received. Here are the translated lyrics, which include a sad farewell to Laredo, Texas:

*The cards arrived
at home for each one,
verifying the registration
those twenty-one to thirty-one.*

*Goodbye, Laredo, highlighted
by your towers and bells,
but we shall never forget
your beautiful Mexican women.*

*They are taking us to fight
in some distant land,
and taking us to fight
the German troops.*

*They are taking us to fight
in distinct directions,
and taking us to fight
with different nations.*

*How far is the journey
over the waves!
Great will be my pleasure
if I will triumph.*

*When I was fighting
I would remember everybody,
and more of my poor mother
who cried so much for me.*

*Goodbye, dear parents,
and the lady I love,
when we are in France
a sigh we will send you.*

*Goodbye, Laredo, highlighted
by your towers and bells,
but we shall never forget
your beautiful Mexican women.*

States were required to register for the draft like all other American males of that age group, in accordance with the Selective Service Act of May 1917. The people of Puerto Rico, who had only just been made U.S. citizens through the Jones Act of March 1917, were subject to the draft just like their fellow Hispanics on the mainland.

Some Mexican Americans fled to Mexico to avoid the draft, but for many others the war was an opportunity to prove their patri-otism. The Zimmermann note, combined with old-fashioned anti-Mexican prejudice, had made many Anglo-Americans suspicious of Mexican-American loyalty. The Justice Department spied on the Mexican-American community in Los Angeles, which they suspected of having been infiltrated by German agents. In Texas vigilante groups harassed and murdered Mexican Americans for their alleged German sympathies. Newspapers warned of the "bronze menace." The slur was proven wrong by the fact that Mexican Americans volunteered to serve in World War I in proportionately larger numbers than the U.S. population as a whole.

Many Hispanic Americans were sent to Camp Cody, New Mexico, where those unable to speak English found their services wasted. Despite the country's large immigrant population, the army only slowly developed a training program designed to work with foreign language speakers in their native tongues. By the time the program was in place, the war was over. Nevertheless, some Hispanic Americans made it to the front to distinguish themselves in battle.

David Barkley of Laredo, Texas, whose Anglo-sounding surname belied his Hispanic ancestry, received the Medal of Honor posthumously for a daring and fatal reconnaissance mission at the Meuse River in France in 1918. Marcelino Serna, a Mexican immigrant from El Paso, Texas, received seven decorations for valor, including the Distinguished Service Cross. He single-handedly captured 24 Germans during the St. Mihiel Offensive of 1918—and then refused to allow a fellow American soldier to murder the prisoners. Another Hispanic American, Nicolas Lucerno from Albuquerque, New Mexico, received the French croix de guerre for destroying two German machine gun emplacements and keeping enemy positions under prolonged fire.

Mexican Americans played an important part on the home front as well. The draft depleted the U.S. work force just when factories and farms needed to step up production to keep up with wartime demand. Immigration from Mexico helped meet the demand, but it was temporarily slowed by the threat of conscription as well as by legislation in 1917 that imposed literacy qualifications and an $8 head tax on immigrants. At the behest of employers suffering labor shortages, the government waived these requirements for agricultural workers from Mexico in 1917 and extended the waiver to railroad and other industries in 1918. From 1917 to 1920, 50,000 Mexicans crossed legally into the United States on a temporary basis, while about 100,000 are believed to have entered without documents.

Even as the immigration flow across the border continued, Mexican Americans began an internal migration, moving out of the Southwest in large numbers for the first time, responding to industrial labor shortages in northern factories. Mexican Americans were soon living throughout the Midwest and Northeast, in such cities as Chicago (which had about 4,000 Mexican Americans by war's end), Detroit, New York, St. Louis, Omaha, Gary, and Kansas City.

Some jobs in the Midwest were agricultural. By 1927 Mexican Americans constituted 75 to 95 percent of sugar beet workers in Michigan, Ohio, Indiana, Minnesota, Colorado, and the Dakotas. Other immigrant groups, such as the Flemish, Germans, and Russians, had previously done this back-breaking and low-paying work but moved up as soon as they had the opportunity, leaving the chore to the Mexicans.

As Mexicans for the first time began to disperse throughout the United States, and as they returned from service in the military, their assumptions and expectations about the manner in which they deserved to be treated in American society changed. The Mexican community became less isolated and less monolithic than it had been in the Southwest, and its members were more aware of the many opportunities that had previously passed them by. Mexican and Mexican-American migration to the Midwest laid the seeds for growth in ethnic consciousness and organization.

CHANGING IMMIGRATION LAWS

Between 1890 and 1914, about 15 million immigrants had come to the United States, most of them from southern and eastern Europe, including Italians, Poles, Russian Jews, Ukrainians, and Slovaks. In the decade after World War I, as the U.S. economy boomed (except for a recession in 1921–1922), employers continued to need laborers. But the flow of laborers from Europe was choked off by tighter immigration laws, instituted largely in response to growing xenophobia against southern and eastern Europeans, who had been coming in great numbers since the late 19th century. Legislation in 1921, 1924, and 1929 established an annual quota for how many people would be accepted from each country, with northern Europeans strongly favored over southern Europeans.

Western Hemisphere countries, including Mexico, were not included in the quota system, which meant that employers seeking cheap labor now looked even more hungrily toward Mexico. With the Mexican Revolution still in progress, hundreds of thousands of Mexicans entered the United States in the 1920s. California alone had an annual increase in its Mexican-American population of 20.4 percent, giving it more than 300,000 people of Mexican descent by 1930. Chicago had 20,000 Mexican Americans by 1925, the largest population of Hispanic Americans outside the Southwest.

Some attempts were made in the 1920s to restrict the flow of Mexicans into the United States. The $8 head tax and literacy requirement were put back in force; these, plus a $10 visa fee, effectively excluded most poor Mexicans from entering the United States legally. Nativists, as those who opposed immigration were called, urged that immigration quotas also be applied to Mexico, but agribusiness and other industries successfully fought any such provisions to protect their access to a supply of low-wage laborers.

Even the existing requirements failed to keep Mexicans out; immigrants simply entered illegally, as undocumented workers. In 1924 Congress established the Border Patrol to try to stop illegal immigration from Mexico. But the patrol's staff of 450 was woefully inadequate to police the 2,000-mile border. Many undocumented workers entered the country with the help of coyotes, professional smugglers of immigrants, who brought them hidden in the backs of cars or trucks. Many waded across the Rio Grande, thus inspiring the creation of a new derogatory term for Mexican Americans: "wetbacks."

Agricultural and other employers were more than happy to hire undocumented workers, knowing that the workers' fear of capture would make them even more vulnerable to exploitation. Employers sometimes even hired coyotes to bring in illegal laborers. Exploitation of Mexican workers was usually confined to low pay, but not always. It was not uncommon for an employer to cheat his workers as well by reporting them to the authorities for deportation after they had picked the crops but before they had been paid.

In 1929 legal immigration from Mexico virtually ceased when the United States began to strictly enforce existing

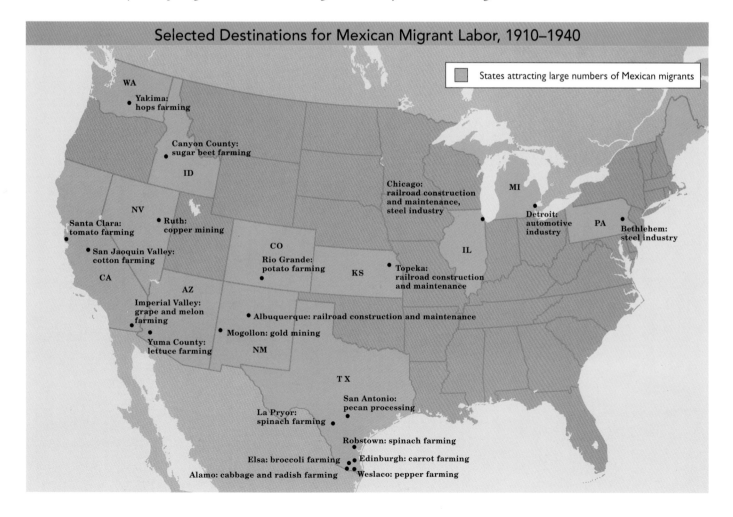

Selected Destinations for Mexican Migrant Labor, 1910–1940

laws. The literacy test was rigidly applied, as were provisions against foreign recruitment of labor and against admission of people likely to become public charges. In Texas the new Texas Emigrant Agent Law, banning out-of-state recruitment of laborers in Texas, added another legal restriction to prospective Mexican immigration. Yet illegal immigration continued. It took the coming of the Great Depression in October 1929 to turn the flow of Mexicans back to Mexico.

MIGRANT WORKERS

Used to harsh exploitation at home, Mexican peasants who immigrated to the United States in the early 20th century were likely to regard as improvements living conditions that native-born Americans would have considered intolerable. The $1 to $3 per day paid to an unskilled agricultural worker in the United States in 1914 would have seemed a pittance to many Americans, but to a Mexican peasant who had received 16 cents per day in Mexico it seemed like good wages.

Nevertheless, the life of a Mexican-American farmworker in the 1910s and 1920s was not an easy one. Job opportunities in the manufacturing and service industries were expanding for Mexican Americans, more of whom found employment in steel mills, construction work, automobile factories, vegetable and fruit canning, meat packing, utility companies, hotels, and restaurants. Yet most Mexican Americans continued to work in the fields, doing the nation's "stoop labor"—so called for the hard and monotonous chore of stooping to pick crops. Stoop laborers typically worked from dawn to dusk in the hot southwestern sun, coming home at night to miserable living conditions—tents, barns, or shacks without running water

THE LUDLOW MASSACRE

In 1913, when a multiethnic group of 12,000 miners in Ludlow, Colorado, working for John D. Rockefeller's Colorado Fuel & Oil Co. began a strike, they were attacked by guards and evicted from company-owned housing, forcing them to live in tents. On April 20, 1914, state militiamen, together with the company guards, attacked the tents, first by shooting at them and then by burning them to the ground. Eighteen people, half of whom were Mexican American, were killed; among the dead were a number of children. Miners from throughout the region retaliated, killing numerous company guards. Finally, the U.S. Army was called in to restore order. President Woodrow Wilson personally asked Rockefeller to negotiate a settlement with the strikers, but he refused.

Migrant Mexican laborers at work picking (top to bottom) carrots, lettuce, and spinach (National Archives)

During a 14-hour battle on April 20, 1914, National Guardsmen soaked strikers' tents in kerosene and set them on fire. The smoke from the blazing tents suffocated 13 women and children. (Library of Congress)

or electricity—and often with bread and beans as their only food.

The work was largely seasonal and migratory. When one crop was picked, the laborers moved by automobile or truck to another field, and then another, often traveling great distances each year. The workers were often recruited through a middleman, the labor contractor (called in Spanish a contratista or enganchista), who was engaged by a grower to supply truckloads of workers for a fixed fee per head. Both contractors and growers were famous for cheating and exploiting workers, withholding wages on various pretexts and supplying food, water, and other necessities at exorbitant prices.

Low wages meant that whole families had to work to make ends meet. Child labor laws and compulsory school attendance were routinely ignored as children joined their parents to labor in the field. Those children who did try to get educations had to change schools often. César Chávez, who later became the most prominent labor leader for farmworkers, attended 36 different schools as a migrant worker growing up in the Great Depression, with eighth grade as his last year of formal education.

In addition to hardships in the workplace, Mexican Americans faced continued persecution on account of their ethnicity. In Texas there were many instances of lynching and mob violence against Mexican Americans, including the excesses of the Texas Rangers, who so terrified the community that the Spanish word rinche (ranger) was used to frighten children into behaving. By 1920 the Ku Klux Klan was vigorously persecuting Mexican Americans in southwestern mining camps.

Despite the migratory character of Mexican-American labor, settled communities of Mexican Americans began to spring up. Laborers often established a colonia, or colony, close to the farms, mines, or railroads where they worked. Along railroad lines, a colonia of boxcars and shacks arose at regular intervals along the tracks being laid by Mexican Americans. Some of these settlements developed into lasting communities.

Within cities, Mexican Americans usually lived in a barrio, or neighborhood, a section of a city predominantly populated by Hispanics. Two forces drew Mexican Americans into barrios: the comfort of living with people who spoke the same language and shared the same culture; and Anglo-American segregation practices, which often forced Mexican Americans to settle in ghettos away from Anglo areas whether they wanted to or not.

Yet despite such growing settlements, Mexican Americans retained strong ties to their homeland. Unlike European immigrants, who endured an arduous and expensive ocean voyage to come to the United States and generally expected never to return, Mexican immigrants had only to cross a border to go home. Many were not permanent residents but temporary ones, sojourners or commuters who worked in the United States during harvesting season and returned home to Mexico in the winter. Some intended to stay temporarily but unexpectedly put down roots and stayed permanently, though with enduring bonds to their homeland. Family ties are important in Mexican culture, as they are for many Hispanics, and regular visits kept the ties alive.

The effect was that Mexican culture thrived even within the United States. New immigrants, permanent and temporary, were constantly arriving and reminding more settled Mexican Americans of the old language and the old ways. Mexican customs and holidays, including the Cinco de Mayo celebrations, also reminded Mexican Americans of their roots. In a tough environment where Anglos regularly exploited and persecuted them, cultural bonds consoled and energized Mexican Americans. On the other hand, those very bonds accentuated the language and cultural differences between Anglos and Mexican Americans, giving nativist Anglos yet another charge to lob at them; as one federal report put it, they had low "assimilative qualities."

THE MUTUALISTAS AND LABOR STRUGGLES

One tradition Mexican immigrants brought with them from their homeland was that of mutualistas, or mutual aid societies. These local self-help groups, first developed in the Southwest during

"There should exist something greater...that will speak higher of us as women, wives, and as Mexicans—that is the betterment of our people, all for country and home."

—Carolina Munguia, cofounder of Círculo Social Feminino de México, a women's group dedicated to help people of Mexican origin, 1939

SELECTED MUTUALISTAS IN SOUTHERN CALIFORNIA IN THE EARLY 20TH CENTURY

Name	Location of Chapter(s)	Description/Goals
Club Mexicano Independencia, or The Mexican Independence Club	Santa Barbara	The Mexican Independence Club was the largest mutualista in Santa Barbara. Only naturalized Mexicans were entitled to membership. It provided workers' compensation, pension plans, death benefits, and home care for those families in need.
Club Mexicano Independencia Feminil, or The Women's Mexican Independence Club	Santa Barbara	The women's chapter of the Mexican Independence Club carried out the same programs as its male counterpart and was responsible for some of the largest-scale social activities in California.
La Unión Patriótica Beneficia Mexicana Independiente, or The Independence Benefits Union	Southern California	The group provided death and medical insurance as well as aid to poor families in the Mexican community, regardless of membership status. It also held fund-raisers for needy family members in Mexico as well as in the community and formed an amateur baseball team.
La Unión Feminil Mexicana, or The Women's Mexican Union	Southern California	The women's chapter performed the same programs as its male counterpart and was responsible for most of the social activities and fund-raisers of both clubs.
La Sociedad Hispano-Americana de Beneficia Mútua, or The Hispanic-American Mutual Benefit Society	Los Angeles	The society provided life insurance, loans, medical insurance, and services to its members.
La Liga Protectora Latina, or The Latina Protection League	Southern California	While the league provided insurance, loans, and other benefits, its membership placed less emphasis on social activities.

the 19th century, were cooperatives or collectives designed to provide security and cohesion in a difficult and sometimes hostile environment. Members included unskilled laborers, artisans, merchants, and professionals. Pooling members' contributions, the mutualistas provided such benefits as burial funds, unemployment compensation, life insurance, medical insurance, education, temporary housing assistance, and relief for the poor. They also provided social and cultural activities, sometimes through women's chapters; these included dances, holiday fiestas, fund-raisers, barbecues, plays, lectures, and discussions.

Some of the mutualistas undertook the task of political organizing and pressing for united action in defense of the civil rights of Mexican-American workers and their families. Some assumed the functions of labor unions, like the Imperial Valley

mutualistas that developed into the Imperial Valley Workers' Union (La Unión de Trabajadores del Valle Imperial) in 1928.

Mexican Americans had been involved in labor organizing and labor strikes since the beginning of the 20th century. In 1901 the Federación de los Trabajadores (Workers' Free Labor Federation), a labor union made up of Mexican Americans, became affiliated with the American Federation of Labor. In 1903 Mexican-American miners went on strike at the Clifton-Morenci copper mine in Arizona, demanding wages and benefits equal to those of Anglos. The Alianza Hispano-Americana, a mutualista founded in Tucson in 1894, supported that strike, although it eventually proved unsuccessful, as did a second strike against the mine in 1915–1917. A later union, the Confederación de Uniones Obreras Mexicanas

(CUOM), founded in 1928, was notable for its broad aims, which included organization of all Mexican-American workers and wage parity with Anglo workers.

Despite some successes of the Mexican-American labor movement in the early 20th century, such as the strike against the Portland Cement Company in Colton, California, in 1917, Mexican Americans often had an antagonistic relationship with organized labor. Anglo labor leaders were among those pressing for immigration restrictions, arguing that Mexicans depressed wages and undermined strikes by accepting low wages. Indeed, it was a common employer practice to import workers from Mexico as strike-breakers—a strategy used, for example, to end a strike organized by the Western Federation of Miners in the Colorado coalfields in 1904. However, the pace of Mexican-American labor organizing accelerated after 1929. That was the year the nation's prosperity ended and the Great Depression began, throwing Mexican Americans into economic distress and persuading many Anglos that it was time to send them back to Mexico.

A TAPESTRY OF HISPANIC AMERICANS: THE 1920S AND 1930S

The Mexican-American community was by far the largest subgroup of Hispanic Americans in the early 20th century, as it is today. But other Hispanic communities also developed at this time, taking distinctive shape in the 1920s and 1930s. These included Puerto Rican Americans, centered in New York City with strong ties to their island homeland; Cuban Americans, driven to the United States by the political turmoil at home; and Spanish Americans, whose increasing immigration numbers in the 1930s were testimony to the traumatic consequences of the bloody Spanish Civil War.

PUERTO RICAN AMERICANS

Since the 19th century, when it housed Puerto Rican patriots against Spanish rule, New York City had been the chief refuge for Puerto Rican émigrés. It

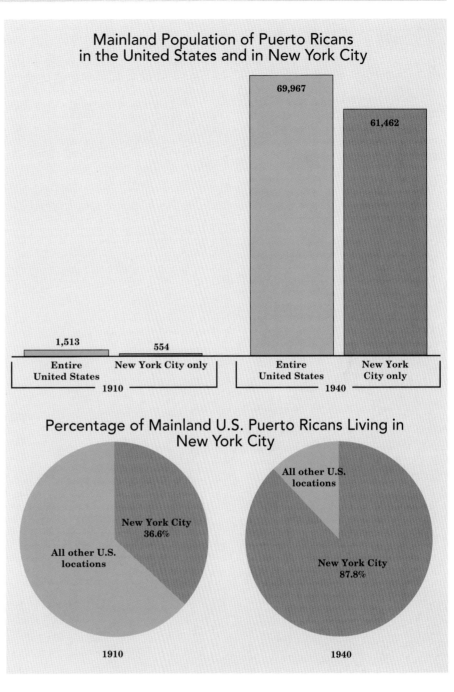

Mainland Population of Puerto Ricans in the United States and in New York City

	1910		1940	
	Entire United States	New York City only	Entire United States	New York City only
	1,513	554	69,967	61,462

Percentage of Mainland U.S. Puerto Ricans Living in New York City

1910: All other U.S. locations; New York City 36.6%

1940: All other U.S. locations; New York City 87.8%

remained so in the early 20th century, when Puerto Ricans migrated there mainly for economic rather than political reasons. Before World War II few Puerto Ricans lived in the United States, but the rate of population growth was rapid. In 1910 only 1,513 Puerto Ricans lived in the entire mainland United States; by 1940, 69,967 lived there—or 46 times as many. Most Puerto Rican immigrants were concentrated in New York City, where 61,462 (87.8 percent) of the 1940 mainland population lived. However, small Puerto Rican satellite communities existed throughout the United States, many of them founded by veterans of

AFRO-CUBAN JAZZ

On an ultimately unsuccessful search for a partner to help him write an opera, African-American poet Langston Hughes traveled to Cuba in 1930. In Havana's cafés, Hughes encountered a form of dance music that he had never heard before. It was, he wrote, "essentially hip-shaking music—of Afro-Cuban folk derivation, which means a bit of Spain, therefore Arab-Moorish, mixed in." The music, he said, spoke "of the earth, life bursting warm from the earth, and earth and sun moving in the steady rhythms of procreation and joy." The music was the rumba, which by the 1940s would be a popular dance in the United States.

Music and race linked Cubans and African Americans. People of African descent were historically a substantial minority in Cuba, and their music, incorporating African rhythms, was part of Cuban culture. In America, jazz was developed largely by African Americans and also incorporated African rhythms. The two cultural styles came together in the collaborations of Cuban-American and African-American jazz musicians like Chano Pozo and Dizzy Gillespie, beginning in the 1940s.

World War I who had settled in the vicinity of where they had been based. Like later immigrants, Puerto Ricans on the mainland retained close ties to their island home, sending letters and visiting when possible.

Despite some improvements under U.S. administration, living conditions in Puerto Rico remained poor. Although the mortality rate fell almost 50 percent from 1901 to 1941, and the illiteracy rate fell about 60 percent, the population almost doubled in that period, due in part to falling mortality. Unemployment and malnutrition were widespread. Under the circumstances, agitation for better living conditions—and in some quarters, an end to U.S. rule—increased. In the late 1930s a brief uprising erupted in Ponce when the police interfered with a Nationalist Party parade; 19 people were killed and almost 100 wounded in the violence.

Cuban Americans

Like Puerto Rican migration to the mainland, immigration of Cubans to the United States remained small compared with that of Mexicans. By the 1930s about 34,000 people of Cuban descent had immigrated to the United States, many of them fleeing the island's chronic political turbulence. Some were refugees of the violent dictatorial reign of Gerardo Machado (president 1925–1933); others came when Machado was overthrown in an army-supported popular uprising in 1933, one that led to the emergence of dictator Fulgencio Batista y Zaldívar. (Batista's domination of Cuban politics from 1933 to 1959 is discussed in chapter 7.)

Among those who fled to the United States when Machado was overthrown was the Arnaz family, which was associated with Machado's government. Their extensive property confiscated, the family sought refuge and a new beginning in Miami in 1943. Desi Arnaz (1917–1986), a teenager at the time, found work as a guitarist and singer in one of Miami's Cuban bands and soon joined the band of Spanish-born Cuban orchestra leader Xavier Cugat (1900–1990). Cugat had himself immigrated to the United States from Cuba in 1921. Arnaz went on to success as a band leader in his own right

and as an actor and television producer, most notably as coproducer and costar with his wife Lucille Ball of the classic situation comedy *I Love Lucy* (1951–1957).

That Arnaz and Cugat should both have found success in music was not unusual in the 1930s and 1940s. At the time Latin music was gaining mainstream popularity, largely through the efforts of Cuban-American musicians like Cugat, whose orchestra, based in New York's Waldorf Astoria, was known not only for its musical style but also for its visual style. His band wore flaming red jackets and featured female dancers. Another Cuban-American veteran of Cugat's band, Machito (1912–1984), dominated New York's Latin music scene from the 1940s onward. Born Frank Grillo in Tampa, Florida, he was raised in Cuba and traveled to New York in 1937, forming his own band in 1940 with brother-in-law Mario Bauza.

Through the performances of such artists, Americans became familiar with Cuban dances like the rumba and with Afro-Cuban instruments like bongos and maracas. Afro-Cuban music also influenced American jazz. American jazz trumpeter Dizzy Gillespie, for example, who blended Cuban rhythms with American bebop, played in the 1940s with Machito and with Afro-Cuban percussionist Luciano "Chano" Pozo.

A pro-Republican poster from the Spanish Civil War (Library of Congress)

Cuban-influenced Latin rhythms have continued to pervade American music from the 1950s, when the mambo was very popular, to the present day.

SPANISH AMERICANS

Another important source of Hispanic immigration to the United States was Spain itself. About 100,000 people immigrated from Spain to the United States between 1900 and 1931. This was a small number compared with the millions who came from other European countries, but it represented an increased rate of Spanish immigration to the United States from that of the 19th century. Steamship travel made the trip faster and cheaper than in previous decades, attracting Spanish farmers and tradespeople who were fleeing poverty, civil turbulence, and, in some cases, military service in their homeland. Spanish immigration to the United States was curbed after the 1920s by the same quota system that limited other immigration, particularly that of southern and eastern Europeans.

Spanish immigrants tended to be better educated and more skilled than other European immigrants. Many settled in New York City or Tampa or went west to work as ranchers or farmers. About 8,000 Spanish immigrants settled in Hawaii from 1906 to 1913 to work in the sugarcane fields; many of them later migrated to San Francisco, California.

In the 1930s the Spanish Civil War (1936–1939) gave Spanish people a new reason to emigrate. The war broke out when right-wing Nationalists, led by General Francisco Franco and his fascist Falange Party, revolted against the left-wing Popular Front leadership of the Second Republic. Nationalist forces controlled southern and western Spain by August 1936, while their opponents, the Loyalists or Republicans, remained strong in Catalonia and the Basque provinces. Fascist Germany and Italy supported Franco with arms and advisers, while the Soviet Union sent aid to the Republicans. Idealists from around the world, including the United States, volunteered to join international brigades fighting for the Republican cause. By the time the Nationalists won in 1939, ushering in Franco's long dictatorship (1939–1975), about 1 million people had died in Spain

Spanish-American musicians at fiesta, Taos, New Mexico, 1940 (Library of Congress)

and more than 500,000 had fled the country, the majority of them never to return.

Because fascism placed strict limits on the intellectual and creative freedom of writers, artists, and academics, intellectuals and artists opposed to Franco had particular cause to leave Spain during or soon after the Spanish Civil War. They included poet Juan Ramón Jiménez (1881–1958), who had been appointed by the Republican government as honorary cultural attaché to the United States. Jiménez first immigrated to Cuba before coming to the United States and ultimately settling in Puerto Rico. He won the Nobel Prize for literature in 1956. Pablo Casals (1876–1973), cellist, composer, and conductor, aided the Republican effort during the war by holding benefit concerts. After the war he vowed he would never return to Spain while Franco was in power, and he never did. He lived in exile in France until the 1950s, when he moved to Puerto Rico, his mother's birthplace. He often traveled to the U.S. mainland to give recitals.

THE GREAT DEPRESSION

The Great Depression, the worldwide economic crisis that in the United States began with the collapse of the stock market on Black Tuesday, October 29, 1929, affected all Americans. But it was particularly hard on two groups: those at the bottom of the economic ladder and those who could be scapegoated by virtue of their race or ethnicity. Mexican Americans were in both groups. American employers who had encouraged Mexicans to immigrate when times were good no longer offered work to immigrants, leaving them without means of subsistence when times were bad. Meanwhile, Anglo-American workers, themselves in dire straits, turned against Mexican Americans more ardently than ever, regarding them as unwelcome competitors for government aid and scarce jobs. The result was the Mexican Repatriation Program, in which hundreds of thousands of Mexican Americans were sent back to Mexico—some forcibly, against their civil rights as U.S. citizens.

Those Hispanic Americans who remained behind benefited from President Franklin Roosevelt's New Deal programs, but often to a lesser degree than did Anglo-Americans. As of 1937, noncitizens, including many Hispanics, were barred from receiving government aid. Even so, Roosevelt has historically been popular among Hispanics. Even more important to the people of Hispanic-American countries than his social legislation in the United States was his Good Neighbor Policy, which reversed, at least temporarily, some of the excesses of American jingoism, or overly blatant nationalism, toward Latin America of previous decades. Ever since Roosevelt's distant cousin and fellow president Theodore Roosevelt had enunciated what became known as the Roosevelt Corollary to the Monroe Doctrine, when he stated that the United States would excercise "an international police power" in the Americas, the United States had frequently sent military troops into Latin America to enforce U.S. will. Under the Good Neighbor policy, the United States promised to respect the rights of Latin Americans.

To cope with the Great Depression, the Hispanic-American labor movement, already in place in the late 1920s, grew more powerful and vocal, as did organized Hispanic-American demands for equal rights with other Americans. Hispanic-American organizations that fought in the 1930s for better working conditions and civil rights included the Confederation of Mexican Workers and the League of United Latin American Citizens. Heroes of the struggle included labor leader Luisa Moreno and U.S. senator Dennis Chávez. Chávez became the first Hispanic member of the U.S. Congress when he was elected to represent New Mexico in 1934. As the Senate's only Hispanic, he fought hard against ethnic and racial discrimination in the workplace and elsewhere and championed better conditions for Puerto Rico in the 1940s. The Guatemalan-born Moreno began life in the United States as a seamstress in New York City sweatshop. The miserable conditions there led her to become one of the first Hispanic labor organizers. During her career, she would organize cigar factory workers in New York, Pennsylvania, and Florida, and pecan processing workers in Texas. Often consulting with Dennis Chávez, she traveled the nation, visiting colonias and barrios and talking to mutualista members.

DEPRESSION AND REPATRIATION

The Great Depression accomplished what years of increasing legal restrictions against Mexican immigration had not: it reversed the flow of immigration between the United States and Mexico. In the early 1930s, more people of Mexican descent returned to Mexico than moved to the United States. Many did so voluntarily, but many—even those with U.S. citizenship—were bullied into leaving through means both legal and illegal in a distinctly anti-immigrant and anti-Mexican climate. For many Anglo-Americans the rationale was clear: why should they share scarce jobs and government relief with "foreigners"?

Enforcement of immigration laws was tightened, preventing new Mexican immigration into the United States. Undocumented workers were found and deported through aggressive raids on Mexican-American communities. Employers, faced with a glut of workers, preferred to hire unemployed Anglo-Americans over Mexican Americans. Meanwhile, laws were passed to establish the same preference for government jobs: California, for example, passed a law in 1931 prohibiting aliens from employment

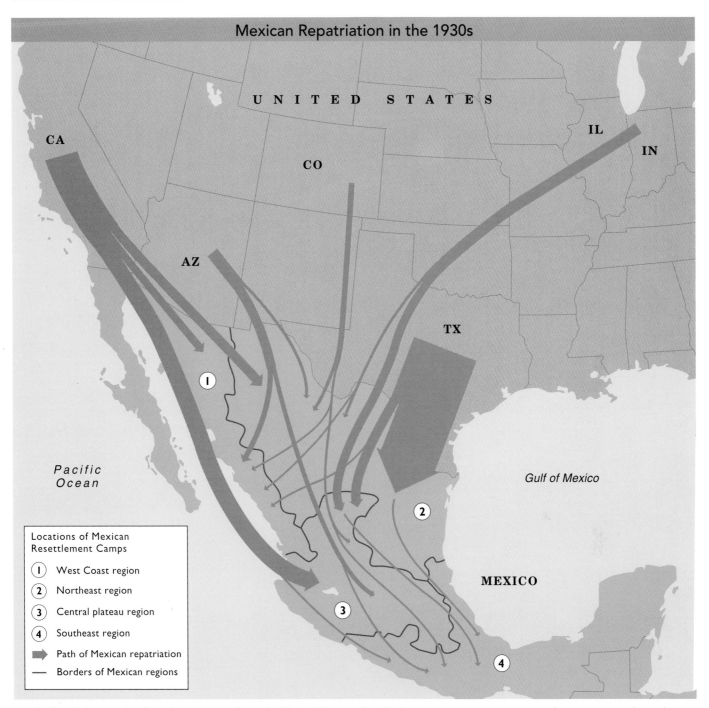

Mexican Repatriation in the 1930s

Locations of Mexican Resettlement Camps

- (1) West Coast region
- (2) Northeast region
- (3) Central plateau region
- (4) Southeast region
- ➡ Path of Mexican repatriation
- — Borders of Mexican regions

To deal with the rapid influx of repatriates from the United States, the Mexican government set up resettlement camps throughout Mexico. The camps functioned as agricultural colonies. Although the exact failure rate of these colonies is not known, many did fail, forcing returnees to travel from camp to camp, to look for work in Mexico's cities, or even to try to return to the United States. The map above illustrates the repatriates' main points of origin in the United States and the regions of Mexico they returned to. The width of arrows signifies the relative numbers of repatriates headed for each destination.

on public works projects. Responding to encouragement from President Herbert Hoover's administration, local government and private agencies across the country organized repatriation programs to send Mexican Americans back to Mexico. Though the programs were designed for aliens, documented and undocumented, in the atmosphere of intolerance even U.S. citizens were intimidated or forced into being repatriated.

The Hoover Administration used many means to persuade Mexican Americans to accept deportation. First, the government tried to convince Mexicans to leave voluntarily. Second, the U.S. Immigration Service began rounding up those immigrants who did not wish to leave, forcing both Mexicans and Mexican Americans to prove that they were in the United States legally. Those who could not were deported to Mexico.

State governments in California, Texas, and Colorado played a role in the repatriation process as well. Mexican Americans applying for welfare relief were steered to "Mexican bureaus," where officials strongly encouraged them to go back to Mexico. If they refused, welfare payments were refused as well. Indignity was part and parcel of repatriation. In Santa Barbara, California, immigration officials herded Mexican-American farmworkers into sealed boxcars as if they were cattle.

As a result of such federal and state government actions and voluntary migration, more than 400,000 Mexican Americans left the United States for Mexico during the 1930s. The largest numbers came from Texas, California, Indiana, Illinois, and Michigan.

The U.S. federal government and various states were not the only authorities promoting repatriation. The Mexican government cooperated with the efforts, as well. Working through chapters of a semi-official Mexican government organization known as the Comisión Honorífica Mexicana, Mexican consuls in the United States served as official links between prospective repatriates and the Mexican government, providing them with information on employment opportunities. Consuls also helped repatriates raise the money needed for the return trip through fund drives and often coordinated the actual journeys.

In addition to the work of its consuls in the United States, the Mexican government aided the repatriation effort in other ways. For example, the goverment abolished import duties on repatriates' belongings, thus reducing the cost of returning to Mexico for those Mexicans who had acquired significant possessions; the Ministry of Interior gave free transport from the border to their final destinations in Mexico. The Mexican Migration Service sped the passage of returning Mexicans through border towns; and during the late 1930s the Ministry of Foreign Relations even recruited U.S.-born Tejanos to colonize land in Mexico.

Although the final destinations of Mexican repatriates cannot be stated for certain, most returned to the towns and villages from which they had come. Others traveled to Mexico's larger cities. It is believed that the majority resettled in northern border states like Nuevo León, Coahuila, Tamaulipas, and Chihuahua, although others returned to states in central Mexico, such as Guanajuato, San Luis Potosí, and Michoacán.

Not all returnees headed for their home towns or for large cities. Some journeyed to Mexican government-sponsored agricultural colonies. Mexico's National Irrigation Commission and other agencies provided land to be settled by returnees.

Many of the repatriate colonies were located in northern Mexico, where large amounts of unsettled land were available. Many repatriates from Texas ended up at one of six National Irrigation Commission– sponsored colonies in northern Mexico. The land required clearing and preparing before being cultivated. Although few records exist that document the success or failure of these colonies, it is known that a number did fail. Some repatriates were forced to move from one colony to another in order to find a successful one, while others left colony life to look for work in the cities. Still other repatriates tried to return to the United States.

Whether returnees to Mexico attempted to settle in Mexican government-

Children of migrant laborers sit on a truck parked at a Farm Security Administration labor camp, in Robston, Texas, in 1942 (Library of Congress)

sponsored farming colonies or not, life back in Mexico was very difficult for them, especially if they had been in the United States for a long time. Their customs were different; they might even find native Mexicans calling them "gringos," a derogatory term for Anglo-Americans. Many American-born people of Mexican descent retraced their steps back north after the Great Depression, when the United States again needed Mexicans for the work force during World War II. But others who attempted to return discovered that their U.S. citizenship had been revoked when they had voted in Mexican elections or served in the Mexican army—eventualities about which they had never been properly warned.

THE NEW DEAL AND THE GOOD NEIGHBOR POLICY

The election of President Franklin Roosevelt (1882–1945; president 1933–1945) brought the United States a vigorous and optimistic leader who instituted many measures to combat the ills of the Great Depression. His domestic reform program, known as the New Deal, included measures that benefited Hispanic Americans.

The New Deal aided Hispanic Americans through direct relief and through jobs programs. The Farm Security Administration established labor camps for migrant farm workers in such regions as the San Joaquin Valley; these camps often had better facilities than those provided by most growers. Federal jobs came through the Federal Emergency Relief Administration in the winter of 1934–1935; after 1935, they came largely through the Works Progress Administration (WPA), which employed Mexican Americans on public works projects such as roads, bridges, and government buildings. The Civilian Conservation Corps (CCC), established in 1933, employed Mexican Americans in surveying and reforestation projects.

However, Mexican Americans faced obstacles to relief and jobs programs that Anglo-Americans did not. Many programs were restricted to those who could establish permanent state residence—a hard task for migrant farmworkers. From 1933 to 1937, New Deal policy changes increasingly barred noncitizens from

REBELLION IN NICARAGUA

In 1909, the United States backed the successful overthrow of Nicaragua's nationalist president, José Santos Zelaya. Two years later, U.S. forces arrived in the Central American nation to forcibly put down popular rebellion and protect the new leader, Adolfo Díaz, a Nicaraguan previously employed by an American-owned mining company. The Marines stayed until 1925, left briefly, and then returned in 1926.

The following year, an anti-interventionist revolutionary leader named Augusto Sandino launched a war against the U.S. military presence and the U.S.-backed conservative government. Although Sandino claimed to be acting in support of the country's Liberal party, when the Liberal presidential candidate won election in 1928, Sandino declared the election unconstitutional, and declared his new goal to be the establishment of a united federation of Latin American states.

Though the United States government saw Sandino as a bandit, his resistance to U.S. forces made him a hero throughout Latin America. Although his army of peasants (which he called "The Army in Defense of the National Sovereignty of Nicaragua") suffered some serious defeats, Sandino's superior knowledge of the local terrain and use of guerrilla tactics allowed he to evaded capture. At one point, he even faked his own funeral to mislead U.S. forces. In 1933, in accordance with President Roosevelt's Good Neighbor Policy, the Marines left Nicaragua. The following year, however, forces under General Anastasio Somoza García assassinated Sandino, then seized power in a coup. The Somoza regime remained in power until 1979, when the dynasty was overthrown, by the National Liberation Front (FSLN), better known as the Sandinistas, in Sandino's honor.

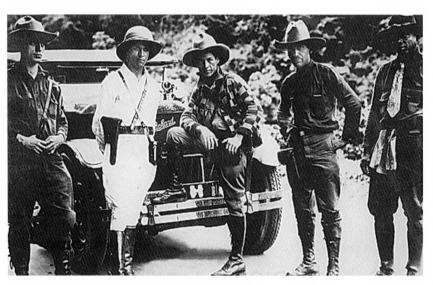

Augusto Sandino (center) and his staff, 1929 (National Archives)

employment and relief, making many Mexican nationals ineligible. In some cases Mexican nationals were able to work, but at lower wages than those received by Anglos.

Despite the shortcomings of New Deal legislation, Mexican Americans and other Hispanics honored Roosevelt as a champion of the poor. The Great Depression established a long-lasting, though not monolithic, preference for the Democratic Party among Hispanic-American voters.

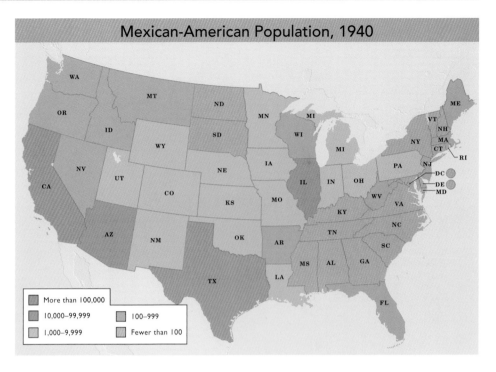

Mexican-American Population, 1940

More than 100,000
10,000–99,999
1,000–9,999
100–999
Fewer than 100

Hispanic Americans also admired Roosevelt for his Good Neighbor Policy toward Latin America. Roosevelt's predecessor, Herbert Hoover, had initiated the policy by preparing the way for the removal of U.S. Marines from Nicaragua and Haiti, both of which had been occupied since the 1910s; the withdrawals were completed, respectively, in 1933 and 1934. But Roosevelt went further, giving the policy its name, "Good Neighbor," and making clear that the United States would no longer intervene militarily in Latin American affairs to suppress insurrections or protect private American business interests. In accordance with this policy, the hated Platt Amendment of 1901, which had compromised Cuban independence, was abrogated in 1934. When Mexico expropriated U.S. oil company properties in 1938, the United States did not go to war but peacefully worked out a compensation agreement. Roosevelt showed his personal respect for Latin Americans by touring the Caribbean in 1934 and becoming, in 1936, the first U.S. president to travel to South America. At least for a time, the era of Theodore Roosevelt's "Roosevelt Corollary" was over.

By formalizing the Good Neighbor Policy, Franklin Roosevelt acted in the best interests of the United States. With the Great Depression squeezing government revenues, the country could ill afford to keep mounting military expeditions all over the hemisphere. The harvest of good relations would pay off during World War II, when the United States enjoyed the close cooperation of Mexico and other Hispanic-American countries on the Allied side.

In keeping with the Roosevelt administration's Good Neighbor Policy with Latin America, First Lady Eleanor Roosevelt paid a goodwill visit to the Dominican Republic in 1934. The first lady is at left, with President Rafael Trujillo (right), and Mrs Trujillo (center). (National Archives)

MEXICAN AMERICANS AND THE NEW DEAL

New Deal Program	Location	Year Established	Impact on Mexican Americans
Interdepartmental Rio Grande Board	New Mexico	1933	Gave New Mexican rangeland to subsistence farmers, Rio Grande Board most of whom were Mexican Americans.
Civilian Conservation Corps (CCC)	Nationwide	1933	Provided work to Mexican-American youths from Corps (CCC) families who qualified for state relief.
Federal Emergency Relief Administration (FERA)	Numerous towns	1933	Provided jobs for many Mexican-American laborers Relief Administration and cities nationwide during the winter of 1934–1935.
Resettlement Administration	Nationwide	1935	Created permanent migrant labor camps in large-scale Administration farming regions, such as the Salt River Valley of Arizona and the San Joaquin and Coachella valleys of California. Facilities at these camps were far better than those usually offered by private growers. Unlike many facilities provided by private growers for migrant labor, these government-run facilities provided wooden or cement shacks, rather than tents, as well as running water. The agency also created mobile camps in other areas during peak seasons. Founded in 1935, the agency was renamed Farm Security Administration in 1937.
Works Progress Administration (WPA)	Nationwide	1935	Hired carpenters, stonemasons, and other construc-Administration (WPA)tion tradesmen as well as unskilled laborers to build bridges, new housing, public schools, and other gov-ernment buildings. The WPA also launched an ambi-tious program called the Federal Writers' Project, which hired writers and artists to bring theater and the arts to those who normally had little exposure to them. In addi-tion, these writers and artists were asked to document the cultural heritage of the nation. This program created a revival of interest in the folk art of Nuevomexicanos, or New Mexicans of Mexican heritage. However, participation in WPA programs was limited to those referred by state welfare agencies, which meant migrant workers were often unable to benefit. In 1939, the program's name was changed to Works Projects Administration.

ORGANIZING FOR A BETTER LIFE

The pace of organized efforts to improve the conditions of Hispanic-American life picked up under the urgent pressures of the Great Depression. This occurred despite the determined efforts of growers and other employers to stop union organizing by any available means, including legislation, warnings about communist infiltration, appeals to anti-immigration sentiment, and old-fashioned intimidation and violence.

In 1933 the Confederación de Uniones de Campesinos y Obreros Mexicanos (CUCOM) was founded, growing out of a strike against strawberry growers in El Monte, California; the strikers won a wage increase. Mexican Americans participated in other strikes in California in 1933, including strikes by pickers of cotton, peas, cherries, peaches, lettuce, and grapes. Another important year in the annals of Mexican-American labor history was 1938, when a pecan strike in San Antonio, Texas, led by the United Cannery, Agricultural, Packing,

A CHRONOLOGY OF LULAC, 1929–1946

1929	The League of United Latin American Citizens (LULAC) is founded in Texas by representatives of several other organizations, including the Order of the Sons of America, the Knights of America, and the League of Latin American Citizens. Its objectives are to improve the social, political, and economic rights of Mexican Americans.
1930	LULAC successfully desegregates hundreds of public places in Texas, including swimming pools, rest rooms, barber shops, beauty parlors, drinking fountains, hotels, and restaurants.
1931	LULAC instigates and funds the first class-action lawsuit (Salvatierra v. Del Rio Independent School District) seeking to desegregate schools in Texas.
1936	To better protect Mexican Americans from discrimination, LULAC urges the U.S. Census Bureau to reclassify Mexicans from the designation of "Mexican" to "White." The change is reflected in the 1940 Census.
1940	LULAC files numerous antidiscrimination lawsuits before the Federal Employment Practices Commission, the first federal civil rights agency.
1941	LULAC launches a campaign to protest discriminatory hiring practices by the Southern Pacific Railroad.
1945	LULAC successfully sues to integrate the Orange County School System, which had been segregated on the grounds that Mexican children were more poorly clothed and mentally inferior to white children.
1946	LULAC files Mendez v. Westminster, in Santa Ana, California, a lawsuit that results in the end of a century of segregation in California's public schools.

and Allied Workers of America (UCA-PAWA), won strikers union recognition and a lower decrease in wages than had been expected. That same year UCA-PAWA organizer Luisa Moreno, a Guatemalan-born labor leader who had immigrated to the United States from Mexico, founded the Spanish-Speaking Peoples Congress, which held its first conference in Los Angeles. More than a labor union, the organization was dedicated to winning equal rights for all Hispanic Americans.

The Spanish-Speaking Peoples Congress was not the first Hispanic-American group to organize for such broad aims. The League of United Latin American Citizens (LULAC), an organization of U.S. citizens of Hispanic descent, was established in the late 1920s in Texas to fight discrimination against Mexican Americans. Largely made up of middle-class people, it encouraged Mexican Americans to learn English, become citizens, and exercise their voting privileges. It sought to end discrimination and segregation in education, housing, and employment and to achieve equal protection under the law. It remains the nation's oldest Hispanic organization.

THE WORLD WAR II ERA

Though precise figures are not known, about 250,000 to 500,000 Hispanic Americans are believed to have served in the U.S. armed forces during World War II. Though most were Mexican Americans, their numbers included 53,000 Puerto Ricans. Yet the record of American valor in combat is only part of the story of how Hispanic Americans contributed to winning the war, and how the war changed their history.

The United States did not immediately enter World War II (1939–1945), but it mobilized to improve its own defenses and to supply countries fighting the Axis Powers (chiefly Germany, Japan, and Italy). This mobilization, which stepped up dramatically once the United States entered the war in December 1941, pulled the country out of the Great Depression. Suddenly jobs in defense and other industries were widely available, the more so as conscription and voluntary enlistment put more than 16 million men in uniform.

During the Great Depression, Mexican Americans had been thrown out of jobs and pushed back to Mexico; now jobs lay open for them, and the United States needed the workers it had only just pushed out. One result was the bracero program, a program for recruiting temporary laborers from Mexico, who were called braceros because they worked with their brazos, or arms (the term was the equivalent of the English phrase "hired hands"). The program, launched in 1942, brought hundreds of thousands of Mexicans into the country during the war, and many more in the years afterward (see chapter 7 for more details).

Another result was upward mobility for Mexican Americans, who now accepted jobs that had previously been closed to them. Mexican Americans migrated from the Southwest to urban areas throughout the country in even greater numbers than in World War I, taking on many kinds of work. Educational opportunities improved; for example, the New Mexico Department of Vocational Education expanded its training programs, teaching such skills as welding and mechanics. Mexican Americans were helped by the Fair Employment Practices Committee, a federal body founded in 1941 to eliminate employment discrimination in defense industries and

HISPANIC WINNERS OF THE CONGRESSIONAL MEDAL OF HONOR IN THE EUROPEAN THEATER

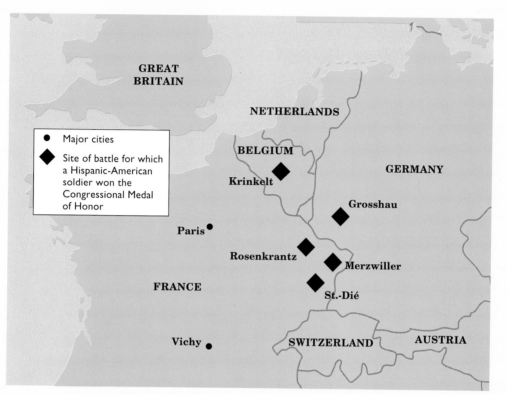

Lucien Adams
Rank: Staff Sergeant
Unit: 30th Infantry, Third Infantry Division
Place: Near St.-Dié, France
Date: October 28, 1945

Marcario Garcia
Rank: Staff Sergeant
Unit: Company B, 22nd Infantry, Fourth Infantry Division
Place: Near Grosshau, Germany
Date: November 27, 1944

Silvestre S. Herrera
Rank: Private First Class
Unit: Company E, 142nd Infantry, 36th Infantry Division
Place: Near Mertzwiller, France
Date: March 15, 1945

José M. Lopez
Rank: Sergeant
Unit: 23rd Infantry, Second Infantry Division
Place: Near Krinkelt, Belgium
Date: December 17, 1944

José F. Valdez
Rank: Private First Class
Unit: Company B, Seventh Infantry Division
Place: Near Rosenkrantz, France
Date: January 25, 1945

government. Though originally aimed at helping African Americans, it enabled many Mexican Americans to obtain jobs they might otherwise not have gained and to achieve parity in wages with their Anglo coworkers.

As for those Mexican Americans who joined the armed forces, they experienced— in many cases for the first time— what it was like to work side by side with Anglo-Americans for a common cause. Hispanic Americans were treated with relatively little discrimination in the armed forces and mostly served in units that integrated them with Anglo-Americans. After World War II, Hispanic-American veterans benefited from the G.I. Bill, which financed higher education and offered low-cost loans to buy homes and establish businesses.

HISPANIC WINNERS OF THE CONGRESSIONAL MEDAL OF HONOR IN THE PACIFIC THEATER

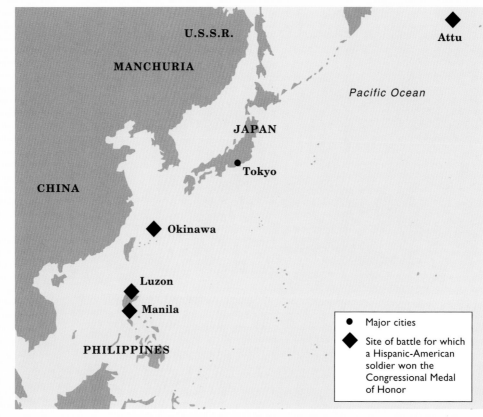

Harold Gonsalves
Rank: Private First Class
Unit: U.S. Marine Corp Reserve (Serving with Fourth Battalion, 15th Marines, Sixth Marine Division)
Place: Okinawa
Date: April 15, 1945

David M. Gonzales
Rank: Private First Class
Unit: Company A, 127th Infantry, 32nd Infantry Division
Place: Villa Verde Trail, Luzon, Philippine Islands
Date: April 25, 1945

Joe P. Martinez
Rank: Private
Unit: Company K, 32nd Infantry, Seventh Infantry Division
Place: Attu, Aleutian Islands (near Alaska)
Date: May 26, 1943

Manuel Perez Jr.
Rank: Private First Class
Unit: Company A, 511th Parachute Infantry, 11th Airborne Division

Place: Fort William McKinley, Luzon, Philippine Islands
Date: Februrary 13, 1945

Cleto Rodriguez
Rank: Technical Sergeant
Unit: Company B, 148th Infantry, 37th Infantry Division

Place: Paco Railroad Station, Manila, Philippine Islands
Date: February 9, 1945

Alejandro R. Ruiz
Rank: Private First Class
Unit: 165th Infantry, 27th Infantry Division
Place: Okinawa
Date: April 28, 1945

Ysmael R. Villegas
Rank: Staff Sergeant
Unit: Company F, 127th Infantry, 32nd Infantry Division
Place: Villa Verde Trail, Luzon, Philippine Islands
Date: March 20, 1945

Even more than World War I, in which fewer Mexican Americans fought, the experience of World War II changed Mexican Americans. Having lost comrades and risked their lives to defend their country, they became more conscious of the world beyond the barrio and the colonia and more determined to demand the rights due to them as Americans.

Hispanic Heroes

Hispanic Americans participated in all campaigns of World War II, in both the European and the Pacific theaters. Many Hispanic Americans were stationed in the Philippines, where their knowledge of Spanish assisted them in communicating with Filipinos, who knew the language from the days when their islands were a Spanish colony. Two units made up of Mexican Americans from New Mexico, Texas, and Arizona fought in the Battle of Bataan in the Philippines. Hispanic Americans also fought on the beaches of Normandy during the D-Day invasion of June 1944.

Relative to their share of the population, Hispanic Americans served in disproportionate numbers in combat divisions and earned a disproportionate share of military honors. Although not all Hispanics served on the front lines, a great number did serve as infantrymen, marines, paratroopers, and tank corpsmen. Seventeen won the Congressional Medal of Honor, five posthumously. An all-Hispanic infantry company, Company E of the 141st Regiment of the 36th Division, was one of the war's most decorated units.

Two stories of Medal of Honor winners, one from Europe, the other from the Pacific, indicate the kind of courage Hispanic Americans showed in the war. José M. Lopez, a native of Mission, Texas, serving as a sergeant in the 23rd Infantry, Second Infantry Division, won his Medal of Honor for uncommon valor near Krinkelt, Belgium, on December 17, 1944. When his company was in danger of being enveloped by an advancing regiment of German infantry, Lopez picked up his heavy machine gun and moved it to one hazardous position after another, to better repel the advance. Almost single-handedly, he held off the enemy long enough to allow his comrades to withdraw. In the process, he killed at least 100 enemy troops, all the while ignoring the threat from tank, artillery, and small-arms fire.

José Lopez survived to tell of his bravery, but another hero was not so fortunate. On April 25, 1945, David M.

Gonzales, a native of Pacoma, California, was serving in Luzon, Philippine Islands, as a private first class in the 127th Infantry, 32nd Infantry Division. His company was pinned down by Japanese fire, and a bomb buried five comrades under rock and sand. Private Gonzales rushed forward through the hail of enemy bullets to help his commanding officer dig out the men. The officer was killed at once by machine-gun fire, but Gonzales kept digging, disregarding the enormous danger. He managed to free three men from being buried alive before being hit by gunfire and mortally wounded. He was posthumously awarded the Congressional Medal of Honor for his action.

Sleepy Lagoon and the Zoot Suit Riots

Despite the sacrifices Hispanic Americans made in the defense of their country in World War II, two wartime incidents in Los Angeles reminded them that the struggle for full acceptance as Americans was far from over. Both of these incidents—the Sleepy Lagoon case and the Zoot Suit Riots—were related to an item of apparel called the zoot suit.

The zoot suit combined a long coat and high-waisted, tight-cuffed pants, and was usually worn with a broad-brimmed hat. A ducktail haircut and hanging watch chain completed the look. In the early 1940s, among others, Mexican-American youths known as pachucos liked to wear zoot suits. For Anglo-Americans infected with war-time xenophobia and egged on by a sensationalist press, the zoot suit was associated with youth gangs, hooligans, and crime.

In August 1942, when a young Mexican American named José Díaz was found dead on a rural road one day after a gang fight at the Sleepy Lagoon swimming hole in Los Angeles, local newspapers and the police accused young zoot suiters. Twenty-two Mexican-American youths who belonged to a gang involved in the fight were tried for the crime. Despite a stunning lack of evidence and flagrant violations of their civil rights, 12 of the defendants were found guilty of murder in January 1943. Supporters formed a Sleepy Lagoon Defense Committee, and nearly two years later, in October 1944, an appeals court reversed

"As a veteran you have equal rights like everybody else, so it gave Mexican Americans new opportunities to go back to school or get benefits. It gave us a feeling of being equal."

—Carlos Samarron, San Antonio, Texas, on his experience as a U.S. Marine

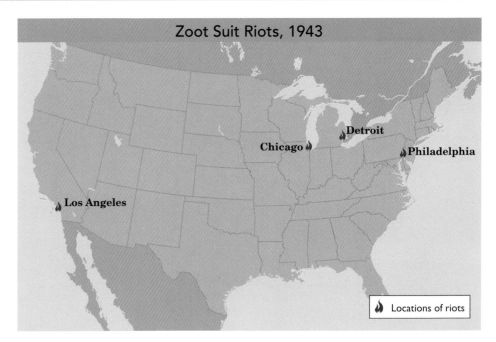

Zoot Suit Riots, 1943

Detroit

Chicago

Philadelphia

Los Angeles

Locations of riots

the convictions and dismissed all charges for lack of evidence.

Despite the dismissal, the high-profile coverage of the trial had served to inflame anti-Mexican sentiment. Regardless of the trial's outcome, many Anglos viewed the episode as confirmation of racist stereotypes—that zoot suiters were by nature criminals. Coming in a time of war when many young Americans were enlisted in the military, the Sleepy Lagoon case called attention to the perceived character of those on trial and ignited some to strike out against them.

As a result, the zoot suiters of Los Angeles suffered more injustices both during and after the trial. Minor skirmishes between Anglo servicemen on furlough and pachucos in zoot suits began increasing in number. Then in June 1943 the tension boiled over. Claiming that some sailors had been attacked by pachucos, hundreds of sailors and soldiers roamed Los Angeles, grabbing, beating, and tearing the zoot suit off of every zoot suiter they could find. For several nights

the riots continued, aimed at any and all Mexican-American youths, whether they were wearing zoot suits or not. The police not only failed to protect the Hispanic victims, they arrested them as if they were responsible. The newspapers, too, blamed the victims, sensationalizing any incident of retaliation by pachucos while lionizing the servicemen for teaching them a lesson.

The riots spread to other cities in California and sparked similar attacks that summer on Mexican Americans in Chicago, Detroit, and Philadelphia. By mid-June the Los Angeles Zoot Suit Riots were over, stopped by military police and the cancellation of overnight passes and leaves. The incident led to earnest official explorations of the possible causes of the riots and short-lived attempts to improve relations between Anglos and Mexican Americans. For Hispanic Americans, Sleepy Lagoon and the Zoot Suit Riots became spurs to fight harder against brutality and prejudice and towards full equality with Anglo-Americans.

LA RAZA UNIDA
The United People and Civil Rights

Since World War II, more Hispanics have come to the United States than in all its previous history. Much of that influx occurred from the mid-1940s to the mid-1970s. The migration had several sources. Mexicans came in increased numbers as a result of the bracero program, an initiative to recruit temporary agricultural labor that was begun during World War II and perpetuated afterward until 1964. The falling cost of air travel made it possible for Puerto Ricans to move to the mainland in numbers large enough to be termed the Puerto Rican "Great Migration." A communist revolution in Cuba in 1959 drove hundreds of thousands of Cubans into exile in the United States, where they were welcomed as political refugees, not subject to the same immigration restrictions as people from most other countries. Political turmoil, economic distress, and lack of opportunity in the Dominican Republic, Central America, and South America brought people from all those regions to the United States despite new immigration restrictions enacted in 1965.

As Hispanic Americans became a more visible presence in the United States, they became more aware of their distinct ethnic identity and more determined to work collectively for their share of the American dream. During the 1960s, César Chávez led Mexican-American farmworkers to strike for better working conditions, and "Chicano," a slang term for Mexican American, became a rallying cry for a new civil rights movement. In various ways—some peaceful, some violent—Hispanic Americans struggled for equal treatment and full political participation. They built new communities that bore the marks of their distinct national origins. But they had not yet begun to reach in any significant way across their national differences. They had not begun to form, in the hopeful phrase of a political party founded at the time, La Raza Unida: The United People.

In 1965, a young playwright named Luis Valdez launched a theater company from the back of a flatbed farm truck in Delano, California. The company, El Teatro Campesino ("farmworkers' theater"), served as cultural offshoot of César Chavez' United Farm Workers (UFW), and its mission was to entertain, to educate and to harness the arts in support striking workers. In fact, the original troupe was made entirely of migrant farmworkers, some of whom were illiterate. The troupe performed their actos, or "short plays" without scripts, props, or lighting, and the actors wore hand-lettered signs around their necks to identify their characters: "grower, " "farmworker," "green grape," "rotten grape" or "raisin." "It was crude and rude and lively, but it mattered," says Valdez.

Valdez himself came from a migrant farmworker family. After graduating from San Jose State University, and a brief stint with the San Francisco Mime Troupe, he returned to Delano to found the Teatro Campesino. Valdez later gained fame for his play *Zoot Suit*, which was produced on Broadway, and for directing the film *La Bamba*, about the life of Mexican-American singer Ritchie Valens.

Although Teatro Campesino is no longer affiliated with the UFW, Valdez remembers those early performances as a form of political art — an outgrowth of the atmosphere of change that was sweeping the nation. Issues of race, class and the Vietnam War were at the forefront of the nation's consciousness. "We saw ourselves as fighting a battle, and we had no idea how it would end," Valdez said in an interview with the organization Tolerance.org. "We had 24 or 25 ranches, a thousand square miles to cover with a roving picket line. We'd start driving before dawn, looking for scab crews, then we'd pull up to the side of the road and start performing."

While Teatro Campesino's early days as a guerilla theater company were very much in the spirit of the 1960s, they also drew on centuries old traditions that were rooted in centuries of Hispanic culture, such as *commedia dell'arte*, Spanish religious dramas adapted for teaching Mission Indians, Mexican folk humor, a

They tell me I'm too head strong, yell too much and incite people

They tell me I am too head strong, yell too much and incite people

But Juarez was my uncle, my father-in-law, Zapata

And now organizing the workers in all of the fields

And now organizing the workers in all of the fields

Because some only eat tortillas with nothing else but chiles

We've been many years, fighting in this strike

We've been many years, fighting in this strike

One grower bit the dust, another's a granddaddy

—from the song "El Picket Sign" by Luis Valdez, founder of Teatro Campesino

Artist Rudy Cuellar, a member of the Royal Chicano Air Force (RCAF), created this poster to promote a performance by El Teatro Campesino. The RCAF, based in Sacramento, California, is an artistic collective founded in 1969 to express the goals of the Chicano civil rights and labor organizing movement of the United Farm Workers. (Poster by Rudy Cuellar, Royal Chicano Air Force Archives, California Ethnic and Multicultural Archives, Special Collections Department, Donald C. Davidson Library, University of California, Santa Barbara)

century-old tradition of Mexican performances in California, and Aztec and Maya sacred ritual dramas.

LATINO CULTURAL ACHIEVEMENT IN THE POST-WAR ERA

By 1971, Valdez began adapting traditional religious plays *La Virgen del Tepeyac* and *La Pastorela* for Christmas celebrations. In doing so, Valdez was not alone. Throughout the postwar era, Latino artistic expression, whether in theater, literature, music, or the fine arts, frequently reflected not only current audience tastes and the contemporary Chicano rights movement, but longstanding Hispanic traditions. In reviving and renewing these artistic traditions during the 1960s and 1970s, Valdez and others were embracing their historical identities as Chicanos, Puerto Ricans, and Cuban Americans.

HISPANIC-AMERICAN THEATER

The theatrical traditions that Valdez drew on dated back to both the religious theater and pageantry of medieval Spain and to the ritual dances of American Indians. In the sixteen and seventeenth centuries, Spanish missionaries fused these traditions together by using theater as a tool

for converting the Indians of Mexico and their mestizo descendants. These plays incorporated the colors, music, and sometimes even languages of Mexico's indigenous peoples. By the eighteenth century a cycle of religious plays dramatizing stories from the Bible, had become popularized. Among them was the *pastorela*, or shepherd's play, which told the story of Satan's efforts to tempt shepherds on their pilgrimage to Bethlehem to pay tribute to the newborn Christ Child. Local productions of the entire cycle of these plays—each imbued with a sense of missionary zeal—took place each year between mid-December and Easter, and involved the entire local community. Despite their Christian nature, these plays frequently had strong elements of slapstick comedy, and often used allegory and masks for actors—folk elements that can be found in the Hispanic theater even today.

While the roots of the Hispanic folk theater go back to the era of Spanish colonization, the first professional Hispanic theater troupes in the United States first emerged in mid-nineteenth century. By the 1840s, itinerant professional theater groups toured the ranchos of northern California, and by the 1870s, local troupes as far afield as Tucson, Arizona and San Antonio, Texas toured regionally.

By the early twentieth century, rail transportation allowed touring companies the ability to reach smaller cities and towns as never before. Mobile makeshift tent and circus theaters soon sprang up on both sides of the Rio Grande, particularly during and after the Mexican Revolution, as thousands of Mexican refugees arrived in the United States, settling in small communities from the border region up to Chicago, New York, and Tampa, Florida. Los Angeles and San Antonio, the U.S. cities with the largest Mexican populations became major Hispanic theater centers. Mexican expatriate playwrights such as Adalberto Elias Gonzalez and Esteban Escalante produced full-length plays that addressed the situation of Mexicans in California. Their extremely popular works helped to solidify Hispanic culture and mores in the United States among the Mexican immigrant community in the face of pressures to assimilate into mainstream American culture.

While the rise of Mexican vaudeville and musicals would displace more serious

Mexican theater in the early twentieth century, that did not mean serious themes did not underlie the presentations. Instead, they were developed within theatrical revues known as *revistas*. *Revistas* usually focused on the lives of the working class. While the early *revistas* on the stages of Revolution-era Mexico City were overtly political, later revistas on both sides of the border were less so. Still, they remained comedic revues that featured comic underdog heroes known as *pelados*, who poked fun at the American and Mexican governments and other authorities. Plots of *revistas* in the American Southwest frequently centered on the misadventures of naïve newcomers to the United States and the underlying real-life cultural shock that the Mexican immigrant community was experiencing. By the late 1920s, and particularly during the Depression-era repatriation crisis, *revistas* reflected the shift from culture shock to outright culture clash. In the face of growing anti-Mexican sentiment in the United States, an even stronger sense of national identity arose in the Mexican-American community of the Southwest. Depression-era *revistas* reflected this by introducing the *renegado*, or thoroughly Americanized Mexican immigrant as a target of satire.

Meanwhile, theater in Hispanic communities in other parts of the United States also blossomed during this era, though with differences. Cuban and Spanish immigrants dominated the turn-of-the century Hispanic theaters in New York City and in Ybor City, Florida. Instead of the Mexican *revista*, Cuban New Yorkers and Floridians frequented *obra bufa cubana*, or Cuban blackface farce. These productions featured slapstick comedy, Afro-Cuban song and dance, and like *revistas* drew material out of current events, gossip and concerns of the community.

During the 1920s and 1930s, New York's Puerto Rican theatrical community produced far more serious works. Puerto Rican playwright José Enamorado Cuesta produced socialist dramas in support of the Spanish Republican cause and the struggles of the working class. Gonzalo O'Neill's plays focused on Puerto Rican nationalism and independence from the United States. Meanwhile, Tampa's Centro Asturiano, one of the city's most important mutual aid societies during the Depression, hosted the only Spanish-language Federal Theater Project in the nation. The Federal Theater Project was a program of President Roosevelt's New Deal, in which the federal government financed artists to develop theater productions in an effort to keep them employed as well as to bring the arts to communities that rarely benefited from live theater.

Post-War Hispanic Theatre

During World War II and the years immediately following, Hispanic theater in the Southwest, New York, Tampa, Florida went through difficult times, as many local venues for live theater converted to moviehouses. In San Antonio, comedic stage actors like Beatriz "La Chata" Noelesca and Pedro "Ramirin" Gonzalez kept the vaudeville tradition barely alive, while other vaudeville performers began making the transition to radio and television.

In New York, 1953 saw the opening *La Carreta* ("The Oxcart") by Puerto Rican author Rene Marqués at the Church of San Sebastian. The play concerned a rural Puerto Rican family and their relocation first to a San Juan slum and then to New York—this dramatizing the real life experience of many of the working-class audience. In 1965 *La Carreta* made it to Off-Broadway in a production starring Raul Julia and Miriam Colón.

With Luis Valdez's founding of Teatro Campesino in the fields of Delano, California in 1965, a groundswell of new "teatro Chicano" (Chicano theater) groups arose throughout the nation. In community centers, church basements, public parks and elsewhere, a new generation of Chicanos used theater in service of a new bilingual, bicultural identity. With the publication of an anthology of Valdez's works in 1971, local teatros had access to his full repertoire. And with it they also received Valdez's theatrical and political canons for presenting el teatro Chicano:

(1) Chicanos must be seen as a nation with geographic, religious, cultural, and racial roots in the Southwest; teatros must further the idea of nationalism and create a national theater based on identification with the Amerindian past;

(2) the organizational support of the national theater must be from within and totally independent;

(3) "Teatros must never get away from La Raza [the people].... If the Raza will not come to the theater, then the theater must go to the Raza. This, in the long run, will determine the shape, style, content, spirit and form of el teatro chicano."

The influence of Teatro Campesino was not limited to Chicanos. In New York, Teatro Cuatro, an improvisational street theater named after its location on Fourth Avenue on the Lower East Side, brought together Puerto Rican, Dominican and other Latin American actors to produce a politically radical people's theater aimed at raising the consciousness of working-class Latinos, across nationality lines.

Another important development in Latino theater in New York was the emergence of the Nuyorican movement. The term Nuyorican means "New York Puerto Rican" and does not signify a specific type of theater. In fact, Nuyorican productions ranged from improvised street theater to works by individual Puerto Rican New Yorkers that were produced for Joseph Papp's Shakespeare Festival or even Broadway. In fact, it was a group of poets associated with both Papp and the Nuyorican Poet's Café on the Lower East Side that best exemplified the movement. These writers, including Miguel Algarin, Lucky Cienfuegos, Tato Laviera and Miquel Piñero, focused on the life and culture of underclass Puerto Ricans in New York. In 1974, Piñero's prison drama *Short Eyes*, won an Obie and New York Drama Critics Award for Best American Play.

The national teatro movement reached its peak in 1976, when five teatro festivals were held to commemorate the American bicentennial. By the 1980s, many Chicano theater groups began to disband, as individual members left to join community theater companies with larger budgets, steadier funding sources, and better facilities. Valdez himself reached mainstream audiences first with his play *Zoot Suit*, which appeared on Broadway in 1979. He then directed the Ritchie Valens biopic *La Bamba* in 1987, and wrote and directed an updated television movie version of *The Cisco Kid* in 1994, starring Jimmy Smits and Cheech Marin.

HISPANIC AMERICANS IN FILM

As discussed in Chapter 6, the Cisco Kid character dates back to the early days of Hollywood. Hispanic Americans in film fell into one of a limited number of racially stereotyped roles—the dark lady, the bandido, the buffoon, or, as illustrated by Cisco, the caballero. In each case, each character reinforced a message that the Hispanic was outside of the mainstream, outside of majority Anglo-American values.

During the war years, Hollywood continued to present Hispanic caricatures in support of the perceived majority values. In 1941, Nelson D. Rockefeller, Coordinator of Inter-American Affairs (CIAA) for Franklin Roosevelt, asked Walt Disney make a goodwill tour of Mexico, Central and South America, in keeping with the administration's Good Neighbor Policy, and the strong desire to prevent any Latin American nations from allying with the Axis Powers. As part of the tour, Disney introduced two new films, featuring Hispanic characters. The first film, *Saludos Amigos*, featured José Carioca, a Brazilian parrot and friend to Donald Duck. The film was so successful that Disney released a sequel, *The Three Caballeros*, which added a third character, Panchito, a Mexican rooster. Together, José Carioca, Donald Duck and Panchito, symbolized what the United States was promoting as the close friendship between Brazil, the United States and Mexico. Although the films played to cartoon stereotypes, they were extremely popular both in Latin America and in the United States. Mexicans appreciated that *The Three Caballeros* presented Mexican traditions such as piñata parties and Christmas *posadas* in a positive light.

Between the end of the war and the late 1960s, Hollywood Westerns provided Hispanic actors with work, but outside of Westerns, roles were generally limited to bit parts. Often, Anglo actors played Hispanic characters. Burt Lancaster, for example, starred in *Valdez is Coming*, Marlon Brando was Mexican revolutionary Emiliano Zapata in *Viva Zapata*, Eli Wallach played the bandit Calvera, in *The Magnificent Seven*, and Paul Newman played the Hispanic lead in *The Outrage*. In 1962's film version of *West Side Story*, the Broadway musical about a clash between white and Puerto Rican gangs,

Rita Moreno in West Side Story (Corbis)

Rita Moreno was the only Hispanic with a significant role.

FINE ARTS

As in the case of Latino theater, works by Hispanic American painters, sculptors and other fine artists in the mid-twentieth century both reflected contemporary trends in fine art while also were rooted in the cultural experiences and history of Latino peoples. During the Great Depression, a number of Hispanic artists found work with the New Deal's Federal Works Progress Art (WPA) Project. Although many large scale murals from this era depicted purely Anglo themes, the work of some Mexican-American artists reflected their heritage. For example, Antonio Garcia, who was born in Monterrey, Mexico and studied at the Chicago Institute of Art, is well known for his mural *Our Lady of Guadeloupe* (1946–47). While employed by the WPA, New Mexico's Edward Chavez painted murals for post offices and other government buildings in Colorado, Kansas, Texas and Wyoming. These murals depicted history, daily life and industry in each of these regions. In his

Indians on the Plains (1943), his subject was the Indians and first white men on the Great Plains.

With the arrival of the 1960s, Mexican-American art, like its theater, took a political turn. The Chicano Art Movement, like the Chicano theater, was overtly political and sought to celebrate and demand and respect for Mexican culture and heritage. Initially, the movement was influenced by the United Farm Workers' struggle, and artists referenced the union's eagle logo frequently. Ernesto Palamino, from Fresno, California, was one of the first Chicano artists. Palamino often used motifs from pre-Columbian cultures as well as contemporary Chicano culture. Luis Jiménez also used pre-Columbian symbols in his sculptural work of the 1960s and 1970s.

Meanwhile, New York's diverse art scene ranged from realism to conceptual and abstract. Puerto Rican painter Pedro Villarini focused on painting objects from his daily life with great precision. Raphael Ferrer, born in Santurce, Puerto Rico, on the other hand, was an installation artist who used everything from hay bales to blocks of ice to create his ephemeral works. And New York-born performance artist Ralph Ortiz was influenced by

Tito Puente (Corbis)

the early twentieth century Dadaist movement. In one of his best-known works, *Piano Destruction Concert*, he hacked a piano to pieces with an ax on national television. Ortiz's "destructive art" was not purely abstract, however. In his series *Archeological Finds*, he used pre-Columbian motifs to symbolize the destruction brought to the Americas by Europeans. In 1969, Ortiz founded El Museo del Barrio, the first museum in the United States dedicated exclusively to Latino arts.

MUSIC

The story of music in Hispanic culture, and in virtually all cultures, is one of tradition, adaptation and the blending of influences. Tex-Mex music for example, is an adaptation of European band music traditions while Cuban and Puerto Rican music is rooted in the use of African percussion and rhythm.

What we know now as Tex-Mex, or Tejano music, has its origins in the mid-nineteenth century. In the 1850s, immigrants from Germany, Poland and what is now the Czech Republic arrived in Texas and Mexico, bringing with them their waltzes, polkas and other popular forms of music and dance. With the start of the Mexican Revolution, many of these Europeans fled northward from Mexico into South Texas, where their music would have a major impact on the Tejanos living in the region. During the early twentieth century, the main form of musical entertainment on the farms and ranches of South Texas were Mexican traveling bands playing Spanish and Mexican story songs on in traditional styles such as corrido and mariachi.

One of the most popular singers of these traditional songs was Lydia Mendoza, who had been taught to play stringed instruments by her mother and grandmother. During the 1920s, record labels like RCA and Paramount had begun producing what it called "race records." In addition to African-American blues singers like Mississippi's Bessie Smith and Texas's "Blind" Lemon Jefferson, the labels also took an interest in Spanish-language music. In 1928, Mendoza and several members of her family recorded for Okeh Records under the name Cuarteto Carta Blanca. By the

mid-thirties, she was recording as a solo singer, and in 1934, "Mal Hombre," her best known song, became a smash hit on Spanish language radio.

By this time, traveling Mexican musical groups had come in contact with areas of Texas with heavier German, Polish and Czech populations. In doing so, they began to incorporate German made accordions with their distinctive "oom-pah" sound, into their own music, which came to be known as conjunto. Among the first and most famous Tejano musicians to popularize the accordion was Narciso Martinez, who is known today as the father of conjunto music. Conjunto soon became the popular music of the working class Tejano. Since that time, others have followed in Martinez's footsteps. Flaco Jimenez, the son of an accordionist and grandson of a man who had learned the instrument from a German immigrant, is the most prominent.

During the 1950s, 1960s and 1970s, some conjunto, as well as mariachi and other traditional Mexican styles became heavily influenced by rock and country music, and drums, electric guitars and keyboards and found their way into conjunto lineups, creating yet another form of hybrid, known as Tex-Mex music. In 1958, a teenager from Valencia, California named Ricardo Valencia, but better known as Ritchie Valens took a traditional mariachi tune called "La Bamba" and gave it a rock and roll beat. Baldemar Huerta, born in San Benito, Texas, became better known as the country singer Freddy Fender. He is best known for his 1974 ballad "Before the Next Teardrop Falls."

While Mexican Americans make up the vast majority of the Hispanic-American population of the United States, Tex-Mex music has always had more of a regional appeal than a widespread commercial impact. On the other hand, an early twentieth century music style emanating from Cuba in the late 1920s, known as "son," has had an enormous global impact. A fusion of Spanish popular music and the African rhythm rumba, son is played on guitar, contrabass, bongos and rounded sticks called claves. As son began to spread and mix with other forms, new instruments were introduced. Flute and violin orchestras, known as charangas, performed a version of son known as the danzon for upper class Cuban audiences. In the 1930s, the Spanish-Cuban bandleader Xavier Cugat founded the Waldorf-Astoria Orchestra in New York, and introduced a highly commercialized (and enormously popular) Latin sound to U.S. audiences.

In the 1940s, bandleader Perez Prado introduced a national craze with new upbeat form of the danzon known as the mambo. A fusion of Cuban music and jazz (or "cubop") became popular after World War II, influencing Dizzy Gillespie and other key jazz figures of the era. New Yorker Frank "Machito" Grillo, who had sung with Xavier Cugat, was a key figure in this genre. Machito would also mentor one of the key figures in the modern Latin music scene in the United States, the Puerto Rican drummer Ernesto "Tito" Puente. *Dance Mania*, one of Puente's best-known records came out in 1958. While Tito Puente played a wide range of Afro-Cuban and other music styles, he is best known as one of the key figures in salsa music, a general term that is sometimes used as an all-encompassing word for Latin music, but more specifically for the fusion of Afro-Cuban and Latin jazz.

Throughout the 1960s, New York remained the center of Latin music in the United States. In addition to Tito Puente, key musicians during the decade included fellow Puerto Rican New Yorkers Ray Barretto and Eddie Palmieri. By the end of the decade, as the hybrid Nuyorican cultural identity emerged, the atmosphere was ripe for and explosion of modern salsa music. Contemporary salsa is said to have been born on the streets of New York. The New York-based record company, Fania Records, introduced many of the early salsa stars, including Johnny Pacheco and Willie Colón.

Latinos in Sports

In 1947, Jackie Robinson, an all-American multi-sport college athlete, broke the major league baseball color line when Brooklyn Dodger general manager Branch Rickey called the African-American Robinson up from the Dodger's minor league affiliate, the Montreal Expos. Over next few years, more African-American athletes would join the majors, as would a growing number of players from Latin America.

There were Latino players in the major leagues before Robinson, though only those with light skin were allowed to play. Some, like Rafael Almeida and Armando Marsans of the Cincinnati Reds, were forced to sign affidavits swearing they were of European and not African descent. Nonetheless, over 40 players, mostly Cubans, played major league baseball between 1902 and 1947. The most prominent was Adolfo Luque, who had a 30-year career as a player and manager.

After Robinson shattered the color line, black and other darker-skinned Latinos joined the game. During the 1950s, Minnie Minoso, Roberto Clemente, Orlando Cepeda, and others helped alter the game forever. Vic Power, a Puerto Rican first baseman who won seven Gold Glove awards in the late 1950s and early 1960s, introduced the one-handed catch at his base, which earned him the reputation from white writers as a "showboat." Frequently, Latino players found that because they spoke little English and therefore got less press attention, their accomplishments on the field were not as well known. Stars like Clemente were branded as "moody", "hot-tempered", or even "troubled" due to his relationship with the press.

In other major sports, Latino participation was much rarer during the 1950s and 1960s. While today there are a handful of Latino football, basketball and even hockey players, there were virtually none in that earlier era. By the end of the 1960s, however, professional golf boasted two major Latino stars: Lee Treviño and Juan "Chi Chi" Rodriguez.

THE BRACERO PROGRAM

Established as an emergency response to wartime labor shortages, the bracero program, which provided for the temporary entry of seasonal farmworkers, became the cornerstone institution in U.S.-Mexican relations for more than 20 years (1942–1964). It was buttressed by American growers, who wanted to protect their low labor costs, and it was tremendously popular with poor Mexicans, who welcomed higher wages, even under exploitative conditions. Before the program ended, it had employed nearly 5 million Mexicans, though many of these were "repeaters"—

Roberto Clemente (Corbis)

Chi Chi Rodriguez (Corbis)

Mexican braceros on their way to the Midwest to farm beets (National Archives)

"[T]hey'd send us into a huge bunk house, where the contractors would come from the growers associations in counties like San Joaquin County, Yolo , Sacramento, Fresno and so on. The heads of the associations would line us up. When they saw someone they didn't like, they'd say, "You, no." Others, they'd say, "You, stay."

—Rigoberto Garcia Perez, former bracero worker, in a 2001 interview with journalist David Bacon

people who were counted again each year they participated. Hundreds of thousands of braceros ultimately settled in the United States.

THE FIRST BRACERO PROGRAM

In July 1942 the United States had been at war for eight months and was looking ahead to an indefinitely long period in which much of its working population would be overseas in uniform. Temporary laborers were needed to fill their places at home. Therefore, the United States and Mexico formally agreed to permit American growers and, later, railroad owners to recruit Mexican braceros, or hired hands, on a temporary basis. Each year the workers harvested beets, cotton, corn, and other crops, then returned to Mexico when the harvest was done. At Mexico's insistence, safeguards protecting the braceros' interests were written into the agreement. Thus, signed contracts between laborers and employers were required, round-trip transportation between Mexico and the United States was to be provided by employers, and minimum guarantees concerning wages and labor conditions were instituted.

In practice, many of the agreement's provisions were routinely violated.

Living conditions were often substandard, with employers providing pest-infested trailers or shacks for housing, and pigs' feet and chicken necks for food. Workers complained of discrimination, physical abuse, and unjust deductions from wages resulting in low net earnings. But considering Mexico's severe unemployment and low wages, the bracero program proved irresistible to many poor Mexicans, some of whom returned year after year to participate in it. When the wartime program wound down in 1947, more than 200,000 Mexicans had been employed as braceros in 21 states.

THE *MOJADOS*

Although growers often circumvented the protections that the bracero program was meant to secure, braceros generally fared better than Mexican laborers who entered the United States illegally. Many of the illegals (who were also known as mojados, or "wetbacks," because they often entered the United States by swimming across the Rio Grande) wound up in Texas, where anti-Mexican prejudice was so strong and incidence of mistreatment so common that the Mexican governement forbid braceros from working in the state.

This ban gave an opportunity to undocumented laborers. However,

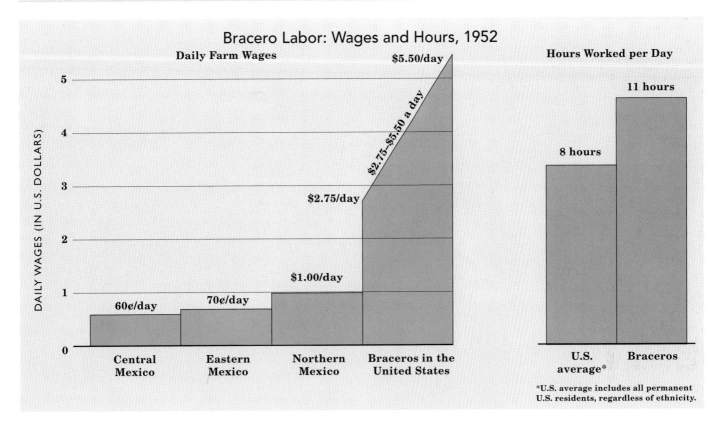

Bracero Labor: Wages and Hours, 1952

Daily Farm Wages

DAILY WAGES (IN U.S. DOLLARS)

- 60¢/day — Central Mexico
- 70¢/day — Eastern Mexico
- $1.00/day — Northern Mexico
- $2.75/day / $2.75–$5.50 a day / $5.50/day — Braceros in the United States

Hours Worked per Day

- 8 hours — U.S. average*
- 11 hours — Braceros

*U.S. average includes all permanent U.S. residents, regardless of ethnicity.

because mojados were not protected from abuse by the rules of the bracero program, they found themselves paid less than the bracero minimum wage and with few, if any, of the benefits offered to braceros. Any mojado who objected was threatened with deportation.

Although the practice of hiring undocumented Mexican workers was officially frowned upon by the U.S.

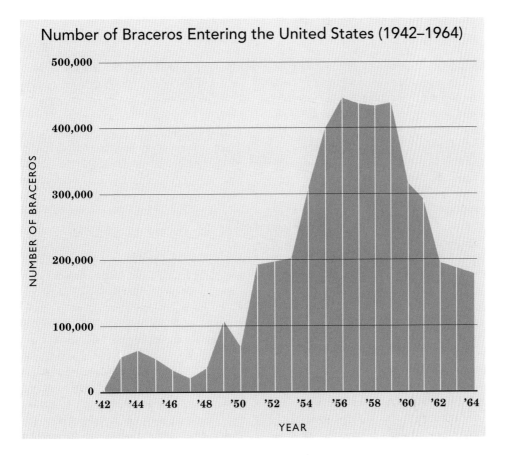

Number of Braceros Entering the United States (1942–1964)

NUMBER OF BRACEROS

500,000
400,000
300,000
200,000
100,000
0

'42 '44 '46 '48 '50 '52 '54 '56 '58 '60 '62 '64

YEAR

HISPANIC HEROES IN KOREA AND VIETNAM

As in all the nation's wars dating back to the American Revolution, Hispanic Americans fought for their country in the Korean War (1950–1953) and the Vietnam War (1954–1975). Nine Hispanic Americans received the Congressional Medal of Honor for valorous action in the Korean War, and one all-Hispanic unit served: the Puerto Rican 65th Infantry Regiment.

Numerous Hispanics received the Medal of Honor for action in the Vietnam era, and analysis of casualty figures indicates that Hispanic Americans in Vietnam laid down their lives in battle in numbers disproportionate to their representation in the population. Also noteworthy in the Vietnam era is Hispanic-American resistance to the war. In 1970 the National Chicano Moratorium Committee was founded to protest U.S. involvement in the war and the high number of Hispanic-American casualties.

federal government, not only did the government frequently ignore the practice, but it also provided growers with legal loopholes to protect it. In 1947, for example, an agreement between the United States and Mexico allowed deported mojados to return to the United States with temporary labor contracts to work for the same employers who had turned them in to the government as illegals. While these temporary contracts were in effect, the migrants could not be deported again. This provision led to a practice known as "drying out the wetbacks," in which employers would report their illegal migrants to the border patrol, which would then ship the laborers back across the border, where they would sign labor agreements and return.

THE EL PASO INCIDENT AND THE SECOND BRACERO PROGRAM

While the practice of "drying out wetbacks" was embraced in Texas, growers in states where the bracero program was not banned made sure that the program was renewed in 1947, even though it was supposed to have terminated shortly after end of World War II. The demand for farm produce was booming, and growers could use bracero labor to hold down wages. Hence the bracero program was renewed with a U.S.-Mexico agreement in 1948.

An event known as the El Paso incident temporarily derailed it, however. Texas cotton growers instituted a maximum bracero wage of $2.50 per 100 pounds of cotton, even though the going nonbracero rate was $3.00. Mexico protested, refusing to supply braceros unless they also received $3.00. In October 1948, under pressure from growers, the U.S. Immigration and Naturalization Service (INS) took an action that circumvented Mexico's resistance: it opened the border at El Paso to Mexican workers, who poured into Texas despite Mexico's efforts to stop them. The Mexicans were then transported to labor camps to pick cotton at the $2.50 wage, which satisfied them if not the Mexican government.

In response to the El Paso incident, for which the United States formally apologized, Mexico renounced the bracero agreement. But the flow of

undocumented workers did not stop, and both governments agreed some controls had to be instituted. In August 1949 a new bracero agreement was instituted, one that penalized growers who hired undocumented workers, legalized undocumented workers already in the United States, and stressed suppression of illegal entry. Dissatisfied with the program's safeguards of worker rights, Mexico took the opportunity to strengthen them when the United States needed to step up the program to supply labor needs during the Korean War (1950–1953). Under Public Law 78, passed in 1951, the Department of Labor took charge of braceros, transporting them and guaranteeing fair labor practices, including a minimum wage at prevailing rates. This agreement led to a great increase in the number of braceros, from fewer than 100,000 in 1950 to nearly 200,000 in 1951.

After the Korean War ended, growers repeatedly persuaded the United States to extend Public Law 78 and continue the bracero program. During the peak period of 1955 to 1959, an average of nearly 430,000 braceros per year entered the United States. From the initiation of Public Law 78 to its demise in 1964, about 25 percent of all seasonal farm workers in Texas, California, Arizona, and New Mexico were braceros.

Several factors led to the end of the bracero program. Demand for labor fell as growers increasingly mechanized their farms. Civil rights and labor organizations protested the program as a way of keeping wages low and exploiting workers. In addition, a $1 per hour minimum wage for braceros, instituted in 1962, made it more expensive for growers to hire braceros, making the arrangement undesirable to growers. In 1964 Public Law 78 at last expired, ending the bracero program.

OPERATION WETBACK

At the same time that the bracero program brought millions of Mexicans to the United States, millions of other Mexicans entered through other means, legal and illegal. Some came on permanent or temporary visas; others came without any documents, slipping illicitly over the border, often with the help of coyotes, or smugglers. Some stayed permanently;

others came and went seasonally. This vast flow of immigration continued after the demise of the bracero program, filling the continuing demand of growers for laborers who would work cheaply. Because illegal Mexican immigrants kept labor costs low in the Southwest, they indirectly pushed Mexican Americans already living there to migrate north in search of increased opportunity.

The government tried to block the flow of undocumented immigration, most notably in a program called Operation Wetback. Launched by the INS in 1954,

Operation Wetback was a military-style program for intensive enforcement of U.S. immigration laws. In its first year, the program, which routinely ignored the civil rights of its targets, resulted in the deportation of about 1 million allegedly undocumented Mexican immigrants. Illegal immigration, as measured by the number of apprehensions and deportations, fell in the years that followed but picked up again once the bracero program ended. During the 1970s, an average of 721,000 undocumented Mexicans were deported each

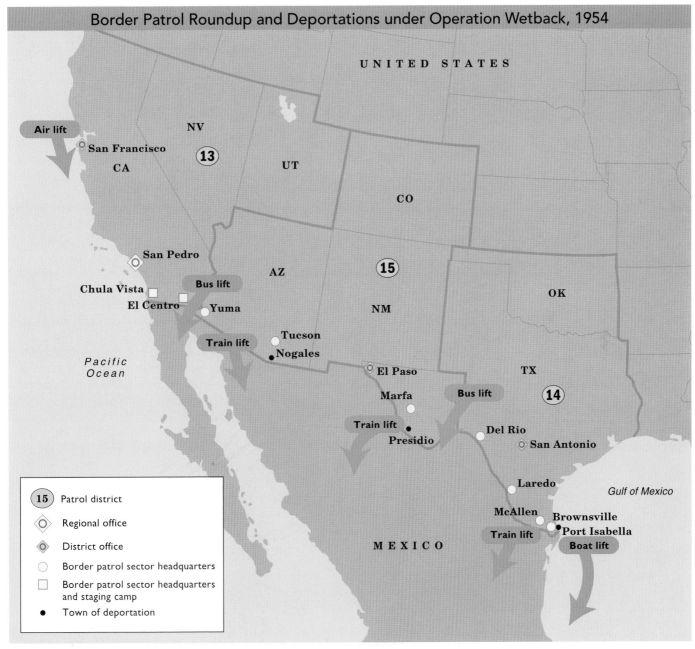

Border Patrol Roundup and Deportations under Operation Wetback, 1954

Legend:
- **15** Patrol district
- Regional office
- District office
- Border patrol sector headquarters
- Border patrol sector headquarters and staging camp
- Town of deportation

In 1954, the U.S. Immigration and Naturalization Service stepped up its policy of deporting undocumented Mexican laborers. Operations were concentrated in the three patrol districts that bordered Mexico and carried out through a combination of border patrol headquarters, staging areas, and regional offices.

PLANE WRECK AT LOS GATOS

Woody Guthrie (Library of Congress)

In early 1948, a charter plane carrying 28 Mexican farm workers crashed en route from Oakland, California, to a federal deportation center in El Centro, in the Southern California desert, killing all aboard. In a brief article about the crash, the New York Times reported merely that "the crash occurred 20 miles west of Coalinga, 75 miles from Fresno." The article neglected to mention any of the names of the victims, only calling them "deportees."

The tragic accident likely would have been lost to history if not for the reknowned folksinger Woody Guthrie. Best known for his anthem "This Land Is Your Land," the Oklahoma-born Guthrie often combined social commentary and a sympathy for working men and women in his songs. After reading about the crash and noting that even in death the victims were recognized not as individuals but simply as anonymous deportees, Guthrie penned a poem titled "Plane Wreck at Los Gatos (Deportees)." His words were later set to music by a former school teacher named Martin Hoffman, and the song has become one of Guthrie's best-loved works.

year; during the 1980s, more than 1 million per year were deported. Uncounted numbers eluded deportation and stayed in the United States.

A NEW DAY FOR PUERTO RICO

In the first two decades after World War II, a tremendous number of Puerto Ricans moved to the mainland United States in what became known as the Puerto Rican "Great Migration." At the same time, those who remained behind in Puerto Rico experienced different kinds of rapid change. Under the leadership of Governor Luis Muñoz Marín, Puerto Rico became a commonwealth with full self-government and it experienced industrialization and economic uplift through a program called Operation Bootstrap. Even so, poverty and the overpopulation that exacerbated it remained chronic features of daily life in Puerto Rico, as did political unrest. Some Puerto Ricans remained dissatisfied with commonwealth status and continued to press for full independence from the United States. A few even turned to terrorism to support their cause. Among these were activists associated with the Nationalist Party who wounded several congressmen and attempted to assassinate President Harry S Truman (1884–1972; president 1945–1953).

Luis Muñoz Marin

Luis Muñoz Marín (1898–1980) was born in San Juan, Puerto Rico, in the year of the Spanish-American War, when the United States won possession of the island from Spain. He was the son of Luis Muñoz Rivera, the patriot who at the time was seeking self-rule for his homeland. The younger Muñoz spent much of his childhood in the United States, receiving his education at Georgetown University in Washington, D.C., and working afterward in New York City as a writer and translator. Conscious of his desire to carry on his father's legacy, he wrote: "I would be a giant, to embrace the mountains that he contemplated in his boyhood, the mountains that shelter his countrymen . . . a giant to complete the work of Luis Muñoz Rivera."

In 1926, Muñoz returned temporarily to Puerto Rico, where he edited La Democracia, a newspaper founded by his father. After another stay in the United States, he returned to Puerto Rico permanently in 1931. There he joined the Liberal Party and served as a senator in the Puerto Rican legislature. He advocated independence but even more urgently wanted to improve the economic condition of Puerto Rico's poor. The issue led him to break with his party in 1936, when he would not support the Tydings Bill, a proposal in the U.S. Congress that would have given Puerto Rico immediate independence at the cost of all economic assistance from the United States. After that bill failed, Muñoz founded the Popular Democratic Party (PDP), with its base in the poor rural farmers known as jibaros. Crisscrossing the island in search of their support, he was the first Puerto Rican politician to make a sustained effort to identify with the jibaros—so much so that their characteristic pava, or straw hat, became the symbol of his party. In 1940 the PDP won a majority in the senate, with Muñoz as president of the senate.

In the 1940s Muñoz came to believe that independence was not the best way to achieve economic uplift. Instead, he believed the island should become a self-governing commonwealth linked to the United States, with Puerto Ricans managing their own internal affairs but drawing on the massive resources of the United States for economic support.

After World War II ended, as a movement for decolonization swept the world, changes in Puerto Rico's governance happened swiftly. In 1946 the United States appointed the first native Puerto Rican as governor, Jesús T. Piñero. In 1948 Muñoz Marín became the first governor (1949–1965) to be elected rather than appointed; he would be reelected three times. Under his leadership, the Commonwealth of Puerto Rico came into being on July 25, 1952, with a new constitution putting the island's internal affairs in the hands of its own elected governor and legislature, though foreign policy would still be in Washington's hands.

Muñoz remains one of the most honored figures in Puerto Rican history, not least for his decision not to run for reelection in 1964, on the view that no one person should remain in power for too long. His handpicked choice, Roberto Sánchez

LUIS MUÑOZ MARÍN AND PUERTO RICAN SELF-RULE

1898 Luis Muñoz Marín, son of Luis Muñoz Rivera, the Puerto Rican freedom fighter and diplomat, is born in San Juan, Puerto Rico. The same year, the United States captures Puerto Rico from Spain during the Spanish-American War.

1917 Passage of the Jones Act gives Puerto Ricans U.S. citizenship and allows men of military service age to be drafted into the U.S. military and serve during World War I.

1922 Muñoz Marín publishes an article in the magazine New Republic condemning the exploitation of Puerto Rican laborers by American businesses. The article prompts U.S. president Warren G. Harding to ask for the resignation of an appointed governor who had mocked the Puerto Rican independence movement.

1924 Puerto Rico's Republican and Socialist Parties, once rivals, unite in support of Puerto Rican independence. The unified party is dominated by the Puerto Rican upper and middle classes.

1928 U.S. president Calvin Coolidge declares that Puerto Ricans can never achieve independence because of a "lethargy of body and soul [which] is the offspring of moral and physical vices that drag down the spirits and lead peasants to such a state of degradation."

1931 Muñoz Marín returns to Puerto Rico to take over the editorship of his father's old newspaper, La Democracia.

1932 Muñoz Marín joins the Liberal Party and is elected to the island's senate for the first time. He gains a national reputation, again by attacking the appointed governor, who is forced to resign within the year.

1936 President Franklin D. Roosevelt pledges $40 million for the Puerto Rico Reconstruction Agency, a social and economic assistance program. Dr. Ernest Gruening, an ally of Muñoz Marín, is appointed commissioner. When a gunman from the radical Nationalist Party kills Puerto Rico's chief of police, E. Francis Riggs, Gruening asks Muñoz Marín to condemn the assassination; he replies that if he is to make such a statement, he will also condemn the police, who had subsequently killed the arrested man under suspicious circumstances. A bill is introduced in Congress to cut all aid to Puerto Rico and grant it independence. Although he supports independence, Muñoz Marín argues that it would be foolish to ask for it immediately since the island needs U.S. support. He declares he will sit out the 1936 election if it is to become a referendum on independence. When he does so, the Liberal Party loses and blames him for the loss.

1938 Forced out of the Liberal Party, Muñoz Marín founds the Popular Democratic Party (PDP).

1940 In order to get the PDP on the ballot, Muñoz Marín collects signatures directly from Puerto Rico's jíbaros, or rural poor. He runs a successful campaign for the Puerto Rican senate. During the campaign, he argues that the primary issue for Puerto Ricans should be not the political status of the island—whether as an independent nation or as a U.S. state—but the problems of poverty, malnutrition, and poor education. Muñoz Marín wins the election and becomes president of the Puerto Rican senate.

1944 Muñoz Marín wins reelection in a landslide. At the same time, he begins to express doubts about whether independence is the best solution for Puerto Rico, having found that many jíbaros fear what that prospect would mean for them economically.

1945 He leads a delegation to Washington, D.C., to press Congress to resolve Puerto Rico's political status. After studying legislation drawn up to grant the Philippines independence, he concludes that independence would greatly harm his efforts to alleviate poverty in Puerto Rico. Instead, he calls for the islands to become a self-governing commonwealth of the United States.

1947 Muñoz Marín initiates Operation Bootstrap. Through the program, he encourages U.S. companies to invest in Puerto Rico by offering them a 10-year exemption from taxes. That same year, Pedro Albizu Campos, leader of the Nationalist Party, is released from an Atlanta, Georgia, prison and returns to Puerto Rico, where he attempts to begin a nationwide revolt.

1948 Although his rejection of independence splits the PDP and leads to the formation of the Puerto Rican Independence Party, Muñoz Marín becomes the first popularly elected governor of Puerto Rico.

1950 President Harry S Truman signs a law allowing Puerto Ricans to write their own constitution. Nationalists nearly assassinate Muñoz Marín. Two days later, two Nationalists attempt to shoot their way into Blair House in Washington to kill President Truman. (Truman and his family are living there during a renovation of the White House.)

1952 Congress approves a constitution under which Puerto Ricans are given control over virtually all internal affairs.

1954 Nationalists wound five congressmen on the floor of the U.S. House of Representatives.

1964 In order to test his party's ability to maintain power without him at the helm, Muñoz Marín retires from the governorship.

1967 In a public referendum, 60 percent of Puerto Ricans vote in favor of continuing Puerto Rico's commonwealth status, 39 percent vote for statehood, and 1 percent for independence.

1980 Muñoz Marín dies in San Juan.

Luis Muñoz Marín (Library of Congress)

"What we have to guard against in this world we live in is not to confuse love for our patria with small, futile and naive concepts of nationalionalism and national state."

—Luis Muñoz Marín, 1951

Vilella, was elected to succeed him, while Muñoz returned to the senate.

THE QUESTION OF INDEPENDENCE

Even while Muñoz negotiated commonwealth status for Puerto Rico and made the most of the island's association with the United States, some Puerto Ricans vigorously opposed any arrangement but independence. That opposition was led by Pedro Albizu Campos (1893–1965), head of the Nationalist Party. Beginning in 1936, Albizu spent several years in prison in Atlanta for conspiring to overthrow the U.S. federal government in Puerto Rico. He regarded Muñoz as a puppet of the United States who was helping to keep Puerto Rico in colonial subjection. In 1950, after President Truman had signed a law authorizing Puerto Ricans to write their own constitution, Albizu organized an uprising in two towns in Puerto Rico, Jayuya and Utuado, and launched an attack on the governor's palace. Gunmen traveling in two cars assaulted the palace, aiming to assassinate Muñoz. They were stopped in a gun battle, while the U.S. National Guard suppressed the uprisings. Thirty-three people were killed in the tumult, and Albizu went back to jail.

Later that year the radical independentistas, or independence activists, took the fight to Washington. Two Puerto Rican Nationalists, Oscar Collazo and Griselio Torresola, assaulted Blair House, Truman's temporary residence while the White House was under renovation. One Nationalist and one policeman died in the gunfight. Truman was unharmed.

The violence was not over. On March 1, 1954, three Nationalists— Lolita Lebrón, Rafael Candel Miranda, and Andrés Cordero—attacked the U.S. Capitol. Shouting "Puerto Rico is not freed!", they fired guns from the gallery of the House of Representatives, wounding five congressmen. They were captured and sent to prison, not to be released until President Jimmy Carter pardoned them in 1979.

Muñoz consistently denounced Nationalist violence. From his experience wrangling for commonwealth status in Washington, he knew that some people in Congress were opposed to granting Puerto Rico greater liberty; it was there-fore important to reassure them that Puerto Rico could govern itself peacefully. After the assassination attempt on Truman, Muñoz wired the president to condemn the "dastardly attempt . . . against your person." Truman replied cordially, saying, "I am sure that the American public understands the irrational and insignificant background of the disorders and does not in the least hold the Puerto Rican government or people responsible for them."

But the desire for independence was not simply irrational. It was part of an internal debate in Puerto Rico that tested Muñoz's political skills at home just as Congressional debates tested them in Washington. Although the Puerto Rican Independence Party (PIP) did not endorse the violent tactics of the Nationalists, they joined them in arguing for independence, while the Statehood Republican Party (PER) advocated statehood. In the midst of vigorous democratic debate, Muñoz managed to persuade the majority of Puerto Ricans to accept commonwealth status and reaffirm it in plebiscites, notably in 1964. Those advocating independence dwindled to a small minority of Puerto Ricans—a minority that sometimes made news beyond its numbers because of terrorist acts on both island and mainland.

OPERATION BOOTSTRAP

Under Muñoz's leadership, Puerto Rico made great strides economically as well as politically. The principal vehicle for economic uplift was Operation Bootstrap, an industrialization program launched by Muñoz in 1947 while he was still president of the Puerto Rican senate. Urging Puerto Ricans to "pull themselves up by their bootstraps," the program aimed to transform the island's economy from one based on agriculture to one based on urban industry. Operation Bootstrap offered tax exemptions to U.S. manufacturing firms willing to establish factories in Puerto Rico. The result was that Puerto Rico became highly industrialized, such that most of its people became city dwellers working in manufacturing and service industries. Thousands of jobs were created, with many jíbaros moving from rural communities to the cities. To provide housing for them, Operation

Puerto Rican terrorist Lolita Lebrón is taken into custody. (Library of Congress)

Bootstrap included a program for building cementos, inexpensive cement houses that Puerto Ricans could buy for $300 each, with 20-year mortgages guaranteed by the commonwealth's government.

Under Operation Bootstrap, private investment in Puerto Rico grew 36 percent per year from 1950 to 1954, and 46 percent per year from 1955 to 1959. The general living standard rose, with average annual per-capita income climbing from $200 in 1940 to $2,000 in 1977, and average life expectancy rising from 48 years in 1940 to 76 years in 1977. New industries broke the island's traditional dependence on sugar exports. In 1972,

Puerto Rico's top 10 manufacturing industries included electrical equipment, scientific instruments, and fabricated metals—industries that had been absent from its top 10 in 1949. By 2000, only 3 percent of Puerto Ricans on the island still worked in agriculture.

By the end of Muñoz's tenure in 1965, there was still much unemployment and poverty in Puerto Rico, particularly by American standards, and conditions would grow worse during an economic slump in the 1970s. But compared with where they had started when Muñoz took power, Puerto Ricans were much better off and had made better

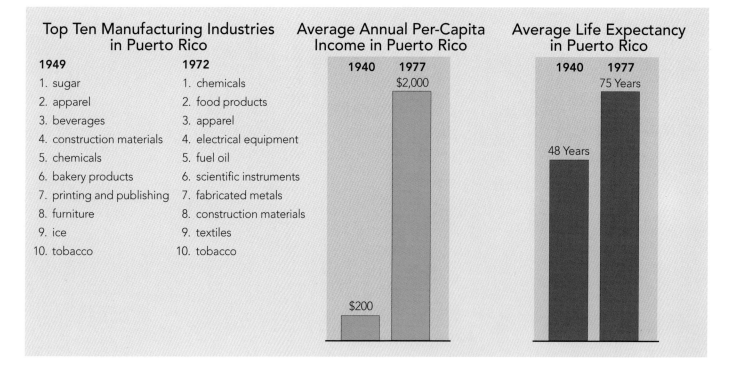

Top Ten Manufacturing Industries in Puerto Rico

1949	1972
1. sugar	1. chemicals
2. apparel	2. food products
3. beverages	3. apparel
4. construction materials	4. electrical equipment
5. chemicals	5. fuel oil
6. bakery products	6. scientific instruments
7. printing and publishing	7. fabricated metals
8. furniture	8. construction materials
9. ice	9. textiles
10. tobacco	10. tobacco

Average Annual Per-Capita Income in Puerto Rico

1940 — $200; 1977 — $2,000

Average Life Expectancy in Puerto Rico

1940 — 48 Years; 1977 — 75 Years

A CULTURAL FLOWERING

As the Puerto Rican–American community grew, it engendered artists, musicians, and writers who gave voice to their experiences. These included poets Juan Avilés and Victor Hernández Cruz and prose writer Piri Thomas, renowned for his autobiographical account of barrio life, *Down These Mean Streets* (1967). Bandleader Tito Puente, born to Puerto Rican parents in Spanish Harlem in 1923, helped popularize the mambo in the 1950s and salsa in the 1970s. His Latin jazz continued the fusion of Caribbean rhythms and American jazz that had begun with Cuban musicians in the 1930s. A Puerto Rican–born musician, José Feliciano, who moved with his family to New York in 1950, became a pop star in 1968 with his Latin-soul recording of The Doors' "Light My Fire."

economic progress than most of their Latin American neighbors. Critics of the Operation Bootstrap policy had charged that the program would increase Puerto Rico's dependence on the United States, and indeed it had made independence less imaginable for many Puerto Ricans. But most Puerto Ricans felt that the program had made effective use of Puerto Rico's relationship with the United States, putting the power of the United States to work for the people rather than against them.

NEW YORK'S PUERTO RICAN COMMUNITY

While Operation Bootstrap improved conditions in Puerto Rico, many Puerto Ricans sought to improve their conditions in a more direct way: by migrating to the mainland United States. As U.S. citizens, they were able to do so without immigration papers. Furthermore the low cost of commercial air travel after World War II made migration affordable to many Puerto Ricans for the first time. From 1940 to 1950 alone, the number of Puerto Ricans in the United States more than tripled, from about 70,000 to 226,000. By the 1970s, nearly 1 million people of Puerto Rican descent lived in New York City alone, giving it an even larger Puerto Rican population than San Juan. Actual

travel from Puerto Rico to the United States during this period was even greater than these numbers indicate, because many migrants returned to Puerto Rico each year, either permanently or temporarily. Net migration—the number of arrivals to the United States minus the number of departures from the United States—was usually a small fraction of each year's total Puerto Rican traffic.

During this Great Migration, New York City remained the principal terminus for Puerto Ricans seeking a better life on the mainland, largely because New York had boasted the largest Puerto Rican population on the mainland since the first immigrants arrived to work in the city's tobacco factories in the late 19th century. They were assisted by the Office of the Commonwealth, founded in New York City in the 1940s. But Puerto Ricans settled in other parts of the country as well, particularly Chicago and New Jersey, where additional Offices of the Commonwealth opened by the mid-1950s; other cities easily accessible from Puerto Rico via a short flight, such as Philadelphia and Miami, were also popular places to settle. The ease of migration out of Puerto Rico was beneficial to the commonwealth, since it acted to relieve population pressure and job competition on the island.

In New York City, Puerto Rican Americans built a community that retained strong cultural ties to the home-

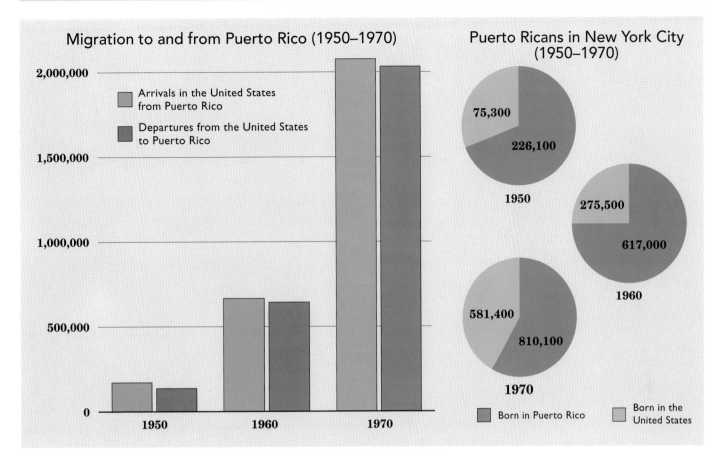

Migration to and from Puerto Rico (1950–1970)

Arrivals in the United States from Puerto Rico

Departures from the United States to Puerto Rico

Puerto Ricans in New York City (1950–1970)

1950: 75,300 / 226,100

1960: 275,500 / 617,000

1970: 581,400 / 810,100

Born in Puerto Rico   Born in the United States

land, ties renewed by the constant flow of migration back and forth. As new, mostly unskilled immigrants, they tended to be poor, working hard in mostly blue-collar jobs for wages that were low by U.S. standards, though high by the standards of Puerto Rico. Many worked in the manufacturing and service sectors as factory hands, garment workers, busboys, and bellhops. Some were migrant farm workers, filling the role on East Coast farms that Mexicans filled in the Southwest. With affordable housing scarce, many Puerto Rican immigrants were forced to live in rat-infested buildings in rough New York City neighborhoods like East Harlem, the Lower East Side, and the South Bronx.

Racial prejudice was a fact of life. Most Puerto Ricans—like most Latinos—are a mix of Spanish, African, and Native American heritage and have light-brown complexions called trigueño (though many gradations of skin tone can be found). This racial mixing so characteristic of Hispanic America has made strict racial categorization neither clear nor especially meaningful to most Puerto Ricans, or most Latinos, for that matter. In the United States, however, the shade of one's skin has always been important, and, as immigrants soon discovered, many Anglo-Americans divide the world into white and nonwhite. Carlos Pérez, a light-skinned mulatto who immigrated to the United States from the Dominican Republic, told historian Peter Winn, "From the minute I arrived at the airport I was treated like a black. Any mulatto, no matter how light, is a black in the United States." During the 1950s, this sense of racial division was so culturally internalized that it was even played out on the Broadway stage. The musical West Side Story memorializes the racial tension in the 1950s between youth gangs living on Manhattan's West Side, an area where Puerto Ricans were increasing in number at that time.

Despite the hardships, many Puerto Ricans in New York City were grateful for their new opportunities. Herman Badillo (1929–), who as a representative from New York became the first Puerto Rican to serve in the U.S. Congress, recalled coming to the city as an orphan in 1941: "I thought I had come into Paradise. I had been starving for seven years and now I got three meals and could eat my fill. . . . [I]nstead of the wide-

In this pro-Castro poster, Castro himself is shown lifting a rifle. (Library of Congress)

spread unemployment I saw all around me in Puerto Rico, most people seemed to have work. This alone was enough to impress me."

Puerto Ricans organized to help themselves, through such organizations as Aspira (Aspire), founded in New York City in 1961 by Dr. Antonia Pantoja to improve educational opportunities for Puerto Rican youths. It advanced this goal through such means as scholarships, financial aid, career and college counseling, educational advocacy, cultural activities, and community action projects. Now a national organization with chapters in several states and Puerto Rico, Aspira no longer restricts itself to aiding Puerto Ricans but instead serves all Latinos.

Other Puerto Rican groups used activism to achieve their goals, such as the Young Lords, a Puerto Rican student activist group founded in New York City in the 1960s. The Young Lords used demonstrations and other forms of protest to draw attention to the educational needs of young Puerto Ricans. They succeeded in bringing about the creation of Puerto Rican studies programs and student organizations at a number of colleges.

As time passed, Puerto Rican Americans in New York City developed a sense that they belonged there. Some came to call themselves Nuyoricans or Neoricans, or Puerto Rican New Yorkers. East Harlem, also known as Spanish Harlem to New Yorkers of non-Hispanic descent, became known to them as El Barrio, the Neighborhood. The Lower East Side became known as Loisaida.

TURMOIL IN THE CARIBBEAN

Even as Puerto Rico shone as a showcase for democracy and economic development, other places in the Caribbean were rife with turmoil. In two of these nations, Cuba and the Dominican Republic, political upheaval brought new waves of Hispanic immigration to the United States. In the former, the depredations of U.S.-supported dictator Fulgencio Batista led to the Cuban Revolution, in which Fidel Castro, in 1959, established the first communist regime in the Western Hemisphere. In the latter, the assassina-

tion of dictator Rafael Trujillo in 1961 began several years of political turbulence, peaking with U.S. military intervention in 1965.

THE CUBAN REVOLUTION

Beginning with his involvement in the uprising that overthrew President Gerardo Machado in 1933, Cuban army officer Fulgencio Batista y Zaldívar (1901–1973) dominated his country for more than two decades. He did so either indirectly through puppet regimes or directly as president (1940–1944, 1952–1958). He ruled openly as a dictator from 1952. Batista's corrupt, repressive regime concentrated wealth in the hands of a small elite, exacerbating the already desperate situation of Cuba's poor and alienating the middle class. Nonetheless, Batista had the full support of Cuba's wealthiest families and of the United States, which appreciated his anticommunist, probusiness stance and his ability to maintain order. Under his rule, Havana became a center for gambling, drugs, and prostitution, controlled by organized crime cartels from the United States.

The beginning of the end for Batista came from an unlikely source: a wealthy sugar-planter's son named Fidel Castro (1926–). Trained by the Jesuits and the holder of a law degree from University of Havana Law School where he became active in politics, Castro was moved by the plight of Cuba's poor and launched a revolutionary attack on the Moncada army base in Santiago on July 26, 1953. The attack failed, and Castro went into exile, but he returned in 1956 to begin a sustained guerrilla campaign, the 26th of July Movement. In what became known as the Cuban Revolution (1956–1959), Castro fought from his base in the Sierra Maestra with forces that included Ernesto "Che" Guevara (1928–1967), an Argentine revolutionary who had trained as a medical doctor before becoming Castro's chief lieutenant. Guevara would later fight for leftist insurgencies in Africa and Latin America before being executed in Bolivia.

Supported by the peasantry and many in the middle class, Castro made Batista's position increasingly untenable. In the early hours of January 1, 1959, Batista fled Cuba by plane. On January 8, Castro's

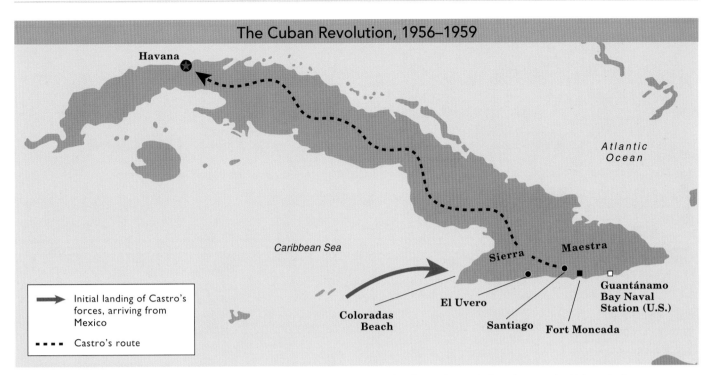

The Cuban Revolution, 1956–1959

Havana

Atlantic Ocean

Caribbean Sea

Sierra · Maestra

El Uvero

Coloradas Beach

Santiago Fort Moncada

Guantánamo Bay Naval Station (U.S.)

→ Initial landing of Castro's forces, arriving from Mexico

- - - Castro's route

In December 1956, Fidel Castro and 81 followers emerged from exile to land in Cuba at Coloradas Beach. Although they were defeated by government forces, they escaped into the Sierra Maestra, a mountainous region of eastern Cuba. The following May, they captured the government garrison at El Uvero. Then, on New Year's Day in 1959, the rebels captured Santiago, eastern Cuba's largest city. When dictator Fulgencio Batista fled the country, Castro and his forces made a triumphant march across Cuba to the capital of Havana.

victorious forces marched into Havana and took power.

Castro claimed at first that his revolution was neither capitalist nor communist. Even so, the cold war between the United States and the Soviet Union, under way since the end of World War II, provided the lens through which the United States viewed the new Cuban leader. The United States put economic pressure on Castro to conform to its vision of democratic capitalism rather than carry out the program of land reform and industrial nationalization he had in mind. Relations between the former allies deteriorated rapidly, and Castro turned to the Soviet Union for aid. Private businesses, including U.S.-owned ones, were nationalized without compensation, and a repressive crackdown on political opponents began. In 1961 the United States cut off diplomatic relations with Cuba and Castro openly declared himself a Marxist-Leninist.

THE BIRTH OF LITTLE HAVANA

Castro's revolution had great appeal for Cuba's rural poor, whose standard of

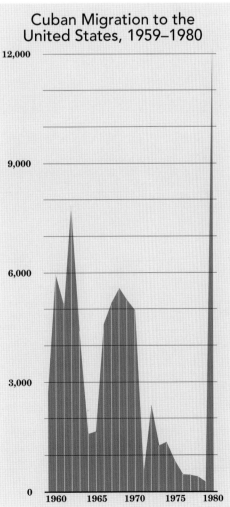

Cuban Migration to the United States, 1959–1980

12,000

9,000

6,000

3,000

0

1960 1965 1970 1975 1980

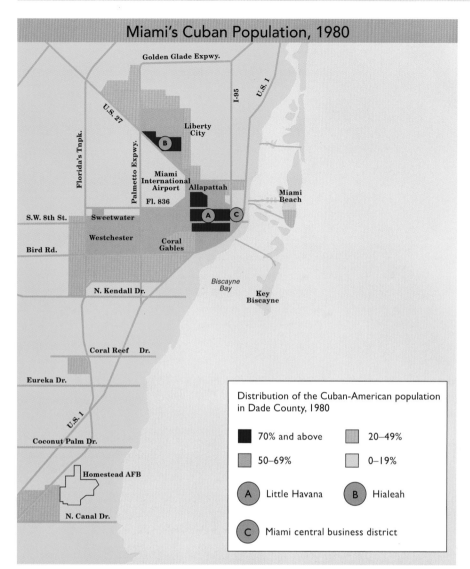

Miami's Cuban Population, 1980

Distribution of the Cuban-American population in Dade County, 1980

- 70% and above
- 50–69%
- 20–49%
- 0–19%

Ⓐ Little Havana

Ⓑ Hialeah

Ⓒ Miami central business district

Support for President John F. Kennedy is shown in a Miami storefront. (Library of Congress)

living, including their access to education and medical care, generally improved under Castro. But wealthy and middle-class Cubans fled by the thousands, most of them to the United States. Some were Batistianos, rich allies of Batista who brought their fortunes with them and were known as "golden exiles." Others were planters, ranchers, businessmen, doctors, lawyers, bankers, civil servants, and teachers. From 1959 to 1962 alone, about 155,000 Cubans fled to the United States; the total reached more than 500,000 by 1973.

The Cuban exiles, as they became known, tended to be highly educated and skilled, and so had greater advantages in finding work than did most other Hispanic immigrants to the United States. They were aided by a government that welcomed them as allies against Castro and communism and gave them permanent residency status, free temporary housing, medical care, financial aid, and job counseling. Their race also aided them: Cuba's upper classes were largely of pure Spanish descent, and were therefore light skinned and not subject to as much racial prejudice as darker-skinned immigrants. Yet with all their advantages, most Cuban exiles had to work hard, for Castro routinely confiscated their life savings and property as a condition of allowing them to leave. Emigration to the United States was banned from 1962 to 1965, and again beginning in 1973, though some Cubans still managed to reach the United States via travel to a third country or clandestine escape by boat.

Most Cuban exiles settled in Miami, where they joined a preexisting Cuban population that had once included Castro himself; he had raised money there in 1955 for his struggle against Batista. Many exiles hoped to return to Cuba after Castro's fall. A considerable number hoped to orchestrate that fall themselves, with U.S. help.

A sleepy retirement town before the Cuban exiles arrived, Miami grew into an international center of finance and trade with the help of the new arrivals. By 2000 its population was more than 60 percent Hispanic. But Cubans spread out to other parts of the country as well, aided by U.S. government efforts to resettle them to relieve the population pressure on Miami. Cities with large Cuban-American communities as of 2000 included Union City,

The Bay of Pigs Invasion, 1961

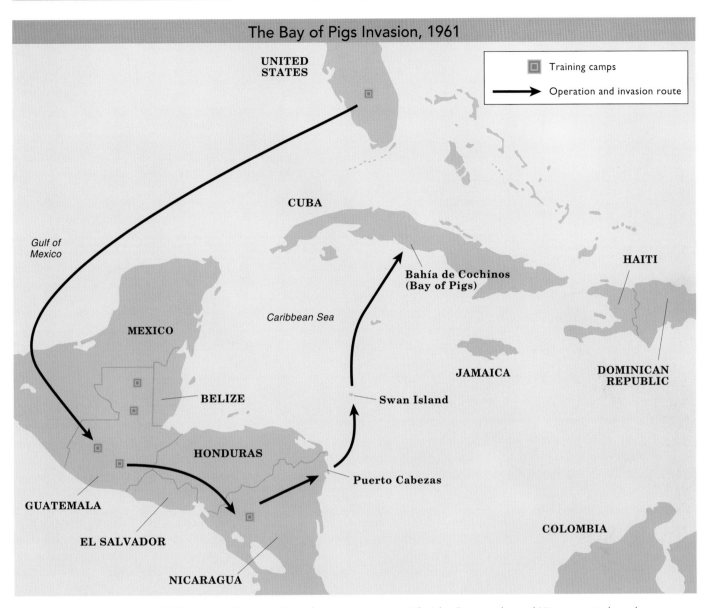

Training camps	
Operation and invasion route	

UNITED STATES

Gulf of Mexico

CUBA

Bahía de Cochinos (Bay of Pigs)

HAITI

Caribbean Sea

MEXICO

BELIZE

JAMAICA

DOMINICAN REPUBLIC

Swan Island

HONDURAS

Puerto Cabezas

GUATEMALA

COLOMBIA

EL SALVADOR

NICARAGUA

On April 17, 1961, a force of CIA-trained Cuban exiles left training camps in Florida, Guatemala, and Nicaragua to launch an invasion of Cuba. Advancing from Puerto Cabezas in Nicaragua and then from Swan Island in the Caribbean, the force landed at Bahía de Cochinos (Bay of Pigs) in Cuba. After occupying the beachhead for two days, they were crushed by Castro's army.

New Jersey; Washington, D.C.; and New York City.

The part of Miami where Cuban exiles concentrated, which became known as Little Havana, is still the center of the nation's Cuban-American community. Spanish became widely spoken there, with the main thoroughfare called Calle Ocho, "Eighth Street." Cuban food and culture became predominant in Little Havana, including such customs as playing dominoes (a Caribbean pastime shared by Cubans with Puerto Ricans and Dominicans) and drinking cafecita, a variety of espresso. In addition, the calendar itself testified to the strong Cuban presence in Little Havana, with such annual events as the January 28 parade in celebration of José Martí and the Carnival parades and balls on the last day before Lent.

BAY OF PIGS AND THE CUBAN MISSILE CRISIS

With the help of the U.S. Central Intelligence Agency (CIA), a group of Cuban exiles in Florida prepared diligently to overthrow Castro's government. On April 17, 1961, about 1,500 exiles launched their invasion at the Bahía de Cochinos, or Bay of Pigs, Cuba. The result was a fiasco. Castro's armed forces decimated the invaders when an expected popular rebellion failed to materialize and President

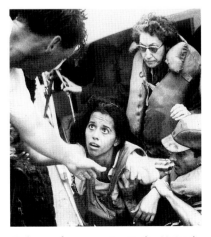

Cuban refugees arrive in the United States in 1964. (Department of Defense)

"The revolution has no time for elections. There is no more democratic government in Latin America than revolutionary government....

If Mr. Kennedy does not like Socialism, we do not like imperialism. We do not like capitalism."

—Fidel Castro, May 1, 1961, in response to the failed Bay of Pigs invasion supported by the United States

John F. Kennedy canceled promised military support at the last minute. About 120 invaders were killed and 1,200 taken prisoner, later to be ransomed for food and medicine. The debacle embarrassed the United States, boosted Castro's popularity at home, and left many Cuban Americans with a hatred of Kennedy's Democratic Party: most have voted Republican ever since. The incident also convinced Soviet leader Nikita Khrushchev of Kennedy's weakness, encouraging him to take strategic action.

In October 1962, U.S. spy planes revealed that the Soviet Union was assembling nuclear missile launching sites in Cuba. Kennedy ordered a naval blockade of Cuba to prevent further military supplies from entering the country and prepared to invade unless the Soviet Union dismantled the missile sites. For two weeks, the world hovered on the brink of thermonuclear war. Finally, Khrushchev agreed to dismantle the sites, and the United States agreed not to sponsor further invasions of Cuba.

With the end of the Cuban missile crisis, the United States effectively accepted that Castro was in power indefinitely. Cuban exiles recognized that they had no realistic hope of overthrowing Castro any time soon, and settled in for a long, perhaps permanent stay. Even so, Cuban exiles remained active in influencing U.S. policy toward Cuba, brooking no relax-

ation of economic sanctions against Castro's regime. A few have even resorted to terrorism to press their cause.

One of the most militant anti-Castro exiles was Orlando Bosch Avila, who through two militant groups claimed responsibility for more than 30 violent acts between 1961 and 1968. Leader of the Revolutionary Recovery Insurrection Movement (MIRR), Bosch and four others were arrested in June, 1965 near Orlando, Florida, with 18 aerial bombs, small arms, and ammunition which the group planned to use to bomb targets in Cuba.

By 1968, Bosch had organized a second group, known as Cuban Power. In January of that year, Cuban Power claimed responsibility for blowing up a B-25 cargo plane at Miami International Airport. Four months later, Bosch ordered the bombing of a British freighter in Key West, Florida, and a Japanese freighter in Tampa, Florida. Using the name "Ernesto, General Delegate of Cuban Power," he cabled the heads of state of Great Britain, Mexico, and Spain warning that ships and planes from their countries would be attacked unless they halted trade with Cuba. Later that summer, 36 pounds of explosives were found chained to the hull of a British freighter. Bosch took responsibility, and some have claimed that explosives were part of a 300-pound supply given to Bosch by the Federal Bureau of Investigation as part of a clan-

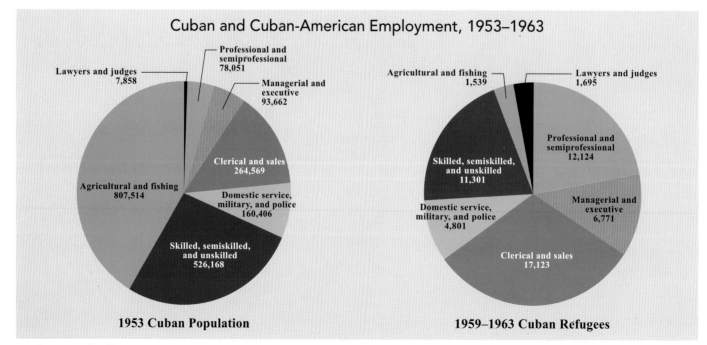

Cuban and Cuban-American Employment, 1953–1963

1953 Cuban Population

- Lawyers and judges 7,858
- Professional and semiprofessional 78,051
- Managerial and executive 93,662
- Clerical and sales 264,569
- Domestic service, military, and police 160,406
- Skilled, semiskilled, and unskilled 526,168
- Agricultural and fishing 807,514

1959–1963 Cuban Refugees

- Agricultural and fishing 1,539
- Lawyers and judges 1,695
- Professional and semiprofessional 12,124
- Managerial and executive 6,771
- Clerical and sales 17,123
- Domestic service, military, and police 4,801
- Skilled, semiskilled, and unskilled 11,301

As these graphs illustrate, a high proportion of the refugees who fled Cuba following Fidel Castro's takeover in 1959 were educated professionals and managers—a far higher proportion than was the case in the general Cuban population under Batista.

destine anti-Castro campaign by the U.S. government.

Although the explosives were removed from the British ship before detonation, Bosch was not deterred. In September 1968 he led an attack on a Polish vessel in Miami, for which he and eight others were arrested and convicted. At the same time, he was also convicted with extortion and conspiracy to damage ships of foreign registry for threatening the three heads of state. In 1972, he was released on parole, at which time he fled the United States for South America.

In the aftermath of Bosch's departure, other groups such as Omega 7, the (José) Martí Insurrectional Movement, and the Cuban Nationalist Movement continued to use violence to press for Castro's overthrow, with sporadic attacks against Cuban government facilities and individuals and against companies suspected of sympathizing with Castro occuring well into the 1980s in New York City, Miami, and Washington, D.C.

UPHEAVAL IN THE DOMINICAN REPUBLIC

On the Caribbean island of Hispaniola, Cuba's neighbor to the east, a different but similarly turbulent chain of events transpired in the 1960s. Soon after the U.S. occupation of the Dominican Republic in 1916–1924 ended, U.S.-trained Dominican military officer Rafael Trujillo (1891–1961) established a dictatorship that he maintained for 31 years, from 1930 to 1961. Like Batista in Cuba, Trujillo used his control of the army and his alliance with both the domestic wealthy class and U.S. interests to retain his grip on power even when someone else served as nominal president. Trujillo developed the country's industrial base and repaid national debts, but corruption was rampant, political dissent was brutally suppressed, and the majority of Dominicans remained poor. His allies at home and abroad gradually became disgusted with his personal avarice, which left precious little for them to share. The Organization of American States imposed economic sanctions against him in 1960 for his involvement in a presidential assassination attempt in Venezuela. Trujillo's rule ended in 1961 with his own assassina-

President John F. Kennedy addresses the nation during the Cuban missile crisis. (Library of Congress)

tion by machine-gun fire, reportedly assisted by the CIA.

After the assassination, family members and cronies of Trujillo continued to dominate the government until 1962, when domestic agitation and international pressure forced President Joaquín

THE DOMINICAN REPUBLIC IN THE 20TH CENTURY

1905 The United States takes control of part of the Dominican Republic in order to protect American business interests.

1916–1924 Following a period of prolonged turmoil and growing Dominican debt to American corporations, the U.S. Marine Corps invades the Dominican Republic. The United States occupies the island until 1924.

1930 U.S.-backed dictator Rafael Trujillo comes to power.

1961 Trujillo is assassinated. Following his death, the administration of U.S. president John F. Kennedy forces his family from Dominican politics with a threat of armed intervention.

1962 Juan Bosch, a reform-minded populist of the Partido Revolucionario Dominicano (PRD), wins the first free presidential election in 40 years.

1963 Bosch is ousted in a military coup and is replaced by a triumvirate.

1965 An armed revolt against the military government escalates into civil war. In the wake of Cuba's 1959 communist revolution, the U.S. government fears a similar result and once more sends in 24,000 marines to restore order.

1966–1978 Joaquín Balaguer, a conservative politician of the Partida de la Liberacion Dominicana (PLD), is elected president, an office he holds for eight years.

1986–1996 Balaguer regains the office and is reelected twice more in 1990 and 1994. In 1996 he steps down due to charges of election fraud. Leonel Fernández of the PLD wins the presidential election.

1998 Democratic elections for the National Assembly give a large majority to the opposition PRD party.

2000 Hipólito Mejía of the PRD is elected president.

American marines stop and search a local Dominican during the U.S. intervention of 1965. (National Archives)

Balaguer, a longtime Trujillo associate, to step down and permit free elections to be held. In the elections of December 1962, Juan Bosch, a liberal opponent of Trujillo who had returned from exile after the dictator's death, was chosen president. His attempts to institute land reform and other forms of social relief earned him castigation as a communist. He was overthrown in 1963 in a right-wing military coup and sent back into exile. Bosch's supporters attempted to overthrow the military junta and restore the elected government in 1965, but the United States regarded the revolt as an open window for communism and sent more than 20,000 marines to close it. Bosch denounced the U.S. intervention, but to no avail. New elections in 1966 were

won by onetime Trujillo puppet Balaguer, who repeatedly won reelection to remain in office until 1978 and from 1986 to 1996. A conservative, he strengthened the economy and maintained domestic stability, often through political repression, without doing much to reduce the endemic poverty of most Dominicans.

Though no great advance in standard of living resulted from the 1961 death of Trujillo, it affected ordinary Dominicans in at least one respect. Trujillo had imposed tight restrictions on emigration, restrictions that ended with his death. Almost immediately, Dominicans began a mass exodus from the island, in most cases heading for the United States in search of economic opportunity. Their numbers included unskilled laborers and skilled and educated members of the middle class. From 1962 through 1972, a mean of 11,445 Dominicans per year were legally admitted to the United States as permanent residents; the figure rose to over 16,000 per year in the 1970s and over 30,000 per year in the 1980s. Many more Dominicans came to the United States illegally, usually by overstaying tourist visas or crossing the narrow Mona Passage that separates their country from Puerto Rico. The channel is turbulent and shark-infested, but those who survive the passage can often pass as Puerto Ricans, who require no passports to fly from the island to the United States.

Most Dominicans settled in New York City, which contained 495,000 people of Dominican descent by 1997, or 60 percent of all Dominicans nationwide. Between 1965 and 1980, Dominicans were the largest group of immigrants to New York City. More than half live in the Washington Heights and Inwood sections of Manhattan; the rest are scattered throughout the city.

Though the United States accepted Dominican applicants, it did not throw open the door to them the way it had with Cuban exiles. Despite the political repression in the Dominican Republic, the United States viewed Dominicans as economic refugees, not refugees from political persecution. They were subject to the same immigration restrictions as other people from Latin America, restrictions that became considerably more stringent than before with the Immigration Act of 1965.

Dominicans protest the U.S. Marine intervention in their country in 1965. (National Archives)

CHANGES IN LATIN AMERICAN IMMIGRATION

Until World War II, the vast majority of Hispanics in the United States were of Mexican descent. After World War II, people from Hispanic nations whose descendants had never before been widely represented in the U.S. population began to migrate to the United States in droves. Besides Puerto Rico, Cuba, and the Dominican Republic, Hispanics also flowed to the United States from the many nations of Central America and South America, though in substantially smaller numbers than from Mexico and the Caribbean.

The availability for the first time of inexpensive commercial air travel was one reason for the dramatic boom in immigration from Latin America; another was the exploding problem of overpopulation of Latin America. Yet another reason for the surge in Latin American immigration was the heightened perception in many Hispanic countries that the postwar United States was a place of prosperity and political stability, one that offered opportunities not to be found in nations chronically poor and unstable. Furthermore, the opportunities were relatively easy to access. There was no prescribed maximum on immigration from Latin America, so the door was as wide as Hispanic newcomers made it. That changed with the Immigration Act of 1965, which considerably narrowed the door for legal entry from the Western Hemisphere.

THE IMMIGRATION ACT OF 1965

Since the 1920s, immigration from the Eastern Hemisphere had been restricted by a quota system that favored immigrants from northern and western Europe over southern and eastern Europe and Asia. Annual immigration from any given country was limited to a percentage of the U.S. population of that ethnic group as listed in the 1890 census. However, this quota system did not apply to Western Hemisphere countries, and Latin Americans enjoyed comparatively greater freedom in immigrating to the United States. The exemption had largely been retained at the insistence of western and southwestern employers, who depended on the unimpeded flow of laborers from Mexico. But after World War II, people

PROVISIONS OF THE IMMIGRATION AND NATIONALITY ACT OF 1965

In 1965, the U.S. Congress amended the nation's long-standing policy of setting immigration quotas based upon the national origin of immigrants. The new law used a system based on reunification of families and needed skills. Although a law that made it easier for families to be reunited across borders benefited most immigrants, immigrants from the Western Hemisphere, including Latin America, had never been subject to quotas to begin with. In fact, for the first time in U.S. history, the 1965 law set an annual ceiling of 120,000 immigrants from the Western Hemisphere. Even with the ceiling, however, Latin America—with Asia—has become the leading source of immigrants to the United States.

The law's provisions are as follows:

a. Abolished the national origins quota system, eliminating national origin, race, or ancestry as a basis for immigration to the United States.

b. It established allocation of immigrant visas on a first-come, first-served basis, subject to a seven-category preference system for relatives of U.S. citizens and permanent resident aliens (for the reunification of families) and for persons with special occupational skills, abilities, or training (needed in the United States).

c. It established two categories of immigrants not subject to numerical restrictions:

1. Immediate relatives (spouses, children, parents) of U.S. citizens, and

2. Special immigrants: certain ministers of religion; certain former employees of the U.S. government abroad; certain persons who lost citizenship (e.g., by marriage or by service in foreign armed forces); and certain foreign medical graduates.

d. The act maintained the principle of numerical restriction, expanding limits to world coverage by limiting Eastern Hemisphere immigration to 170,000 and placing a ceiling on Western Hemisphere immigration (120,000) for the first time. However, neither the preference categories nor the 20,000 per-country limit was applied to the Western Hemisphere.

e. It introduced a prerequisite for the issuance of a visa that an alien seeking to enter the United States would not replace a currently employed worker in the United States or adversely affect the wages and working conditions of similarly employed individuals in the United States.

from many parts of the Western Hemisphere began to take advantage of it.

Statistics attested to the rising tide of immigration from Hispanic America. While the number of immigrants from all of Latin America in the 120 years from 1820 to 1940 had amounted to only 13.5 percent of the total from Europe (4.4 million immigrants from Latin America, 32.5 million from Europe), the total number of Latin American immigrants from 1951 to 1960 leapt to 77 percent of the European total for that period (1 million from Latin America, 1.3 million from Europe).

Partly because of concern that the United States might be overwhelmed by Latin American newcomers, U.S. leaders in the 1960s reconsidered the lack of restrictions on Western Hemisphere immigration. The reconsideration was also motivated by concern for civil rights. Demands had been growing to eliminate the quota system, with its racist bias against certain ethnicities. If there had to be ceilings on immigration, some congressmen reasoned, they should be equally applied—and not just to the Eastern Hemisphere, but to the Western Hemisphere as well. The resulting law, the Immigration Act of 1965, tightened Latin American immigration at the same time that it eliminated unequal quotas.

Under the new law, a maximum of 170,000 immigration visas per year would be granted to the Eastern Hemisphere and 120,000 to the Western Hemisphere. Later, in 1979 and 1980, the two separate ceilings were merged into a single, reduced, worldwide ceiling of 270,000 visas. Under the 1965 law, no single country in the Eastern Hemisphere could receive more than 20,000 visas, a restriction extended to the Western Hemisphere in 1976. The 1965 law and its amendments established a preference system to determine which visa applications would receive greater priority, with family ties to U.S. citizens or permanent residents as the primary criterion and labor market skills as a secondary one. Political or religious refugees received special consideration, though until 1980 refugee status was largely restricted to people fleeing communist countries.

The ceilings on Latin American immigration proved to be woefully low compared with the demand. Many people who wished to immigrate had virtually no chance of being able to do so legally. The result was that many desperate Latin Americans decided to immigrate illegally. Some came by obtaining student, tourist, or temporary visas and quietly remaining in the United States after these expired. Others traveled to Mexico first and slipped across the border to the Southwest, as undocumented Mexican workers had long done. A number of Latin Americans, like the Dominican immigrants described previously, traveled first to Puerto Rico and flew to the mainland from there; still others, like the Cubans fleeing Castro, hazarded their way to Florida shores by boat. Whatever the path of entry, illegal immigration from Latin America has been a persistent problem in the United States from the enactment of the 1965 restrictions to the present day.

IMMIGRATION FROM SOUTH AMERICA

Until World War II, immigration from South America was exceedingly small. Afterward, it contributed significantly to the United States's ballooning Hispanic-American population. Of the roughly 1.5 million South Americans who immigrated to the United States from 1820 to 1995, more than 90 percent arrived since 1950. Though some came from non-Hispanic countries like Brazil and Guyana, most came from the continent's Hispanic nations.

The availability of affordable commercial air travel after World War II was a major factor in increased immigration, at least for middle-class individuals who could afford a plane ticket. Since the cost of air travel was outside the range of most poor South Americans, immigrants from that continent tended to be better educated and more prosperous than those from other parts of Hispanic America. Yet they had reason to seek a better life. South America's population more than doubled between 1960 and 1990, putting a strain on the continent's resources. After World War II, many South American nations industrialized and modernized their economies, creating social dislocation and unrest as peasant farmers flocked to urban areas only to find themselves unemployed or underemployed, living in squalid shantytowns. In most countries,

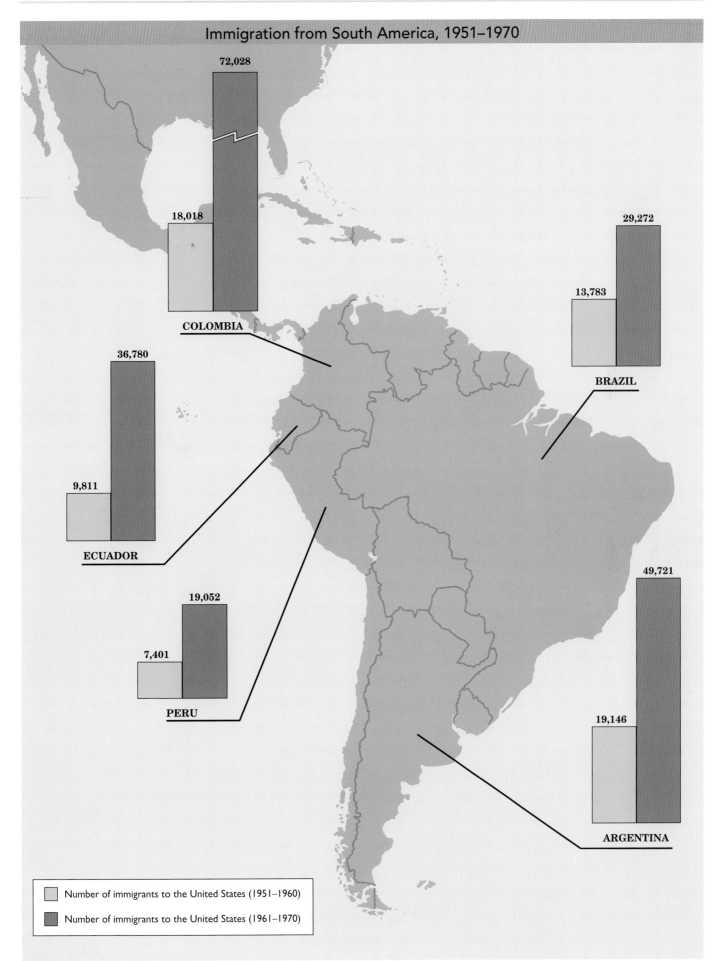

Immigration from South America, 1951–1970

72,028

18,018

COLOMBIA

36,780

9,811

ECUADOR

19,052

7,401

PERU

29,272

13,783

BRAZIL

49,721

19,146

ARGENTINA

Number of immigrants to the United States (1951–1960)

Number of immigrants to the United States (1961–1970)

political instability had been a fact of life since independence, but the changing social conditions made the situation even more chaotic, as coups and revolts led to blindingly rapid changes in constitutions and presidents.

Military rule was instituted in Ecuador in 1972, Uruguay in 1973, Argentina in 1976, and Peru in 1962, 1968, and 1975. Leftist insurgencies rocked such countries as Bolivia and Colombia. In Chile in 1973, President Salvador Allende, the country's elected leader, was overthrown and killed in a right-wing coup by General Augusto Pinochet, reportedly with covert help from the United States, which feared Allende's left-wing views. In many countries, such as Chile and Argentina, murder, torture, and terror became common tactics for suppressing dissent.

Under these conditions, the United States seemed like a beacon of tranquillity and opportunity. From 1951 to 1960, about 92,000 South Americans immigrated legally to the United States. From 1961 to 1970, the number nearly tripled, to 258,000. It rose again in the 1970s (to 296,000) and 1980s (to 462,000). During this same period, many other South Americans moved to the United States illegally, though the precise number is not known.

By far the largest group of South Americans came from Colombia. There the era after World War II was marked by perpetual political crisis, as Liberal and Conservative factions battled for power. Liberal Party leader Jorge Eliécer Gaitán was assassinated in Bogotá in 1948, setting off a civil war between Liberals and Conservatives known as La Violencia (1948–1958) that killed about 200,000 people. In the 1950s Colombia suffered two coups, in 1953 and 1957. In the 1960s the country was besieged by guerrilla and paramilitary activity from left and right. Under such stress, nearly 150,000 Colombians fled their country for the United States in the 1960s and 1970s alone. Smaller but still substantial numbers came from Ecuador, Peru, Argentina, Chile, and Venezuela.

South Americans have settled principally in the cities of the East Coast as well as in San Francisco, Los Angeles, and Miami. As of 1990 the largest concentrations of people of South American descent were in New York, New Jersey, Florida, and California, with smaller populations in Texas, Massachusetts, Connecticut, Pennsylvania, Maryland, Virginia, and Washington, D.C. The largest community of South Americans in New York City today lives in Jackson Heights, a neighborhood in the borough of Queens. The neighborhood is well stocked with Hispanic restaurants, newsstands, travel agencies, and grocery stores.

IMMIGRATION FROM CENTRAL AMERICA

Immigration to the United States from Central America increased from the 1940s to the 1970s, but not to the same degree as from other parts of Hispanic America. In the 1950s, 45,000 people immigrated to the United States from Central America—a small number by the standards of Mexico or Puerto Rico, but relatively large considering that until 1950 only 71,000 Central Americans had ever done so. Panama, Honduras, Guatemala, El Salvador, and Nicaragua combined sent nearly 75,000 immigrants to the United States from 1961 to 1970—a growing number, but still fewer than came from the Dominican Republic alone in the same period. The numbers began to increase in the 1970s (to a combined total of 113,000), but truly phenomenal growth would not occur until the 1980s (to 425,000).

Behind the growing numbers lay a history of worsening civil and economic chaos. In the 1950s Panama and Honduras were the largest source of the region's immigrants, generally middle-class, skilled people in search of economic opportunity. But as a result of civil wars and other conflicts in Guatemala, El Salvador, and Nicaragua, by the 1970s, hordes of refugees fleeing violence and dire poverty were arriving from those countries, in a wave that grew dramatically larger in the 1980s.

Historically, the region had strong links to the United States. Beginning in the 1840s, American companies invested millions of dollars in agriculture and mining, forming alliances with wealthy families in the region. The United States supported various right-wing strongmen as dictators to maintain order, such as Anastasio Somoza (1896–1956), who ruled Nicaragua from 1936 until his

Migrant Labor Routes

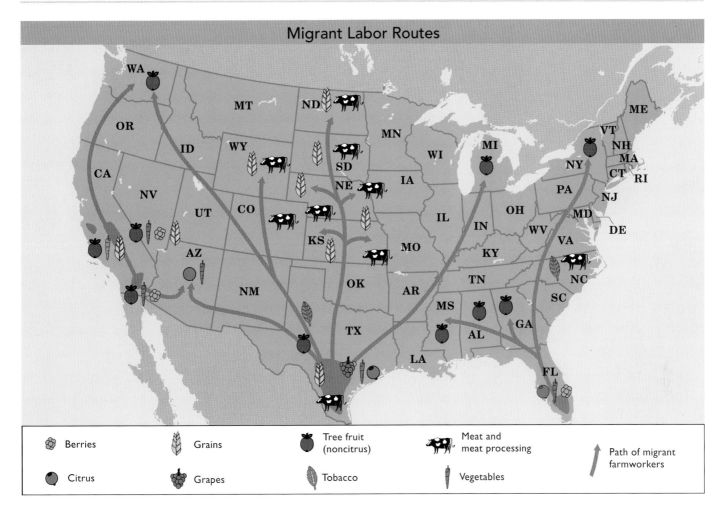

Berries	Grains	Tree fruit (noncitrus)	Meat and meat processing	Path of migrant farmworkers
Citrus	Grapes	Tobacco	Vegetables	

death and founded a dynasty to perpetuate it afterward; and Omar Torrijos Herrera (1929–1981), who ruled Panama from 1968 until his death. In 1954 the United States covertly assisted in the overthrow of Guatemalan president Jacobo Arbenz Guzmán (1951–1954), whose left-wing land redistribution policies had angered both American communist-hunters and the United Fruit Company, a U.S. company that had invested heavily in Guatemala.

Central America's political and social tensions boiled over in the 1960s and 1970s in numerous conflicts. In Guatemala, leftist guerrillas launched a civil war against the ruling elite that lasted 36 years, from 1960 to 1996, the longest civil war in Latin American history. In 1969 more than 2,000 people died in a conflict between El Salvador and Honduras called the Soccer War, so named because it was sparked by El Salvador's defeat of Honduras in a soccer series, though it stemmed from deeper tensions over heavy Salvadoran immigration to Honduras. In the late 1970s left-wing rebels initiated offensives against

government forces in El Salvador and Nicaragua.

By disrupting economic life, war exacerbated the poverty already faced by most of the region's inhabitants. For many Central Americans, the only hope lay north—in the United States. They came legally when possible, illegally when necessary, often traveling overland through Mexico, then crossing the border. They settled most heavily in Los Angeles, though Central American communities also sprang up in New York, Florida, and other places where Hispanic Americans were already living.

THE FIGHT FOR RIGHTS

As the Hispanic-American population of the United States grew in the 1960s and 1970s, a movement for civil rights and cultural recognition grew among the nation's largest ethnic subgroup of Hispanic Americans—those of Mexican descent. It sprang up in the context of the African-American civil rights movement

The poster above promotes the United Farm Workers' strike and boycott against California grape growers. (Private collection)

of the 1950s and early 1960s and the numerous progressive and radical left movements of the late 1960s and early 1970s. But the Mexican-American civil rights movement took its own distinctive shape. Behind all the activism lay a growing sense of ethnic identity as Chicanos, and a dawning awareness of the ties that bound Chicanos to all other Latinos, or Hispanic Americans.

HERNANDEZ V. TEXAS

In 1954, the same year in which the landmark case Brown v. Board of Education overturned educational segregation directed against African Americans, the Supreme Court rendered a similarly significant ruling for Hispanic Americans. Pete Hernandez was a Mexican American convicted of murder in Texas, a state that had long segregated people of Mexican descent just as it did people of African descent. Signs in restaurants and other public places stated this prejudice in so many words, with phrases like "No Dogs, Negroes, Mexicans." Local juries, including the one in Jackson County, Texas, that tried Hernandez, typically contained no Hispanics even when Hispanics were a substantial part of the population. In fact, at the time of Hernandez's trial, Jackson County had not had a single Hispanic serve on a jury for more than 25 years.

In *Hernandez v. Texas*, Hernandez's lawyers, Carlos C. Cadena and Gus C. Garcia (the first Hispanic Americans to argue in front of the U.S. Supreme Court), were faced with a challenge. In order to reverse Hernandez's conviction, they needed to establish that people of Mexican descent constituted a separate class of people in Jackson County, distinct from "whites." To do that, Cadena and Garcia called attention to the very public attitudes of the Anglo majority—as evidenced by signs that segregated Mexicans from Anglos in public places.

To buttress their case, Cadena and Garcia elicited admissions from county officials and business leaders that they themselves viewed Mexican Americans as distinct from "whites" and that very few Mexicans were asked to participate in local business and community groups. Additionally, Cadena and Garcia demonstrated that Mexican-American children were required to attend a segregated school through fourth grade. Finally, they observed that right on the county courthouse grounds at the time of the case's initial hearing, there were two men's toilets, one unmarked, and the other marked "Colored Men" and "Hombres Aqui" ("Men Here").

Having established Mexican Americans as an identifiable class of people in Texas, Cadena and Garcia had to prove that Mexicans as a group had been discriminated against. To do so, they relied on the precedent set in Norris v. Alabama, which showed that although many African Americans in Alabama were qualified to serve on juries, a consistent pattern of exclusion over a long period of

The mural above in an El Paso park displays the thunderbird, a symbol of pride in La Raza Unida. (National Archives)

time could be shown. The Norris case had established a "rule of exclusion," which had also been applied to other cases to prove discrimination.

Cadena and Garcia then showed that 14 percent of the population of Jackson County were either Mexican or had Latin American surnames, and that 11 percent of the males over 21 bore such names—underlining the point that Hispanics were a clearly identifiable group. The county tax assessor then testified that 6 or 7 percent of the freeholders on the tax rolls of the county were of Mexican descent. Since property taxpayerswere by state law qualified to serve on juries, argued Cadena and Garcia, only discrimination could explain the lack of Mexican jurors in the county. Although lawyers for the state argued that county commissioners had not discriminated against Mexicans but had only chosen jurors on the basis of qualifications, the court ruled that rationale to be insufficient, and ordered Hernandez's conviction to be overturned.

The court's ruling extended to Mexican Americans the equal protection clause of the 14th Amendment, making them the first minority group besides African Americans to receive that explicit recognition. On that basis the court overturned Hernandez's murder conviction. The court also made it easier for other Hispanics to use the courts to combat discrimination.

César Chávez and the United Farm Workers

By the early 1960s the lot of migrant farm workers had not substantially improved since the early 20th century, when southwestern growers first established the practice of hiring people of Mexican descent to pick the nation's fruits and vegetables. Wages were low, housing and food abysmal, education and health care scarce. Workers were often cheated of their wages or forced into debt. Attempts had been made throughout the century to organize migrant workers to demand better treatment, but little progress had been made.

Into the arena stepped César Chávez (1927–1993), an Arizona-born son of migrant farmworkers, who had also spent time laboring in the fields doing migrant work. In 1952, Chávez was approached by

THE ALIANZA FEDERAL DE MERCEDES

1963 The Alianza Federal de Mercedes (Federal Alliance of Land Grants) is incorporated by Reies López Tijerina.

1966 On October 15, Tijerina and 350 supporters commandeer the Camp Echo Amphitheater in Kit Carson National Forest, in northern New Mexico, and proclaim themselves leaders of the new state of Pueblo de San Joaquín de Chama. When park rangers attempt to intervene, Tijerina orders that they be arrested for trespassing.

1967 On June 5, members of the Alianza make an armed attack on a courthouse in the village of Tierra Amarilla to make a citizen's arrest of District Attorney Alfonso Sánchez. During the struggle, a jailer and a police officer are wounded. Although the New Mexico National Guard arrests 40 Alianza members at a nearby campground, Tijerina escapes. He is captured on June 10 and tried for conspiracy for the Kit Carson National Forest occupation. While the conspiracy charge is dismissed, Tijerina is found guilty of assault and sentenced to two years in prison. The decision is appealed.

1968 On November 12, a jury finds Tijerina not guilty in the first of two trials for the Tierra Amarilla raid.

1969 Tijerina loses the appeal of his assault conviction in the New Mexico District Court, and when he appeals to the U.S. Supreme Court, the Court, headed by Chief Justice Warren Burger, refuses to hear the case. In November, Tijerina is convicted and sentenced to two concurrent prison terms for his role in the assault on the county courthouse in Tierra Amarilla.

1971 Having served three years of his terms in federal prison, Tijerina is released on parole.

an activist named Fred Ross who worked for a voter registration group called the Community Service Organization (CSO) about becoming a volunteer. According to Chávez, Ross "did such a good job of explaining how poor people could build power that I could even taste it." While working for CSO, Chávez met Dolores Huerta, a former elementary school teacher who had also worked as a migrant laborer. Growing up, Huerta learned about the plight of laborers firsthand. After her mother had earned enough money to buy a hotel, she rented rooms to braceros and other field workers, often allowing them to stay for free so that they would also have money for food.

In 1962 Chávez and Huerta broke from the CSO when they decided the time had come to form a union for migrant workers. That year they founded the National Farm Workers Association, a union that would later become the United Farm Workers, a member of the AFL-CIO. Pressure from the union helped end the bracero program, which had long thwarted labor organizing by supplying growers with a continually replenished

Dolores Huerta (United Farm Workers)

CÉSAR CHÁVEZ
AND THE UNITED FARM WORKERS MOVEMENT

1942 U.S. and Mexican governments reach an agreement to allow Mexican migrant farmworkers into the United States as temporary workers during annual harvest seasons. The Mexican government agrees to the program as a method of safeguarding the treatment of its citizens working on the U.S. farms.

1947 Labor organizer Ernesto Galarza makes an unsuccessful attempt to organize farmworkers.

1952 César Chávez, a Mexican American born in Arizona, joins the Community Service Organization (CSO), a grassroots political movement founded by activist Saul Alinsky. The group's main focus is voter registration.

1953 The U.S. Immigration and Naturalization Service launches Operation Wetback, arresting and deporting more than 3.8 million persons of Mexican descent through 1958. Many U.S. citizens are deported unfairly, including political activist Luisa Moreno and other Mexican-American leaders.

1955 Dolores Huerta, a former elementary schoolteacher, joins the CSO.

1958 César Chávez becomes general director of the CSO.

1962 Chávez and Huerta resign from the CSO to organize the National Farm Workers Association (NFWA) in Delano, California.

1964 The bracero program finally ends, in part due to pressure from the NFWA and its supporters. That same year, President Lyndon Johnson signs the Civil Rights Act of 1964. The new law prohibits racial discrimination and establishes affirmative action programs to remove discrimination in advertising, recruitment, hiring, job classification, promotion, wages, and conditions of employment.

1965 On September 8, Filipino farmworkers from the Agricultural Workers Organizing Committee strike the Di Giorgio Corporation, a large grape grower in the San Joaquin Valley of California, demanding recognition of their organization and higher wages. The following week, Chávez and Huerta lead the NFWA in a vote to join the Agricultural Workers Organizing Committee strike. Following the vote, the National Farm Workers Association launches a grape boycott, targeting the Di Giorgio Corporation and Schenley Industries, another grower. On December 15, Walter Reuther, president of the United Auto Workers (UAW), flies to Delano, California, to support César Chávez. He divides a $5,000 strike contribution between the National Farm Workers Association and the Agricultural Workers Organizing Committee. His presence pressures the AFL-CIO, the nation's largest union, to support the farm labor strike.

1966 From March 17 to April 11, César Chávez and the National Farm Workers Association march from Delano to the California capital in Sacramento to publicize their strike. They arrive on Easter Sunday. On August 22, the NFWA and the Agricultural Workers Organizing Committee unite to form the United Farm Workers Organizing Committee (UFW). Shortly thereafter, the Di Giorgio Cororation grants the UFW membership a contract.

1968 On February 15, Chávez begins a 25-day fast at Forty Acres, near Delano, California. He proclaims that the fast is to show penitence for morale problems in the United Farm Workers and to discourage threats of violence against his followers. Shortly thereafter, he appears in court to respond to an injunction filed by the Giumarra Corporation aimed at prohibiting picketing by the UFW. Chávez is too weak from his hunger strike to testify, and the incident gains national attention and sympathy. On March 10, he breaks his fast at a Catholic mass in Delano's public park with 4,000 supporters at his side, including Senator Robert Kennedy.

1970 The UFW wins a major victory when 40 growers in California's Coachella Valley ask to negotiate contracts with the union. Huerta leads two months of negotiations that result in better pay, a union hiring hall, creation of formal grievance procedures, restrictions on the use of pesticides, rehiring of strikers, and employer contributions to a health fund. In another victory, grape growers in Delano sign three-year contracts with the UFW. Meanwhile, when Chávez refuses to call off a lettuce boycott, he is jailed and then released, pending an appeal to the California Supreme Court.

1972 In August, the UFW files suit in Phoenix, Arizona, to bar the enforcement of the Arizona Agricultural Relations Act, a law that would have prohibited picketing during harvesttime. That same year, the UFW helps defeat Proposition 22, a California bill that would have restricted workers' right to organize boycotts.

1973 In the spring, the Teamsters Union forms the Agricultural Workers Organizing Committee to compete with the UFW. On April 13, Chávez calls for UFW strikes after the growers sign agreements with the Teamsters. On August 16, Juan de la Cruz, a 60-year-old UFW member, is shot to death by a strike breaker. The strikes last through November 1974.

1975 California governor Edmund Brown Jr., an ally of Chávez's, signs the Agricultural Labor Relations Act, a landmark piece of legislation that establishes collective bargaining for the state's farmworkers.

César Chávez
(AFL-CIO)

supply of nonunion labor. From 1965 to 1970, the union sponsored a strike demanding union recognition and higher wages from growers of California table grapes. For inspiration Chávez turned to the nonviolent resistance philosophy and tactics of Indian leader Mohandas Gandhi and African-American civil rights leader Martin Luther King. Chávez called resolutely for nonviolence from his followers and used La Huelga, or "The Strike," to draw national attention to the plight of migrant farm workers, most of them Mexican American. He also stressed the importance of cultural heritage, encouraging Mexican Americans to be proud of their history. Building public sympathy through such tactics as a dramatic 25-day fast in 1968 (which caught the attention of presidential candidate Robert F. Kennedy, who visited Chávez to pledge his support), he sought and achieved a national grape boycott. At the time, Chávez summed up his motivation this way: "We are poor, but we have something the rich do not own— our bodies and our spirits and the justice of our cause." La Huelga ended with growers accepting union demands and negotiating agreements to improve the workers' condition.

In later years Chávez had difficulty getting growers to honor their agreements and faced other obstacles, such as jurisdictional issues with the Teamsters Union. But he had made an important step in improving the lives of migrant farm workers. In addition, he helped Mexican Americans achieve a new level of self-awareness and self-respect and presented an enduring example of Mexican-American leadership.

The Chicano Movement

LULAC, founded in the 1920s, had sought only to protect the civil rights of Mexican Americans. The Community Service Organization (CSO), founded in the late 1940s, focused on voter registration drives to elect Mexican Americans to office. The Mexican American Political Association (MAPA), founded in the 1950s, helped John F. Kennedy win election as president. But some Mexican Americans began to question the assimilationist drive of such organizations. Rooted partly in the example of Chávez, partly in earlier efforts, Mexican

SELECTED EVENTS IN THE CHICANO MOVEMENT, 1968–1973

1968 The Mexican American Legal Defense and Educational Fund (MALDEF) is founded in San Antonio, Texas, becoming the first national Chicano civil rights organization. The Ford Foundation announces that it will help fund MALDEF activities. The poet Alurista (Alberto Baltazar Urista) organizes the Movemiento Estudiantil Chicano de Aztlán (MEChA), uniting local and regional Chicano student organizations nationwide.

1970 In July, a National Chicano Moratorium Committee anti-Vietnam War march and rally in Houston, Texas, draws 5,000 people. The following month, a second rally is held in East Los Angeles's Laguna Park, this time attracting 30,000. Before breaking up the rally with tear gas and billy clubs, the police prevent Chicano activists Rodolfo "Corky" González and Albert Gurule from speaking before arresting both men on charges of robbery and carrying concealed weapons. (The two are later acquitted.) When some members of the crowd respond by throwing rocks, chaos ensues, and two bystanders are killed. A tear gas canister is thrown into a nearby restaurant, striking and killing Mexican-American journalist Ruben Salazar, whose columns in the Los Angeles Times had provided a powerful voice for the Chicano movement.

1972 A new political party, La Raza Unida (The United People), holds its first national convention in El Paso, Texas. Delegates decide to promote Chicano candidates for local elections instead of supporting major party candidates in national elections. José Angel Gutiérrez is elected national chairman.

1973 Texas lawyer Vilma Martínez becomes general counsel for MALDEF, beginning an influential career that will help lead to the passage of the Voting Rights Act of 1975. (The act granted special considerations, such as bilingual materials at the polls, to Hispanic voters.) With the support of La Raza Unida, José Angel Gutiérrez wins election as a judge in Zavala County, Texas.

Americans actively sought political and social change in the 1960s and 1970s. Many of these activists were more vocal and radical than their predecessors. They emphasized difference from Anglos and spoke of themselves proudly as Chicanos, a slang term abbreviated from Mexicanos and previously used by Anglos in a derisive sense.

The new Chicano groups included the Brown Berets, founded in East Los Angeles in 1967. A paramilitary organization of youths in brown berets, its members spoke of themselves as brown rather than black or white and organized to defend their neighborhoods against crime and police brutality. They also provided social services, such as food drives, and took part in public protests. In 1969 Chicano boxer, poet, and activist Rodolfo "Corky" González drafted El Plan Espiritual de Aztlán, "The Spiritual Plan of Aztlán," which called for the creation of a separate Mexican-American state in the Southwest, using the name of the mythical homeland of the Aztec. Throughout the Southwest, Chicano students demanded

Rodolfo "Corky" González (Colorado Historical Society)

SELECTED CHICANO ORGANIZATIONS

Organization: Brown Berets
Date founded: 1967
Region: Los Angeles metropolitan area
Activities: Defending neighborhoods against crime and police brutality, providing social services, including education, food drives, and health care

Organization: Movimento Estudientil Chicano de Aztlán (MEChA)
Date founded: 1968
Region: National
Activities: Promoting higher education for Chicanos, encouraging communication among Chicano high school and college students, fighting for the civil and human rights of Chicano students, promoting cultural awareness and pride

Organization: Mexican American Legal Defense and Education Fund (MALDEF)
Date founded: 1968
Region: National
Activities: Promoting and protecting the civil rights of Mexican Americans through class action litigation, community education, and leadership training

Organization: National Chicano Moratorium Committee
Date founded: 1970
Region: National
Activities: Protesting U.S. involvement in the Vietnam War, in particular the high number of Latino deaths and casualties during the conflict which the group attributed, in part, to a lack of Latino representation in command

Organization: La Raza Unida
Date founded: 1972
Region: National
Activities: A political party with the primary goal of organizing campaigns to get Chicano and Hispanic candidates elected to public office

better educational facilities and academic courses on Mexican-American culture and history. That culture was enriched through a new wave of Mexican-American arts and letters, including the books of José Antonio Villarreal, Rudolfo Anaya, and Tomás Rivera; the theatrical performances of Luis Valdez's Teatro Campesino; and the murals of artists Judy Baca and Manuel Martínez.

One organization turned separatist sentiment into violence. In 1963 Reies López Tijerina founded the Alianza Federal de Mercedes (Federal Alliance of Land Grants) to take back by force the lost land that had belonged to Chicanos before the U.S.-Mexican War. In 1966 the group occupied part of Kit Carson National Forest in New Mexico. The following year they raided Rio Arriba county courthouse in Tierra Amarilla, New Mexico, to try to make a citizen's arrest of District Attorney Alfonso Sánchez. More attempted arrests of prominent officials followed, along with prison time for Tijerina.

Less dramatically but more successfully, the Mexican American Legal Defense and Educational Fund (MALDEF), founded in 1968, used such means as class action litigation and community education to promote Mexican-American civil rights. Texas lawyer Vilma Martínez, MALDEF's general counsel from 1973, helped bring about passage of the Voting Rights Act of 1975, which gave special consideration to Hispanic voters. La Raza Unida (The United People), a Mexican-American political party, was founded in 1970 by José Angel Gutiérrez to elect Chicano candidates to public office.

The Chicano rights movement succeeded in making Mexican Americans more self-aware and self-confident, proud of their heritage and insistent on equal treatment under the law. It was part of the larger movement for social change that marked the 1960s and early 1970s, running parallel to movements in other Hispanic-American communities, such as the Puerto Rican groups Aspira and the Young Lords. By and large, however, Hispanic Americans continued to see themselves not as one large group, but as many distinct ones—people variously rooted in Mexico, Puerto Rico, Cuba, the Dominican Republic, or the many countries of South America and Central America. They had not yet begun to fulfill the promise inherent in the name of the party of the time, *la raza unida*.

A CHANGING COMMUNITY

In the waning years of the 20th century, Hispanic Americans were one of the country's fastest growing minorities. By the year 2000 they represented about 12 percent of the population and were projected to continue growing rapidly. Though natural increase played a role, much of the growth in the Hispanic-American population during this period resulted from continuing heavy immigration from Hispanic nations. Many of the newcomers arrived from Mexico, Puerto Rico, Cuba, and the Dominican Republic, places that had been active sources of migration in the period from 1945 to 1975 as well. But Central America and South America, which had previously sent smaller numbers of immigrants, opened their own floodgates during this period.

MEXICAN AMERICANS

The Mexican-American community of the late 20th century had many faces. There were the Mexican Americans who had migrated from their traditional heartland in the Southwest to other parts of the country. There were those who stayed in the border region, creating a culture with strong ties to northern Mexico. There were the second- and third-generation Mexican Americans, likely to assimilate as other immigrant groups before them had. But there were also millions of newcomers from Mexico, many coming with the required immigration documents, many without them.

A Changing Population

Since World War I, Mexican Americans had been migrating in considerable numbers north from the Southwest to other parts of the United States. The pace of this internal migration increased in the late 20th century. The majority of the country's 13.5 million Mexican Americans (as counted in the 1990 census) still lived in the Southwest—California, Texas, New Mexico, and Arizona. But other states had also become home to large Mexican-American populations.

By 1990 Illinois had between 500,000 and 1 million Mexican-American residents—the same range as Arizona. Washington, Nevada, Colorado, Michigan, and Florida each had between 100,000 and 500,000 Mexican Americans—the same range as New Mexico. In numerous states the number of Mexican Americans was between 20,000 and 100,000; these were as far-flung as Oregon and Idaho in the Northwest, Iowa and Missouri in the Midwest, New York and Pennsylvania in the Northeast, and North Carolina and Georgia in the Southeast.

While most Mexican Americans of the early 20th century were migrant farmworkers, those of the late 20th century worked in varied occupations. A disproportionate number labored in low-skill, low-paid positions, but an increasing number were in skilled or white-collar jobs, including college professors, teachers, journalists, lawyers, doctors, and bankers. Industries in which Mexican Americans developed a growing presence included construction, trucking, oil, garment manufacturing, assembly-line manufacturing, hotel and restaurant operations, retail sales, gardening, and domestic work.

By the 1970s a growing number of Mexican Americans were merchants and entrepreneurs, members of a small but expanding Mexican-American middle class. Many of these businesses were small, barrio-based service operations, such as restaurants, groceries, and contracting firms. Mexican-American businesses made up the lion's share of Hispanic-American businesses, which grew by 200 percent in the 1970s and continued to increase in the 1980s. By the early 1990s there were more than 800,000 Hispanic-owned businesses.

As Mexican Americans spread throughout the country, they continued their tradition of forming community organizations to provide mutual aid and political organizations to advocate for

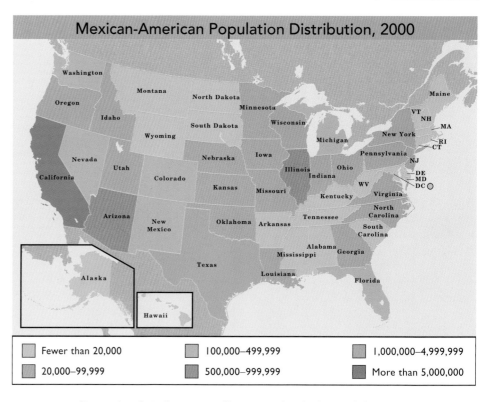

Mexican-American Population Distribution, 2000

☐ Fewer than 20,000	☐ 100,000–499,999	☐ 1,000,000–4,999,999
☐ 20,000–99,999	☐ 500,000–999,999	☐ More than 5,000,000

greater equality and political power. All this organizing had a measurable impact. During the 1970s, the number of Mexican Americans elected to public office increased 200 percent.

Even so, the problems facing Mexican Americans remained substantial. As of the late 1990s, 28 percent of Mexican Americans lived in poverty, a greater proportion than the 23.5 percent of 1981. The high school dropout rate among Mexican Americans was 50 percent. Despite some gains, Mexican Americans are still underrepresented in terms of elected officials. Many Mexican Americans are recent immigrants, enduring the hard times often faced by new arrivals, perhaps with well-founded hopes of bettering their condition in the future. But many Mexican Americans born in the United States inherit the poverty of their parents and seem unable to change it. The children of migrant worker families, for example, are still unlikely to receive adequate education and health care, despite the advances wrought by the farmworkers movement of the 1960s and 1970s.

IMMIGRATION LAW AND THE U.S. ECONOMY

As it had been for most of the 20th century, the United States at the century's end continued to be a magnet for Mexicans in search of a better life. At the same time, the relationship between the U.S. and Mexican governments evolved—as did the relationship between the American majority population and Mexican immigrants in the United States as the economic and social forces at work on both sides of the border ebbed and flowed.

From 1965 to 1976, a generally prosperous era in the United States, prospective Mexican immigrants benefited by not facing the ceiling of 20,000 visas per country that was then applied to the Eastern Hemisphere. By the late 1970s, with the United States facing an economic downturn, the flow of illegal aliens from Mexico became a major issue in domestic politics and in U.S.-Mexico relations. Due to this pressure, in 1976, the U.S. Congress extended the immigration ceiling to cover Western Hemisphere countries. At the same time, various provisions of immigration law permitted the number of legal immigrants to average more than 20,000 per year, and all told, more than 600,000 Mexicans immigrated legally to the United States during the 1970s.

Likewise when a deep U.S. recession intensified U.S. anti-immigrant sentiment in the early 1980s and more Americans began accusing "foreigners" of taking away jobs, Congress again responded, passing the Immigration Reform and Control Act (IRCA) of 1986.

Illegal Immigration and the Mexican Economy

The Immigration Reform and Control Act (IRCA) of 1986 took action to control future immigration by beefing up the Border Patrol and making it unlawful to knowingly employ undocumented aliens, with penalties prescribed for employers who did so. Nonetheless, the act also conceded the impossibility of deporting all those who had ever entered illegally. It offered amnesty and legal status to undocumented immigrants who had entered the United States before 1982 and remained there since, as well as to immigrants who could demonstrate that they had engaged in farmwork for a sufficiently long period in more recent years.

IRCA had some impact in reducing illegal immigration, but its force was diluted by the ease with which undocumented workers could obtain counterfeit documents "proving" their legal status to employers, who could then evade prosecution for not verifying the status. The act also resulted in some cases of unfair discrimination against Hispanics in general, as employers decided the best way to avoid prosecution was not to hire Hispanics. In an attempt to continue a tough attitude toward illegal immigration, Congress enacted another immigration law in 1996, this one including penalties for undocumented aliens who try to legalize their status by marrying a U.S. citizen. But Mexicans continued to flow into the country illegally despite all such efforts.

In many ways, the provision of IRCA that undocumented farmworkers be offered amnesty and legal status highlights the very complex relationship between Mexico and the United States on both legal and illegal immigration. That migrant laborers were singled out for amnesty while other recently arrived undocumented aliens were not illustrates that regardless of changing immigration laws, both the U.S. and Mexican economies rely on the maintainance of a steady flow of inexpensive Mexican labor to work American farmlands. Thus, even as IRCA tightened border patrols in the 1980s, more than 1 million Mexicans were able to immigrate legally to the United States—representing about one-sixth of all legal immigration during that decade.

IRCA's provisions tightening border patrols were not put into place to stem legal immigration, however. In addition to the flow of legal immigrants, many Mexicans entered the United States illegally during the final decades of the 20th century. Often they tried to immigrate legally but found that the backlog of applications made it virtually impossible that they would be admitted soon or ever. Precise figures are unavailable, but the number of people captured and deported to Mexico each year for lacking proper immigration documents is an indication of the number, since at least as many Mexicans can be expected to elude capture and remain in the United States. During the 1970s, the average number of people so deported was 721,000 per year; in the 1980s and 1990s, the average number went up to 1 million a year.

As the flow of illegal immigration increased, the U.S Border Patrol became more effective at monitoring the border, using everything from more patrol officers and improved training to helicopters, movement sensors, and night-vision goggles. As the Border Patrol became more effective, the coyotes who aided Mexicans in crossing the border illegally became more ingenious. Coyotes set up operations in Mexican border cities, where aspiring immigrants paid them $300 and up for assistance in immigrating illegally.

A favorite coyote technique was to drive openly through immigration checkpoints with immigrants hidden in vehicles. The immigrants would then be delivered to the nearest large city. Another technique was to avoid immigration checkpoints and instead drop clients off at a remote desert location south of

TOP 20 ILLEGAL IMMIGRANT POPULATIONS BY STATE, 1996

California	2,000,000	Colorado	45,000
Texas	700,000	District of Columbia	44,000
Florida	540,000	Maryland	44,000
New York	540,000	Michigan	37,000
Illinois	290,000	New Mexico	37,000
New Jersey	135,000	Pennsylvania	37,000
Arizona	115,000	Oregon	33,000
Massachusetts	55,000	Connecticut	29,000
Virginia	55,000	Georgia	32,000
Washington	52,000	Nevada	24,000

Note: Illegal immigrant figures represent all nationalities.

Estimated Illegal Immigrants from Latin America in the United States, 1996

UNITED STATES

MEXICO:
2,700,000

2.1 million overstays

3.9 million border crossings

DOMINICAN REPUBLIC:
50,000

HONDURAS:
90,000

Atlantic Ocean

GUATEMALA:
165,000

NICARAGUA:
70,000

EL SALVADOR:
335,000

Pacific Ocean

COLUMBIA:
65,000

ECUADOR:
55,000

PERU:
30,000

The numbers in the map above indicate amounts of people (by country) who illegally immigrated to the United States in 1996.

the border. The clients then crossed the border on foot and rendezvoused with a partner of the coyote at a prearranged spot, from which they would be driven to a city.

Since such operations were by necessity unregulated, clients put their lives on the line each time they trusted a coyote. More than once, they were abandoned to die of thirst in the desert or left confined in a vehicle. In Texas in 1987, 18 undocumented aliens were discovered by the Border Patrol locked in a boxcar, where they had suffocated to death.

The rising tide of immigration resulted in part from worsening economic conditions in Mexico. Inflation, unemployment, and foreign debt rose in Mexico in the 1970s, and declining oil prices in the 1980s damaged Mexico's ability to repay debt. The currency was devalued and capital fled the country. Mexico required an emergency loan from the United States in 1982 to salvage its economy, and in 1995 a currency crisis

was resolved only by a bailout package from the United States and the International Monetary Fund.

According to many economists, Mexico's financial trouble stemmed from its emphasis on nationalization and government economic control that dated to the Mexican Revolution. During the 1980s and 1990s, Mexico tried to improve its economic outlook by cutting government spending and adopting policies of liberalization and privatization. In 1994, in the hope of attracting jobs and foreign investment, Mexico joined Canada and the United States in signing the controversial North American Free Trade Agreement (NAFTA), which eliminated most trade barriers among the three countries.

Reduced protection of state industries and cuts in social programs only made things worse for some Mexicans, adding to the rising social tensions. In 1994 a guerrilla uprising of poor Native Americans who called themselves the

NAFTA will cause a giant sucking sound as jobs go south.

—Ross Perot, Independent candidate for President, 1992

Zapata Army of National Liberation arose in the Mexican state of Chiapas, partly in response to fears about NAFTA's impact at home. The increasing social tensions contributed to a liberalizing of Mexico's political system, as the long-reigning Institutional Revolutionary Party (PRI) gave up some of its hold on power. But the tensions also contributed to continued heavy immigration, legal and illegal, to the United States.

By the late 1990s, people from Mexico were by far the largest group of foreign-born people in the United States. Seven million people living in the United States in 1997 had been born in Mexico; the next largest groups of foreign-born people, Filipinos and Chinese, numbered only 1.1 million each. Mexicans also far outstripped other Hispanic foreign-born groups. Cubans, the next largest Hispanic foreign-born group, numbered 913,000; Dominicans 632,000; and Salvadorans 607,000.

Mexican workers in a foreign-owned factory, or maquiladora, in Mexico (Corbis-Bettmann)

El Norte

Even more than in the past, the U.S.-Mexico border region in the late 20th century took on the distinctive character of an extra-national region, one that transcended national boundaries. In this region it became increasingly common for work-ers to commute from Mexico every day to work in jobs in the United States, then return home to Mexico at night. Many Mexicans laboring in various fields—including construction, service, and agriculture—came to prefer this arrangement because higher U.S. wages buy more in Mexico, where prices are lower. Others did it because they preferred Mexican culture; still others saw no significant difference

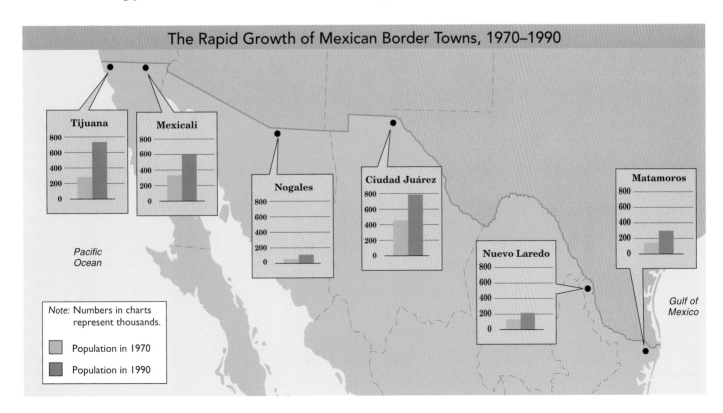

The Rapid Growth of Mexican Border Towns, 1970–1990

Tijuana

Mexicali

Nogales

Ciudad Juárez

Nuevo Laredo

Matamoros

Pacific Ocean

Gulf of Mexico

Note: Numbers in charts represent thousands.

Population in 1970

Population in 1990

"There have been 23 studies of the impact of NAFTA on jobs in the United States. Twenty-two of them have shown that it will cause an increase in jobs in the United States."

—Vice-President Al Gore, 1993

between Mexico and El Norte, "The North," at least in the borderlands. On both sides, in cities close to the border, Spanish was widely spoken and customs were a blend of Mexican and American. Said one Mexican commuter in the Tijuana, Mexico, area: "There is no real difference in living on this side. I can watch the Chargers and Padres on television just as easily from over here, so I'm not really losing any of the convenience or benefits I had."

In some cases, Mexican women would commute into the United States to give birth. Shortly before her baby was due to be born, a pregnant woman would cross into the United States with a temporary visa or no visa, give birth in the United States so that the child was born a U.S. citizen, then return to Mexico. That way, the child could choose to live in the United States in later years without legal difficulty, and, upon reaching adulthood, could even sponsor his or her parents and other family members. The practice continued to blur the lines between who was a Mexican and who was a Mexican American.

While Mexican workers flowed northward looking for employment, American employers during this period increasingly flowed southward looking for workers. This trend ballooned because of Mexico's establishment in the 1960s of the Border Industrialization program, or maquiladora program. This program used the incentive of reduced or eliminated duties on international shipping to encourage the establishment of maquiladoras, foreign-owned factories on Mexican soil near the border, with products assembled in Mexico from imported parts, then exported back to the United States. The program allowed employers both to pay workers lower wages than American workers enjoyed and to avoid the United States's more stringent environmental protection laws. The employment opportunities brought a rush of Mexicans into such border towns as Tijuana, Nuevo Laredo, and Matamoros. By 1993 maquiladoras employed about 600,000 workers. In 1994 NAFTA increased the influence of the border region by creating a North American free trade zone. The agreement imposed some antipollution restraints on maquiladoras, but enforcement has been lax, and pollution on both sides of the border has continued.

NAFTA: PRO AND CON

To increase economic growth, the governments of Mexico, the United States, and Canada signed the North American Free Trade Agreement (NAFTA) in December 1992. NAFTA's purpose is to erase economic boundaries by creating a regional free-trade zone that will benefit all three nations. Since 1994, when the program went into effect, many trade tarriffs have been lowered and others have been eliminated. NAFTA, like the maquiladoras, is not without controversy, however. Some of the arguments in favor of and against NAFTA are listed below:

Pro:
• The treaty helps North America compete against European and Asian nations that have also eliminated regional trade barriers.
• NAFTA helps increase cultural ties to Mexico, the ancestral home of millions of Americans.
• NAFTA will boost the Mexican economy, which will slow down illegal immigration to the United States.

Con:
• Although the negotiations reached side agreements that impose some antipollution restraints on maquiladoras, many of those laws are not enforced, and the rapidly growing population in Mexico's border region has only increased pollution on both sides of the border.
• NAFTA allows U.S. corporations to exploit low-wage Mexican workers.
• Although NAFTA has created some jobs on the U.S. side of the border, many profitable corporations have closed factories in the United States in order to open factories in Mexico.

LANGUAGE AND EDUCATION

Some Anglo-Americans living in the border region during the late 20th century were unhappy about the increasing Mexican influence. Much of the anger on the part of conservative Anglos and others has crystalized around the issue of bilingual education. Ever since the U.S. Supreme Court ruled in the 1974 case of *Lau v. Nichols* that public schools should be in effect required to provide bilingual education programs for students who needed them, some have argued that bilingual education programs are a subversive force undermining national unity. In the late 1970s, an English Only movement emerged, calling for the "defense" of the English language, with Spanish treated as the enemy. The movement spawned a Washington, D.C.–based organization called U.S. English, which prodded many states to approve legislation making English the official language. Under the presidency of Ronald Reagan (1981–1989), federal spending on bilingual education was routinely cut.

While all Hispanic Americans are affected by the debate, the issue has affected Mexican Americans in particular since they make up a higher percentage of the foreign-born Hispanic population in the United States than all other Hispanic immigrant groups combined. Hispanic immigrants want their children to learn English, for they recognize that it is the primary language of advancement in the United States. Yet the debate over bilingual education has continued to the present day, a symbol of underlying tensions between the Hispanic minority and the non-Hispanic majority.

In 1998, a coalition of civil rights groups in California lodged a lawsuit to block Proposition 227, an English Only initiative passed by voters that year. The groups argued that the initiative violated the Equal Educational Opportunity Act of 1974, Title VI of the Civil Rights Act of 1964, and other federal laws guaranteeing the right of non-English-speaking students to appropriate language programs, which ensure meaningful access to equal educational opportunity. Joe Jaramillo, staff attorney for the Mexican American Legal Defense and Education Foundation (MALDEF), put it this way:

> *Proposition 227 violates the fundamental right of national origin minorities to participate on an equal basis in the political process of advocating for effective educational programs for their children. This Proposition shuts off the basic means to advocate for or to change local educational programs designed to overcome students' language barriers. We're now forced to turn to the courts to vindicate the rights of parents and students to advocate for effective and appropriate education programs for limited English proficient children.*

Jaramillo was joined by Juana Flores, a mother of two daughters who were enrolled in bilingual classes in San Francisco schools. Speaking through an interpreter, Flores said, "Although I do not speak English well I have been able to help my children with school. As parents, the more we are involved the more our children are going to see that education is

Young Chicanos in El Paso's barrio near the Mexican border, 1972 (National Archives)

important. If they take away bilingual education they are going to take away our communication with the teachers, and we will no longer feel welcome at the schools, nor will we be able to participate in the school community."

Not all Hispanic Americans—nor even all Mexican Americans—see the bilingual education issue the same way. Two years before the passage of Proposition 227, a Los Angeles parents group called Las Familias del Pueblo (Village Families) organized a boycott of a local school that they claimed refused to teach their children English. As one parent, Lenin Lopez, put it in Spanish, "A lot of us want our kids to learn Spanish so they can write to their grandpas or whatever. But I want my children to learn English so they won't have the problems that I've had." Although the principal of the school in question tried to explain that her school's had decided to begin English classes by the third grade, a year earlier than they had previously been taught, many studies had shown that young non-English- speaking children also needed a solid grounding in their native languages before learning English. Nonetheless, the debate illustrates that finding the best means of adapting to a new culture is never easy.

DOMINICANS AND PUERTO RICANS

The Spanish-speaking Caribbean—Cuba, the Dominican Republic, and Puerto Rico—continued to be important sources of Hispanic migration to the United States in the late 20th century. As of 2000, the Dominican-American community was among the most recently developed Hispanic-American groups. Their numbers had swiftly come to rival those of Cuban Americans. Mostly poor and living in urban areas, Dominican Americans were facing socioeconomic problems similar to those Puerto Rican Americans have historically faced.

DOMINICAN IMMIGRANTS

Already growing in the 1970s, Dominican immigration skyrocketed in the 1980s and 1990s. In the 1980s more than 20,000 Dominicans on average were legally admitted to the United States each year; in the 1990s, the annual average number

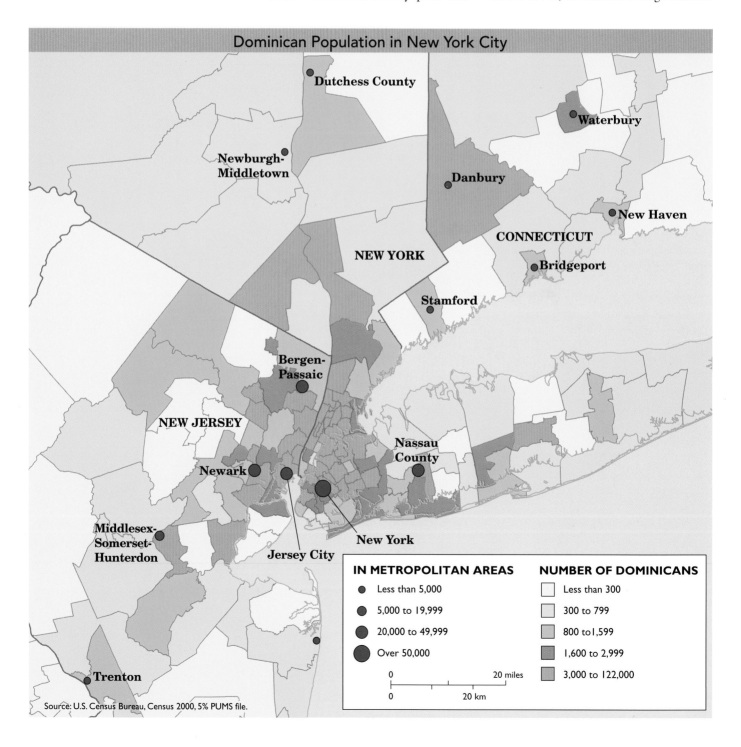

Dominican Population in New York City

IN METROPOLITAN AREAS

- ● Less than 5,000
- ● 5,000 to 19,999
- ● 20,000 to 49,999
- ● Over 50,000

NUMBER OF DOMINICANS

- Less than 300
- 300 to 799
- 800 to1,599
- 1,600 to 2,999
- 3,000 to 122,000

0   20 miles
0   20 km

Source: U.S. Census Bureau, Census 2000, 5% PUMS file.

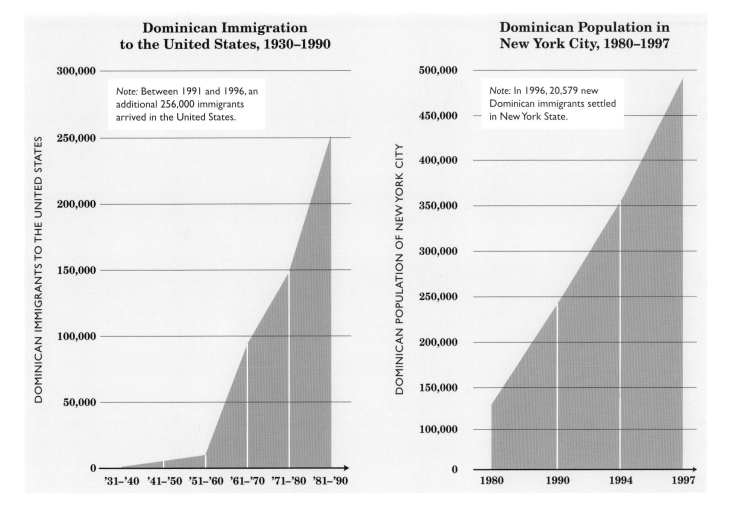

Dominican Immigration to the United States, 1930–1990

DOMINICAN IMMIGRANTS TO THE UNITED STATES

Note: Between 1991 and 1996, an additional 256,000 immigrants arrived in the United States.

300,000
250,000
200,000
150,000
100,000
50,000
0

'31–'40 '41–'50 '51–'60 '61–'70 '71–'80 '81–'90

Dominican Population in New York City, 1980–1997

DOMINICAN POPULATION OF NEW YORK CITY

Note: In 1996, 20,579 new Dominican immigrants settled in New York State.

500,000
450,000
400,000
350,000
300,000
250,000
200,000
150,000
100,000
0

1980 1990 1994 1997

climbed even higher, to more than 40,000. An uncounted number immigrated illegally. The total population of Dominican Americans by century's end was close to 1 million, comparable to the Cuban-American population.

Like their predecessors in previous decades, Dominican Americans arrivals since the 1980s have concentrated in New York City. Although some Dominicans came from the better-educated, urban stratum of society, and thus were able to adjust quickly to urban life in the United States, their lack of English and other disadvantages often led them to take jobs below their abilities. Together with the many unskilled, blue-collar laborers who also arrived in New York from the Dominican Republic during the same period, educated Dominican immigrants faced many economic challenges since arriving. At a time when manufacturing jobs were declining in the United States—and particularly in New York City—in favor of lower-paying service jobs, Dominican workers often suffered unemployment and underemployment.

Many found work in the hotel, restaurant, and garment industries and as domestics.

The economic progress of Dominican New Yorkers has been difficult to assess because the 2000 U.S. Census did not separate figures for Dominican Americans from Hispanic Americans in general, even though they did make the distinction for Mexicans, Cubans, Puerto Ricans, and Central and South Americans. Although members of the Dominican-American community protested this policy after census forms were mailed out, and Dominican community groups instructed individuals to write in "Dominican" instead of "Hispanic" on the form, federal government statistics on Dominican Americans were not collected. Nonetheless, it is known that as of 2000, Dominican immigrants made up the largest foreign-born group in New York City. Manhattan's Washington Heights neighborhood was largely Dominican by 2000.

It is also clear that unemployment and poverty remain a concern for Dominican Americans. Kinship networks have helped, with new immigrants finding support in relations who had immigrated earlier. Voluntary associations have also provided assistance. For example, New York's Alianza Dominicana, founded in the 1980s, offered youth services, substance abuse prevention, employment training, and other services. Ties to home remained strong; many Dominican Americans regularly sent money to family members left behind and made return trips to visit them.

Dominican-American neighborhoods are enlivened by Dominican culture, manifested in the dance music called merengue, Caribbean cuisine, community clubs celebrating Dominican history and culture, and Dominican flags in storefront windows, along with names of Dominican provinces and towns. Dominican Americans have founded many retail businesses—grocery stores, beauty parlors, travel agencies—to serve their community. A study in 1991 showed that about 70 percent of all bodegas (grocery stores catering to Hispanics) in New York City were owned by Dominicans.

Still, Dominican Americans were underrepresented in white-collar occupations, and their community continued to face an array of problems, including unemployment, drug addiction, crime, and low educational attainment. According to a study by the City University of New York, By the late 1990s more than 54 percent of Dominican New Yorkers over the age of 25 had not finished high school, and only 4 percent had finished college. On the other hand, the Dominican presence in higher education was growing, and in 1992 a Dominican Studies Institute was founded at the City University of New York (CUNY), where Dominicans tend to be the largest subgroup of Hispanic Americans.

PUERTO RICAN AMERICANS: LIFE ON THE MAINLAND

Migration from Puerto Rico to the mainland United States slowed after the heyday of the 1950s and 1960s but continued. As of 1997, about 2.7 million people of Puerto Rican ancestry were living on the U.S. mainland, a number equal to 71 percent of the 3.8 million living in Puerto Rico. If current trends continue, people of Puerto Rican ancestry living on the mainland United States will soon outnumber those remaining on the island.

On the U.S. mainland, Puerto Rican Americans remained concentrated in the metropolitan New York City region, though substantial populations could also be found in Florida, Pennsylvania, New Jersey, Connecticut, Massachusetts, Illinois, and California (each of which had between 100,000 and 500,000 people of Puerto Rican descent in 1990). An increasing number of Puerto Rican Americans worked in white-collar professional and technical jobs. Second- generation Puerto Rican Americans were likely to be better educated and more prosperous than their parents. As of the late 1980s, median earnings for Puerto Rican men were higher than for any other Latino group in the United States except for Cubans. Although Puerto Rican Americans are more likely to be poor than the general population—and also poorer, on average, than Mexicans, Cubans, Central and South Americans—69 percent lived above the poverty line as of 1999.

The majority of Puerto Rican Americans were blue-collar workers. Like Dominican Americans, they were hurt by the flight of manufacturing jobs from New York City in the late 20th century. Many Puerto Rican Americans continued to endure poverty and its related problems, including broken families, low educational attainment, drugs, and crime. As of the late 1990s, Puerto Rican–American families were more likely to be headed by a single parent, usually a female, than families in any other Hispanic-American group.

As the 20th century drew to a close, the Puerto Rican community in New York City was increasingly well represented in government. By the mid-1990s more than 20 Puerto Rican Americans were serving in elected positions in New York, including Fernando Ferrer, Bronx borough president since 1987, and U.S. Congressman José Serrano. The Puerto Rican–American community was visible in many other ways, including the annual Puerto Rican Day parade in June, one of New York City's biggest public events. It is marked by avid waving of the Puerto Rican flag and wearing of the pava, the traditional straw hat of the Puerto Rican jibaro, or farmer.

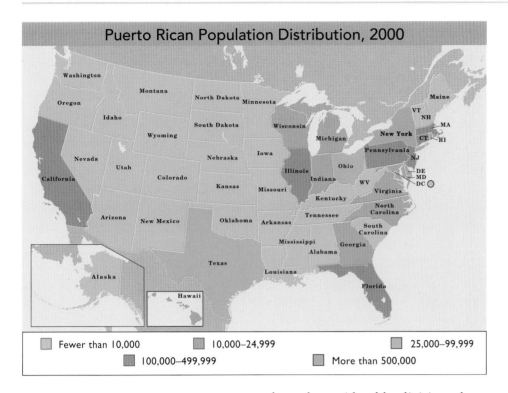

Puerto Rican Population Distribution, 2000

□ Fewer than 10,000   □ 10,000–24,999   □ 25,000–99,999
□ 100,000–499,999   □ More than 500,000

PUERTO RICANS: LIFE ON THE ISLAND

At the end of the 20th century, Puerto Rico continued to be economically successful by the standards of other Caribbean nations, but not by the standards of the United States. In 1995 Puerto Rico's per-capita gross product of $7,662 was a third of the average U.S. citizen's income on the mainland but was nearly twice as high as the Dominican Republic's per-capita gross income and six times as high as Cuba's. As of the mid-1990s, unemployment hovered at about 15 to 20 percent, and at least half of the population of Puerto Rico lived below the U.S. poverty line.

Puerto Rico's status remained controversial, and the actions of a few independentista terrorists remained highly visible in the century's closing decades. For example, in 1983 a terrorist group called Los Macheteros ("bearers of machetes," the traditional Caribbean sword) gained notoriety for robbing $1.7 million from an armored car company in West Hartford, Connecticut. However, few Puerto Ricans advocate outright independence from the United States. In a 1993 plebiscite, only 4 percent of Puerto Ricans voted for independence.

Though independence from the United States is not a popular option for most Puerto Ricans, the 1993 vote showed considerable division about whether Puerto Rico should remain a commonwealth or become a state. The 48.6 percent of voters who opted to retain commonwealth status carried the day, but with only a slight margin over the 46.3 percent of voters calling for statehood. Statehood would give Puerto Ricans full representation in Congress, but it might also bring economic problems, since federal tax exemptions for businesses and individuals would come to an end. If Puerto Rico does ultimately become a state, it will be the first with an almost entirely Hispanic population.

CUBA AND CUBAN AMERICANS

The story of the Cuban-American community since the 1970s has inevitably been intertwined with the political relationship between the United States and Cuba—just as it had in the years immediately following Castro's takeover in 1959. Although the United States has not trained and sponsored a direct invasion of Cuba since the Bay of Pigs fiasco, and the former Soviet Union has not attempted to place nuclear weapons in Cuba since the Cuban missile crisis ended, the U.S. government and the government of Fidel Castro continued to play games of political brinksmanship against each other.

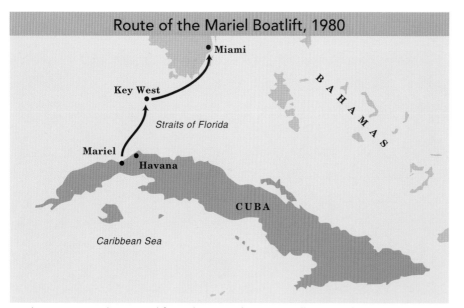

Route of the Mariel Boatlift, 1980

Under pressure at home and from the United States to allow people to leave Cuba, Fidel Castro decided to permit open immigration from April 21 to April 26, 1980, out of the port of Mariel. During this period, some 125,000 Cubans fled to the United States, many of them poor and far less educated than the initial exile group of the 1960s. Many were criminals Castro had released from prison, and many others were mentally ill. Most were quickly processed by American officials at Fort Chafee, Arkansas, and other bases. But thousands—including many falsely accused of crimes or of being mentally ill—were detained for months.

"The news media tended to focus on the 'undesireables' that the Castro government forced onto the boats.... The majority of those who arrived in the U.S. were decent, hard-working folks, who simply wanted to be reunited with their family members, or have new opportunities; but their stories were buried in larger stories with very sensationalistic headlines."

—Maria C. Garcia, author of *Havana USA*, a history of the Cuban exile community

THE MARIEL BOATLIFT

From 1973, Fidel Castro for the most part banned emigration from Cuba to the United States. But in 1980 the Cuban dictator temporarily lifted the emigration ban, allowing about 125,000 people to leave by boat from the port of Mariel. Known as Marielitos, the people in the Mariel boatlift were demographically unlike previous generations of Cuban immigrants, who had largely been well educated, middle class, and white. Most Marielitos were poor, less educated, and of African descent. A small percentage were convicted criminals and mentally ill patients, though many sensationalist news reports in the United States made it seem like most of them were sick or criminal. About 2,700 Marielitos (2 percent) were refused permission to enter the United States, either because of criminal records or crimes committed upon arrival.

Because of a combination of factors—racist sentiment, economic anxiety, fear of rising crime, and concern about rising immigration—many Americans gave the Marielitos a cold reception, unlike the welcome they had extended to earlier newcomers from Cuba. One New Jersey automobile worker said, "Those Cubans—we should put them back on their boats and sink them. We don't have enough work for our own people." With the boatlift coming at the height of a major economic recession in the United States, this anti-immigrant attitude was fairly commonplace—and not just aimed at Cubans. Other Hispanics, as well as immigrants from Asia and elsewhere, were targeted for blame. Even the popular name for Marielitos signaled that they were percieved as different from earlier arrivals from Cuba. While earlier Cuban immigrants had been given the noble title "exiles," these immigrants were called by the scruffier term "refugees."

As for the Marielitos who were refused entry, most languished in American prisons for years, detained in diplomatic limbo while Cuba and the United States faced off over the issue of their return. Not until some Marielitos led prison riots in 1987 did the United States take action to hear their cases, permitting some to stay in the United States and others to return to Cuba.

CUBA AND THE COLLAPSE OF THE SOVIET UNION

Throughout the 1980s, episodes like the Mariel boatlift were played out in the context of cold war relations between the United States and the Soviet Union, Cuba's primary financial backer. While Castro's socialist ideology placed him squarely within the pro-Soviet camp in the cold war era, Cuba's bond with the Soviets was cemented by massive Soviet financial support for the island's economy at least as much as by shared ideology. In the face of a U.S. trade embargo in force since 1960, Cuba depended on the Soviet Union for trade and assistance. U.S. officials accused Cuba of serving as the Soviet Union's proxy, giving arms and military support to leftist forces in other nations to spread Soviet control throughout Central America and the Caribbean. The United States responded with its own military aid—for example, to the anticommunist government of El Salvador and the right-wing Contra rebels in Nicaragua (described later in this chapter). In 1983 a U.S. invasion overthrew the Cuban-supported government of Grenada.

The United States put pressure on Cuba in other ways as well, notably by aiming the anticommunist station Radio Martí at Cuba beginning in 1985. Immigration policy remained a sore point, with the United States wanting to control the flow of immigrants to avoid another inundation of refugees as in the Mariel boatlift, and Castro wanting to restrict emigration to the United States except when politically useful. Despite these restrictions on emigration, Cubans unhappy with the Castro regime managed to make their way to American shores. Some came by way of travel to a third country, like baseball pitcher Livan Hernández, who defected to Mexico in 1995 and was soon playing for the Florida Marlins. Others came on leaky boats or rafts made of inner tubes.

The collapse of the Soviet Union in 1991 ended the cold war and put Cuba in a difficult position. Still unable to trade with the United States and now bereft of its main source of foreign aid, Cuba suffered economic deterioration. But Castro retained his grip on power, with cold war tensions persisting. In 1996 Castro launched a crackdown on dissidents and shot down two private planes operating out of the United States. The United States reacted by tightening its economic embargo, adding penalties for foreigners investing in Cuba. While Cuba and the United States have made some progress in improving relations, some Americans have strongly opposed a complete lifting of sanctions, among them the Cuban exiles who fled when Castro came to power.

The Elian Gonzalez custody battle in 2000 highlighted the unresolved issues still separating the United States and Cuba. It began in late 1999, when American fishermen rescued the five-year-old boy off the coast of Florida. Attempting to flee Cuba, his mother and

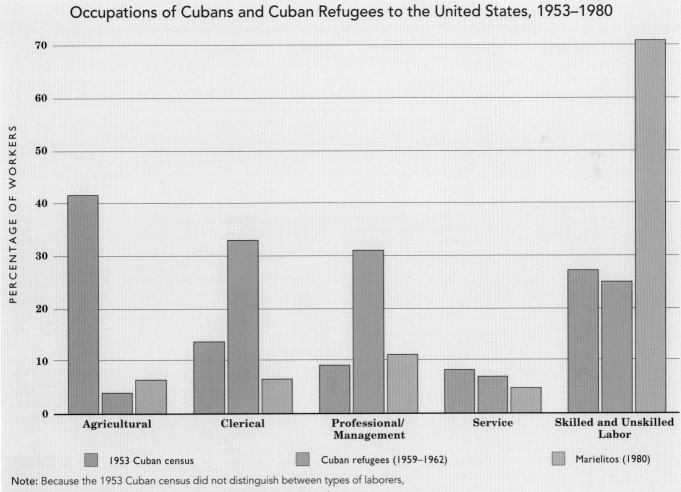

As the graphs above indicate, the Mariel boatlift refugees were less skilled than either earlier refugee groups or the Cuban population as a whole, as reflected by the prerevolution 1953 Cuban census. Many Americans accused Castro of using the boatlift to "dump" undesirable members of Cuban society on the United States.

several others had crowded into a motorboat that had capsized, killing Elian's mother and 10 others and leaving Elian to float on an inner tube for two days before being rescued. The U.S. Immigration and Naturalization Service (INS) placed the boy in the custody of relatives in Miami's Little Havana neighborhood. Elian's father, Juan Miguel Gonzalez, who had remained in Cuba, asked to have the boy returned; Castro supported his wish, sponsoring anti-American demonstrations to put pressure on the United States. Passions in the United States ran high, with the boy's Miami relatives and others insisting that the mother's wish to secure freedom for her son from Castro's dictatorship should be honored. Other Americans argued that the father's right to custody of his son trumped the issue of whether the United States or Cuba had a superior form of government. When Gonzalez came to the United States to take custody of Elian pending a court decision on the case, negotiations for transferring him from the care of his Miami relatives failed, prompting the U.S. Justice Department to seize the boy in an armed raid on their house. In the end, the courts ruled in favor of permitting Elian to return to Cuba with his father, leaving behind renewed awareness of unfinished business between Cuba and the United States.

A VIBRANT COMMUNITY

Cuban Americans remain most strongly concentrated in Florida, particularly Miami and surrounding Dade County, home to more than 700,000 people of Cuban descent. But Cuban-American communities exist in many other areas as well. As of 1990, New York, New Jersey, Connecticut, and California each were home to between 25,000 and 100,000 Cuban Americans; Texas and Illinois each had 10,000 to 25,000 Cuban Americans.

Cuban Americans made numerous contributions to the commerce and culture of the United States in the last 25 years of the 20th century. With their bilingual advantage, Cuban-American businesspeople in Miami spearheaded a strong and growing trade with Latin America, converting the city into a commercial gateway to the southern part of the Western Hemisphere.

During this period the Cuban community in the United States offered novelists like Oscar Hijuelos, author of the novel The Mambo Kings Play Songs of Love (1989), and pop musicians like Gloria Estefan and her Miami Sound Machine. Cuban-American baseball players like Livan Hernández continued the tradition of excellence begun by Tony Oliva, a hitter and later coach for the Minnesota Twins beginning in 1964. In this field their major rivals seemed to be

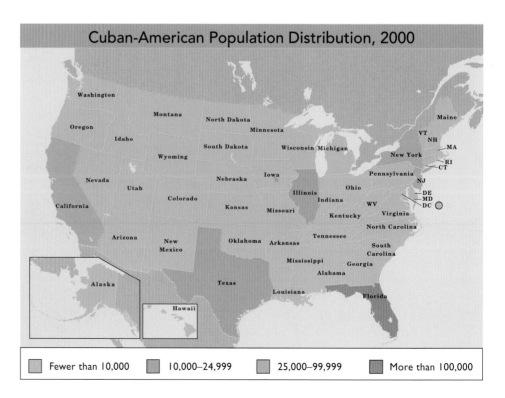

Cuban-American Population Distribution, 2000

Fewer than 10,000 | 10,000–24,999 | 25,000–99,999 | More than 100,000

Dominican-American baseball players, who also came from a country with a strong baseball tradition.

As the children and grandchildren of the first Cuban exiles who had fled Castro matured, significant cultural differences emerged between the old and new generations of Cuban Americans. The latter have been less likely to share their parents' loathing of Castro and have had little yearning to return to a free Cuba. These young, upwardly mobile Cuban Americans (YUCAs, as they are known) could speak both English and Spanish, but preferred English. While their parents and grandparents may have considered the United States nothing but a temporary way station, these younger Cuban Americans saw in it their permanent home.

CENTRAL AMERICANS

Though Central American immigration had been on the rise since the end of World War II, the flow of immigrants from that region took a sharp upturn in the 1980s, driven by the cold war–related civil wars that wracked the region during the decade. In the 1980s, 425,000 Central Americans immigrated legally to the United States, and far many more are believed to have come illegally. The largest number of legal immigrants came from El Salvador; by 1997 there were 607,000 Salvadoran-born people living in the United States, not much fewer than the country's 632,000 Dominican-born people. Many other immigrants came from Guatemala and Nicaragua.

Turmoil at Home

In the 1980s El Salvador, Guatemala, and Nicaragua all experienced dire civil wars. In all three cases the conflicts arose in radically unjust societies, where a tiny elite controlled most of the country's wealth, leaving the majority of the population in desperate poverty and political oppression. The U.S. government under Presidents Ronald Reagan (1981–1989) and George Bush (1989–1993), however, viewed the conflicts as theaters of the cold war, where anticommunist forces had to be supported, and communist, or even

ELIAN'S RETURN TO CUBA: CLASHING VOICES

On June 28, 2000, Elian Gonzalez returned to Cuba with his father, Juan Miguel Gonzalez, after a bitter custody battle with Elian's U.S. relatives, who believed he should remain in the United States on political grounds. This was Gonzalez's statement before leaving the United States, translated from Spanish:

> I would like to thank the North American people for the support they have given us and to the U.S. government. I think that this has allowed me to meet very beautiful and intelligent people in this country, and I hope that in the future this same friendship and this same impression that I have of the U.S. people, that the same thing can become true between both our countries, Cuba and the U.S. I am very grateful for the support I have received. I am extremely happy of being able to go back to my homeland, and I don't have words really to express what I feel.

This was the statement made a short time later by Armando Gutierrez, a spokesperson for the Lazaro Gonzalez family, who had cared for Elian in Miami and fought his return to Cuba:

> Elian's arrival and the subsequent fight for his life was like a wake-up call for the Cubans in Miami. Many had become complacent with our lives in the United States of America. Young and old, rich and poor, so many have forgotten the crisis in our country that brought us to this country. Elian's mother brought him to this great country seeking the promise of our Statue of Liberty. She and her son were among the huddled masses yearning to breathe free. How tragic that unlike the immigration of so many Americans, myself included, Elian Gonzalez cannot yet be free. Lazaro Gonzalez wants everyone to know that the family will still fight for Elian to be free regardless of where he's at.

left-leaning, forces had to be countered, lest the Soviet Union expand the foothold it had already established in Cuba.

In El Salvador a left-wing guerrilla insurgency known as the Farabundo Martí National Liberation Front (FMLN) waged war against the country's government from 1980 to 1992. Because the U.S. government viewed the FMLN as a Soviet-Cuban proxy, they supported the Salvadoran government with money, arms, and military advisors, despite mounting evidence from international human rights groups that government forces and progovernment, right-wing, paramilitary groups called "death squads" were conducting systematic murder and torture. Among atrocities linked to the Salvadoran government in 1980 were the assassination of Archbishop Oscar Arnulfo Romero, an advocate for the country's poor, and the 1980 rape and murder of four American churchwomen.

In 1992 Salvadoran president Alfredo Cristiani finally negotiated a peace treaty

Central American Immigration to the United States, 1961–1996

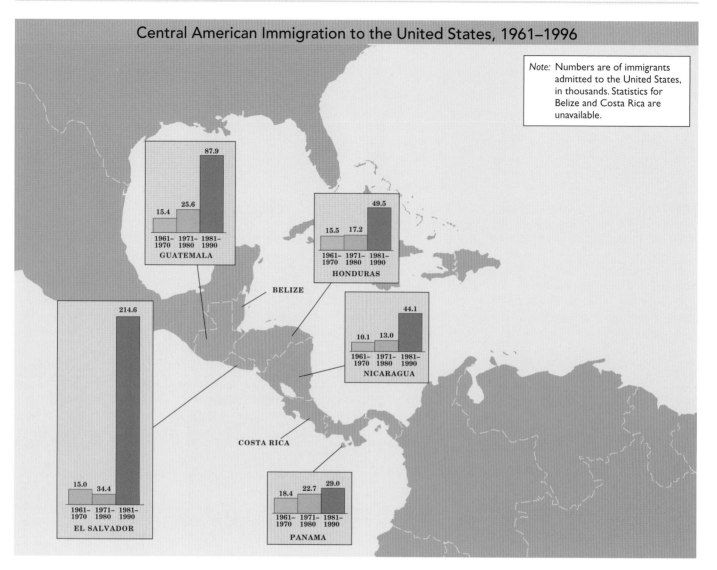

Note: Numbers are of immigrants admitted to the United States, in thousands. Statistics for Belize and Costa Rica are unavailable.

GUATEMALA
15.4 — 1961–1970
25.6 — 1971–1980
87.9 — 1981–1990

HONDURAS
15.5 — 1961–1970
17.2 — 1971–1980
49.5 — 1981–1990

NICARAGUA
10.1 — 1961–1970
13.0 — 1971–1980
44.1 — 1981–1990

BELIZE

EL SALVADOR
15.0 — 1961–1970
34.4 — 1971–1980
214.6 — 1981–1990

COSTA RICA

PANAMA
18.4 — 1961–1970
22.7 — 1971–1980
29.0 — 1981–1990

with the FMLN, ending the civil war, which had killed about 75,000 Salvadorans. The FMLN laid down its arms and was converted into a legitimate political party. A "truth" commission was established to investigate the government's human rights violations.

In Guatemala's even longer civil war, from 1960 to 1996, the left-wing guerrilla insurgency called the Guatemalan National Revolutionary Union (URNG) fought against another U.S.-backed government and its own associated set of right-wing death squads terrorizing the populace at the merest hint of dissent. About 100,000 people were killed and about 40,000 disappeared. The war ended with a peace accord between rebels and a more democratic system of government in 1996, with concessions on each side.

In Nicaragua in the 1980s, the United States supported not the government but the rebels. Until 1979 the United States had given its support to the Somoza

dynasty of dictators, founded in 1936. But the last member of that dynasty, Anastasio Somoza Debayle, was overthrown in a revolution in 1978–1979—a revolution led by yet another left-wing insurgency, this one the Sandinista National Liberation Front (FSLN), named in memory of Augusto Sandino, the guerrilla leader who had struggled against the U.S. military occupation of Nicaragua that lasted from 1926 to 1933. The new Sandinista government redistributed land and enacted social reforms, but the Reagan administration viewed it as another Soviet-Cuban proxy and sought to undermine it with a trade embargo and by funding and training a right-wing guerrilla insurgency called the Contras. Part of the U.S. aid to the Contras came from the Reagan administration's illegal sale of arms to Iran, in what was called the Iran-Contra scandal. The civil war in Nicaragua lasted from 1983 to 1990, when the Sandinistas, under U.S. pressure, held national elections and lost to opposition leader Violeta Barrios de Chamorro.

The other Hispanic nations of Central America—Costa Rica, Honduras, and Panama—experienced fewer troubles in the 1980s and therefore generated fewer refugees seeking safe haven elsewhere. Costa Rica has a long tradition of relative stability and democratic government, owing in part to the abolition of its army in mid-century. Honduras, which borders Guatemala, El Salvador, and Nicaragua, received massive aid from the United States during this period; it had some civil disorder and economic trouble, but not on the scale of its neighbors. Panama remained fairly stable, though only under the harsh dictatorial hand of Manuel Noriega. Noriega's excesses eventually led the United States to turn against him. U.S. troops invaded Panama in 1989, capturing Noriega and bringing him to the United States, where he was tried and convicted for drug trafficking. With hundreds of Panamanians killed in the U.S. invasion and damage estimated at $2 billion, immigration out of Panama increased, though not to the degree that had occurred elsewhere in Central America.

IMMIGRANTS OR REFUGEES?

With their countries in turmoil, Salvadorans, Guatemalans, and Nicaraguans fled in vast numbers to other nations. In Guatemala alone, about 1 million people became refugees during the civil war, seeking shelter not only in the United States but in other Central American countries and Mexico.

Even though many of the Central Americans who made their way to the United States were fleeing oppressive, violent governments, they had a hard time proving to U.S. officials that they were political refugees. Under U.S. immigration law, political refugees received special consideration and were not subject to the same restrictions as other immigrants. But because the United States was publicly aiding the governments of El Salvador and Guatemala, U.S. officials were not inclined to acknowledge that the hundreds of thousands of Salvadorans and Guatemalans begging for political asylum had really been politically persecuted by those governments. Instead, newcomers

THE SANCTUARY MOVEMENT

During the 1980s, civil war, political turmoil, and the the covert involvement of the administrations of U.S. presidents Ronald Reagan and George H. W. Bush in Central America combined to ignite protests in the United States. Out of these protests came the sanctuary movement, an effort that involved hundreds of churches and other religious organizations across the United States and Canada, through which refugees—mostly from El Salvador and Guatemala—were smuggled out of their home countries and into the United States, where, in violation of U.S. law, they were sheltered in church basements, private homes, and elsewhere. Angered that the U.S. government denied Salvadorans and Guatemalans fleeing violence at home the same political asylum status given to those leaving Nicaragua, leaders of the sanctuary movement argued that U.S. government was refusing to grant asylum because it refused to acknowledge that its Guatemalan and Salvadoran allies were violating their own citizens' human rights.

In 1982, Southside Presbyterian Church in Tuscon, Arizona, became the first church in the United States to declare itself a sanctuary, becoming an important stop in what movement activists came to call an "underground railroad." Among the refugees the church aided was a Guatemalan woman identified at the time as "Juana Beatriz Alvarez." The wife of a labor leader who had been killed in 1984, the woman soon realized that she too was in danger when she noticed that she was frequently being followed.

According to a series of articles in the *Arizona Daily Star* newspaper, the woman, whose real name was Marta, then made a dramatic escape to the United States in 1984. Fleeing north over Guatemala's border into Mexico, she was met by Jim Corbett of Southside Presbyterian. The two then flew to Hermosillo; drove to Nogales, Sonora; walked across the U.S. border; and finally drove the last stretch to Tucson. After a stay in Tucson, a terrified Marta continued to move from shelter to shelter, to keep ahead of U.S. federal agents who hoped to extract incriminating evidence from her that would help them arrest Corbett.

In 1985, after paid informants for the Immigration and Naturalization Service infiltrated Tucson's sanctuary movement, eight local activists were convicted of alien smuggling. None served time in prison, recieving probation instead, but as Rev. Fife of the Southside Presbyterian Church told the *Arizona Daily Star,* the episode was an "extraordinarily difficult time." Nonetheless, he added, "it was a joy to be a part of a movement that was standing up for human rights."

who entered without the proper immigration visas were regarded as illegal immigrants and subject to deportation as such, unless they could prove a "well-founded fear of persecution"—which in most cases was impossible to prove.

Nicaraguan refugees were treated more sympathetically than refugees from El Salvador and Guatemala because they were fleeing the Sandinista government, which U.S. officials regarded as Marxist and therefore by definition oppressive. Even Nicaraguans, however, were subject to shifting factions in the U.S. government; they were sometimes welcomed, sometimes not. The cause of the refugees was aided by the sanctuary movement, operated by a national network of churches and synagogues that sheltered undocumented Central American

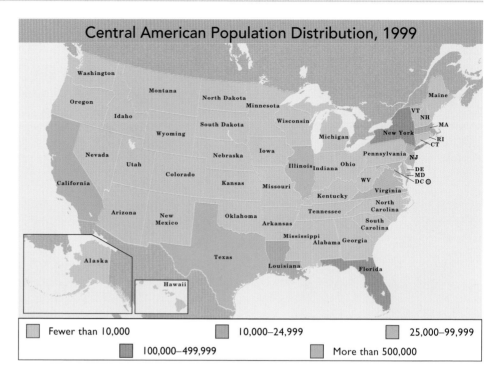

Central American Population Distribution, 1999

Fewer than 10,000 | 10,000–24,999 | 25,000–99,999 | 100,000–499,999 | More than 500,000

refugees for moral and religious reasons, despite the threat of fines and imprisonment. The U.S. government successfully prosecuted some leaders of the sanctuary movement but, due to public opposition to U.S. policy in Central America, found it politically inadvisable to punish them to the full extent of the law or to prosecute all the cases it might have.

The end of the civil wars in the 1990s brought a decrease in the number of new refugees from Central America but also made it more difficult for Central American refugees whose cases were still pending to win political asylum. A 1996 law tightened an avenue for gaining legal status, one that required applicants to show only that they had resided in the United States for several years and that leaving the country would constitute an extreme hardship. According to the Illegal Immigration Reform and Immigrant Responsibility Act of 1996, a maximum of 1,000 aliens per fiscal year could be granted asylum by the United States or admitted as refugees. The law also provided for a new category of immigration status known as "withholding of removal," available to refugees in the United States who could show a likelihood that their lives or freedom would be threatened if they were returned to their country of origin. However, the rules governing withholding of removal required applicants to prove that it was more likely than

not that they would be persecuted—again, a difficult or impossible condition to prove. Therefore, the ultimate legal status of many refugees of Central America's civil wars remained uncertain by the close of the 20th century.

The largest community of Central Americans in the United States was in Los Angeles, where about 350,000 Salvadorans and 110,000 Guatemalans lived as of 1990. The Pico-Union section of Los Angeles had a particularly large concentration of Central American immigrants. New York and Florida also had large Central American populations, each numbering between 100,000 and 500,000; Texas, Illinois, Virginia, Maryland, and New Jersey each had 25,000 to 100,000 Central Americans.

Many Central Americans in the United States held blue-collar jobs in manufacturing, agriculture, construction, restaurants, and domestic work. Some others worked in white-collar, middle-class professional careers. Nicaraguans who fled their country after Somoza's overthrow were especially affluent, much like the Cuban exiles who initially fled Castro. Many Nicaraguans settled in Miami, where they could commiserate with Cuban exiles who shared their anti-communist sentiment and helped procure aid for them. By 2000 Miami's Nicaraguan community was populous enough that one area of the city was known as Little Managua.

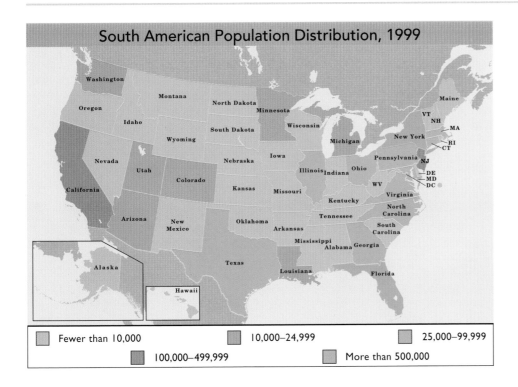

South American Population Distribution, 1999

Fewer than 10,000   10,000–24,999   25,000–99,999   100,000–499,999   More than 500,000

SOUTH AMERICANS IN THE UNITED STATES

South Americans immigrated to the United States in great numbers in the last 25 years of the 20th century. In the 1980s alone, 462,000 South Americans were legally admitted to the United States, and an unknown number came illegally. The most came from Colombia. According to the U.S. Census Bureau, 286,000 Colombian-born people lived in the United States in 1990, nearly double the 144,000 counted in 1980. Many immigrants also came from Ecuador. According to INS annual reports, 101,452 Ecuadorans immigrated in the period 1966–1987, compared with 187,560 Colombians. Substantially fewer immigrants came from other South American Hispanic countries, though in total they contributed to the growing South American presence: from 1966 to 1987, Argentina was the source of about 57,000 immigrants, Peru 38,000, and Chile 37,000.

By the end of the 20th century, the South American population in the United States probably comprised close to 1 million people but it was not a unified community. South America includes nine Hispanic nations—Argentina, Bolivia, Chile, Colombia, Ecuador, Paraguay, Peru, Uruguay, and Venezuela—along with three non-Hispanic nations (Guyana, Suriname, and Brazil) and French Guiana, an overseas department of France. Though sharing a common language, South America's Hispanic nations are fiercely independent and have a long history of fighting and competing with one another as well as, sometimes, cooperating. Hence, South American immigrants tend to identify themselves by their individual nationalities, not as South Americans.

Still, some general trends on their home continent during this period - affected many of the nations from which Hispanic South Americans migrated, and some general points can be made about their reasons for immigrating to the United States and about the communities they established.

A WAVE OF LIBERALIZATION

As in previous years, the quest for economic opportunity rather than fear of political persecution was the most important factor driving South Americans to immigrate to the United States in the late 20th century. Like Central America, South America had its share of military regimes, revolutions, persistent guerrilla wars, and right-wing death squads in the 1970s and 1980s, but by the end of the 1980s a liberalizing spirit was in evidence. In the face of mounting foreign debt, international recession, and high inflation, South American countries privatized many of their state-owned industries and undertook fiscal austerity measures. Inflation was curbed, though unemployment and poverty rose as well. One by one, countries established viable, democratically elected governments to replace the continent's military juntas: Ecuador in 1979, Peru in 1980, Bolivia in 1982, Argentina in 1983, and Chile in 1990.

By the 1990s South America was generally under democratic rule but still plagued by poverty, some guerrilla insurgencies, and the ghosts of its unstable political past. In Ecuador in 1997, the Ecuadoran congress deposed President Abdala Bucaram, an eccentric and controversial leader, for "mental incapacity." In Peru, President Alberto Fujimori, elected in 1990, became increasingly authoritarian as he struggled to suppress the Tupac Amaru Revolutionary Movement and the Maoist, Andean-based guerrillas called the Shining Path.

In Colombia in the 1980s, drug cartels came to control large areas where coca and cannabis were grown for illegal export. In the 1990 election campaign, the drug traffickers assassinated several presidential candidates. The U.S. government, concerned about the flow of narcotics into the United States, pressured Colombia to suppress the drug trade, offering military and economic aid in support of that cause. But by 2000, U.S. aid to Colombia was itself controversial, as human rights organizations complained about the Colombian government's human rights abuses, and guerrillas retaliated against the latest U.S.-Colombian drug effort by crossing into Ecuador to kidnap several foreign oil workers, including five from the United States.

SOUTH AMERICAN COMMUNITIES

As of 2000, South Americans in the United States were most heavily concentrated in New York, New Jersey, California, and Florida, which each had more than 100,000 South Americans. But other states, such as Texas, Illinois, Massachusetts, and Connecticut, also had substantial South American populations. Many South Americans made their home in the borough of Queens in New York City, particularly the neighborhood called Jackson Heights, known as "Chapinero" to some of its Colombian residents, after a suburb of Bogotá.

Because they usually arrived in the United States with fairly high levels of education and skills, South American immigrants have generally prospered more than those from Mexico and Puerto Rico, though not so much as those from Cuba. South Americans were often eager to assimilate, but they also retained strong ties to their homeland. Among South American couples in the United States, one spouse might become a U.S. citizen and the other retain citizenship in the country of birth, so that the couple had the option of returning home easily. They often sent their children to Catholic schools rather than public schools, maintaining the links between South American culture and Catholicism. They retained a sense of their distinct national heritages, often forming Argentine-American or Peruvian-American associations and social clubs. Restaurants in ethnic enclaves featured distinctive national dishes, such as Peruvian anticuchos (skewered cow's heart) or Bolivian-style beef.

South Americans also retained some of the differences that divided them at home, such as the color line that separates Colombia's costeños, darker-skinned people of mixed African, Native American, and Spanish descent, from white Colombians of European descent. The two groups rarely associate in South America, and in cities like Chicago, the costeño and white Colombian communities have continued to remain mostly separate. Rooted in a variety of places and histories, South Americans added strongly individual flavors to the eclectic mix of Hispanic-American culture.

HISPANIC AMERICA TODAY

In 1967, when the U.S. population hit a milestone 200 million, the U.S. population was 84 percent white, 11 percent black, four percent Hispanic and one percent Asian and Pacific Islander. In 2006, when the U.S. population reached 300 million, the population makeup had changed to 66 percent white, 12 percent black, four percent Asian and Pacific Islander and nearly 15 percent Hispanic. Of those 100 million new Americans, 36 percent were Hispanic, and the total Hispanic population had grown from just 8.5 million in 1967 to 44.7 million in 2006.

Not surprisingly, this enormous population shift has had a profound impact on American culture, economics, and politics. While Americans of all ethnic backgrounds danced to the sounds of Latin musical artists like Ricky Martin and Gloria Estefan in the 1990s or Jenifer Lopez, Shakira and Yankee Daddy in the 2000s, politicians on local, state and federal levels eagerly courted Hispanic voters, even though Latinos do not typically vote as a monolithic bloc. Although Hispanic Americans are still underrepresented at the highest levels of power and many Latinos still live in poverty, business leaders also increasingly understand the economic clout of the Hispanic-American community, and Hispanic American-owned businesses are a rapidly growing force in the American economy.

This view was especially pronounced among Republican voters, particularly in Iowa, which held the nation's first 2008 presidential caucuses earlier that month. According to Iowa Republicans, the issue of illegal immigration was the single most important issue facing the nation, topping the state of the economy, the Iraq War or terrorism. In fact, Republican Senator John McCain of Arizona, who would go on to win his party's nomination, garnered considerable heat from the conservative wing of his party for working with the liberal Senate icon Edward M. Kennedy of Massachusetts to craft a compromise immigration reform bill that would have allowed some illegal immigrants to remain in the country with a guest visa as long as they paid a $1,500 fine. Former Massachusetts governor Mitt Romney, one of McCain's competitors for the nomination, accused McCain of offering "amnesty" to illegal immigrants, a charge McCain denied. For his part, Romney argued that any immigration reform must start with securing the U.S.-Mexican border and issuing tamper-proof cards to all non-citizens so that employers could verify their legal status before hiring them. Yet the deep reliance of the American economy on cheap, illegal labor from Latin America was underscored when the public learned that the landscaper hired by Mr. Romney to care for the front lawn of his mansion used illegal day laborers from Guatemala.

"The [African-American] civil rights slogan was 'We shall overcome.' Ours is going to be we shall overwhelm."

—Christy Haubegger, Editor, *Latina* magazine

THE CONTINUING DEBATE ON IMMIGRATION

Meanwhile, the tensions over legal and illegal immigration have grown, becoming an even greater concern in the U.S. Congress, in the 2008 presidential race, and in the minds of many American citizens than ever before. According to a January 14–16th, 2008 nationwide poll of 1000 adults conducted by *Fortune* Magazine, 60 percent felt that the immigration issue was either extremely or very important to them.

THE MIGRANT WORKER DEBATE

Tensions between proponents of stricter enforcement of immigration laws and illegal migrant farm workers and day laborers are made infinitely more complicated by the U.S. labor force's deep reliance on migrant farm workers and day laborers. According to one recent survey, more than two million year-round and seasonal migrant farm workers, including 100,000 children, work in the United States. About two-thirds are immigrants, and more than

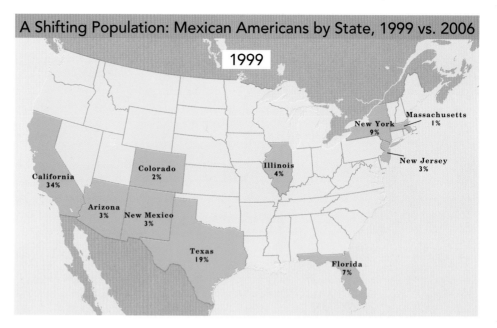

A Shifting Population: Mexican Americans by State, 1999 vs. 2006

1999

Massachusetts 1%
New York 9%
New Jersey 3%
Illinois 4%
California 34%
Colorado 2%
Arizona 3%
New Mexico 3%
Texas 19%
Florida 7%

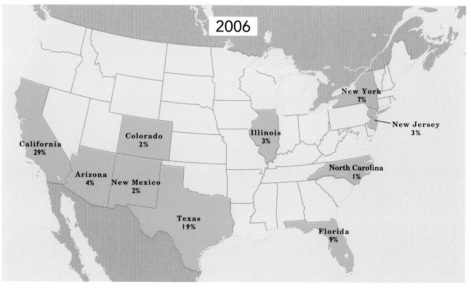

2006

New York 7%
New Jersey 3%
Illinois 3%
California 29%
Colorado 2%
Arizona 4%
New Mexico 2%
North Carolina 1%
Texas 19%
Florida 9%

three-quarters were born in Mexico. Meanwhile, half of all migrant farm workers are estimated to be unauthorized, illegal workers. Only 25 percent of all farm workers in the United States are U.S. citizens.

Critics of illegal immigration frequently argue that Mexican farm workers are taking jobs away from jobless American citizens. Little evidence supports this claim. In fact, agricultural work is among the lowest paid, most dangerous occupations in the American economy. Most farm workers receive poverty wages. Three out of four earn less than $10,000 a year, and only 14 percent have full-time work. Three out of every five farm worker families live below the federal poverty line. Making matters worse, farm workers live in harsh conditions as migrant housing often lacks plumbing or working appliances, and are often located next to pesticide-laden fields. Even so, farm workers must spend more than 30 percent of their income on housing.

In addition, farm workers are disabled with injuries and illness at a rate three times that of the general population. In California, the average death rate for farm workers is five times that of workers in other industries. According to a study published by the Institute for Global Communications, pesticides poison approximately 300,000 farm workers in the U.S. annually. And when farm workers get sick, they rarely have health insurance. In one 1997–1998 study, only five percent of farm workers reported having employer-paid health insurance to cover non-work-related illnesses, only 28 percent received any kind of compensation for work-related illness, and just

Place of Birth of Agricultural Workers in the U.S.

Mexico, 76%

United States, 23%

Central America, 2%

Other, 1%

Note: Due to rounding, figures do not add up to 100%.

one percent of workers used Social Security or disability insurance. What's more, very few farm workers were able to take advantage of "social safety net" federal programs like Medicaid, Food Stamps, or the Women, Infants and Children program.

Many studies have shown that Americans pay less for their food than citizens in most other industrialized nations. However, large-scale farm employers argue that higher wages and benefits will force them to raise prices to an unacceptable level. According to author Eric Schlosser, "Maintaining the current level of poverty among migrant farm workers saves the average American household $50 a year."

Whether a $50 annual increase in food prices for a household is truly unacceptable to keep migrant workers out of destitute poverty is at best unclear. Advocates for farm workers are quick to point out the disparity between wages in large scale agriculture. While the average farm worker earns roughly $7,500 a year, the CEO of Archer Daniels Midland received over $3 million in salary and bonuses in 2005, as well as an additional $8 million in stock options. Critics of these wage disparities point out that because the H-2A Visa program that governs the temporary legal status of these workers prevents them from collectively organizing, there is little incentive for farm employers to increase wages for field workers. This fact may also explain

why the H-2A guest worker program expanded so rapidly during the 1990s. In North Carolina, for example, the number of H-2A guest workers rose from just 168 in 1989 to 10,500 by 1998.

According to the U.S. Department of Labor, roughly 75,000 temporary workers were employed in 2007 nationwide under the H-2A program, and that an estimated 600,000 to 800,000 immigrants are working illegally on American farms. In 2007, the AgJOBS Act of 2007 would have granted amnesty to illegal immigrants working in the agriculture industry. The Bush administration responded by proposing a "streamlining" of the program's regulations. According to the administration, wages required under the program were actually higher than prevailing wages, and the application process was too complex. According to AFL-CIO president John Sweeney, "The Department of Labor will hurt both immigrant and U.S.–born labor alike if it goes ahead with its plan to strip a number of workers' rights from the H-2A agricultural guest worker program."

On the other hand, critics of the program argue that these changes are needed. According to the conservative Heritage Institute, the formula used to determine worker wages is flawed, leading temporary farm workers to receive pay that is higher than the wages paid to farm workers not enrolled in the program. By changing the pay formula, employers would have the right to hire workers for less money. The

Images (top and above) from a 2007 farmworkers rights march on the headquarters of Burger King. (Photos by Alan Pogue)

Administration proposals also would loosen the application requirements by allowing agribusinesses to employ migrant workers already in the United States for up to 120 days while visa applications for immigrant workers are pending. Finally, the proposals would establish a pilot program that would record biographic or biometric information about each migrant worker before they could leave the farm site at the end of the harvest. This program would be aimed at ensuring workers do not overstay their visas.

Regardless of the fate of these H-2A program proposals, there are other factors that drive down farm worker wages and living conditions. One such factor is the widespread use by growers of farm labor contractors. By contracting out hiring, growers can avoid liability for labor law violations.

Another is the consolidation of the U.S. agricultural system. Since the 1980s, large food retailers have increasingly purchased directly from a shrinking number of grower-shipper conglomerates. By 2004, 20 food retailers controlled more than half of retail grocery sales in the nation. Walmart alone accounted for 19 percent of all grocery sales, giving a single company extraordinary power over the prices paid to producers.

The number of fast food and cafeteria restaurant chains are also consolidating. For example, A&W, KFC, Taco Bell, Long John Silver's, and Pizza Hut are all owned by Yum Brands!, which contracts with Unified Foodservice Purchasing Co-op to supply produce for all their restaurants. For this reason, every tomato purchased by Taco Bell comes from a single food broker, who buys tomatoes from just five or six growers. This arrangement allows a small group of produce buyers to dictate prices for the entire U.S. market, forcing many small farmers out of business and keeping wages paid to migrant crop pickers artificially low. In Florida alone, the number of tomato farms dropped 38 percent during the five years between 1992 and 1997. Today, the top 10 Florida growers ship 70 percent of all tomatoes sold in the United States.

With this kind of power, charge industry critics, supermarket chains, food-service conglomerates and wholesalers can demand rock-bottom prices, often negotiating prices with growers prior to planting. These pre-purchase agreements short the risk to growers, who view labor as the only expense they can control. Growers claim that a shortage of legal workers willing to do farm work "forces" them to hire illegal immigrants, whose fear of deportation often stops them from challenging the low wages and poor living conditions. An example of this downward wage pressure can be seen in wages paid to tomato pickers. In 1980, they earned minimum wage by picking just over seven buckets of tomatoes. By 1997, pickers had to fill

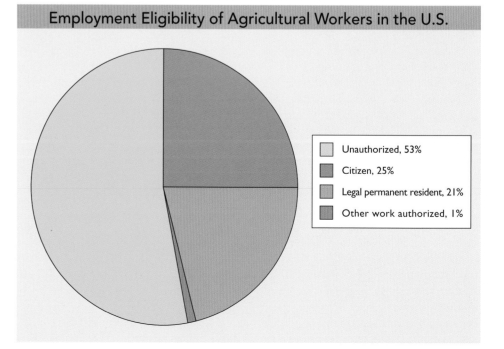

Employment Eligibility of Agricultural Workers in the U.S.

Unauthorized, 53%
Citizen, 25%
Legal permanent resident, 21%
Other work authorized, 1%

A migrant laborer in the tomato fields outside Immokalee, Florida (Photo by Scott Robertson)

13 buckets. In 2004, pickers in Immokalee, Florida, the fastest tomato pickers had to fill between 100-150 buckets in order to earn just $40-$60 a day, while slower pickers earn about $28 a day by filling 70-80 buckets a day. Working seven days a week, for 10-12 hours a day, these workers earn just $7500 during harvest season.

One Florida farm worker organization, the Coalition of Immokalee Workers (CIW), has had some success bringing the public's attention once again to the treatment of Florida farm workers, much as the United Farm Workers did a generation ago in the fields of California. In the spring of 2005, following a 4-year national boycott campaign, Taco Bell and the CIW came to an agreement by which Taco Bell would pay its tomato pickers an additional one cent per pound picked—nearly doubling their pay at the time. At the time that the agreement was signed, Yum! Brands also announced an historic initiative to address the ever-deepening poverty and decades of degradation faced by farmworkers in Florida. At that time, Taco Bell called on its fast-food industry counterparts to join in paying fair wages and better conditions the workers who pick their tomatoes.

In April, 2007 McDonald's came to a similar agreement with the CIW, but went even further than Taco Bell. McDonald's also signed on to work with the CIW to develop an industry-wide mechanism for monitoring labor conditions in the fields and investigating workers' complaints of abuse. After the CIW-McDonald's accord was announced, Taco Bell's parent company, Yum! Brands, agreed that all of its other restaurant chains—A&W, KFC, Long John Silver's, and Pizza Hut—would also adhere to the higher standards. As of early 2008, CIW was focusing much of its efforts on Burger King, the largest fast food chain in the nation still refusing to follows the lead of McDonald's, and the Yum! Brands chains.

THE MINUTEMEN

As the federal government has been debating the best method of containing illegal immigration from Mexico and elsewhere in Latin America, the flow of migration has continued. Frustrated by the federal response, anti-immigration activists Jim Gilchrist and Chris Simcox cofounded an organization in early 2005 known as the Minuteman Project. (In December 2005, the organization split in a dispute over funding, with Gilchrist forming the Minuteman Project, Inc. and Simcox forming the Minuteman Civil Defense Corps.)

The Minutemen monitor the United States–Mexico border's flow of illegal immigrants. While some carry weapons, their stated purpose is to "provide law enforcement agencies with incriminating evidence of deliberate violations of state or federal immigration, tax or employment law." Calling itself "a citizens' Neighborhood Watch on our border," the group was won both praise and condemnation as vigilantes. Soon after the group was founded, California governor Arnold Schwarzenegger praised group, saying it had been doing "a terrific job" and welcoming Minutemen to patrol the border between California and Mexico. On the other hand, the Southern Poverty Law Center has condemned the Minuteman Project and its local chapters as an extreme nativist group and the Anti-Defamation League has noted that Neo-Nazi and white supremacist groups have worked alongside the Minutemen although there is no official known connection between the groups.

Relations between the Minutemen and the federal government is mixed. Although President George W. Bush has declared his opposition to "vigilante" border patrols, the official stance of the U.S. Border Patrol is that it "continues to appreciate the efforts of civilians who contact law enforcement authorities regarding suspicious activity."

NAFTA AND ILLEGAL IMMIGRATION

As discussed in the previous chapter, the North American Free Trade Agreement (NAFTA), which eliminated most trade barriers between the three countries, went into effect in 1994. In the decade and a half since NAFTA's appearance, the trade agreement has faced widespread criticism. Labor unions in the United States argued that the agreement has cost millions of American workers their jobs as factories have shutdown at home and moved to Mexico. Environmentalists had argued that looser environmental laws in Mexico has led to a rise in pollution in the border region. Indigenous peoples in southern Mexico have risen up against new social tensions that NAFTA and economic reforms have brought to their land.

While proponents of NAFTA argued that the agreement would help bring the benefits of free trade to Mexico, many studies have found that the agreement had the unintended effect of pushing illegal immigrants north to the United States at an unprecedented level. In the first decade after the agreement was signed, millions of Mexican farmers have been forced off their land, unable to compete with cheap American farm commodities flooding the Mexican market. Some estimates suggest that as many as 1.7 million Mexican subsistence farmers have migrated north to work in border region *maquiladoras* or in the fields and cities of the United States. Some NAFTA critics estimate that as many as 15 million may end up displaced by NAFTA, with about five million projected to eventually head of the United States.

In Mexico itself, free-market reforms have led to severe government cutbacks. In the first seven years under NAFTA alone, the Mexican government slashed

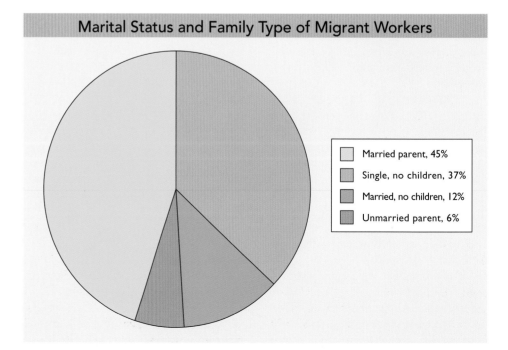

Marital Status and Family Type of Migrant Workers

- Married parent, 45%
- Single, no children, 37%
- Married, no children, 12%
- Unmarried parent, 6%

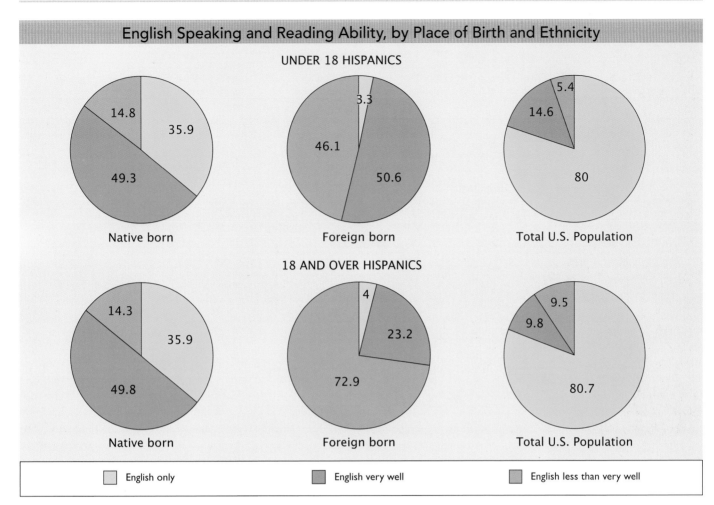

English Speaking and Reading Ability, by Place of Birth and Ethnicity

UNDER 18 HISPANICS

Native born — 14.8 / 35.9 / 49.3

Foreign born — 3.3 / 46.1 / 50.6

Total U.S. Population — 5.4 / 14.6 / 80

18 AND OVER HISPANICS

Native born — 14.3 / 35.9 / 49.8

Foreign born — 4 / 23.2 / 72.9

Total U.S. Population — 9.5 / 9.8 / 80.7

English only   English very well   English less than very well

its agricultural programs 90 percent. Prior to NAFTA, many Mexican farmers received as much as a third of their incomes from farm-support payments. In the immediate post-NAFTA years between 1995 and 2000, that percentage fell to about 13 percent. (In the United States, corn growers still receive 40 percent of their income from U.S. government subsidies.) What's more, 25 percent of all corn in the United States is now shipped to Mexico, which critics argue, keeps Mexican corn prices at artificially low levels. By 2004, 80 percent of rural Mexicans live in poverty, and 60 percent in what is considered extreme poverty. Meanwhile, hunger has increased as purchasing power has plummeted. The price of tortillas (which studies have shown account for 59 percent of the Mexican population's caloric intake) increased roughly 40 percent between 1994 and 2003.

Conditions in Mexico are contributing to push both legal and illegal Mexican labor across the U.S. border, where labor contractors and large agribusinesses welcome the opportunity to pay them at rates that are barely better than subsistence level. Because even the lowest pay and poor conditions in the United States are still often better than what is possible at home, these workers are willing to risk arrest and their personal safety for the chance to earn money in the United States to send home to their families.

The Federal Response

Not all illegal immigrants travel to the United States alone and send money home. Numerous illegal immigrants have their families with them in the United States. An examination of some demographics relating to migrant farm workers highlights the complexity of the issue. About 56 percent of all illegal farm workers are male and about 39 percent are female. In total, 45 percent of all farm workers are married and have children. Some of those children are the children of illegal immigrants, but having been born in the United States, are U.S. citizens themselves. As such are entitled to the full rights of equal protection under the law, as

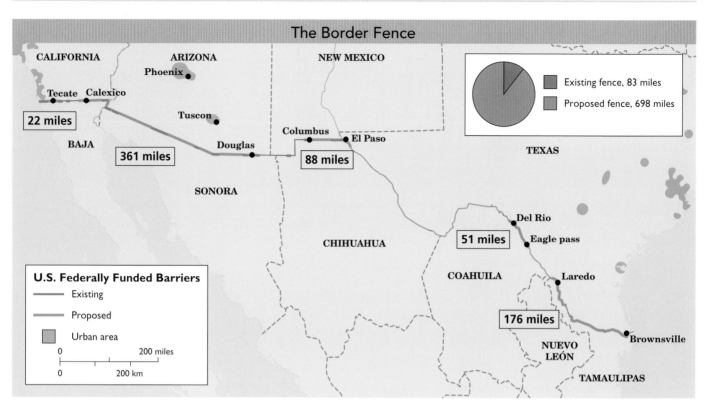

The Border Fence

CALIFORNIA

ARIZONA

NEW MEXICO

Phoenix

Tecate Calexico

22 miles

Tuscon

BAJA

Columbus

El Paso

Douglas

361 miles

88 miles

SONORA

TEXAS

| | Existing fence, 83 miles |
| | Proposed fence, 698 miles |

Del Rio

51 miles Eagle pass

CHIHUAHUA

COAHUILA Laredo

U.S. Federally Funded Barriers

Existing

Proposed

Urban area

0   200 miles

0   200 km

176 miles

Brownsville

NUEVO
LEÓN

TAMAULIPAS

well as equal access to federal and local government assistance programs, such as financial assistance for education, Medicaid, and free school lunches.

In many cases, these children are far more acculturated into the mainstream of American culture than their parents. Although statistics for the language abilities of illegal Hispanic immigrants alone are not available, other statistics show that more than 85 percent of all U.S. –born Hispanics who are under 18 speak English either as their only language or speak it very well.

The fact that many children of illegal aliens are themselves U.S. citizens has complicated the response of state and local governments to the immigration issue. Many local and state governments have argued that providing benefits to unauthorized immigrants imposes a major financial drain. A 2002 study found that the largest costs relating to illegal immigrants are Medicaid ($2.5 billion); treatment for the uninsured ($2.2 billion); food assistance programs such as food stamps, WIC, and free school lunches ($1.9 billion); the federal prison and court systems ($1.6 billion); and federal aid to schools ($1.4 billion). In response, many states have moved to deny illegal immigrants government assistance. For example, in 2005, the Virginia House of Delegates voted to deny Medicaid and

other benefits to illegal immigrants. The Virginia bill required immigrants prove their legal status before receiving some state and local benefits.

On the federal level, there is widespread agreement that current immigration laws are in need of reform. Most argue in favor of tighter border security, but there is little agreement on how to proceed toward that goal. What's more, there is a bitter split on the problem of what to do about those aliens already here illegally. In the U.S. House of Representatives, a variety of new restrictions have been proposed, including making it a felony to be in the United States illegally, stiffening penalties on employers who hire illegals, requiring churches to check the legal status of its parishioners before helping them, and erecting a new fence along the U.S.-Mexican border.

In 2005, Republican Senator John McCain, Democratic Senator Edward Kennedy, and others co-sponsored the Secure America and Orderly Immigration Act. The bill, which won bipartisan support, including that of President Bush, aimed to secure U.S. borders and improve the enforcement of current immigration laws.

The bill proposed the creation of a new visa category known as an "H-5A." According to the McCain-Kennedy bill,

400,000 H-5A visas would have been issued annually to "essential workers" who are nonagricultural or highly skilled employees. The bill also allowed spouses and children of the visa applicant to legally join the person applying for the visa in the United States. H-5A visas were to allow foreign workers to perform a job for initially three years, with a possible extension later.

The bill also toughened enforcement policies by requiring employers to certify an employee's status through a central database. Business owners who hired illegal workers faced fines up to $20,000 and up to six months in prison.

Despite these tough enforcement mechanisms, the McCain-Kennedy bill was widely condemned by conservative members of Congress, and failed to win passage. The most controversial aspect of the McCain-Kennedy bill was that it would have allowed aliens already in the United States to pay a fine and their back taxes and then stay in the United States legally. To anti-immigration forces, this amounted to an amnesty for illegal immigrants. An alternate bill, introduced by Republican Senators Jon Kyl of Arizona and John Cornyn of Texas required illegal immigrants already in the United States to leave the country within five years and then reapply for legal status. That bill also failed to pass.

Although conservatives praised the Kyl-Cornyn bill as an improvement, many argued that it did not adequately address illegal entry at the border. Increasingly, anti-immigration forces called for an extended border fence that would run the full 700 miles along the U.S.-Mexico border. Proponents of the border fence pointed to a 14-mile stretch of fencing built by the federal government along the San Diego-Tijuana border during the 1990s. Prior to the construction of that stretch of fence, the San Diego-Tijuana region was of the primary points of illegal crossings, as just a single strand of cable served as the border marker for much of the 12-mile stretch. Today, that cable is gone, replaced by a triple fence system made up of, first a 10-foot high wall made of welded metal panels and then a 15-foot high steel mesh fence. In some of the most heavily trafficked parts of the San Diego-Tijuana area, there's also a smaller chain link fence. Between the two main fences is 150 feet of "no man's land" which the U.S. Border Patrol sweeps with flood lights, trucks, and surveillance cameras. Since this fence system appeared, apprehensions of illegal immigrants have dropped from about 100,000 a year to only about 5,000 a year.

It is this success that led anti-immigration activists to call for a similar fence that runs the full 700 miles between the United States and Mexico. Despite his initial opposition to such a fence, just before the Congressional elections of

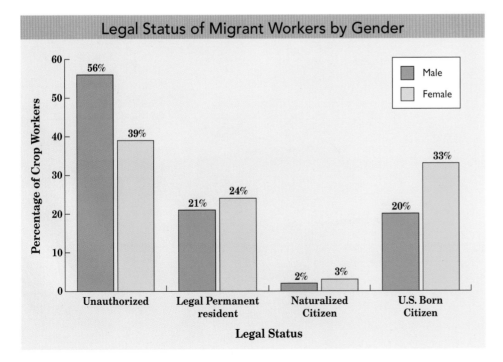

2006, President Bush authorized the building of such a fence.

Democrats argue that the new legislation is impractical and pointless. For one, Congress appropriated only a fraction of the billions of dollars needed to build the fence. What's more, geography makes the construction daunting. Through much of Arizona, the U.S.-Mexico border traverses steep desert cliffs and deep ravines.

Advocates for Mexican immigrants argue that as the fence is constructed through more heavily populated regions of the border zone, illegals will take more expensive, more dangerous and more desolate routes through dry desert. In fact, since the fence was built in the San Diego-Tijuana area, an estimated 3,600 people have died trying to cross the border into the United States.

Some have also argued that the border fence might also have the ironic consequence of keeping some people in the United States who might otherwise go back to Mexico. Many migrants used to come to the United States for a number of months out of each year and then return to their families. More recently, some are

not only deciding to stay but they are bringing their families with them.

A New Sanctuary Movement

The tension over illegal immigration has spurred an angry response from the Latino Community. In March, 2006, half a million people in Los Angeles, as well as thousands more in other cities nationwide marched to protest against tightened immigration laws. In addition, the Sanctuary Movement, which had been active in the 1980s, has returned as well. As discussed in Chapter 8, the Sanctuary Movement of the 1980s was an interfaith response to the thousands of mostly Salvadoran and Guatemalan refugees who were arriving in the United States illegally, fleeing the life-threatening conditions and human rights violations they faced during a period of U.S.-backed civil wars at home.

Although the United States often granted refugee status to civilians fleeing the civil war in socialist-led Nicaragua, the United States denied refugee status to

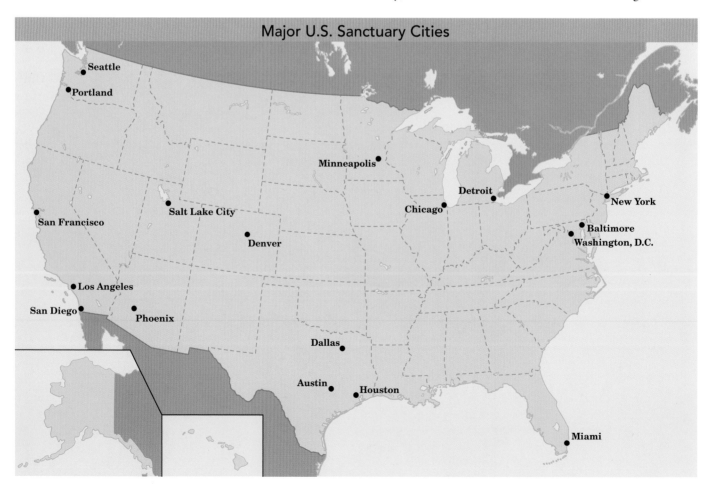

Major U.S. Sanctuary Cities

those who were fleeing the U.S.-allied right-wing governments of El Salvador and Guatemala. Many Catholic, Protestant and Jewish congregations and temples in the United States responded by offering these refugees shelter and social services, while also working to change federal immigration policy. Leaders of these congregations also pledged to protect the safety and identities of the refugees under their care, even risking arrest and jail to do so.

In 2007, a 21st century version of the Sanctuary Movement was born. The previous August, Elvira Arellano, a Mexican immigrant in the United States illegally since the late 1990s, failed to appear at an immigration hearing following her arrest for working under a false Social Security number. Because Arellano had had a son in the United States in 2002, her son was a U.S. citizen. Fearing deportation and separation from her son, Arellano took sanctuary in the tiny Adalberto United Methodist Church in Chicago, where she remained for a year. When she left the church to attend an immigrants rights rally in Los Angeles, she was arrested and deported to Mexico. In the wake of her arrest, an interfaith association called Clergy and Laity United for Economic Justice, began building a new coalition under the banner "New Sanctuary Movement" to continue to press for the right of religious congregations to "publicly provide hospitality and protection to a limited number of immigrant families whose legal cases clearly reveal the contradictions and moral injustice of our current immigration system."

THE DEMOGRAPHICS OF HISPANIC AMERICA

By the middle of the 21st century, Hispanic Americans are expected to account for one-quarter of the U.S. population. Because most Hispanic Americans are young, the population is likely to continue growing rapidly throughout most of the century as many people come of age and begin building their own families.

As the Hispanic-American population grows, much of the population remains centered in the Southwest,

LEADING CAUSES OF DEATH AMONG U.S. HISPANICS

Hispanic Males
1. Heart disease
2. Cancer
3. Accidents
4. HIV/AIDS
5. Homicide
6. Stroke
7. Chronic liver disease and cirrhosis
8. Diabetes
9. Suicide
10. Pneumonia and influenza

Non-Hispanic White Males
1. Heart disease
2. Cancer
3. Stroke
4. Asthma, emphysema, and other lung diseases
5. Accidents
6. Pneumonia and influenza
7. Suicide
8. Diabetes
9. Chronic liver disease and cirrhosis
10. HIV/AIDS

Hispanic Females
1. Heart disease
2. Cancer
3. Stroke
4. Diabetes
5. Accidents
6. Pneumonia and influenza
7. Asthma, emphysema, and other lung diseases
8. Kidney diseases
9. Chronic liver disease and cirrhosis
10. Blood poisoning

Non-Hispanic White Females
1. Heart disease
2. Cancer
3. Stroke
4. Asthma, emphysema, and other lung diseases
5. Pneumonia and influenza
6. Accidents
7. Diabetes
8. Alzheimer's disease
9. Kidney diseases
10. Blood poisoning

Northeast, Florida and Illinois. The Hispanic-American population in California grew by nearly seven percent from 2000 to 2007; in Florida during the same period, the Hispanic population grew by more than 2 million, or by more than 12 percent. Nonetheless, other regions have also seen dramatic increases: Arkansas, Georgia, South Carolina, Tennessee, and North Carolina were the five fastest growing from 2000 to 2006, with growth rates ranging from 54.9 percent to 60.9 percent.

As of 2002, over 90 percent of Latinos lived in urban areas, compared to less than 80 percent of whites. Almost half lived in a central city, compared to 21 percent of whites. In fact, in 2000, about 31 percent of all Hispanic Americans lived in one of 10 metropolitan areas—Los Angeles, New York City, Chicago,

Miami, Houston, Riverside-San Bernadino, California, Orange County, California, Phoenix, San Antonio, and Dallas. Yet, smaller Latino destination cities like Raleigh, Atlanta, Greensboro, Charlotte, and Orlando are all growing faster in Hispanic population than the more traditional destinations.

One of the main reasons for the rapid growth of the Hispanic-American population is a high rate of immigration. All told, as of 2005, just 59.5 percent of all Hispanic-Americans were born in the United States.

INCOME, POVERTY, HEALTH, AND EMPLOYMENT

High rates of immigration help explain why a 2002 study showed that nearly 73

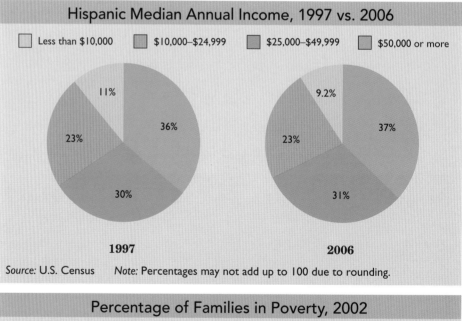

Hispanic Median Annual Income, 1997 vs. 2006

☐ Less than $10,000 ☐ $10,000–$24,999 ☐ $25,000–$49,999 ☐ $50,000 or more

1997

11%
36%
23%
30%

2006

9.2%
37%
23%
31%

Source: U.S. Census   *Note:* Percentages may not add up to 100 due to rounding.

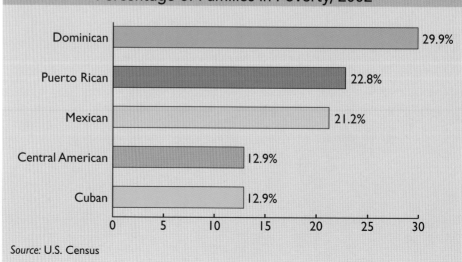

Percentage of Families in Poverty, 2002

Dominican	29.9%
Puerto Rican	22.8%
Mexican	21.2%
Central American	12.9%
Cuban	12.9%

Source: U.S. Census

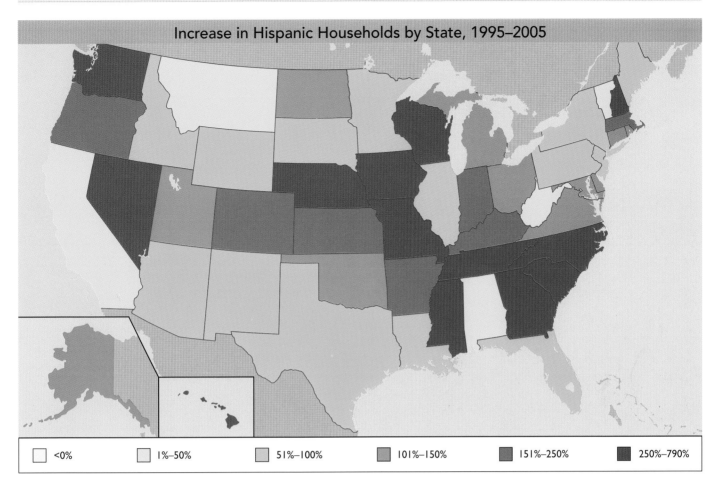

Increase in Hispanic Households by State, 1995–2005

<0%	1%–50%	51%–100%	101%–150%	151%–250%	250%–790%

percent of all Hispanic-Americans over the age of 18 who arrived in the United States after 2000 report that they speak English "less than very well." In turn, language may in part explain why, on average, Hispanic Americans are poorer than any other ethnic group in the United States except Native Americans. A 2006 survey showed that nearly a third of all Hispanic Americans earned less than $25,000 a year. Poverty rates for different Hispanic ethnicities varied widely in a 2002 study, however, ranging from a low of 12.9 percent in the case of Cuban Americans to a high of 29.9 percent in the case of Dominican Americans. The survey also reported poverty rates of 22.8 percent for Puerto Ricans living in the United States, 21.2 percent for Mexican Americans and 12.9 percent for both Central Americans and Cuban Americans.

Behind Hispanic poverty lie several factors. Many Hispanics are recent immigrants with few skills, working in low-wage occupations. Hispanics are twice as likely as whites to be employed in unskilled jobs and 50 percent more likely to labor in the service sector. In some cases, as with Mexican-American migrant workers in the Southwest, generations of discrimination have contributed to keeping their earnings low.

Higher than average poverty rates impact other spheres of life, such as health and crime. In 2000, for example, 27.9 percent of Hispanics were victims of violent crimes, compared with 26.5 percent of non-Hispanic whites. In the area of health care, Hispanic Americans tend to be less healthy than non-Hispanic whites, for example, receiving less frequent prenatal care and experiencing higher rates of death in childbirth. (The U.S. Census Bureau often compares Hispanic demographic data to those of non-Hispanic whites, instead of using data for the U.S. population as a whole. It is for that reason that the comparison is used here.)

Signs of improvement in the health and well-being of Hispanics as a whole are somewhat mixed. Individual Hispanic Americans are more than twice as likely to lack health insurance as the general population, with 34.1 percent of Hispanics lacking coverage, while just 15.8 percent of the general population lacked coverage. Back in 1992, the median earnings for year-round, full-time Hispanic males was 63.1 percent that of non-Hispanic white males. In 2006, however, the median earnings of Hispanic males had risen, though modestly, to 65.1 percent of that of non-Hispanic white males. On the other hand, median earnings of Hispanic females actually fell in relation to median earnings of non-Hispanic white females during the same period—78.1 percent in 1992 to 75.8 percent in 2006.

While there is still deep poverty in many Hispanic communities, recent years have also seen the growth of a Hispanic middle class. In one of the most positive signs of this trend, the rate of homeownership—the percentage of families owning the house or apartment in which they lived—among Hispanics reached 49.5 percent in 2005, up from 42.8 percent in 1996. Unfortunately, this improved percentage still dramatically lags behind the total for all Americans in 2005: 68.9 percent.

EDUCATION

Not surprisingly, the number of Hispanic Americans enrolled in the nation's schools has risen dramatically in the last few decades. In 1972, only 6 percent of high school students were Hispanic. By 2004, the percentage had jumped to 17 percent. Yet low educational achievement has remained a concern: only 58.5 percent of Hispanic females and 48 percent of Hispanic males graduated from high school in 2004. Even among those who do graduate, Latinos are underrepresented in advance science and math classes or in gifted and talented programs. Post-secondary education rates are also low: in 2007, only 19 percent of Latinos between ages 25 and 34 had an Associates, Bachelor's or advanced degree, compared with 48 percent of non-Hispanic whites.

While language barriers have proved to be one roadblock to Latino success in more rigorous classes, a bigger problem may be the lack of advanced classes in schools serving mostly Latino and other minority students. According to a 2005 study by Achieve, Inc., although 74% of minority girls want to enroll in advanced courses, but only 45% of their schools offer these courses. Similarly, although two-thirds of minority boys have an interest in taking advanced mathematics courses, fewer than half attend schools that offer these courses.

Black and Hispanic students are generally less likely than their white and Asian peers to participate in gifted and talented programs. In comparison to white students, Blacks and Hispanics are less than half as likely to be enrolled in gifted and talented programs, and a third as likely as Asians. Specifically, an estimated 7.5% of white and 10% of Asian/Pacific Islander students are placed in gifted programs; only 3% of Hispanic and 3.5% of Black students are placed into these programs.

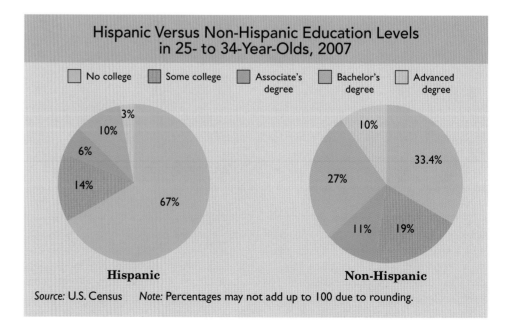

Hispanic Versus Non-Hispanic Education Levels in 25- to 34-Year-Olds, 2007

☐ No college   ☐ Some college   ☐ Associate's degree   ☐ Bachelor's degree   ☐ Advanced degree

Hispanic: 3%, 10%, 6%, 14%, 67%

Non-Hispanic: 10%, 33.4%, 27%, 11%, 19%

Hispanic   **Non-Hispanic**

Source: U.S. Census   *Note:* Percentages may not add up to 100 due to rounding.

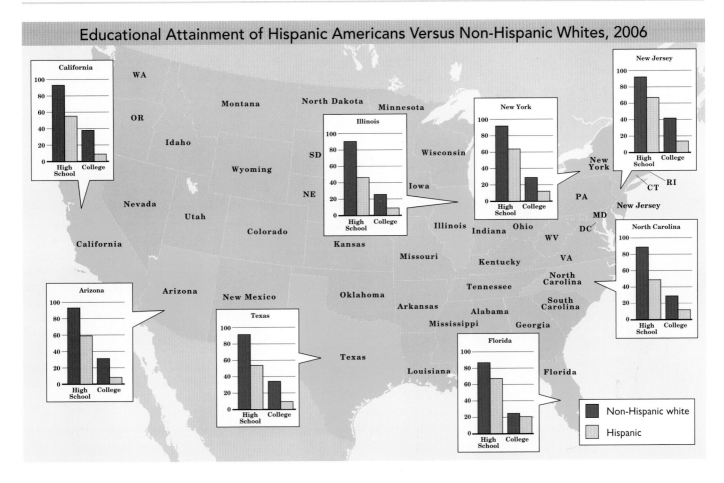

Educational Attainment of Hispanic Americans Versus Non-Hispanic Whites, 2006

POLITICAL POWER

Though they composed nearly 15 percent of the population in 2006, Hispanic Americans have historically been under-represented in Congress and as a share of the electorate. As of 2001, there were only 23 Hispanic members (less than 5 percent) in the House of Representatives and no Hispanic senators. By 2008, there was a modest increase, with 25 Hispanic members in the house and 3 Hispanic senators. These still low numbers correlate closely with the number of Hispanic voters who go to the polls. In the 2000 election, for example, only 32 percent of eligible Hispanics voted.

Analysts point to several factors that have kept Hispanic voter participation down. Poverty and lack of education, or lack of English, probably affect Hispanic voting patterns. Also, many Hispanics are not yet U.S. citizens, and thus are not eligible to vote. Yet another factor that impacts the number of Hispanics in Congress is geography—the fact that much of the country's Hispanic population is heavily concentrated in a few states translates into fewer seats for Hispanic politicians.

Where Hispanics do represent a sizable portion of the electorate, they form a powerful—and powerfully courted—voting bloc. Many of the states with large Latino populations—California, Texas, Illinois, and Florida, for example—are key battleground states in any presidential election. For this reason, many politicians have gone to great lengths to win the favor of local Hispanic communities.

Although Hispanics do not vote as a bloc and there are Democratic and Republican voters in every Latino nationality group, the Cuban community in Florida has generally voted Republican while most other Hispanic Americans have traditionally leaned Democratic. In 1996, more than 70 percent of Hispanics voted for President Clinton. In 2008, Hispanic voters continued to express their loyalty to Clinton by strongly favoring New York Senator (and former first lady) Hillary Clinton over her Democratic challengers in the primaries. But Latinos do not vote strictly along party lines, and both parties often eagerly seek them as a key swing vote. The Republican Party receives more money in campaign contributions from Hispanic Americans than

Bill Richardson, governor of New Mexico, also served as a U.S. congressman and as Secretary of Energy during the Clinton Administration. (House of Representatives)

does the Democratic Party because of the support of Cuban Americans, who usually vote Republican and who are the most affluent Hispanic subgroup.

What is more, Hispanic voting patterns have become increasingly unpredictable. As of 2004, 24 percent of Hispanic voters considered themselves independent voters with no allegiance to either Democrats or Republicans. Forty-nine percent were Democrats, and 27 percent were Republicans.

In the end, blanket statements about Hispanic voting patterns are problematic. Many considerations enter into the voting decisions of Hispanic Americans. Some are moved by conservative social values, such as support for family and religion. Often, they have supported vouchers for parochial schools. But many lean to the left on such issues as civil rights and spending on social programs. Since so many Hispanic Americans are immigrants, U.S. immigration policy has been of particular concern, as has the issue of bilingual education, which has periodically roiled regions with heavy immigration. In 1996, for example, voters in California passed Proposition 227, limiting bilingual education, over considerable Hispanic opposi-

tion. Most Hispanics consider bilingual education an effective way of helping immigrant children compete academically and make the transition to English-only classes; many also think that Hispanic culture and language generally need to be taught more in school.

Not surprisingly, Latinos have followed the immigration debates closely. A 2006 survey found that 42 percent of native born Latinos believe that the large immigration rights marches of that spring had a positive effect on the way the American public thinks about illegal and undocumented immigrants, while 24 percent felt they had a negative impact and 16 percent felt they had no impact. Foreign-born Latinos were more positive, with 60 percent believing the marches impacted public perception positively, 18 percent negatively, and 12 percent believing they had no effect. What's more, three quarters of Latinos surveyed believed that the immigration debate in Spring 2006 would drive more Latinos to the polls that November. (Latino voting did, in fact, increase.)

There are thousands of Hispanic elected officials, most in local and state offices, and many appointed Hispanic officials as well, such as Bill Richardson,

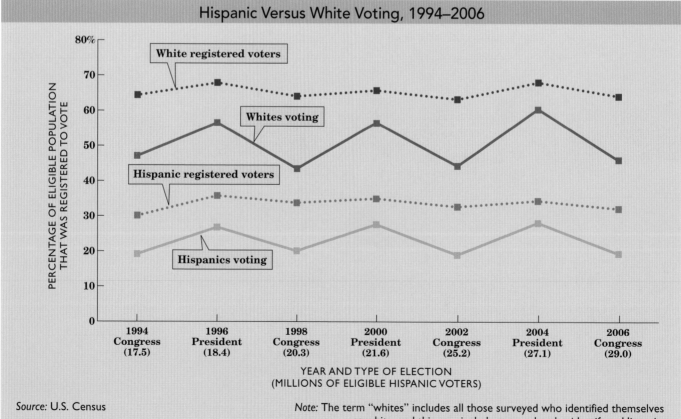

Hispanic Versus White Voting, 1994–2006

PERCENTAGE OF ELIGIBLE POPULATION THAT WAS REGISTERED TO VOTE

White registered voters

Whites voting

Hispanic registered voters

Hispanics voting

| 1994 Congress (17.5) | 1996 President (18.4) | 1998 Congress (20.3) | 2000 President (21.6) | 2002 Congress (25.2) | 2004 President (27.1) | 2006 Congress (29.0) |

YEAR AND TYPE OF ELECTION
(MILLIONS OF ELIGIBLE HISPANIC VOTERS)

Source: U.S. Census

Note: The term "whites" includes all those surveyed who identified themselves as white, and this may include some who also identify as Hispanic.

HISPANIC AMERICANS IN CONGRESS

The Hispanic Americans who have served in Congress from 1822 to the present are as follows (in chronological order by dates of office):

Senate

1928–1929	Octaviano Larrazolo
1935–1962	Dennis Chávez
1964–1977	Joseph Manuel Montoya
2005–	Ken Salazar
	Mel Martínez
2006	Robert Menendez

House of Representatives

1822–1823	Joseph Marion Hernández
1853–1857	José Manuel Gallegos
1856–1861	Miguel Antonio Otero
1863–1865	Francisco Perea
1865–1867	José Francisco Chaves
1871–1873	José Manuel Gallegos
1877–1878	Romualdo Pacheco
1877–1879	Trinidad Romero
1879–1881	Mariano Sabino Otero
1879–1883	Romualdo Pacheco
1881–1884	Tranquilino Luna
1884–1885	Francisco Antonio Manzanares
1899–1901	Pedro Perea
1901–1905	Federico Degetau
1905–1911	Tulio Larrinaga
1911–1916	Luis Muñoz Rivera
1913–1927	Ladislas Lazaro
1915–1917	Benigno Cárdenas Hernández
1917–1932	Félix Córdova Dávila
1919–1921	Benigno Cárdenas Hernández
1921–1923	Néstor Montoya
1931–1935	Dennis Chávez
1931–1941	Joachim Octave Fernández
1932–1933	José Lorenzo Pesquera
1932–1939	Santiago Iglesias
1939–1945	Bolívar Pagán
1943–1956	Antonio Manuel Fernández
1945–1946	Jesús T. Piñero
1946–1965	Antonio Fernós-Isern
1957–1964	Joseph Manuel Montoya
1961–1998	Henry B. González
1963–1993	Edward R. Roybal
1965–1969	Santiago Polanco-Abreu
1965–1997	Eligio "Kika" de la Garza II
1969–1973	Jorge Luis Córdova Díaz
1969–1989	Manuel Luján Jr.
1971–1977	Herman Badillo
1973–1977	Jaime Benítez
1973–1979	Ron de Lugo
1977–1985	Baltasar Corrada del Río
1978–1990	Robert Garcia
1979–1989	Anthony Lee Coelho
1981–1995	Ron de Lugo
1982–2001	Matthew G. Martínez
1983–1997	William B. Richardson
1983–2001	Solomon P. Ortiz
1983–1999	Esteban Torres
1985–1992	Jaime B. Fuster
1985–1993	Ben Blaz Garrido
	Albert G. Bustamante
1989–	Ileana Ros-Lehtinen
1991–	Ed López Pastor
1992–1993	Antonio J. Colorado
1993–1997	Frank M. Tejeda
1993–2001	Carlos Antonio Romero-Barceló
1993–2004	Robert A. Underwood
1993–2006	Robert Menéndez
1993–2007	Henry Bonilla
1993–	Xavier Becerra
	Lincoln Díaz-Balart
	Luis Gutiérrez
	Lucille Roybal-Allard
	Nydia M. Velázquez
1996–	Silvestre Reyes
1997–2004, 2007	Ciro D. Rodriguez
1997–	Rubén Hinojosa
	Loretta Sanchez
1999–	Joe Baca
	Charles A. Gonzalez
	Grace Napolitano
2001–2004	Aníbal Acevedo-Vilá
2003–	Dennis Cardoza
	Mario Diaz-Balart
	Raúl Grijalva
	Devin Nunes
	Linda Sanchez
2005–	Henry Cuellar
	Luis Fortuño
	John Salazar
2006–	Albio Sires

who came to national attention as secretary of energy in the Clinton administration's second term and then went on to become governor of New Mexico and run for the Democratic nomination for president in 2008. The first Hispanic mayor of a major American city was Henry Cisneros, who held that office in San Antonio, Texas (1982–1990), before going on to serve in the Clinton cabinet. President George W. Bush also chose several Hispanics for his cabinet, including Mel Martinez as secretary of Housing and Urban Development and Alberto Gonzales, first as White House counsel, and later, as Attorney General. The Republican Martinez later left the Bush Administration to represent Florida in the Senate, joining Democrats Ken Salazar of Colorado and Robert Menendez of New Jersey.

Latina members of Congress include, among others, longtime representative Ileana Ros-Lehtinen, Cuban American from Miami, a Republican; Puerto Rican Nydia Velázquez, a Democrat from New York, and two Mexican-American sisters, Loretta and Linda Sanchez, both from Southern California. In addition, Hispanic-American civic leaders serve in many other capacities, such as Dennis Rivera, a New York City labor leader of Puerto Rican ancestry, and Antonio Gonzalez, president of the Southwest Voter Registration Education Project (SVREP), which since its founding in 1974 has been active in registering Latinos and encouraging them to vote.

THE TEXAS REDISTRICTING CONTROVERSY

In addition to the level of voter participation in congressional elections, another factor that influences national election results is the ethnic make-up of state congressional districts. Beginning in 2002, this issue came to a head in Texas, as Republican party leaders worked to remap congressional district in the state to favor their party. In 2002, Republicans won control of the Texas state legislature for the first time in 130 years, and immediately set about trying to redraw Texas congressional districts to favor Republican candidates for Congress. To support their argument, Republicans argued that the way districts were drawn for the 2002 election unfairly led to a Democratic 17-15 edge in House seats representing Texas, even though Texans had voted statewide for Republicans by an by an 18-14 margin. After a long partisan struggle, the Republican-controlled legislature enacted a new congressional districting map, Plan 1374C. In the 2004 congressional elections, the impact of the new map was felt as Republicans won 21 seats to the Democrats' 11. In 2006 Republicans won 19 seats, and Democrats won 13.

The Texas redistricting was extremely controversial, particularly because of the role played by Republican majority leader Tom DeLay, who had made it clear that his goal was to establish a permanent Republican majority in the Texas Congressional delegation.

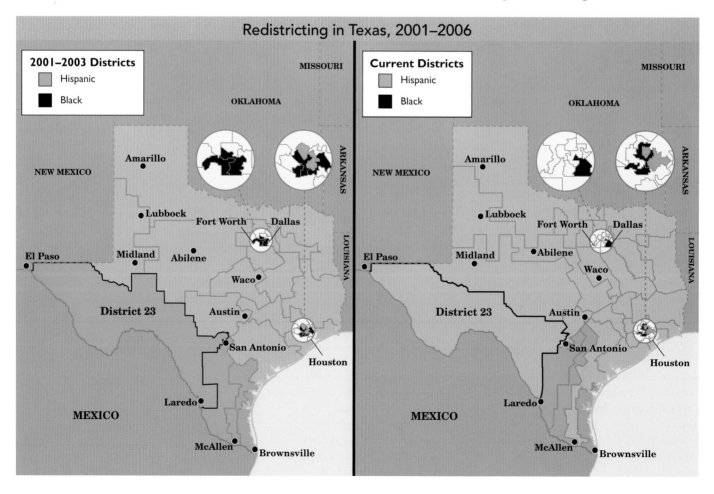

Redistricting in Texas, 2001–2006

For Texan Latinos, who are generally Democrats, the redistricting was especially controversial. Arguing that the plan was unconstitutional and would weaken Latino influence, the League of Latin America Citizens (LULAC) sued Texas Governor Rick Perry. The case ultimately reached the U.S. Supreme Court, where the Court threw out portions of the redistricting, requiring Texas lawmakers to readjust boundaries. Nonetheless, Texas Republicans have been able to maintain their majority in the House.

ACHIEVEMENT IN BUSINESS

Just as Hispanic Americans have grown as a political force, they have also grown as an economic force. By 2004 they represented $700 billion in annual purchasing power and is projected to reach $1 trillion by 2010, nearly three times the overall national rate of consumer purchasing power over the past decade. There are approximately 2 million Hispanic-owned businesses in the country that generate almost $300 billion in annual gross receipts. By 2010, there will be 3.2 million Hispanic firms generating $465 billion, more than triple the number of Hispanic businesses in operation back in 1992. Though most of these were small firms owned by a single proprietor, the number of Hispanic-owned companies grew 82 percent since 1997, making them among the fastest-growing business segments in the nation.

Of those Hispanic businesses, Latinas owned 553,618. By 2004, Hispanic women-owned businesses employed 320,000 and generated $44.4 billion in sales nationwide. The 10 states with the greatest number of Hispanic women-owned firms in 2002 were California (17 %), Texas (18%), Florida (16%), New York (14%), Arizona (13%), Illinois, New Jersey, Massachusetts, New Mexico and Colorado.

Among the oldest Hispanic business success stories has been Goya Foods, founded by Spanish-American businessman Prudencio Unanue in 1936. Based in Secaucus, New Jersey, Goya specializes in foods marketed to Hispanic Americans (but increasingly to Americans in general as well). By the end of the 20th century, it was one of the country's 500 largest private companies, enjoying $620 million a year in annual revenue. Meanwhile, San Antonio-based TerraHealth, Inc., which specializes in healthcare and military support, was the fastest-growing Hispanic-owned company in the United States in 2006 with reported growth of 8,339 percent since 2001. Numerous magazines, newspapers, radio and television stations, and web sites were catering to Hispanic Americans. Latinos were also prominent in businesses that had nothing particularly to do with Latinos. For example, Cuban American Roberto C. Guizeta (1931–1997), who fled Castro's revolution in 1960, became chairman and chief executive officer of Coca-Cola by the 1980s.

Latinos have had a long, successful history in media and journalism. The roots of the nation's largest Spanish-language television network, Univision, date to 1955, when Raul Cortez founded KCOR-TV, Channel 41 in San Antonio, Texas. With the 1962 addition of KMEX-TV in Los Angeles, Cortez began the Spanish International Network (SIN), the first foreign-language television network in the United States. Over the next quarter century SIN added stations throughout the Western United States, as well as in Chicago, Florida, and New York City. In 1986, Cortez sold SIN to a partnership between Hallmark Cards and Mexico City-based Televisa, the largest media company in the Spanish-speaking world. Univision was an immediate success, largely due to the import of the Chilean variety show *Sábado Gigante*, and the signing of Cristina Saralegui, who became the top Spanish-language talk show host. Then in 2006, Univision announced that it accepted a $12.7 billion dollar bid from a group of private equity investors led by TPG Capital, L.P. and Thomas H. Lee Partners. Although federal regulators approved the sale, Univision stockholders have contested the sale, and a trial began in April, 2008.

Telemundo, founded in Puerto Rico in 1954, is the second largest Spanish language network in the United States. The station is the only Spanish-language network broadcasting telenovas, or Spanish soap operas. In 2002, NBC Universal, a division of General Electric, purchased the network.

In 2004, the nation's two largest Spanish-language newspapers, the Los Angeles-based *La Opinión* and the New York-based *El Diario La Prensa* merged to

LEADING HISPANIC-OWNED BUSINESSES, 2007

Company	Location	Business	Year Founded	2006 Revenue (in millions)
Brightstar Corporation.	Miami, FL	Value added services	1997	3.6 billion
Burt Automotive Network	Centennial, CO	Auto sales and service	1939	$2.06 billion
Molina Healthcare Inc.	Long Beach, CA	Medical services	1980	$2 billion
Related Group of Florida	Miami, FL	Real estate development	1979	$1.4 billion
Prestige Builders Partners LLC	Miami Lakes, FL	Real estate development	1994	$1 billion
MasTec Inc.	Coral Gables, FL	Telecommunications	1969	$949 million
International Bancshares Corp.	Laredo, TX	Financial services	1966	$786 million
Ancira Enterprises Inc.	San Antonio, TX	Auto sales and service	1983	$629 million
The Diez Group	Dearborn, MI	Steel sales and services	1973	$513 million
Lopez Foods Inc.	Oklahoma City, OK	Meat products	1979	$465 million
Quirch Foods Co.	Miami, FL	Food distribution and wholesaling	1967	$453 million
Greenway Ford Inc.	Orlando, FL	Automotive sales and service	1994	$452 million
General Real Estate Corp.	Milami, FL	Real estate development	1994	$441 million
Sedano's Supermarkets and Pharmacies	Miami, FL	Supermarket and pharmacy chain	1962	$437 million
Lou Sobh Automotive	Duluth, GA	Automotive sales and service	1990	$420 million

form ImpreMedia. In 2007 ImpreMedia announced the purchase of *Hoy*, New York's second large Spanish-language newspaper. Both *El Diario/La Prensa*, headed by Rossana Rosado, and *La Opinión*, headed by Monica Lozano, have Hispanic women as publisher/CEOs.

Despite the long history of these television and newspaper media outlets, advertising in Spanish-language media can be undervalued. An FCC study in the late 1990s showed that advertisers often chose not to place ads on radio stations serving Hispanic- and African-American audiences. When they did include those stations in their ad campaigns, advertisers paid the broadcasters an average of 63 percent less for the same ads reaching the same size audience on mainstream stations. The rationale for such practices rests, at least in part, on old-fashioned bigotry. In one case, the study reported that a major soap company told a Hispanic broadcaster that an ad was not needed because Hispanics do not bathe as much as whites.

LATINOS IN THE ARTS SINCE 1975

The same penchant for mixing that has characterized Hispanic culture since antiquity, when Celts, Iberians, Carthaginians, and Romans mixed on the Iberian Peninsula, characterizes it in the United States. Hispanic Americans regularly cross ethnic lines to marry Hispanics of different national ancestry—for example, Mexicans with Puerto Ricans and Cubans with Nicaraguans. Hispanic Americans also freely intermarry with Anglo-Americans and African Americans, letting Hispanic culture mingle with that of their spouses. Examples abound in popular culture. For example, singer Mariah Carey, born in New York City in 1970, is the daughter of an Afro-Venezuelan father and an Irish mother. Another example is actor and playwright John Leguizamo, whose background is Colombian–Puerto Rican.

FINE ARTS

Since the flowering of the Chicano art movement in the late 1960s and early 1970s, a diverse range of Latino artists have had an impact on American art. One of the best known is Judy Baca, a Mexican-American from Los Angeles. Baca is known for her brightly colored urban murals, the most famous of which is the Great Wall of Los Angeles, which stretches for a half mile. To create this work, Baca recruited other artists and scholars, as well as local children to create a work that is both artistic and communal.

Richard Serra, born in San Francisco in 1939, remains one of the most highly regarded American sculptors working today. His large scale sculptures of metal, concrete, and other materials are usually created for specific outdoor sites, and some have stirred considerable controversy. His 120-foot long Tilted Arc, from 1981, became a cause célèbre when office workers in lower Manhattan demanded its removal from a public plaza.

Serra's paintings have also generated controversy. In 2006, Serra's "Stop Bush," a stark painting of a hooded Iraqi prisoner at Abu Ghraib prison, highlighted the artist's opposition to the president's war policy in Iraq. The work was featured at the Whitney Museum's 2006 biennial exhibit.

On the East Coast, Jean-Michel Basquiat, a half Haitian, half-Puerto Rican artist from Brooklyn, was embraced as an 1980s star of the downtown New York art scene. Basquiat, who began as a graffiti artist, and t-shirt artist, emerged from the urban hip-hop scene and was strongly influenced by hip-hop culture and multiculturalism. He worked closely with Andy Warhol, who became a mentor and great influence on him, as were earlier artists like Picasso and Matisse. Although Basquiat died of a heroin overdose at age 27, by the 21st century he had become regarded as one of the great neo-expressionists of his era.

Hispanic Americans in the Performing Arts

Mariah Carey and John Leguizamo are just two examples of Hispanic performers who have gained widespread popularity in recent years. The rich diversity of Hispanic-American actors and musicians and their increased popularity illustrates not only the growing "crossover" appeal of Hispanic artists, but also the extent to which Hispanic culture has itself become part of the mainstream. In previous eras, Hispanic actors were all but invisible. Rita Hayworth (born Margarita Carmen Cansino) was Spanish American, but with her hair dyed auburn and an Anglo-sounding name, she "passed" for Anglo with the GIs in World War II who treasured her pinup and with the movie fans who enjoyed her in films like *Gilda* (1946). Anthony Quinn often played some kind of ethnic—a Greek in *Zorba the Greek* (1964)—but few moviegoers know he is Mexican American.

Nowadays, being Hispanic is more acceptable for an actor. Jennifer Lopez (who is also a singer), Salma Hayek, Cameron Diaz, Rosie Perez, and

THERE IS A GALLERY IN SPANISH HARLEM

In the cultural ferment of the late 1960s and early 1970s, the Puerto Rican community in New York City's El Barrio established several cultural institutions to showcase Puerto Rican arts. These included the art museum El Museo del Barrio, the Nuyorican Poets Café, and the art gallery Taller Boricua. ("Boricua" is a popular name for "Puerto Rican," from the indigenous Arawak name "Borinquen" for Puerto Rico.) In 2000, Taller Boricua, which has now evolved into the Julia de Burgos Cultural Center, celebrated its 30th anniversary.

A red-brick castle on Lexington Avenue between 105th and 106th Streets, the Julia de Burgos Cultural Center is named for a great Puerto Rican poet who died in El Barrio. The center is home not only to Taller Boricua, but to Los Pleneros de La 21, a bomba and plena performance group; the Puerto Rican Traveling Theatre, which offers acting classes; and the Heritage School, a junior high school.

"There are very few venues where Latino artists can bring their work to the community," Yasmin Ramirez, curator of a show at Taller Boricua called "Fresh Produce," told Latino.com in 2000. "Julia de Burgos brings the new, the old, and the experimental all to one place." The center is not only for people of Puerto Rican descent, but for all residents of El Barrio, who also include Mexicans, Dominicans, and other Hispanic Americans.

Puerto Rican Reggaeton stars Daddy Yankee, at left, and Pitbull, right. (Corbis)

Rosie Perez has appeared in numerous films since her debut in Spike Lee's Do the Right Thing. (Movie Star News)

Elizabeth Peña are a few Latinas who have reached wide audiences as film actresses. Latino movie stars have included Antonio Banderas, Edward James Olmos, Andy Garcia, John Leguizamo, Benicio Del Toro, and the late Raul Julia, who died in 1994. Spanish-American Martin Sheen (born Ramon Estevez) established an acting dynasty, with sons Emilio Estevez and Charlie Sheen following in his footsteps. Hispanic-American television actors have included Freddie Prinze, the first Puerto Rican–American to become a major television star, who played Chico in the 1970s sitcom *Chico and the Man* and died in 1977 (his son, Freddie Prinze Jr., starred in the 1999 big-screen hit *She's All That*), and Jimmy Smits, star of the television dramas *L.A. Law* and *NYPD Blue*. Broadway performers of Hispanic ancestry have included Chita Rivera and Rita Moreno—the latter holding the distinction of having won all four major entertainment awards: an Oscar, a Tony, an Emmy, and a Grammy.

A number of great 20th century jazz musicians and singers, mentioned in earlier chapters, are Hispanic Americans—Xavier Cugat, Tito Puente, and Celia Cruz—as is the classical cellist Pablo Casals. Hispanic-American pop and rock sensations from the 1950s to the present have included Ritchie Valens, Joan Baez, Carlos Santana, Jerry Garcia, Linda Ronstadt, and Gloria Estefan. In the 1990s, Selena (1971–1995), star performer of the style known as Tejano music, entranced Mexican-American audiences until her untimely shooting by a disgruntled employee. Recent pop music stars have included Ricky Martin, Marc Anthony, Mariah Carey, Jon Secada, Shakira, Reggaeton star Daddy Yankee, and Christina Aguilera. Not all Latino performing artists fit in these categories. Supermodel Christy Turlington is Hispanic American. So is Vanna White, the woman who turns the letters on the TV game show Wheel of Fortune, and Geraldo Rivera, the journalist and broadcaster.

HISPANIC ATHLETES

Sports is another area in which Latinos have had high-profile success. Many Hispanic Americans love fútbol (soccer, known as football outside the United States), which is popular across Latin America. Their enthusiasm has helped make it popular in the United States as well. Tab Ramos, an Uruguayan American, is among the great Hispanic-American soccer players.

In several Hispanic countries, baseball is as much the national pastime as it is in the United States. At the start of the 2007 Major League season, there were 750 players on opening day rosters, of which were 149 were foreign-born Latinos and 33 were Latinos born in the United States. The Dominican Republic alone provided one out of every nine players in the Majors in 2005. Of 895 players on active rosters and disabled lists that year, an astonishing 101 were Dominican. Heading into the 2008 season the New York Mets boasted 14 Latinos on their active roster of 25 players.

Singers Mark Anthony and Jennifer Lopez join New York mayor Michael Bloomberg at the front of the city's annual Puerto Rican Day Parade. (Corbis)

MAJOR STYLES OF LATIN MUSIC

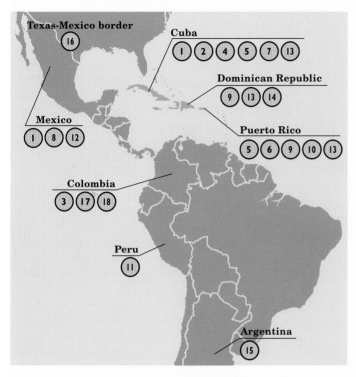

1. Conjunto: A small instrumental group, highlighted by trumpet in its Cuban variety and accordian in the Mexican variety. Backing instruments include piano, bass, conga, and bongos, as well as vocals. Mexican conjunto music played by groups is known as norteño.
2. Cubop: A nickname for Afro-Cuban jazz, which first blossomed in the 1940s, fusing improvisational bebop jazz of that era with Latin percussion and rhythms. The form was popularized by artists such as Dizzy Gillespie and Machito.
3. Cumbia: A Colombia-based, accordion-led style that fuses Andean Indian music with African and European influences.
4. Danzón: A highly syncopated music form that is one of the earliest styles of Afro-Caribbean music, danzón was introduced to Cuba from immigrants from Haiti and Louisiana in the 17th century.
5. Guaracha: This song and dance style, featuring alternating rhythms, started in Cuba and became popular in Puerto Rico and New York City from the 1920s to the 1940s.
6. Jíbaro: Rural Puerto Rican music featuring guitar, cuatro, maracas, güiro, and vocals.
7. Mambo: An instrumental Cuban dance style that became immensely popular in New York City from the 1930s to the 1950s.
8. Mariachi: Mariachi is an urban style of Mexican folk music. While mariachi bands originally consisted of two violins, a

vihuela (a small five-string guitar), a jarana (a larger five-string guitar), and a harp, the harp was replaced at the turn of the 20th century by a guitarrón (a large, acoustic four-string bass guitar). Since the 1930s, two trumpets have also been included in the ensemble. Mariachi bands are also known for their elaborate, highly embroidered costumes, which include sombreros, short bolero jackets, and vaquero pants.

9. Merengue: A music born in the Dominican Republic and imported to Puerto Rico and the United States during the 1930s, merengue is usually accompanied by a small accordion, a two-headed drum called the tambora, and a singer who plays the güiro.
10. Plena: A style of Puerto Rican street music that is played on panderetas (hand-held frame drums), güiros, harmonica, and accordion.
11. Quechua: A traditional music form named after the Quechua Indians of Peru, who are descended from the Incas. Quechua is often accompanied by the waltzlike huayno dance.
12. Ranchera: Literally meaning "ranch song," rancheras were a key element in the Mexican political theater of the early 20th century. Ranchera lyrics usually focus on powerful expressions of patriotism. This music is very popular to this day.
13. Salsa: Salsa is a mixture of African, Cuban, Puerto Rican, and Dominican styles first popularized in the United States during the 1970s. Salsa is usually played by a band of eight to 10 musicians, including piano, bass, conga drums, timbales, bongos, cowbell, trumpet, cuatro, and one or two singers. Salsa stars include Celia Cruz and Tito Puente.
14. Son: A very highly syncopated Cuban dance music that has had a strong impact on Hispanic music in New York City. Son is sometimes also called rumba.
15. Tango: The tango, an Argentinian dance form, became a worldwide sensation during the early 20th century. Featuring a solo vocalist accompanied by a guitar, tangos often feature lyrics that stress long, sentimental narratives. Perhaps because of the dance's overt sensuality, tangos have often been condemned.
16. Tejano: In its broadest musical context, Tejano refers to the broad range of pop music from the Texas-Mexico border region. Also referred to as Tex-Mex, Tejano often blends mainstream rock or pop music with traditional Mexican genres, particularly the accordion-based conjunto. The Tejano sound, therefore, can vary from the countrified sound of Freddy Fender to the pop ballads of Selena.
17. Vallenato: Vallenato, once the music of Colombian rancheros, or ranchers, is an increasingly popular music. Vallenato features the accordion backed by instruments like the scraper, handdrum, and bass guitar.

The first Latino baseball player to be admitted to the Baseball Hall of Fame was Puerto Rican legend Roberto Clemente (1934–1972). Current Hispanic-American baseball stars included Albert Pujols, Manny Ramirez, David Ortiz, Pedro Martinez, Vladimir Guerrero, Alex Rodriguez, Johan Santana, and Alfonso Soriano, and José Reyes.

In golf, notable Hispanic-American athletes have included Juan "Chi Chi" Rodriguez and Mexican Americans Lee

José Reyes of the New York Mets dives into a base. On Opening Day of the 2008 Major League Baseball season, 14 of the Mets' 25 players were Latinos, reflecting the increased prominence of Hispanic players throughout the game. (Corbis)

Treviño and Nancy López. In boxing, Mexican American Oscar de la Hoya won a gold medal at the 1992 Olympics. Pancho Gonzalez, Gigi Fernandez, and Gabriela Sabatini are Hispanic-American tennis stars. Felipe López in basketball gives a further idea of the range of Hispanic-American athletes.

ACHIEVEMENTS IN SCIENCE

Few people now emigrate from Spain to the United States; only 1,321 came in 1995. But Spain has been responsible for sending some great scientists to the United States. Among them was Severo Ochoa (1905–1993), who was a corecipient of the 1959 Nobel Prize in physiology or medicine for isolating an enzyme that allowed him to carry out the first test-tube synthesis of RNA (ribonucleic acid). Another was Luis W. Alvarez (1911–1988), who won the 1968 Nobel Prize in physics for research on the detection and nature of subatomic particles. In 1979, with his son Walter Alvarez, he proposed the now widely held theory that a comet or asteroid caused the extinction of the dinosaurs.

In addition to theorizing about asteroids and comets, Hispanic Americans have also made in-person investigations of outer space. The first Latino astronaut in space was Costa Rican American

Franklin Chang-Diaz in 1986. Since then, Dr. Chang-Diaz has logged over 1,200 hours of space flight on five additional missions.

The first Latina astronaut in space was Ellen Ochoa in 1993. In that year, she served on board the space shuttle *Discovery* during a nine-day mission during which the crew conducted atmospheric and solar studies in order to better understand the effect of solar activity on the Earth's climate and environment. Dr. Ochoa used a Remote Manipulator System (RMS) to deploy and capture the Spartan satellite, which studied the solar corona.

Among the organizations that have been established to encourage Hispanic-American science education and participation in scientific careers is the Society for the Advancement of Chicanos and Native Americans in the Sciences. Composed of science professors, industry scientists, K-12 educators, and students, the group promotes opportunities in graduate science education for Latinos, Native Americans, and other minority students.

TRADITIONS AND CULTURE

In New York City, the annual Hispanic Day parade, held on the Sunday of Columbus Day weekend, celebrates the diversity that is Hispanic America. Floats from many countries, cheered by thousands of flag-waving Hispanics, proceed along Fifth Avenue. Typical of the spectators was a woman from the Bronx at the parade in 2000 who waved two flags—that of El Salvador, where she was born, and of Ecuador, where her husband was born.

Hispanic culture encompasses many things. It includes the quinceañera, an elaborate celebration of a girl's 15th birthday that is traditional among Cuban Americans and has spread to some other Latino communities. Another tradition in Hispanic culture is the piñata, the decorated container full of candy and toys that Mexican-American children break at parties, and that has spread to Anglo culture. Other traditions include dominoes, a favorite game of Puerto Ricans and other Caribbean Hispanics, and hammocks, an invention the Arawak bequeathed to the Spanish as an ideal place for a siesta, or afternoon nap (itself a time-honored Hispanic custom).

IMPORTANT CONCEPTS IN HISPANIC FAMILY STRUCTURE

La Familia

The Hispanic family incorporates the concept of *la familia* (the greater family), which includes members of the immediate household and any blood relatives.

Members of the extended family usually live together in the first stages of immigration, when newcomers need support adjusting to their new environment.

Family Ideology

Hispanics and Hispanic Americans place high worth on the ideal of family values. Family ideology serves as a guide for behavior and defines the ideal roles of each family member. The ideal family is usually patriarchal, headed by a father embodying the concept of "machismo," whereby men are imbued with dominant qualities such as strength and responsibility. In reality, however, women are often the decision makers of the family, especially in the United States, where women tend to be the primary wage earners.

Compadrazgo

This is a strong friendship relationship, in which friends are seen as members of the family. *Compadrazgo* serves as both the extension of kinship to nonrelatives and the strengthening of bonds within the family. This special relationship sometimes includes godparenthood. In this case the friends usually sponsor the child in baptism and confirmation ceremonies and are best man and bridesmaid at the weddings. Parents may choose close friends or relatives to become godparents (*padrinos* or *madrinos*) to their children. Godparents usually have special responsibilities toward the child and will take the parental role if the parents pass away.

The strongest relationship is between the child's parents and godparents, who call each other *compadres* and provide each other with help, care, and support. *Compadres* also provide shelter for new immigrants of either family, access to jobs, and a supportive base for acclimatization.

Parentesco

Prevalent in Mexican-American households, *parentesco* (kinship) is the extension of family sentiment to strangers from the same country of origin.

Confianza

Confianza (trust) is central to the principles of *compadrazgo* and *parentesco* among Hispanic Americans. This forms the basis of all relationships, signifying a bond of special feeling, respect, and intimacy.

Latino culture includes many different styles of music: the Puerto Rican/Cuban blend called salsa, the Colombian-based cumbia, the Argentinean tango, the Dominican merengue, and the Mexican mariachi band. It includes many cuisines: the chili con carne and tortilla chips of Tex-Mex cooking; the mole poblano sauce of central Mexico, which combines chili peppers, garlic, bananas, onions, and unsweetened chocolate; the lechón asado, or roast suckling pig, of Cuba; the asopao, or chicken and rice dish of Puerto Rico; the comida criollas, or creole foods, shared by Puerto Rico, Cuba, and the Dominican Republic.

Hispanic Americans do not necessarily practice medicine the same way as other Americans. Mexican Americans may seek medical help from curanderos and curanderas, healers who combine Catholic faith-healing with herbology and Aztec and Mayan beliefs and may also act as parteras, or midwives. Puerto Rican neighborhoods often have their own brand of folk medicine, practiced in botánicas, stores that sell herbs and natural medicines along with candles, statues, and other articles related to Santería, the syncretistic Caribbean religion.

Religion is an area of great diversity among Hispanic Americans. Most are

Roman Catholic but with regional touches that reflect the tendency to mix traditions and create local adaptations. Mexican-American Catholicism has aspects of Aztec religion (visible in the iconography of Mexico's patron saint, Our Lady of Guadalupe); Guatemalan Catholicism has aspects of Mayan religion.

Each Hispanic subgroup's religious calendar is adapted to regional differences. Mexican Americans celebrate All Souls' Day, November 2, as El Día de los Muertos, "The Day of the Dead," decorating their homes with skeletons and going to cemeteries with gifts of food and flowers for the deceased. In July, Puerto Ricans celebrate the Fiesta del Apóstol Santiago, honoring St. James the Apostle with music, dancing, and traditional costumes.

Not all Hispanics are Catholic. A growing number are evangelical Protestants, and some are Jewish.

Catholicism blends with West African Yoruba elements in Santería, which was developed by enslaved Africans and is still practiced by many Puerto Ricans, Cubans, Venezuelans, and other Latinos. Worshippers pray to santos, or saints, who are fused with Yoruba deities. Animal sacrifice, food-sharing rituals, and charms and potions are part of the religion.

The particular nationality of Hispanic Americans affects their memories and outlook. A Cuban exile may count the years until democracy returns to Cuba, while Latinos from other countries may admire Fidel Castro and his brother Raul, who succeeded him in 2008, for having stood up to the United States. A Peruvian American and Ecuadoran American may get along fine until the subject of old Peruvian-Ecuadoran wars comes up—at which point their friendliness may turn into hostility. A Costa Rican American thinks back to a relatively peaceful home-

A DIVERSITY OF HEROES

The legacy of Hispanic culture has had so many facets that it would be difficult to choose and rank the most influential Latinos of the century. But the online community Latino.com attempted to do just that by asking its members to choose "Latino.com's Hispanic Heritage Heroes." The resulting Top 20 list reflects the diversity of the Hispanic-American experience, combining as it does patriots and movement leaders, such as Pancho Villa and César Chávez, along with current celebrities like Jennifer Lopez. Noting that many users nominated "mamá y papá, not to mention los abuelitos, tìas y tìos" (grandparents, aunts, and uncles), the staff of Latino.com recognized "family" as an honorable mention.

The Top 20 heroes were:
 1. César Chávez, Mexican-American labor organizer
 2. Ernesto "Che" Guevara, Argentine revolutionary (known for his role in the Cuban Revolution)
 3. Edward James Olmos, Mexican-American actor
 4. Gloria Estefan, Cuban-American singer
 5. Tito Puente, Puerto Rican–American bandleader and composer
 6. Selena, Mexican-American singer
 7. Ricky Martin, Puerto Rican–American singer
 8. Jennifer Lopez, Puerto Rican–American actress and singer
 9. Marc Anthony, Puerto Rican–American singer
10. Dolores Huerta, Mexican-American labor organizer
11. Emiliano Zapata, Mexican revolutionary
12. Roberto Clemente, Puerto Rican–American baseball player
13. Carlos Santana, Mexican-American musician
14. Pancho Villa, Mexican revolutionary
15. Celia Cruz, Cuban-American singer
16. Rita Moreno, Puerto Rican–American actress
17. Gabriel García Márquez, Colombian novelist
18. Frida Kahlo, Mexican painter
19. Fidel Castro, Cuban leader
20. Rigoberta Menchú, Guatemalan human rights activist

Traditional dancers in Arizona celebrate the Mexican holiday Cinco de Mayo. (The Viesti Collection)

land, but a Salvadoran may awake with nightmares from post-traumatic stress disorder, the result of having witnessed atrocities in the civil war.

Because they come from different nations, Hispanic Americans celebrate different national holidays. Mexican Americans celebrate Cinco de Mayo on May 5. In July many Colombian Americans celebrate Colombian Independence Day. One spot on the calendar unites all Hispanic Americans: National Hispanic American Heritage Month, from September 15 to October 15, a period that includes Columbus Day, which many Hispanics call El Día de la Raza.

Common Strands

Despite their varied backgrounds, nearly all Hispanic Americans share some traditions. One is the importance of family, la familia, which includes not only the nuclear family itself but also the extended one of grandparents, aunts, uncles, and cousins. Another is the institution of compadrazgo, in which close friends become virtual members of the family, serving as compadres (literally coparents) to the family's children. Often compadres act as godparents to the child, sponsoring the child at baptism as well as helping out as needed as the child grows up.

Another common feature of Hispanic-American culture is the concept of machismo, or manhood, whose broad dimensions non-Hispanics often fail to grasp. To be macho is to be responsible, upright, brave, strong, and able to provide for one's family. The concept of machismo also implies superiority to women and paternalistic dominance over the family, though those notions are regularly undermined in the United States, with its doctrine of equality between the sexes and its widespread phenomenon of women as joint or even primary wage earners.

As immigrants or near-descendants of immigrants, many Hispanic Americans share basic immigrant experiences, like saving money every week to send remesas, or remittances of money, home to their families in the old country. They tend to be fluent in Spanglish, a mix of Spanish and English handy for communication between people whose grasp of one language or the other may be limited, or who simply prefer to think in two languages.

Latinos share a common experience of encountering prejudice and misunderstanding on the part of non-Hispanics. Like other recent immigrant groups, Hispanics know all the pejorative names used to insult them and are aware of the stereotypes used to demean them: Colombians as drug dealers; Puerto Ricans as knife fighters; and Hispanics in general as hot-blooded, lazy, and unstable. They know that a Guatemalan may be regarded as a Mexican and an Ecuadorian assumed to be a Puerto Rican. Under such circumstances, many Hispanic Americans choose to work together to promote an understanding of Hispanic culture and to demand respect and equal rights. Aware of all that unites Hispanic peoples, they take pleasure in coming across a fellow Latino, even if that person is from an entirely different Hispanic background.

THE HISPANIC NATION

Hispanic Americans today are not just one people, but many. They differ in their customs, their histories, and their ways of interacting with the larger American society. They differ even on what to call themselves—Hispanic, Latino, descendants of a certain country (Peruvian American, Chicano)—or whether to dispense with labeling themselves by ethnic ancestry and simply call themselves American.

But Hispanic Americans also share common characteristics. All descend from people who spoke Spanish, and many still speak it themselves, with varying levels of proficiency. They share cultural traits, like devotion to family, and most share a religious background, Catholicism. Further, Hispanic Americans face common problems. Many, though not all, are of mixed race and face prejudice from those who regard nonwhites with suspicion. Many are immigrants or closely related to immigrants, and thus have a strong interest in policies related to immigration and bilingual education. As a group, Hispanic Americans suffer from relatively lower income and educational attainment than Americans as a whole.

In the late 20th and early 21st centuries, as Hispanics from various countries met and mingled in the United States, they noted the commonalities that unite them and distinguish them from other Americans. They have begun to celebrate as a common heritage the historical roots that unite them and the heroes who represent them. In so doing they have become more conscious of themselves as Hispanic Americans and more conscious of the power they can wield if they work together.

SELECTED BIBLIOGRAPHY

Acuña, Rudolfo. *Anything But Mexican: Chicanos in Contemporary Los Angeles.* Verso Books: New York, 1996.

_____. *Corridors of Migration: The Odyssey of Mexican Laborers, 1600-1933.* Tucson AZ: University of Arizona Press, 2008

_____. *Occupied America: A History of Chicanos, Sixth edition.* Boston: Longman, 2006.

All-Media Guide. "All-Music Guide." Available online. URL: http:// www.allmusic.com/amg.html. Downloaded February 3, 2008.

Assis, Moises, and Robert M. Levine. *Cuban Miami.* New Brunswick, NJ: Rutgers University Press, 2000.

Boorstin, Daniel J. *The Discoverers: A History of Man's Search to Know His World and Himself.* New York: Random House, 1995.

Bradley, David. *The Encyclopedia of Civil Rights in America.* Vol. 3. Armonk, NY: M. E. Sharpe Inc., 1998.

Bucavalas, Tina, et al. *South Florida Folklife.* Jackson: University of Mississippi Press, 1994.

Calavita, Kitty. *Inside the State: The Bracero Program, Immigration and the I.N.S.* New York: Routledge, 1992.

Carr, Raymond. *Spain: A History.* New York: Oxford University Press, 2000.

Chabrán, Richard, and Rafael Chabrán, eds. *The Latino Encyclopedia.* New York: Marshall Cavendish, 1996.

Chapman, Victoria, and David Lindroth. *Latin American History On File.* New York: Facts On File, 1996.

Chasteen, John Charles. *Born in Blood And Fire: A Concise History of Latin America, Second Edition.* New York: W. W. Norton, 2005.

Coe, Michael D. *Mexico: From the Olmecs to the Aztecs.* New York: Thames and Hudson, Inc., 1994.

Dalleo, Raphael and Elena Machado Saez. *The Latino/a Canon and the Emergence of Post-Sixties Literature* . New York: Palgrave MacMillan, 2007.

Dary, David. *The Santa Fe Trail: Its History, Legends, and Lore.* New York: Alfred A. Knopf, Inc., 2000.

Davis, Mike, and Roman de la Campa. *Magical Urbanism: Latinos Reinvent the U.S. Big City.* New York: Verso, 2000.

De Genova, Nicho. *Latino Crossings: Mexicans, Puerto Ricans, and the Politics of Race and Citizenship.* New York: Routledge, 2003.

Department of Commerce and Labor. *Statistical Abstract of the United States, 1904.* Washington, DC: Government Printing Office, 1905.

Dietz, James. *Economic History of Puerto Rico.* Princeton, NJ: Princeton University Press, 1986.

Dye, Alan. *Cuban Sugar in the Age of Mass Production.* Palo Alto, CA: Stanford University Press, 1996.

Ebright, Malcom. *Land Grants and Lawsuits in Northern New Mexico.* Guadalupita, NM: Center for Land Grant Studies, 1993.

Eisenhower, John S. D. *Intervention!: The United States and the Mexican Revolution, 1913–1917.* New York: W. W. Norton & Company, 1995.

Firmat, Gustavo Perez. *Life on the Hyphen: The Cuban-American Way.* Austin: University of Texas, 1994.

Fernández-Shaw, Carlos. *The Hispanic Presence in North America from 1492 to Today.* Updated ed. New York: Facts On File, Inc., 1999.

Ferriss, Susan, and Ricardo Sandoval. *The Fight in the Fields: César Chávez and the Farmworkers Movement.* New York: Harcourt Brace and Company, 1997.

Flanders, Stephen A. *Atlas of American Migration.* New York: Facts On File, Inc., 1998.

García, Maria Cristina. *Havana USA: Cuban Exiles and Cuban Americans in South Florida, 1959–1994.* Berkeley: University of California Press, 1997.

Gonzalez, Juan. *Harvest of Empire: A History of Latinos in America.* New York: Viking, 2000.

Gonzalez-Pando, Miguel. *The Cuban Americans.* Westport, CT: Greenwood Publishing Group, 1998.

Grosfoguel, Ramón. *Colonial Subjects: Puerto Ricans in a Global Perspective.* Los Angeles: University of California Press, 2003

Guerin-Gonzalez, Camille. *Mexican Workers and American Dreams.* New Brunswick, NJ: Rutgers University Press, 1994.

Haney López, Ian F. *Racism on Trial: The Chicano Fight for Justice.* Cambridge, MA: Belknap Press, 2003.

Hardin, Stephen, and Gary S. Zaboly. *Texian Iliad: A Military History of the Texas Revolution.* Austin: University of Texas Press, 1994.

Henretta, James. *America's History.* New York: Worth Publishing, 1996.

Jiménez, Carlos M. *The Mexican American Heritage.* Berkeley, CA: TQS Publications, 1994.

Johnson, Paul. *A History of the American People.* New York: HarperCollins, 1999.

Josephy, Alvin M. *War on the Frontier: The Trans-Mississippi West.* Alexandria, VA: Time-Life Books, 1994.

Kanellos, Nicolas, ed. *The Hispanic American Almanac.* Detroit: Gale Research, 1993.

Kanellos, Nicolas, and Gristelia Perez. *Chronology of Hispanic-American History: From Pre-Columbian Times to the Present.* Detroit: Gale Research Inc., 1995.

Lewin, Stephen, ed. *The Latino Experience in U.S. History.* Paramus, NJ: Globe Fearon Educational Publisher, 1994.

Lewis, James E. *The American Union and the Problem of Neighborhood: The United States and the Collapse of the Spanish Empire, 1783–1829.* Chapel Hill: University of North Carolina Press, 1998.

Library of Congress. "Hispanic Americans in Congress, 1822–1995." Available online. URL: http://lcweb.loc.gov/ rr/hispanic-congressmunozrivera. html. Downloaded on October 17, 2007.

LULAC – League of United Latin American Students. "History of LULAC." Available online. URL: http// www.lulac.org/ About/History.html. Downloaded on November 2, 2007.

Maclel, David, Isidro Ortiz, and Maria Herrera-Sobek. *The Chicano Renaissance* Flagstaff: University of Arizona Press, 2000.

Maclel, David, and Maria Herrera-Sobek. *Culture Across Borders: Mexican Immigration & Popular Culture.* Flagstaff: University of Arizona Press, 1998.

Manucy, Albert. *Sixteenth Century St. Augustine: The People and Their Homes.* Gainesville: University Press of Florida, 1997.

Masud-Piloto, Felix Roberto. *From Welcomed Exiles to Illegal Immigrants: Cuban Migration to the U.S., 1959–1995.* London: Rowan and Littlefield, 1996.

Mazón, Mauricio. *The Zoot-Suit Riots.* Austin: The University of Texas Press, 1989.

McKay, John, et al. *A History of World Societies.* 5th ed. Boston: Houghton Mifflin, 1999.

Meier, Matt, and Feliciano Ribera. *Mexican Americans/American Mexicans: From Conquistadors to Chicanos.* New York: Hill and Wang, 1993.

Meyer, Michael, and William H. Beezley. *The Oxford History of Mexico.* New York: Oxford University Press, 2000.

Meyer, Michael, William L. Sherman, and Susan M. Deeds. *The Course of Mexican History.* New York: Oxford University Press, 1998.

Monaghan, Jay. *Chile, Peru, and the California Gold Rush of 1849.* Berkeley: University of California Press, 1973.

Munoz, Carlos. *Youth, Identity, Power: The Chicano Movement, Revised and Expanded Edition.* New York: Verso Books, 2007.

Ngai, Mae M. *Impossible Subjects: Illegal Aliens and the Making of Modern America.* Princeton NJ: Princeton University Press, 2005.

Nelson, William Allan, ed. *Webster's Biographical Dictionary.* Revised ed. Springfield, MA: G&C Merriam, 1995.

Novas, Himilce. *Everything You Need to Know About Latino History.* New York: Plume, 2007.

Office of the Deputy Secretary of Defense for Military Manpower and Personnel Policy. *Hispanics in America's Defense.* Washington, DC: Government Printing Office, 1980.

Olson, James, and Susan Wladaver-Morgan. *Dictionary of United States Economic History.* Westport, CT: Greenwood Press, 1992.

Pantojas-Garcia, Emilio. *Development Strategies as Ideology.* Boulder, CO: Lynne Rienner, 1990.

Paterson, Thomas. *Contesting Castro: The United States and the Triumph of the Cuban Revolution.* New York: Oxford University Press, 1994.

Phillips, Charles. *Encyclopedia of the American West.* New York: Simon & Schuster Macmillan, 1996.

Pierson, Peter. *The History of Spain.* Westport, CT: Greenwood Publishing Group, 1999.

Pitt, Leonard. *The Decline of the Californios: A Social History of the Spanish-Speaking Californians, 1846–1890.* Berkeley: University of California Press, 1999.

Pitt, Leonard, and Dale Pitt. *Los Angeles A to Z.* Berkeley: University of California Press, 1997.

Reddy, Marlita. *Statistical Record of Hispanic Americans.* Detroit: Gale Research, 1993.

Rodriguez, Jaime E. *The Independence of Spanish America.* Cambridge: Cambridge University Press, 1998.

Romo, David Dorado. *Ringside Seat to a Revolution: An Underground Cultural History of El Paso and Juarez, 1893-1923.* El Paso TX: Cinco Puntos Press, 2005.

Rosales, Francisco. *Chicano!: The History of the Mexican American Civil Rights Movement.* Houston, TX: Arte Público Press, 1997.

Russell, Cheryl. *The Official Guide to Racial and Ethnic Diversity: Asians, Blacks, Hispanics, Native Americans, and Whites.* Ithaca, NY: New Strategist Publications, 1996.

Russell, Joel, et al. "The 1998 Hispanic Business 500." *Hispanic Business, Inc.* (June 1998): 50–92.

Samora, Julian, and Patricia Vandel Simon. *A History of the Mexican-American People.* Notre Dame, IN: University of Notre Dame Press, 1993.

Suro, Roberto. *Strangers Among Us: Latinos' Lives in a Changing America.* New York: Vintage, 1999.

Thernstrom, Stephan, ed. *Harvard Encyclopedia of American Ethnic Groups.* Cambridge, MA: The Belknap Press, 1980.

UCLA Committee on Latin American Studies. *Statistical Abstracts of Latin America, 1957.* Los Angeles: Latin American Publications, 1957.

U.S. Bureau of the Census. "American Factfinder." 2000 Census Detailed Tables—Sample Data (STF3). Available online. URL: http://factfinder. census.gov/java_prod/dads.ui.pbq. PopBuildQueryViewShowTableViewTable. Downloaded January 7, 2008.

———. *Statistical Abstracts of the United States, 2007.* Washington, DC: Government Printing Office, 2007.

U.S. Department of Agriculture. "The North American Free Trade Agreement." Available online. URL: http://www.usda.gov/ info/factsheets/nafta.html. Downloaded June 1999.

Villegas, Benjamin, William Ospina, and L. Enrique Garcia. *Mestizo America : The Country of the Future.* Bogota, Columbia: Villegas Editores, 2000.

Viva Zapata. "Mexico." Available online. URL: http://www.geocities.com/CapitolHill/3102/ipzap.html. Downloaded May 18, 1999.

Walker, Dale L. *Bear Flag Rising: The Conquest of California, 1846.* New York: Forge Books, 2000.

Whalen, Carmen Teresa and Victor Vazquez-Hernandez, eds. *The Puerto Rican Diaspora: Historical Perspectives.* Philadephia PA: Temple University Press, 2005

Winders, Richard Bruce. *Mr. Polk's Army: The American Military Experience in the Mexican War.* College Station: Texas A&M University Press, 1997.

Ybarra, Lea, Manuel Monterrey, and Edward James Olmos. *Americanos: Latino Life in the United States.* Boston, MA: Little, Brown and Company, 1999.

Zinn, Howard. *A People's History of the United States: 1492 to the Present.* New York: HarperCollins, 1999.

INDEX